640
BHG

Making A Home

Making a Home

Better Homes and Gardens® Books • Des Moines, Iowa

Better Homes and Gardens® Books
An imprint of Meredith® Books

Making a Home

Editor: Linda Hallam

Senior Associate Design Director: Richard Michels

Contributing Editors: Jilann Severson, Diane Witosky

Photographers: King Au, Douglas Smith, Lark Smothermon

Illustrator: Buc Rogers

Copy Chief: Terri Fredrickson

Managers, Book Production: Pam Kvitne, Marjorie J. Schenkelberg

Contributing Copy Editor: Jane Woychick

Contributing Proofreaders: Maria Duryée, Gretchen Kauffman, Jennifer Mitchell, Susan J. Kling

Indexer: Kathleen Poole

Electronic Production Coordinator: Paula Forest

Editorial and Design Assistants: Kaye Chabot, Mary Lee Gavin, Karen Schirm

MEREDITH® BOOKS

Editor in Chief: James D. Blume

Design Director: Matt Strelecki

Managing Editor: Gregory H. Kayko

Executive Shelter Editor: Denise L. Caringer

Director, Retail Sales and Marketing: Terry Unsworth

Director, Sales, Special Markets: Rita McMullen

Director, Sales, Premiums: Michael A. Peterson

Director, Sales, Retail: Tom Wierzbicki

Director, Book Marketing: Brad Elmitt

Director, Operations: George A. Susral

Director, Production: Douglas M. Johnston

Vice President, General Manager: Jamie L. Martin

BETTER HOMES AND GARDEN® MAGAZINE

Editor in Chief: Jean LemMon

Executive Interior Design Editor: Sandra S. Soria

MEREDITH PUBLISHING GROUP

President, Publishing Group: Stephen M. Lacy

Vice President, Finance and Administration: Max Runciman

MEREDITH CORPORATION

Chairman and Chief Executive Officer: William T. Kerr

Chairman of the Executive Committee: E. T. Meredith III

All of us at Better Homes and Gardens® Books are dedicated to providing you with information and ideas to enhance your home. We welcome your comments and suggestions. Write to us at: Better Homes and Gardens Books, Shelter Editorial Department, 1716 Locust St., Des Moines, IA 50309-3023.

If you would like to purchase any of our books, check wherever quality books are sold. Visit us at bhgbooks.com.

CONTENTS

INTRODUCTION

MAKING YOUR HOME
PAGE 4

CHAPTER 1

ORGANIZATION
PAGE 9

CHAPTER 2

CLEANING ROUTINES
PAGE 51

CHAPTER 3

SURFACE CARE
PAGE 71

CHAPTER 4

FURNISHINGS CARE
PAGE 103

CHAPTER 5

KITCHEN KEEPING
PAGE 125

CHAPTER 6

LIVING & DINING ROOMS
PAGE 159

CHAPTER 7

BEDROOMS & BATHS
PAGE 183

CHAPTER 8

LINENS & LAUNDRY
PAGE 205

CHAPTER 9

HOUSE SYSTEMS
PAGE 231

CHAPTER 10

HOME ENVIRONMENT
PAGE 263

CHAPTER 11

ENTERTAINING
PAGE 289

CHAPTER 12

ETIQUETTE
PAGE 315

CHAPTER 13

RECORDS & REFERENCES
PAGE 335

CHAPTER 14

RESOURCES
PAGE 355

CHAPTER 15

INDEX
PAGE 369

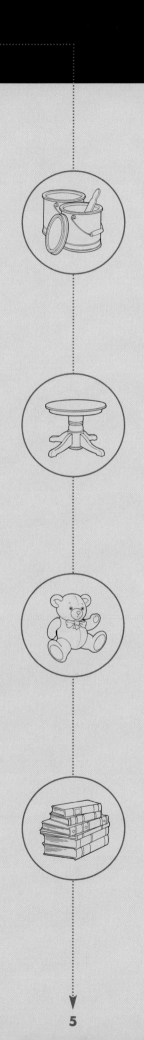

Making Your Home

I've often thought about what makes a home. I've concluded that the true measure of home is not about the past or the future. Home is about making the most of your life and your family's life every day. In the midst of finishing this book and starting others, I often think of the hard lessons I've learned through the years as my family and I

make our home. The most important one I've learned is to create a home and a life that you and your family enjoy. I think of planning, organizing, cleaning, cooking, and maintaining as the tools to making the home we want.

I've researched and written *Making a Home* because home is the most important place in the world. My premise for the book is as simple as the tabbed, ringbound format—a well-organized, clean, and safe home creates a peaceful, comfortable environment for you and your family. My goal for *Making a Home* is to provide accurate, current, concise information to help you safely and economically organize, furnish, clean, maintain, and enjoy your home.

There are no magic solutions, but with some thought and practice, you can make a home that nurtures you and your family. Last night, for instance, I worked until 6:30 and had dinner on the dining table for my youngest son, Forrest, and me by 7:15. (My husband Steve was working late.) We had a pork loin roasted slowly in a crockery cooker all day, fresh asparagus that Forrest sautéed in olive oil, and admittedly instant (but garlic-roasted) potatoes from the pantry. We put on a new Eric Clapton compact disc and looked up a painter we like in an art book.

Every day doesn't go this smoothly. It certainly didn't when Forrest and his older brother Dallas were small. But through the

years, I've made my home and family my priority, and I've found that thinking ahead, planning, stocking, and setting reasonable routines and expectations for children do work. I've devoted a chapter and a number of tip boxes in *Making a Home* to setting up time-saving routines that incorporate my experiences.

House and home have been a special interest of mine since I was a child. I grew up in the house where my mother was born, the house my grandmother lived in from the day she married until the day she died 72 years later. When I think of what it means to make a home, I think first of this rambling old house, with a big front porch where we still take family snapshots.

I learned through the years that home is more than a house, no matter how filled it is with memories. Home is where you live your life every day. In our years of marriage, Steve and I have lived in five houses in three states. Twenty years ago, we married under a flowering pear tree in the backyard of the small house I rented. As soon as we could, we bought our first house, a post-World War II box on the affordable side of town.

That house, with floor-length windows in the living room, faced west so we planted a fast-growing tulip poplar tree in the front yard to block the afternoon sun. When we lived in this house, we and our friends, mostly reporters like us on the daily newspapers, were only a few years out of college. We had baby and wedding showers, backyard barbeques, and welcome back and goodbye parties for our

mobile friends. For several years, a friend arrived by Model-T Ford in a Santa Claus suit for our annual children's Christmas cookies party.

When our boys were small, we moved to a bigger city so I could work at a magazine and Steve at a university—better hours for parents than daily newspapers. My new boss told us about a neighborhood of affordable houses and good public schools.

The house we bought on a quiet circle was a few years older, $20,000 more expensive, and minus the carport of our first house. Our budget was tight so we became dedicated do-it-yourselfers, and I was forced to become an organized working mother. We hung a porch swing the week we moved in. We redid the kitchen ourselves by painting the cabinets white and putting in a new vinyl floor. We even refinished the wood floors in the other rooms. With two small, active boys and several pets, I could have used the cleaning tips I've learned as I researched *Making a Home*.

Through the years, we painted every room at least once. I chose a salmon pink for the exterior (it had been dark red).

The change was so dramatic that Forrest didn't think it was his house—and refused to get out of the car—when he came home from his day at nursery school.

In this little house, I refined the cleaning, shopping, cooking, and laundry routines that still work for me and that I adapted for *Making a Home*. We do the laundry on Thursday night and clean the house on Saturday. Saturday afternoon I plan our meals for the week and do the grocery shopping. Through the years, I learned to do some of the cooking for the next week in advance and to use a crockery cooker. I found the week goes much smoother if we start each Monday with a clean house, fresh laundry, meals and food for the week ahead, and up-to-date paperwork.

Such cleaning and organizing are important parts of *Making a Home*, but savoring life at home is the heart of the book. That's why I've included sections on children's books, the family library, birthday parties, wedding and baby showers, summer cookouts, and

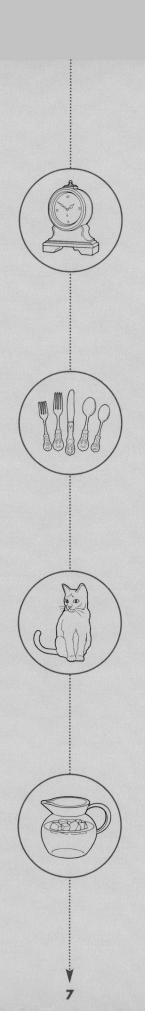

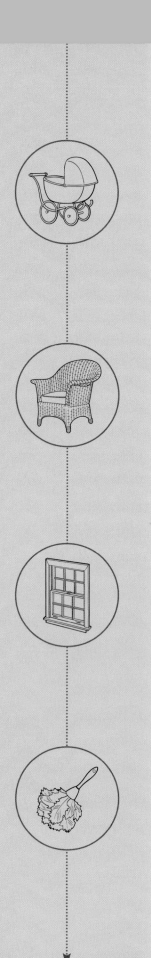

overnight guests, all the enjoyable and happy things I remember from our little pink house.

Eventually we moved a few miles away in the same school district. This sprawling split-level ranch needed TLC. It suffered from dated carpet and an overgrown but lushly planted back garden. We painted the open living and dining room a month after we moved in, right before we hosted my office Christmas party.

We finally had space for bigger parties. On a very hot summer afternoon, we called guests at the last minute to tell them to wear shorts when our air-conditioner broke before an engagement party. Because I like to entertain and have always had time and budget constraints, I've included fun, easy, and simple entertaining ideas in *Making a Home*.

We moved across the country after Dallas graduated from high school. A smaller house suited our lifestyle and college-strapped budget. We like walkable neighborhoods and found one with brick cottages, including our little house that was built in 1941. The house has an attic bedroom, a screen porch, and a basketball hoop. When it's warm, the porch is our living room. I read there by lamp light on summer nights, as does Dallas when he comes home from college. Forrest sets up his easel and paints. Some day I want a house with porches on all four

sides and a big dining room for our extended family. Until then, I'll make my home in this cottage or wherever life takes us.

I hope *Making a Home* will be useful to you and your life at home. And I hope that the information, advice, and sources in *Making a Home* will help you save time and money and create a

safe and comfortable haven of calm and order in your life. You can make the home you want for yourself and your family. Making a home isn't the easiest thing you'll ever do, but I promise it is the most worthwhile. Please call or e-mail me if you have any comments or suggestions.

Linda Hallam, editor, *Making a Home*, lhallam@mdp.com

The Whole-House Plan

- WHAT DO YOU REALLY NEED?,11
- WHERE DO YOU WANT TO KEEP IT?,11

Whole-House Solutions

- FAMILY ENTRY,16
- MUDROOM,18
- LIVING AREAS,19
- THE KITCHEN,27
- BEDROOM AND CLOSET,31
- KIDS' ROOMS AND NURSERY,34,36
- BATH AND POWDER ROOM,39
- FAMILY MEDICINE CABINET,41
- HOME OFFICE,42
- LAUNDRY ROOM,43
- ATTIC AND BASEMENT,44
- GARAGE AND STORAGE SHED,46

Super Solutions

- IDEAS FOR UNUSED SPACE,14
- SUGGESTIONS FOR DECLUTTERING,14
- STORING MUSICAL INSTRUMENTS,20
- STYLISH HOOKS AND PEGS,21
- RECYCLING TIPS,25

Apartment or Condo

- SPACE SAVERS,47
- IDEAS THAT WORK,47

Storage Safety

- SPECIAL CONCERNS,48
- HELPFUL SHELVING,49

Renting Space

- HOW TO FIND,50
- QUESTIONS TO ASK,50

The Whole-House Plan

Who doesn't dream of a place for everything and everything in its place? Most of us do—no matter how small or large our residence and how much storage we have. Every household chore is easier when your home is well-organized and relatively clutter-free. When you have to pick up and declutter before every cleaning or cooking chore, even small tasks seem monumental. Use this chapter to organize your furnishings and possessions. Choose from furniture-quality built-ins to budget retail solutions. In between, you'll find products at every price to solve almost any storage problem. Before you get started, keep in mind that you'll have more success by controlling the amount of possessions under your roof. If you don't own something, you don't have to store it or clean it.

SETTING PRIORITIES

What do you really need? If you are drowning in clutter and stuff, create a workable, reasonable plan. Set a time, such as a weekend, to go through your home and review its contents; then systematically get to work, room by room and closet by closet. (Allow extra time if you are dealing with notorious out-of-sight areas such as attics, basements, and garages.) Set a goal of clearing out one room per week or one room every two weeks, depending on your time and possessions. If you want quicker results, block out one hour each day, perhaps after the children are in bed if you are a parent. As you work, divide the items you don't need in that room into one of four boxes: trash, sell, donate, or store someplace else. Purchase boxes with lids and use the space under your beds or at the backs of closets if storage is limited. When you've cleared your home of its excess, you can find workable storage solutions.

Where do you want to keep it? Don't rush off to the store for home storage containers. Your solution will be more effective if you give thought to the things that you store. Tackle the most problematic areas first, such as the back door entry or mudroom. Before you make hard-and-fast decisions, keep a notebook handy for a few weeks to jot down your thoughts about clutter and storage issues. Keep these questions in mind: Where are you when you reach for an item? Where are you when you set it down? Is it something you seek out and find when you need it—keys, cold-weather gear, or the turkey roaster? Or is it an item that you want to remember—such as a library book or tape or a child's school

TIPTAG №1

Storage Fixes

DROP OFF SPOT:
- Identify a consistent place for items in transit, such as mail and school papers.
- Train every family member to use this area for items coming in and going out of your home.
- Install shelves and hooks at a back door. At a front door, add a basket for mail and a shelf in the coat closet for bulky items.

ONE STEP SOLUTIONS:
- Have baskets, bins, and shelves within easy reach for every family member.
- Set aside 30 minutes each week to transfer items, such as bank papers, into your filing system.

project—that isn't part of your daily routine?

Remember, as you assess your needs, that some specialized storage products and custom designs become obsolete when your family size or interests change. Before you invest in a storage solution of any price, ask "What else could this hold or organize?"

Super Solutions

SURVEY YOUR ROOMS

You'll have success with storage if you think of it as a whole-house organization project. By looking at the big picture, you'll see where to shift items and functions—and storage— for better organization. For example, if your children pile papers and school supplies in the dining room, the solution lies in creating study and storage areas in their bedrooms. If your small bedroom closet is packed with the clothes you wear, a solution may be to adapt the space with double-hung rods; you also can store out-of-season clothes at your dry cleaners to free up closet space.

As you survey your space, incorporate storage, particularly in small rooms and homes, as part of the decorating scheme. For example, a bookcase or étagère can organize collections, books, and magazines. If space is tight, such as in small apartments, attractive bins and boxes can be added to the bookcase to neatly conceal personal papers, bills, and work or school projects.

BASIC HELPERS

Don't overlook the obvious as you plan storage solutions. Some proven storage methods are so effective that they call for special recognition:

Hooks and pegs: These classic solutions were used for storage long before closets. Hooks and pegs come in a variety of styles, sizes, materials, and finishes and work well in areas where convenience and visible storage are beneficial, such as near the back door. Widen your horizons as you shop for these utilitarian items. Rather than a plastic stick-on hook, look for more decorative styles. Examples of decorative alternatives include metal coat and hat hooks, detailed wooden pegs, vintage doorknobs, or a find from the plumbing aisle. Flea markets, home-furnishings stores, and gift shops also sell specialty items, such as old doorknobs mounted on boards that can be used for decorative storage.

Roll-out shelving: Available at home centers and mass-market stores, this type of shelving comes in a range of widths and tiers. It works well for bringing items in the back to the front. If the load is light enough, a basket functions the same way.

For long wear and service, look for well-made, smooth, plastic-coated metal shelving or heavy-duty plastic shelving. Colors typically are white, tan, or other neutrals.

Contain Your Clutter

Newspapers:
Lightweight and attractive, wire mesh bins are ideal for back-door recycling. Handles make it easy to carry to the car or garage.

Newspapers:
Classic stackable bins are sized for newspapers but also work at the back door for recyclables such as bottles and cans.

Magazines and Catalogs:
Wire mesh bins with handles allow you to neatly store mail, magazines, and catalogs before sorting.

Magazines and Catalogs:
For items that you plan to keep for weeks or months, woven baskets provide neat and handsome storage.

Mail and Letters:
Busy households are neater with designated interim storage. Stash items that need weekly attention on a desk or counter.

Invoices and Receipts:
Upright organizers are for desk or counter storage. Use for papers that are kept for several weeks before filing, such as bills.

Whole-House Solutions

When storage and organization affect the enjoyment and function of your home, it's time to find answers. When space is tight and you have a lot to store, think creatively to tame your clutter. Use the following ideas for help.

USE OVERLOOKED STORAGE SPACE

At your feet: Build shallow drawers into the toe-kick space beneath base cabinets. Fitted with a touch-latch release, they can be opened with a tap of your toe.

In the wall: Carve out shallow display shelves between wall studs. This can be ideal for a kitchen or bath where many small items, such as spices or toiletries, are stored. Space flanking a fireplace also is a natural for storage.

Behind the wall: Cut a short stack of shelves, drawers, or even a closet into a wall backed by unfinished space, such as attics or dormers.

Under the stairs: This sometimes roomy space may be the most overlooked for home storage. Angled and deep, the space can be fitted with a series of pull-out, pantry-style shelving units that will swallow books, files, sporting equipment, games, and more.

Around a window or door: Take advantage of this wall space to build maximum decorative shelving for books and collectibles. To avoid sagging shelves, use ¾-inch plywood and restrict spans to no more than 24 inches between vertical supports. Have the top of a window seat built with hinges for concealed storage. In a young child's room, sliding panels are a safer alternative to avoid pinched little fingers.

In the built-in (banquette seating): Include built-in seating in compact dining areas. Have seating built with open space underneath to store books or have doors installed to conceal items stored under the seat. Another solution: Have seating built window-seat style with hinged tops to store larger items.

HOLD A GARAGE SALE

As you sort, clear, and organize, prepare for a garage sale. Designate a holding area, such as a corner of your basement or a closet shelf or two. Wash and neatly fold items. Keep masking tape and markers in the designated area. Price and identify each item before you store it. When the garage sale weekend arrives, you'll have a big task out of the way.

DONATE TO CHARITY

Declutter and do a good deed. Donate unwanted clothing and household items to a charitable organization. (Children's and infant's clothes are in particular demand.) Check to see if the organization will pick up large items, such as furniture. Some charities offer this service. It may also depend on the condition of the item. As an added benefit, any items donated to charitable organizations may be tax deductible. Keep a list of your donations, the condition of each item, and your receipt from the organization. If the item is valuable, take a snapshot or a digital photograph for your records. If you have an questions about what and how much is deductible, check with your tax preparer or the local office of the Internal Revenvue Service. For more information on charitable deductions, visit the IRS at www.irs.gov.

HIRE A PRO

If your time is limited and you have the money, get a grip on organization by hiring a professional. A professional organizer can offer advice and services tailored to you and your family. Areas normally covered are space and storage planning, managing paper, and busting clutter. Find a professional organizer in your area through the National Association of Professional Organizers at www.napo.net. Franchised or locally owned closet component firms also may offer space planning and storage advice along with installation fees for their products. Check with shops that sell closet organizing components.

Front Entries

This is the first peek visitors have into your home. While the goal is an attractive, uncluttered, functioning space, how it is set up depends on your residence and family. Don't allow this important part of your home to be even a temporary dumping ground.

DEFINING THE SITUATION

Organizing starts with the space. If the family uses a side or back door, mail and packages may be the main front-entry organizing issues. If this is the entry everyone uses, or if you live in an apartment or condominium unit with only one door to the outside, you'll need an aggressive corralling and controlling strategy. Realistically assess how much stuff enters and leaves your home through this area. Think about how long items need to be in the entry area before they can be stored.

SEASONAL CONCERNS

Because this is an entry from the outdoors, cold-weather and rain gear, such as coats, boots, slickers and umbrellas, may need to be stored nearby. In a snowy locale, a bench where you can take off or put on boots, with nearby storage for boots, gloves, and hats prevents tracking slush and outer wear through the house.

smartideas

Sell Your Surplus

CONSIGNMENT SHOPS
Look into shops that resell clothing and home furnishings. Clothing should be clean, repaired, and in good condition. Furniture and home furnishings should be in salable condition. Expect to receive a percentage of the sales price without investing the time and energy of a garage sale.

TRADE-IN OPTIONS
Look into variations of trade-in policy for items such as infant's and children's clothing. Both types are often outgrown or are rarely worn before they wear out. Ask about policies for trading in infant furniture, such as cribs, or items such as baby carriers or car seats.

IDEAS THAT WORK

■ If you buy or build a house, don't overlook the convenience of a coat closet near the front door. A bench for changing shoes, perhaps with a storage rack, encourages neatness.

■ Control incoming and outgoing mail, keys, and small packages with a hall chest. Find a style—from traditional to contemporary—and a size that fits your space. Use the top drawer or a tray on the top for mail. If the family primarily uses this entry, school papers, books and tapes to be returned to the library or video rental store, and other transit items can be stored neatly in the chest.

QUICK FIXES

No room for a chest? Hang a shelf for mail and keys. Have a local carpenter craft one to your specifications or check with companies and local retailers.

No coat closet? Install a coat rack and rotate seasonal coats and rain gear to avoid clutter. An umbrella stand is an old-fashioned convenience that serves a practical purpose.

Family Entries

Depending on the layout of your home, you and your family may enter through a garage or carport or a side or back door. Whether this is a back-stoop space or part of the porch or kitchen, the family entry has the potential of becoming the family dumping ground. Because guests may not use this entry, it's tempting to let clutter pile up. Here are organizing ideas to control the stuff of life.

DEFINING YOUR NEEDS

Consider how you and your family use the entry—and what comes and goes each day. Use the space to keep the household running smoothly. Items should be needed daily or frequently. Pet owners find it convenient to keep leashes at this entry. Bottom line: The less unnecessary stuff you keep in this busy area, the better.

SEASONAL CONCERNS

The family entry stores rain and winter gear, such as slickers, umbrellas, hats, jackets, and boots. During the school year or special camp programs, sports equipment, book and athletic bags, and lunch boxes typically pass through this area.

IDEAS THAT WORK

■ If space allows, plan or redesign the family entry with built-ins. Designate one wall as a mini locker with a built-in unit for sports gear. Measure the sizes of key pieces of equipment, such as tennis rackets, baseball bats, and hockey sticks, and have shelves built to size. Purchase bins or buckets to corral smaller items such as tennis balls and baseballs. Use this area for sports gear in active use. Organize out-of-season gear in the garage or basement.

■ Allow a separate shelf or two, preferably with racks for drying, for

---

TIME SAVER

Front Door Organizers

•

Place a small chest or narrow table as near as possible to the front entry. Designate this as your transit area. Hang an attractive rack, pegboard, or shelf for additional organizing efforts. Hang a hat rack for shopping bags, jackets, and backpacks.

Bookshelf Construction

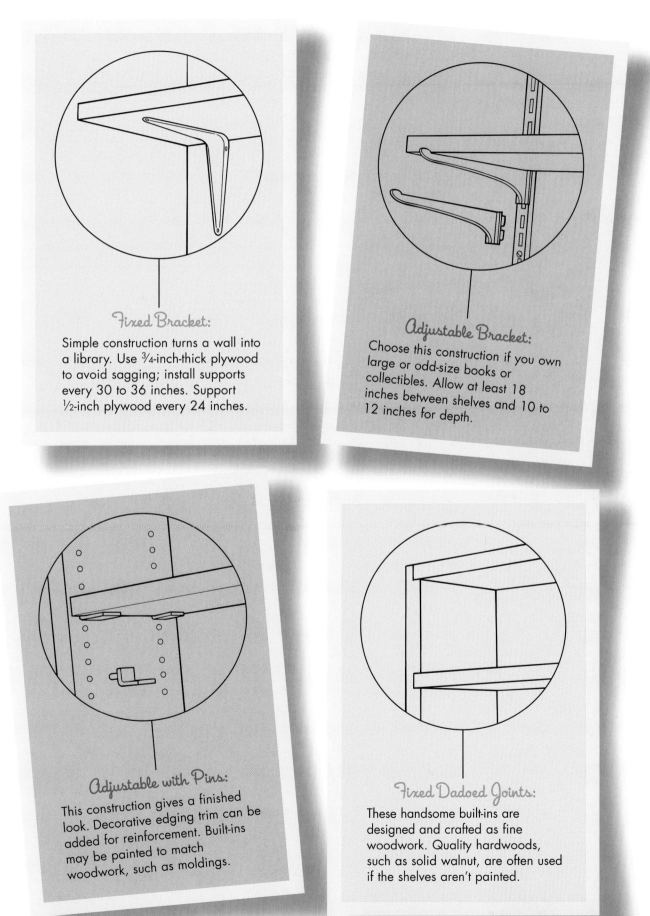

Fixed Bracket:

Simple construction turns a wall into a library. Use ¾-inch-thick plywood to avoid sagging; install supports every 30 to 36 inches. Support ½-inch plywood every 24 inches.

Adjustable Bracket:

Choose this construction if you own large or odd-size books or collectibles. Allow at least 18 inches between shelves and 10 to 12 inches for depth.

Adjustable with Pins:

This construction gives a finished look. Decorative edging trim can be added for reinforcement. Built-ins may be painted to match woodwork, such as moldings.

Fixed Dadoed Joints:

These handsome built-ins are designed and crafted as fine woodwork. Quality hardwoods, such as solid walnut, are often used if the shelves aren't painted.

dirty or muddy athletic shoes. If space permits, designate sections of the built-in for individual shelves or bins for each child or adult who plays a sport. A nearby bulletin board is a convenient way to keep game and practice times on the calendar.

QUICK FIXES

If you or your child needs a place to pull off boots or change from athletic shoes, add built-in seating with handy sports storage. With a simple plywood addition, perhaps crafted as window seat with a hinged lid, you'll have a place to neatly stash gear. Apply a tough enamel paint to stand up to daily life. Or, purchase a sturdy unfinished chest and add racks and bins inside for shoes or gear. Purchase a heavy-duty, wide bench and add bins below the seat to keep gear handy and out of family foot traffic.

Mudrooms

Once a common feature of country houses, mudrooms are a practical way to keep your house clean—especially if you live in a climate with months of wet or snowy weather. In traditional farmhouse design, the mudroom was the working entry from the outdoors into the house. In current design, country or country-style houses may be designed with a combination laundry and mudroom—or with a combination mudroom and potting area. A small bathroom, with a shower or at least a sink, may be included for cleanups. If space is tight, a mudroom can be an expanded back-entry area with storage for outdoor gear, a place to change and store shoes and boots and leave soiled outdoor clothing. Shelves, racks, hooks, and pegs provide storage and keep items from being strewn throughout the house.

DEFINING YOUR NEEDS

Decide what you need before you plan your mudroom. Do you live in the country and have outdoor animals or do you garden much of the year? Do you work in an occupation that requires you to clean up or store gear? Do you walk to work or walk from the bus stop or train and need a neat place to leave your boots and coat to dry? Do your children play a variety of outdoor sports? Will you combine your mudroom with another function, such as doubling as laundry room? Will a small bath or a sink for washing up be included in the plan? Each situation demands its own storage solutions.

SEASONAL CONCERNS

The name says it all. Mudrooms were originally designed to keep mud from the farmyard out of the house. There's still a good reason to designate such a space. In some climates, your concern may be dust and dirt or winter salt and sand from the city streets. If boot or shoe storage is only seasonal, consider placing shoe or boot racks in the mudroom when needed.

Living Areas

Whether you call this area a living room, family room, or great-room, the furnishings in this space are what make your residence a home. How do you organize and store family photographs, books, magazines, travel souvenirs, collections, musical instruments, electronic gear, and perhaps toys and games?

DEFINING YOUR NEEDS

Consider the type of living area you have. Do you have the traditional formal living room and a family room or den? Do you have only one living room, or a combination living area and dining room? If you have just one living area, how do you use it?

THE FORMAL LIVING ROOM

In homes with two or more living areas, the living room is usually used for conversation and entertaining rather than active family living. Storage is based on appearance and style rather than strictly utilitarian concerns. Some home styles, such as the bungalow, feature built-in shelves flanking the fireplace. Current home styles may include a small living room off the entry that doubles as a library. The addition of built-in bookshelves may be all it takes to convert a room into a dual-purpose library and formal sitting room. To add interest to a living room, paint the backs of the built-ins a dramatic color, such as red. If your budget allows, have the built-ins constructed with base cabinets that complement the room's woodwork for concealed storage. This can be an ideal solution if you want a television or other electronic equipment in the room.

THE FAMILY ROOM OR DEN

Second only to the kitchen in family activity, the family room has its own unique organization and storage needs. In open plans, the family room is usually part of the kitchen and close to a secondary entry. Whether that entry is a mudroom or a side or back door, clutter in the area must be controlled to preserve the appearance and functioning of the family's main living space. (See pages 16–18 for ideas.) Because this is where the family lives, the daily clutter of life—such as newspapers, magazines, mail, books, hobbies, projects, videos, and perhaps the computer—can take over. If clutter and stuff are problems for your family, hone in on the various cluttering activities and plan your storage accordingly.

The position of the television in the living room or den—tucked away or open and visible—dictates how much storage is open and

Home Remedies

OLD-FASHIONED FIXES

Organize with Pegs

Shaker-style pegs are an easy and attractive way to add back-door storage. Purchase a shelf unit with pegs to hang hats, gloves, and scarves. The shelf above provides room for open storage or for concealed storage in baskets and bins. Install two levels of pegs to double the available storage. Less used items stowed on the lower level will be covered by frequently used items on the top row.

Get Hooked on Hooks

Reduce time spent looking for misplaced items. Hang tiny hooks or a low shelf next to the peg rack to organize keys or catch sunglasses, garage door openers, and other often misplaced items.

how much is concealed. For many families, built-ins, wall-mounted bookshelves, or bookcases with bins or baskets are requirements for keeping things under control.

If children use the family room as a play area, a toy box and bins for blocks and other small items are essential. Large sturdy baskets for toys and books are another option. Window seats also add additional, accessible storage.

THE GREAT-ROOM

This combination room offers challenges and opportunities for organization. Because the space is open and visible, plan for concealed storage as well as open shelving. Built-in seating with storage can expand your options in the dining and living areas of a great-room. If built-ins aren't practical in your situation, purchase freestanding storage units that offer a combination of open shelves and concealed storage.

For additional concealed storage, use trunks or ottomans with hinged lids. Arrange baskets or bins inside these pieces to keep small items or crafts neat and organized. If you like a vintage look, shop for a bookrack and accent table combination that can add chair-side storage. Plan built-ins for electronic and computer equipment or purchase storage units geared to your needs. Computer cabinets designed to resemble armoires when the door or doors are closed are practical in open spaces.

MUSICAL INSTRUMENTS

These valuable pieces deserve special care in your organization plan. Your piano will hold its tune much longer if it is placed against an interior wall. This instrument is sensitive even to overnight temperature swings through an outside wall. Pianos also need humidity. If the air in your home is dry from the climate or from indoor heating, compensate with a combination humidifier-sensor attachment available for pianos. (Check with a piano dealer for a source and proper installation.)

If you own brass, wind, or string instruments, keep them in their cases, which may have humidifier and sensor attachments. (If your instrument is old, check out the possibilities of a new case for safer storage.) If you are storing an instrument for use in years to come, such as an older child's band instrument for a younger sibling, store it in a climate-controlled part of your home, never an unheated attic or dank basement.

Remove all tuning slides and valves from brass instruments, such as trumpets and tubas; then wrap each piece in tissue paper or cloth. Don't use plastic because it retains moisture. Remove the reeds of a clarinet, oboe, and other woodwind instruments. For stringed instruments, such as violins and cello, turn the keys to release the pressure from the strings; store the instruments in their

BUDGET STRETCHER

Bar Keeping

Convert a vintage armoire or wardrobe into a liquor cabinet or bar. Reinforce shelves to store heavy bottles. Add a wine rack or two. Attach under-shelf, track-style hangers designed for footed glasses. Fill flat baskets with corkscrews, stirrers, cocktail napkins, and coasters.

Decorative Hooks and Pegs

Hall Hooks:
No coat closet? Install handsome chrome- or brass-plated hooks near the front door. Also hang on the back of your bathroom door for robes or extra towels.

Country Pegs:
Hang wherever you need extra storage. Pegs work well at the back door for everyday gear and shopping bags. Also add to your kitchen, children's room, or laundry.

Rustic Iron Hooks:
Need heavy-duty hooks for backpacks or book bags? Reminiscent of Early American ironwork, these sturdy hooks are just the ticket. Hang one for each family member.

Contemporary Chrome:
For modern style, look for sleek designs for your kitchen, bath, hall, or entry. Chrome hooks are a stylish solution for everything from coats to kitchen towels.

Instant Closet:
When one or two hangers won't do, add a multipronged hanger at your family entrance. This shapely, sturdy design organizes with two rows of staggered hooks.

Handy Cup Hooks:
Unbeatable for saving space and for organizing, cup hooks simply screw into the undersides of shelves for quick storage. Use for open shelves too.

cases, fitted with a humidifier and sensor to prevent cracking.

ENTERTAINING

Adapt vintage, secondhand, or reproduction wardrobes or armoires as television cabinets. Measure your television, including the depth, before shopping for such a piece. Some storage pieces are too shallow to hold a television. Normally, the back of the unit will have to be drilled or cut for wiring, and well-supported shelves added. These units are usually large enough to also house the video cassette recorder and tapes. As an alternative, use such a unit for a compact disc player, compact discs, and tapes.

A butler's tray is a classic solution for working a bar into a living room. If you use a butler's tray, pour liquors or sherry into decanters. Vintage tea carts on wheels or vintage or reproduction metal utility carts also serve the purpose.

IDEAS THAT WORK

▪ Install floor-to-ceiling metal shelving tracks on one or more walls in your family room or den. Have ¾-inch thick, 10- to 12-inch-deep plywood planks cut to fit the wall, and hang them from adjustable brackets. Support the shelves at least every 24 inches to prevent sagging. Use stock molding and other stock detailing to trim basic built-ins or freestanding storage pieces. Look for detailing at home centers and at specialty woodworking shops that carry reproduction trim, often based on 19th- and early-20th-century styles.

▪ Fit shelves to the slope of a vaulted ceiling. Use the centered wall space above the door for extra display. Build in sturdy shelves to display heavy collectibles. Use ¾-inch plywood rather than ½-inch and reinforce with edging strips. Vary heights and widths to accommodate your collectibles.

▪ Before anchoring shelves to the wall, check access to electrical outlets and wiring boxes. Be certain you have the number of outlets and electrical boxes you need now and in the future. When possible, divide shelving into groups of three—an odd number is more visually pleasing than an even number.

▪ Think beyond the obvious for storage and display. Look at a variety of pieces, such as metal baker's racks, for shelving options.

SPACE SAVERS

Hang a painting, print, or photograph from a vertical bookcase support for prominent display. The piece immediately takes on importance and conserves valuable wall space.

▪ Buy your display pieces ready-made and painted or stained. Accessory and decorating shops and home decorating catalogs sell shelves and brackets, including ledges for art and framed photography. Measure spaces and order to fit. Stack several shelves for the display you need. Shop for a ready-made wall-mounted cabinet or a hanging corner cupboard. These are ideal for organizing

SPACE SAVER

Plate Racks For Storage

•

Three-tiered metal plate racks, available from home furnishings stores and catalogs, are ideal for quick storage. Use a plate rack to group potted plants in a sunny living or dining area, to organize soaps and towels in a bath, or for counter storage in a small kitchen.

a collection of small objects.

■ Turn a closet into a library by removing the door, replacing the trim, and adding interior shelves. Measure a love seat or sofa and have shelves built on either side for a recessed nook.

■ House a television in a cabinet to create a room divider between open living and dining areas. Maximize use of the space by incorporating bench seating with storage into the room divider. Have the bench crafted so the top lifts for magazines, videocassettes, table linens, or other items you like to keep handy.

Even rooms with 8-foot ceilings have enough space for a bookshelf over the door. The same idea can work with wide cased openings if you reinforce the spans every 24 inches. Have shelving built from floor to ceiling on the unbroken wall in a small den to create a library effect. Add handsome boxes or baskets with tops for concealed storage. Buy matching boxes or baskets in identical or in graduated sizes. If you save magazines, purchase specially sized containers for a neat appearance.

QUICK FIXES

Add a pair of étagères, freestanding open shelves, to a living room to display collectibles. Convert baskets or trunks into cocktail or coffee tables. Inside, store throws, magazines, or newspapers. If space is extremely limited, use trunks or baskets on stands for side tables.

If flea market is your style, stack vintage suitcases for side tables. Use the interiors to store games, magazines, or seasonal throws.

Purchase large flat baskets to store newspapers. If reading material takes over your living areas, add one or more magazine racks. Clear out newspapers daily and magazines every week or two. Move magazines you want to save to specially designed storage units or stack them neatly on bookshelves.

Seriously desperate for living room storage? Use the space under a skirted particleboard table to temporarily declutter a room of magazines or books. Purchase tables, such as glass-top patio tables, that include shelf-style bases. Place a console table behind a sofa or against the wall and add squared wicker baskets or trunks with tops. Stack magazines in flat baskets under a console table.

In informal living areas, think creatively to maximize storage. Add a shelf around the perimeter of your room for basket or bin storage. Purchase metal, European-style magazine bins and attach to the wall. Make books and magazines you plan to keep part of the decor by neatly stacking oversized books to serve as small tables. (Keep

TIP TAG № 2
Paper Clutter

LETTERS AND BILLS:
• Buy flat baskets, wire bins, or wood boxes for in and out boxes.
• Use a metal vertical sorter and file folders to sort bills. Set aside 30 minutes each week for personal paperwork, including children's schoolwork and reports.
• Organize paperwork with a metal filing cabinet and tabbed folders. Store in a closet if space is tight.

NEWSPAPERS:
• Use a basket or magazine rack to keep daily papers handy.
• Buy a flat basket to organize newspapers for recycling. Designate a recycling spot.

coasters nearby to protect your books from glasses and cups in case anyone wants to use your stacked books as a handy side table.) Likewise, stacks of design or travel magazines can be attractive on the lower shelf of a bookcase.

Dining Areas

Whether your home has one dining area or both formal and informal dining spaces, storage in or near the dining area is the key to organization and function. Built-ins can be customized to your needs, but freestanding wardrobes, cupboards, and armoires adapt well and can add style to your setting.

SEASONAL CONCERNS

If you use some items, such as holiday china or serving pieces, only occasionally, consider storing them elsewhere. This will free up valuable space for the dinnerware and glasses you use frequently. When you entertain during the holiday, a bar cart may work better than keeping a bar set up year around.

SPACE SAVERS

Turn an interior wall of your dining room into a sideboard by installing floor-to-ceiling cabinets. Use the top cabinet to store little-used or seasonal items, such as holiday decorations. This arrangement provides much-needed storage in houses built without basements or attics. It's also better than garage storage for temperature and humidity control, especially in damp climates.

In a small dining room, build a wall of cabinets and open shelves around the window. Include a wine rack for handy storage. Find room for a built-in china cabinet by using space between wall studs. This shallow storage works for glasses and plate display. Fit a compact corner cupboard into a small dining area. Look for vintage pieces or paint or stain an unfinished one. Use the top of the cupboard for extra display or for plants that require little light.

IDEAS THAT WORK

■Maximize storage and function with a built-in sideboard or server for china, flatware, linens, and serving pieces. Measure your plates, trays, and serving pieces for a custom fit. Add a built-in china cabinet with glass doors on both sides to define a dining area without blocking light.

In an informal dining area, take advantage of the counter between the kitchen and dining room by attaching glass shelves with metal supports. Glass keeps the look open and adds display. If you have curved wood shelves, common in homes built in the 1940s and 1950s, replace them with glass.

■Consider something other than a matching dining room suite. You can often get better buys on antique, vintage, reproduction, or contemporary sideboards sold separately. If stained pieces aren't

---

BUDGET STRETCHER

Create Your Own Server

•

No space for a conventional server or sideboard? Purchase a vintage or reproduction demilune (half-round) chest or other small chest. Line the drawers with special silver-storage cloth to slow tarnishing if you are storing sterling silver or silver-plated pieces.

What You Can Recycle

Glass:
Rinse food jars to avoid attracting pests to your recycling. Glass bottles, such as wine bottles, may be returnable to markets for deposit.

Newsprint:
Stack neatly in a box or bin to save space. In some areas, newspapers have to be tied with twine. Donate magazines to nonprofit groups.

Metal Cans:
Rinse to avoid attracting pests. To save space, open the lids and flatten by stepping on them. Plastic lids may have to be sorted with plastics.

Drink Cans:
Beer and soft-drink cans are often returnable for deposit at grocers or recycling centers. Some cities require cans to be sorted from paper.

Boxes:
In areas that recycle boxes, flattening may be required. If recycling isn't an option, school and community groups often need sturdy, clean ones.

Plastics:
Depending on your area, plastic bottles may be returnable for deposits— or recyclable through city pick up. Rinse, as sugars and milk attract pests.

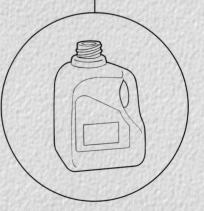

compatible, prime and paint the sideboard or detail with a decorative paint finish. Look for pieces that are compatible in scale and style. Use a narrow console table, such as a metal and glass piece, for a server in a small dining area. This type of piece takes up much less space than a conventional sideboard.

▪ Put your library to work with double duty. If you are a collector or have a home library, have floor-to-ceiling bookshelves installed on one or more walls of your dining room. Have shelves build around cased opening and flanking windows to create a library ambiance.

QUICK FIXES

Replace solid doors with glass-paned ones to update an old server. Have an old sideboard refinished with a combination of colors and finishes and updated hardware. Replace pulls on a built-in or freestanding server; look at some of the fun motifs on the market, such as knives and forks, stylized leaves, or animals. To stretch your dollar, mix these special pulls with plain ones from a home center. Or mix plain pulls of different colors.

Combine two metal or sturdy wood wine racks with a glass or painted plywood top for a server with storage. Place away from direct sun to avoid damage to your wine. Purchase a commercial serving stand from a restaurant supply company and top with a decorative, tole-type tray for a server.

Make a sideboard server by skirting a plywood base and having a plywood top cut to fit. Use a heavy cloth, such as tightly woven linen, for pleats or gathers. Take advantage of the space underneath—with baskets, a wicker trunk, or stackable plastic bins or boxes—for extra out-of-sight storage. For organizing, buy a pair of stacked, pullout vinyl bins on stands and place them underneath to organize linens and serving pieces.

Butler's Pantry

Traditionally the butler's pantry is a small room between the dining room and kitchen used for storing china, silver, glassware, serving pieces, and linens. This arrangement works well for families who entertain and need extra storage and serving pieces. However, many of the convenient organizing ideas of the traditional butler's pantry also can be incorporated into dining rooms and informal dining areas. Although storage in a butler's pantry is often custom-built, stock pieces, such as plate and glass organizers and lazy Susans, can turn a closet or even a sideboard into your own version of this handy pantry.

DEFINING YOUR NEEDS

Before you plan a butler's pantry, determine exactly what you want to store. A combination of open and concealed storage provides accessibility and a convenient way to store more utilitarian objects.

Storage Specifics
•

Shop organizing stores or websites (see sources on pages 357-368) to find storage tailored to your needs. Items include dispensers for bread, pet food, canned drinks, paper plates, and plastic bags; stacked inserts to double drawer storage; and holders for liter-size bottles.

If you are beginning to set up a household, plan storage space for future serving pieces, such as large trays and coffeemakers.

PANTRY POINTERS

Fit stock under-the-counter cabinets with easy-slide drawer glides and wood dividers sized to your china. (Check with a kitchen cabinet firm.) Put stock plastic or wire dividers into drawers, and line them with antitarnish cloth if you store silver pieces there. If you use easy-drawer glides for bar storage, reinforce the drawers to support the weight of liquor bottles.

Keep tablecloths, runners, place mats, and napkins neat and unwrinkled with a pullout unit constructed from oversize wooden dowels mounted inside a frame.

Adapt storage to specific needs: Have an upper shelf custom made for stemware storage, or install tracks (available at hardware stores) on the underside of a shelf. Use dowels from a home center or lumber store for vertical plate storage. Such cabinets often are open on both sides for easy access.

SPACE SAVERS

Construct your own butler's pantry by building shelving around a window in a back hall, laundry room, or kitchen. Choose adjustable shelves so you can store items of various heights.

If you have a closet in your dining room or nearby in a hall or kitchen, use the space for a butler's pantry. Purchase plastic stacking bins for dishes and glasses and hang tracks under shelves for wine glasses. Install old-fashioned cup hooks for cups and mugs. Use flat, lined baskets for stainless flatware. If you have silver or silver plate, store it in a chest to avoid tarnishing. Purchase racks, such as foldout racks used for tea towels, to hang table linens on the back of the door. Use the top shelf for large serving pieces, such as chafing dishes, or items that you use infrequently, such as coffee carafes and punch bowls.

QUICK FIXES

Add a baker's rack or cupboard to create a handy mini butler's pantry. Shop for a baker's rack with wide lower shelves for a convenient serving counter.

The Kitchen

DEFINING YOUR NEEDS

Storage is the key to how well your kitchen functions. No room in the house is more storage-oriented. How much and what kind of storage you need depends on the size of your family, how much you

Home Remedies

KITCHEN FIXES

Creative Storage

Add style and personality to your kitchen as you find creative storage uses for interesting items. Use a new or vintage fish poacher to organize oils and condiments on the counter. Store rarely used items in large bowls or crocks arranged along cabinet tops. Collect pitchers and crocks to hold wooden spoons and serving utensils.

Handy Holders

Purchase a wooden expandable rack with pegs to hang mugs. Store spices in test tubes with corks, neatly in a rack. Organize small envelopes in berry baskets. Corral family flatware in a divided basket. Use one compartment for everyday cotton or paper napkins.

cook, your lifestyle, and your cooking style. Before you get started, ask yourself:

▸Do you need utensils and cookware for entertaining and trying out new cuisines and recipes? Do you have time for entertaining?

▸Do you like to do a special type of cooking?

▸Do you need cookbook storage? What appliances do you use?

▸Do you like utensils, small appliances, mugs, and other items within easy reach? Do you prefer clean, uncluttered countertops?

▸How frequently do you go to the grocery store? Do you cook primarily from the freezer or the pantry? Do you need space for refrigerated and unrefrigerated fresh produce?

▸Where does your family eat most of its meals? Is it convenient to keep table linens, dinnerware, and flatware in the kitchen?

PANTRY POINTERS

Carve out a pantry from a sliver of wall space. When space is narrow but deep, fit the space with pullout shelving to put items at your fingertips; install shallow shelves between wall studs to store cans one row deep.

Store rice, beans, flour, cornmeal, cereal, and dry staples in sealed see-through containers. You'll keep pests away and always know supply levels. Also use containers for small packets of sauce mixes that can get lost in the pantry. Squared containers are more space-efficient than round containers.

CABINETS AND SHELVES

Consider options other than standard base cabinets. Standard cabinets are cheaper to build and install, but custom-made cabinets with both deep and shallow drawers may better organize kitchen items. Plates and bowls can be stored in drawers if you use dividers. Existing cabinets can be retrofitted with pullouts. Check with a local cabinet firm for options.

SPACE SAVERS

Maximize work space by keeping appliances on the counter that you use every day. Hang utensils from wall-mounted hooks or pegboards. Attach a magnetic timer to the rack.

If you have a blank wall and need storage, install a counter-to-ceiling metal grid and hang cookware and utensils from S-hooks. Mount a narrow shelf on the backsplash to keep salt and pepper, mugs, and frequently used items off the counter. Such storage might seem convenient for spices, but spices are better stored in a cabinet away from heat.

Hang a shelf over a window. A mesh metal shelf with S-hooks can hold items on its underside. Purchase a new or vintage hanging cabinet or corner cupboard for open storage in your kitchen. If an old piece has a timeworn finish, clean it up and enjoy the patina. Buy ready-made picture ledges, available from decorating shops and

SPACE SAVER

Cabinet Keepers

•

Fit cabinet doors with racks to easily find cookware lids and canned goods. This is also a good space-stretcher for a small pantry. Install a rack for trash bags. Organize shelves with revolving racks for spices and other staple ingredients.

Kitchen Storage Ideas

Drawer Divider:

Protect, sort, and organize everyday flatware with handy dividers. Laminate and wood divider boxes are sturdy and easy to clean. Double dividers fit deep drawers.

Double Lazy Susan:

Create accessibility and maximize cabinet storage with a lazy Susan. Models with an adjustable top shelf provide room for tall canned goods, spices, and condiments.

Spice Stairs:

Forget the aggravation of lost spices with staggered shelves that let you see what you have on hand. Sources for handy kitchen storage are on page 360.

Wire Produce Baskets:

Use attractive and durable baskets to neatly organize nonrefrigerated produce, such as bananas, potatoes, and onions. These baskets also store kitchen linens.

specialty catalogs, and have a frame shop rout grooves for plates. Hang them around your kitchen as plate racks.

IDEAS THAT WORK

■ For the ultimate in accessible storage, use open wall storage and open under-the-counter storage in place of conventional cabinets. Vary the heights of shelves or install adjustable shelves to expand your options. Use sturdy decorative baskets for items such as produce.

■ Retrofit existing base cabinets with pullout bins, racks, and lazy Susans for tight corners. Use baskets or color-coded plastic trays if you need to store easy-to-lose items. If you frequently use heavy kitchen equipment, such as a mixer or food processor, consider storing it on its own pullout and pull-up tray. Check with kitchen designers, custom dealers, or cabinetmakers for installation.

■ Think recycling. A standard base cabinet is normally sized to hold two kitchen bins—an easy way to divide glass from plastic. For easy recycling, adapt one side with a pullout shelf and vinyl-coated racks.

Home centers, discount stores, and shops specializing in organizing offer a wide selection of products. If space allows, an antique or reproduction dresser or dry sink adds kitchen display and handy concealed storage. Install cup hooks for a neat look.

QUICK FIXES

Use drawer dividers for utensils instead of plastic organizers that quickly fill up with stuff. Visit a discount store, home center, or organizing specialty store to find ways to customize a kitchen. Add items such as lazy Susans to make corners accessible.

Find new uses for standard items. Stools, benches, and bookcases, all available from unfinished furniture stores, are ideal for attractive storage. (Remember, cookbooks need storage too.) Place a narrow table against a wall and arrange baskets underneath.

Products such as racks for glasses and hooks for cups and inside-the-door attachments utilize every bit of space.

Be neat and selective when concealed storage space is tight. As you buy cookware, collect only one or two types that display well together. This is more attractive than a hodgepodge of styles and materials. If you don't have a pantry, add shelves at the back of the kitchen door to store canned goods and seasonal items.

Forget custom. Buy and hang a decorative shelf for spices. Use large decorative jars to hold bulk quantities of foods. Before buying jars for this purpose, ask whether the finishes are safe for food.

Compensate for minimal storage. Purchase a multitiered plate rack to keep everyday plates handy. Use acrylic or natural woven baskets with several compartments, such as those designed for buffets, to store frequently used flatware and napkins. Tailor basket storage to your style. Use a chrome-plated steel basket with handles to keep fresh fruit neatly arranged, or store kitchen towels in a simple wire basket with wood handles. Collect baskets in one style and arrange on the top of cabinets—if space allows—to hold kitchen items, such as extra tools or napkins, when space is very tight.

Bedrooms

This is the most personal room of your home. Unless you constantly strive to be neat and tidy, it's easy to let down your guard and give in to clutter and chaos. When you get a handle on organization, however, you are on the way to creating a peaceful retreat. For more information on closet organization, see page 36.

DEFINING YOUR NEEDS

Normally a bedroom has at least a small closet, but beyond that, consider what you need and want for bedroom storage.

▸Do you need storage space for clothing beyond the closet and conventional chest or dresser? (You may have a small closet, or two people may share a standard-size closet.)

▸Do you have space for additional storage pieces?

▸Do you have to store seasonal clothing and bedding in the bedroom?

▸Do you use the bedroom for a home office, study, library, computer room, or hobby room?

▸Do you need to store papers and records in your bedroom?

SPACE SAVERS

Choose perforated clothes hampers that are too handsome to hide. They keep dirty clothes out of sight and organized for the laundry. Buy two: one for washable clothing and one for dry cleaning only. In a country- or cottage-style bedroom, use white wicker hampers to keep clothes for the laundry or cleaners. Shop antiques stores or flea markets for vintage hampers.

In a bedroom with little or no storage, use decorative storage cubes with lift-off lids. These work well for matching bedside tables or at the foot of the bed in place of a more conventional blanket chest. Specialty home decorating stores and catalogs carry variations of the versatile storage wood cube.

Use the space under a bed for heavy duty plastic or cardboard storage boxes. (Purchase boxes with tight-fitting lids to keep out dust.) This space works well for out-of-season items, such as sweaters or blankets. Use it for belongings you don't need every day but that require climate control, such as photographs, books, and heirloom linens. Skirt a particleboard table and use the space

TIPTAG №3

Repurpose

RACKS AND PEGS:

• Install a plate rack and use it to display dishes and saucers.

• Hang an expandable wood or plastic wall-mounted hat rack for tool or basket storage. Hang a second to keep coffee mugs handy. Hang mesh shopping bags from the racks to store produce.

• Add Shaker pegs or a hat rack at the back door for shopping bags.

BASKETS:

• Hang a basket or two from your pot rack for kitchen linens, such as tea towels and cotton napkins.

• Fill flat baskets with everyday flatware and cooking utensils, such as wooden spoons.

underneath for stacked boxes. Some plywood table bases are made with a shelf for stacked boxes. Add a padded or wood bench and use the space underneath to stash out-of-season items in wicker suitcases or other decorative boxes.

IDEAS THAT WORK

If space allows, use the most classic storage of all—the desk. Choose one with the drawer space you need. A small writing table can work if you need minimum storage for supplies. Other ideas:

- Take advantage of bedroom walls with floor-to-ceiling bookshelves.
- Box in windows with shelves above and window seats below to use every bit of space for storage and display.
- Buy a bed with integral, under-the-mattress storage. Check with a full-service furniture store.
- Get double duty out of your nightstand by placing a decorative box from an import store on a stand. Such decorative hinged boxes, which work well as lamp tables, are easy to access and handy for tissues, glasses, reading material, and miscellaneous clutter.
- Get both storage and style from interesting mismatched vintage furniture. Try a burnished metal dresser or a 1930s dressing table with drawers for style. Look for a nicely shaped piece to paint.
- When you need maximum storage for items such as hats and bulky duvets or quilts, add a vintage or reproduction trunk or chest at the foot of the bed. Affordable wicker is easy to move.

QUICK FIXES

Hang fabric panels on wire line or a drapery rod suspended from the ceiling to add concealed storage in a room. Choose washable cotton fabrics that complement your decorating scheme.

Purchase matching bookshelf units to turn your bedroom into a reading nook. Choose a contemporary or traditional style and paint or stain for a look compatible with your decor.

Add storage to a traditional-style bedroom furnished with antiques. Shaker boxes in graduated sizes or wicker or wooden boxes enhance the look while hiding necessities and clutter. Use an antique steamer trunk or wood trunk for blankets, pillows, out-of-season clothing, or extra reading material.

Be creative with specialized storage. Add wood, woven, or art-paper-clad decorative boxes to store papers, magazines, crafts projects, or mending supplies. Cover a plain cardboard box and its removable top with heavy gift paper, brown kraft paper, or colorful wallpaper scraps for affordable, attractive storage.

Use the space on your dresser or the top of a chest. Stack matching decorative boxes in graduated sizes to keep items such as earrings, costume jewelry, socks, tights, hose, or scarves handy for the morning rush. Control dresser-top clutter with colorful boxes in varying shapes, sizes, and materials to hold small pieces of jewelry.

Guest Room with Storage

Create a guest room and add storage to your home office, den, or living room with a fold-down bed unit. These modular units can be ordered with open shelving that doubles as side tables for guests, plus a desk and files. Units also can be installed between bookcases.

Organized Clothes Closet

Separates:

Hang double bars, at 82 and 42 inches, to maximize your usable closet space.

Bags and Hats:

Use boxes to protect hats from dust. Group purses and totes upright by size and season.

Long-Hanging Clothes:

Long dresses need a minimum of 69 inches. Use wood or padded, hangers, not wire ones.

Shoes and Boots:

Organize on shelves or racks off the floor. Use shoe trees in leather shoes and boots.

Low-Hanging Clothes:

Clean before hanging. Use pants hangers to avoid creases and cedar blocks for moth control.

Folded Clothes:

Stack by season and style. Use zippered bags or storage boxes; never store in dry cleaning plastic bags.

Create affordable dresser-top storage with a lipped serving tray from a gift shop or import store. Substitute a flat basket. If the bottom of the piece is rough, glue on felt squares to prevent scratching.

If clothes are spilling out of your closet, buy a freestanding clothes rack and angle it in a corner behind an attractive screen. Buy a new or vintage screen or make your own by hinging bifold doors from a home center and painting or covering them with wallpaper.

Kids' Rooms

Parents already know that children need lots of storage. Unless children have a playroom, the bedroom is the repository for their possessions. (Train your children from an early age not to store or leave toys, books, and school projects in the living or family rooms.)

DEFINING YOUR CHILDREN'S NEEDS

The ages of children are obvious factors, but also consider needs for schoolwork, projects, and hobbies. A small, low bookcase, storage cubes, and a toy box are sufficient for preschool-age children. When children enter elementary school, add shelves and a desk for basic school supplies. If your children have computers in their rooms, include storage for disks and games. When a room is shared, designate individual storage for each child.

SPACE SAVERS

Work with a carpenter or cabinetmaker to design and build a twin-size platform bed with drawer storage underneath. Pullout drawers are safer than toy boxes because they don't have the hinged lids that can pinch little fingers or trap young children inside. Drawers work well for older children's extra bedding, sweaters, sports equipment, projects, and collections.

Purchase a bed designed with storage. Check with stores that handle youth furniture. Consider modular furniture for a built-in look that's movable. Pair up storage pieces with a desk along a wall or in a closet. Incorporate a trunk on casters for clothes storage and a bedside table.

Install Shaker pegs or hooks near the bedroom door. To make and install a Shaker peg rack, cut a 1×3 inch pine board to length. Using wood glue, glue the board to the wall. Cut two pieces of ½-inch-wide decorative molding the same length; nail them flush to the top and bottom of the board with finishing nails. Drill holes for 3-inch-long Shaker pegs 5 inches apart; glue pegs into holes.

IDEAS THAT WORK

■Build a low, corner bookcase with smoothed edges for safe and accessible storage. Measure what you plan to store before you design and install shelves. Plan for adjustable sizes rather than standard symmetrical arrangements. (Measure some bigger toys to ensure that the shelves are adequate size.) Avoid sharp angles and corners that can hurt children.

■ Consider weight loads. Architects often specify ¾-inch-thick birch plywood for bookshelves; spans should be no more than 30 to 36 inches between supports. If you use a thinner plywood, such as ½-inch, reinforce it with supports every 24 inches.

■ Think long-term storage needs. Children's bedrooms tend to be small; take advantage of every bit of space by building removable shelves in one end of the closet. Store everyday toys and games on low shelves.

■ Look at material alternatives. Economical painted particleboard, rather than laminate or birch plywood, works fine for built-ins.

■ Acquire storage pieces that can be used through the teen years, then placed in other rooms or settings. A dresser and armoire that are ideal for baby clothes and diapers will work equally well for jeans and sweaters. Buy sturdy storage pieces that grow with children. Check construction warranties before you purchase child-size versions of office furniture. As soon as children have homework, buy a desk with storage. As a budget-stretcher, shop for a vintage or unfinished desk to paint. Standard desks are 30 inches high; computer stands are usually about 26 inches high.

■ Place the bed against the back of a freestanding wardrobe, making a walk-in dressing area behind the bed. If the piece isn't finished on the back, staple or glue fabric to cover rough edges.

■ For children in upper elementary or middle school, look for chests to paint and use for storage. Add plastic drawer dividers or stackable storage so items don't get lost in a deep chest.

QUICK FIXES

Paint an unfinished chest or toy chest with blocks of color for color-coded organization. Make a sturdy desk from painted wood or metal filing cabinets. Paint or stain a 4-foot-long, 1-inch-thick wood plank or door that fits the depth of the cabinets.

Stack flea market suitcases to create a bedside or occasional table with storage. Buy sturdy large baskets, open or with tops, or large hampers for instant storage. Purchase plastic crates for a room divider with storage. Link two rows of plastic crates for a room divider that has access from both sides. Stack and tie two pairs of crates so there is knee space between. Lay a plywood top with rounded corners, sanded smooth and painted, across the crate pairs for a desk. Place heavy objects on the bottom for stability.

smart ideas

Tiny Toys

LOST AND FOUND

Building sets, games, crayons, puzzles, and assorted small items can be the bane of a parent's existence. Keep such easy-to-lose items out of the toy box, where they can be lost forever. Instead, purchase drawer organizers and caddies made for flatware and cleaning supplies. Store on shelves out of the reach of younger children.

COLOR CODING

Even the youngest child soon learns colors and shapes. Purchase bins and boxes in bright colors and tape pictures of items, such as toy cars or doll clothes, on the boxes to avoid confusion at cleanup time.

Nurseries

You'll be surprised at how much storage your baby needs. The basics are a chest for clothes and a changing table with open shelves to keep supplies handy. As your baby grows, organize the closet with double rods for hanging clothes and add bookshelves and a toy chest.

IDEAS THAT WORK

■ Center the crib on the wall and add matching storage units on either side for a built-in look. In a tiny nursery, borrow space from a closet by removing sliding or bifold doors. Add a smaller baker's rack for easily accessible storage.

■ When space is really tight, purchase a small corner cupboard for extra storage. (Bolt it to the wall so it can't tip over.) Purchase a crib or changing table with integral storage underneath. Stretch your budget by purchasing a secondhand chest or dresser and painting it bright colors.

QUICK FIXES

Buy a child-size coatrack to hang little outfits, or hang special dress up outfits from a decorative Shaker peg rack. Hang a small display cabinet or decorative shelves or brackets on the wall. Install an expandable rack with pegs for little jackets, mittens, and caps.

Closets

Closet space seems to be in perpetually short supply. This is especially true if you live in a pre-1960 house or apartment, both of which are notorious for small closets. If your closets are miserably small, add freestanding storage pieces, such as a wardrobe or armoire, for hanging clothes. With planning and myriad organizing products, you can maximize the storage in every closet. Double rods for hanging shirts, slacks, blouses, and suits are a first step. This works well for children's closets too. Plan for special items, such as hats, that are easily crushed on closet shelves.

SPACE SAVERS

Attach pegs, hooks, or racks to the insides of closet doors to make extra storage for hats, ties, scarves, and belts. Use hooks only for robes and belts because most clothing does not hang properly from hooks. The backs of closet doors also can hold racks or cloth pouches for shoes and small items. If you can't hang double rods and still need more storage, utilize the space under hanging shirts or blouses with a low chest, a wicker hamper for out-of-season clothes, or stackable storage units. Add clear plastic bins in children's closets to organize toys without concealing them from view.

IDEAS THAT WORK

■ Get shoes, luggage, and other items off the floor. Use shoe racks, shelves, and hanging bags. Store little-used items, such as luggage,

Dust-Free Storage Boxes

Sleek Plastic:

When you need to see what you have stored and labeled, use practical plastic boxes. The graduated sizes, which can also hold crafts supplies, fit on shelves.

Classic Cardboard:

Reinforced with metal corners, paper-covered cardboard boxes organize papers, documents, letters, and memorabilia. Use for a small home office or study center.

Budget Stretchers:

For quick storage or to organize a closet or dressing area, consider easy-to-assemble cardboard drawers to corral everything from compact discs to socks and hose.

Chic Canvas:

Clothing items, such as seasonal sweaters, or evening bags and shoes deserve a protected environment. Such boxes are ideal for all items you want to keep dust-free.

under the bed or in a utility area. Organize shelf space by stacking sweaters and storage boxes. Plan storage according to your needs and clothes.

■ Organize your closet to streamline the morning routine. Group clothes by purpose. Business and dress clothes together, casual together, crossover in the middle. Arrange by color and style for new outfits. Line up shoes by purpose and color; keep standbys where they are easy to find. Keep small items in a central spot; keep jewelry in a shallow drawer.

■ Maximize a walk-in closet by adding a small chest. Padded lingerie chests have traditionally been used in closets; any small chest will work as long as it fits the space.

■ Take advantage of the variety of styles of closet organizers. Ready-made vinyl-coated shelving units in various configurations are sturdy and economical. Look for racks or shelves that attach to closet walls or doors or try freestanding units.

■ Replace sliding closet doors, often found in houses built in the 1940s and 1950s, with easier-to-access bifold doors. Paint the doors to match the wood trim.

■ Turn a spare room into a walk-in closet. Fit it with bookshelves for folded items, double-hung rods for short items, and large shallow drawers for jewelry and scarves. Add a freestanding clothes rack on wheels if more storage is needed. Put in stacks of shoe shelves. Install a bank of built-in closets across a room wall.

■ Build shelving, drawers, or rod space into the dormer areas.

QUICK FIXES

Organize closet shelves with creative solutions such as reproductions of classic hat boxes. Look for thrift store boxes, small suitcases, or hat boxes. Place a comfortable chair near your closet to slip on shoes. Install decorative hooks to hang the day's clothes and a mirror to check your appearance.

If your bedroom closet is large, buy a cart for your portable television. Save bedroom floor space by rolling it out only when you want to watch it.

Remove your clothes from dry cleaner bags—humidity inside the bags can cause yellowing. Cedar blocks next to your clothes can have the same effect. Let your clothing air before hanging in the closet to allow body moisture to escape. The clothes will stay clean and fresh longer, require less dry cleaning, and last longer.

CEDAR CLOSETS

Cedar closets and chests can help protect your clothing and textiles from insects and mildew. The cedar closet or chest must be tightly fitted, and clothing and textiles must be freshly laundered before storage. To make a cedar closet effective, eliminate airflow under the door and through electrical outlet covers, open screw holes, or

FAMILY FRIENDLY

Lower the Bar

•

Drop a closet rod to a height children can reach; use upper rods for out-of-season clothing. Use hanging closet organizers, such as shoe or sweater bags, to keep clothing at eye level. Install a few decorative hooks nearby for hanging robes and sweaters.

holes made by hooks. Cedar chests are often a good choice because they can be fitted with tight sides and heavy lids.

Line a closet with cedar by placing the cedar over existing dry wall or studs. Purchase ¼-inch tongue-and-groove boards or 4×8 panels featuring a cover of cedar chips. Panels are easy to install and budget-priced, and they boast as much fragrance as expensive boards. Don't use the cedar intended for decks; it doesn't have the same properties.

Maintain the cedar scent: Leave the cedar panels or boards unfinished to enjoy the aroma. If the cedar loses its fragrance or its surface becomes hard, sand lightly to restore. Cedar blocks and chips do not prevent moth damage.

If the closet is in a perpetually damp place, find an alternative location and solve the moisture problem. Common culprits include improper drainage around the house and improper appliance venting. Never attempt to cover damp walls with insulation and vapor barriers.

Baths & Powder Rooms

It's a rare bathroom that is equipped with just the storage space for your particular needs and supplies. To get a fresh start on organizing, clear the bath of linens, lotions, tools, and medications that you no longer use. Nearly every surface and space can be used to boost your bath's storage space and efficiency—walls, doors, corners, and nooks.

DEFINING YOUR NEEDS

Consider how you use the bath. If a couple or several family members share the bath, designate shared and separate zones. If guests also use this bath, plan for storage that declutters and keeps the bath neat and presentable. Also keep in mind what items you store in the bath and how the space functions. For example, if this is your makeup and hairstyling area, you'll need storage for the various items you use.

SPACE SAVERS

Think shelves and more shelves. Add a shelf with brackets over the tub. If storage needs are great, add a second shelf over the door. Make every inch count with shallow shelves between wall studs. For extra storage when the medicine cabinet is overflowing, install a clear acrylic shelf on brackets above the sink. Use plastic canisters or small pieces of vintage or contemporary pottery.

For freestanding storage, add a small cupboard, chest, or corner étagère (a freestanding shelving unit). If wall space allows, include a

TIPTAG № 4
Closet Space Guide
HOW HIGH TO HANG:
Closet components, including rods and plastic-coated wire shelving, are sold at discount stores and home centers. Use them to create the storage you need.
- Long dresses. . .69 inches
- Robes. . .52 inches
- Dresses. . .45 inches
- Pants (cuff hung). . .44 inches
- Men's suits. . .38 inches
- Skirts. . .35 inches
- Women's suits. . .29 inches
- Blouses or shirts. . .28 inches
- Pants (double hung). . .20 inches
- Double-hung rods. . .82 and 42 inches
- Single rods. . .66 and 72 inches

hanging cupboard or other decorative shelving unit.

Hang hooks for towels and robes. If you have children, hang hooks at heights that encourage children to hang robes and towels. Sew fabric loops on towels that young children use so that towels are easier to hang on hooks. Remember to hang a hook on the back of the door too. Metal hooks, in a variety of styles and finishes, give a sleek, updated look. A door-hinge towel rack also works well and doubles as a robe or clothing hook.

IDEAS THAT WORK

▪ Skirt the sink vanity by sewing hook-and-loop tape to gathered fabric. For a lush look, measure the exposed sink with a tape measure and triple the measurement to determine yardage. Glue the loop attachment to the sink so that the skirt can be removed for laundering. Add a storage basket, wicker hamper, or stackable containers underneath for concealed storage. Never store cleaners or medicines in this under-the-sink area.

▪ Convert a chest or small sideboard into a vanity and have a marble or granite top cut to fit. Or start with a self-rimming sink to keep the water off the original wood top. To be sure your project will work in an existing bath, consult a plumber and a skilled carpenter. The top drawers of a chest may have to be reshaped if you want to retain them for storage.

▪ Install roll-out drawers—similar to those used in kitchen cabinetry—for deep storage at your fingertips. Mount racks on the inside of cabinet doors. Make cabinet space more accessible and convenient in a bath: Have cabinet doors removed and replace the lower shelf with a laundry bin.

▪ Clear the countertops by using wall-mounted hooks or pegs topped with shelving for blow dryers or curling irons.

QUICK FIXES

Declutter by boxing up the essentials that line the bath counter. A hair dryer can fit nicely in a decorative storage box. Use small boxes in complementary patterns and colors for easy-to-lose items such as earrings and pins.

In a powder room, use a dough bowl, wood bowl, or pottery piece for guest towels. Metal or wicker baskets also work well for towels. Use a vintage dish for guest soaps or a small plate rack with decorative plates to hold guest soaps.

Turn bathroom essentials, such as cotton balls and cotton swabs, into decorative accessories by storing them in sturdy clear plastic canisters topped by metal lids, arranged on a tray for neat storage.

Add a small butler's tray on a stand for towels and other essentials. Turn a metal basket, such as a vintage egg basket with a handle from a flea market, into a decorative container for rolled towels or extra rolls of toilet tissue.

HEALTHY HOME

Maximize the Medicine Cabinet

•

Replace a small mirror-front medicine cabinet with one that spans the width of the countertop. Choose one that has shelf space behind the entire mirror. Add small baskets to organize items such as nail clippers and tweezers.

Family Medicine Cabinet

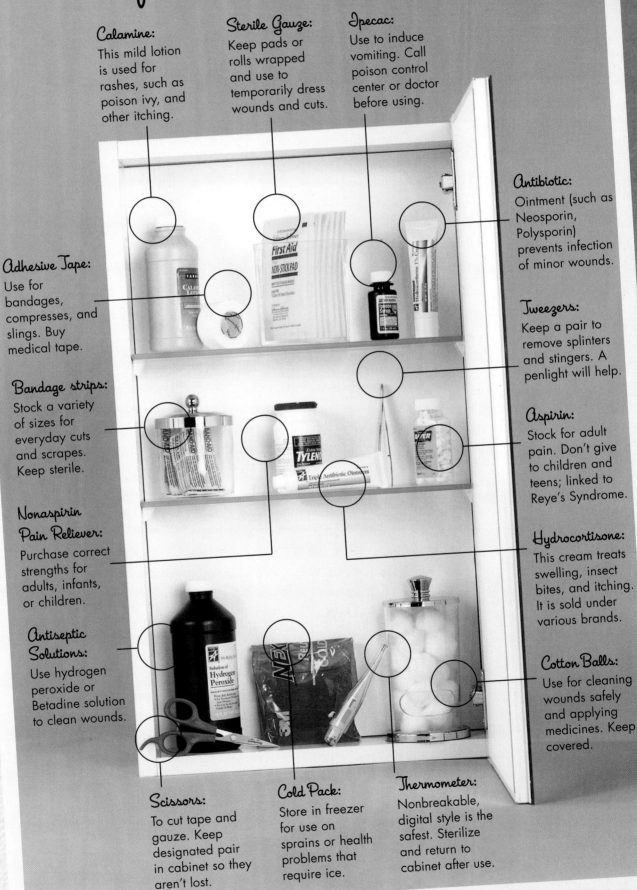

Calamine: This mild lotion is used for rashes, such as poison ivy, and other itching.

Sterile Gauze: Keep pads or rolls wrapped and use to temporarily dress wounds and cuts.

Ipecac: Use to induce vomiting. Call poison control center or doctor before using.

Antibiotic: Ointment (such as Neosporin, Polysporin) prevents infection of minor wounds.

Adhesive Tape: Use for bandages, compresses, and slings. Buy medical tape.

Tweezers: Keep a pair to remove splinters and stingers. A penlight will help.

Bandage strips: Stock a variety of sizes for everyday cuts and scrapes. Keep sterile.

Aspirin: Stock for adult pain. Don't give to children and teens; linked to Reye's Syndrome.

Nonaspirin Pain Reliever: Purchase correct strengths for adults, infants, or children.

Hydrocortisone: This cream treats swelling, insect bites, and itching. It is sold under various brands.

Antiseptic Solutions: Use hydrogen peroxide or Betadine solution to clean wounds.

Cotton Balls: Use for cleaning wounds safely and applying medicines. Keep covered.

Scissors: To cut tape and gauze. Keep designated pair in cabinet so they aren't lost.

Cold Pack: Store in freezer for use on sprains or health problems that require ice.

Thermometer: Nonbreakable, digital style is the safest. Sterilize and return to cabinet after use.

Ready the Bath For Guests

•

For each guest, set a handled basket filled with sample size toiletries, such as shampoo, toothpaste, and bath salts, and washcloths on the bathroom counter. Also make sure each guest has a towel rack or hook.

Home Offices

Everyone needs an organized, dedicated home office. This can be a small nook used for paying bills and filing important papers or an entire room for a home-based business. The key to making the most of your space—however small or large—is paying attention to tasks.

SPACE SAVERS

Consider a computer table or storage unit that folds out from a freestanding wardrobe. Or if you like the appearance of a wardrobe or armoire, have a cabinetmaker convert the unit into your own mini office with sturdy, supported shelves.

When you hang open shelving, take advantage of the space over windows and doors. Use collected baskets to organize supplies and papers, mixing sizes and styles to meet your storage and organization needs.

IDEAS THAT WORK

■ Include a built-in desk with drawers and built-in bookshelves in your designated work space. Such an arrangement allows the family room, bedroom, or kitchen to double as an office.

■ Have a cabinetmaker design and craft a vertical pullout storage cabinet for office storage. Include plywood organizing dividers, open bulletin boards, and a small bulletin board for notes and reminders.

■ Transform a window nook into an office with a pull-down, tambour-door built in (similar to the type used for rolltop desks). The door pulls down to conceal the computer and keyboard. Add file drawers below and, if space allows, floor-to-ceiling cabinets to keep papers and supplies out of sight.

■ Get the greatest value for your money with well-planned, creative, concealed storage. Have cabinets constructed as plywood storage cubes. Install doors that slide back and forward to conceal equipment and supplies.

■ When built-ins don't meet your needs, choose freestanding office unit components. Home decorating catalogs, office furniture stores, home supply warehouses, and discount and home center stores sell units in a range of prices and styles. A local carpenter may be able to build a unit for your specific needs.

■ Purchase affordable cube-style shelving units from home furnishing stores or home product catalogs. Color-code by painting the interiors in a mix of your favorite vibrant colors. Add plastic bins and storage boxes from home organizing and discount stores. Use pottery, flowerpots, or decorative woven baskets to hold pens, pencils, and scissors.

QUICK FIXES

Organize desk drawers with plastic divider trays or boxes to store pens, paper, paper clips, tape, and stamps. Use file folders to keep papers neat and organized.

Make your own desk with storage by using two contemporary-style filing cabinets to support a glass top. (Make sure the edges are beveled for safety.) Use the files rather than piling papers on the desk top. Stack clear or colored bins for dust-free storage.

Organize open storage with matching metal record bins—available from shops and catalogs that specialize in storage solutions and from some discount stores. Substitute flat baskets for in and out boxes. Use larger baskets for mail, magazines, and projects. Add baskets with handles, including the divided baskets designed for buffet flatware.

Conceal less-than-decorative items on open shelves by storing them inside wicker attaché cases, baskets with tops, well-made picnic baskets, or vintage suitcases.

Have fun with baskets old and new. As you visit crafts and antiques shows, shop for sturdy split oak or twig baskets made by folk artists or interesting Native American baskets.

Use wicker trunks and bins to store larger items. They are ideal under work counters or desks. Visit import or specialty gift stores for out-of-the-ordinary storage options. Footed boxes, stacked band boxes, and small leather trunks can neatly hold office supplies in style.

The Laundry

If you have a choice, floor plans with separate laundry rooms or combination laundry and mud or hobby rooms are ideal for storage and organization. However, a corner of the kitchen or a closet can work well if you add organizing shelves on brackets, racks, and durable baskets.

SPACE SAVERS

Convert a closet into a laundry room with stackable storage units. Install racks for laundry supplies on the back of the closet door. If your washer and dryer are closed off by louvered bifold doors, install racks and deep shelves above the appliances for supplies and laundry baskets. Vinyl-coated mesh shelving units, available at stores that specialize in organizing products and at some discount stores, are economical and sturdy.

Install a closet rod for clothes that drip dry or that you hang directly from the dryer. Use double rods if you hang primarily shirts and slacks. Add a rack for socks and similar items. Locate the rack as close to the washer as possible because socks notoriously disappear during washing. Hang a sturdy shelf behind the washer

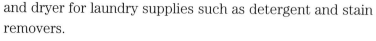

and dryer for laundry supplies such as detergent and stain removers.

IDEAS THAT WORK

■ Remember the basics. You'll be dealing with dirty and clean clothes and with wet, damp, and dry clothes. Plan storage accordingly.

■ If space allows, build in a counter for folding and sorting. Include open shelves for sorting bins. Store an ironing board and iron in the laundry room. If the room doesn't have a storage closet, hang the ironing board from a heavy-duty storage hook. Add a utility shelf for items such as the iron and spray starch.

Attics & Basements

Your attic may have space to spare, but use it carefully. Heat and radical temperature swings make it unsuitable for many items. However, the attic is a fine place for storing items that aren't temperature sensitive, such as holiday decorations, pottery, and housewares. Clothes, blankets, and linens can be stored for a single season. (If you don't have closet space for furs or leather clothing, store them at the cleaners.)

ATTIC IDEAS THAT WORK

Clean clothing and textiles before storage. If insects have been a problem in the past, spray the baseboard with an all-purpose household insecticide. Fabrics need to breathe: Hang clothing and linens from a garment rack or rod hung from the rafters. Keep it dust-free by covering the rack with a clean cotton sheet. Store folded clothing in an acid-free cardboard box or one lined with a clean cotton sheet. Don't store clothing or textiles in plastic because moisture trapped inside can cause mildew. If you prefer, purchase garment bags designed for long-term clothing storage.

Alternative: If you have lots of clothing to store, purchase cardboard clothing boxes with hanging rods from moving companies.

Precaution: Don't risk storing valuable or heirloom clothing, such as a wedding gown, in an unfinished attic or basement. Wedding and christening gowns should be professionally cleaned and professionally packed. Store in a climate-controlled area, such as on a shelf of a bedroom closet.

BASEMENT BASICS

Moisture is the chief storage concern in a basement. Mildew can be a particular problem in climates with long or hot and humid summers. Keep flooding or excess moisture at bay with a sump pump, floor drain, dehumidifier, or a combination of these. Check to make sure they are working properly. (See page 281 for more on dehumidifiers.) With precautions, an unfinished basement without ventilation, heating, and cooling can be used for items that are

TIME SAVER

Storage
That
Organizes
•

Think accessibility and convenience when you plan garage storage. Install a pegboard or vinyl-coated metal grid system with hooks and hangers for small items and hand tools. Group by function and job. Install heavy-duty hooks for large shovels and rakes.

Not in Basement or Attic

Fur and Leather:
Heat, changes in temperatures and moisture levels, and pests can seriously damage expensive or vintage coats and wraps.

Wood Furniture:
Changes in humidity and temperature can cause wood to expand and contract, resulting in cracks and splits in solid and veneered pieces.

Books:
Mildew and dust are the chief villains here. But rodents can be harmful too. Changes in moisture are damaging to old leather-bound books.

Stuffed Toys:
Squirrels, chipmunks, and mice that find refuge in the attic love these toys. Humidity and moisture in the basement also cause damage.

Photographs:
Moisture, mildew, and temperature and humidity changes are harmful. Attic heat can destroy slides and photographic negatives.

Formal Dresses:
Basement moisture and mildew are the worst offenders, but dust and attic pests can be problems. Don't risk a wedding or formal dress.

unaffected by moisture, such as extra dishes, pottery, glassware, hand tools, and plastic or metal toys. Hang hand tools, such as saws and hammers, on pegboard or a rack to lessen the chances of rusting from the damp environment.

Garage & Storage Shed

The aboveground garage or carport is often used for storage. Sheds are similar in function, although they usually offer less square footage for storage. Tuck-under garages are like basements and should be treated as such for storage purposes. To get the most from your garage or shed, first clear it of unwanted items. Make a list of what you expect to store; then go to work setting up storage.

IDEAS THAT WORK

■Look up for overhead space. Tubular steel hooks can hang tools, sporting goods, ladders, lumber, and lawn furniture out of the way.

■Check out home centers and storage stores for bench kits—choose a system that can be expanded over time.

■Build a loft to store luggage, patio furniture, and other bulky items. Include a locked metal chest or cabinet for dangerous tools. Store pesticides, herbicides, and other chemicals in this cabinet.

■If you have an open carport and space allows, add a locked closet area for secure storage. Open carports are unsuitable for storage because hazardous items are exposed; other items, such as tools or sports gear, may be tempting to thieves.

■Take advantage of the space under the deck if it is at least 4 feet off the ground. Use this space for items that can be safely exposed to the weather, such as the barbeque grill, wheelbarrow, or outdoor toys. For a neat appearance, screen the storage area with lattice or paneling from a home center or lumberyard.

QUICK FIXES

Install a pegboard and hooks for small items such as garden and hand tools. Group tools by function. Claim a couple of feet from the far end of a garage for a tool bench or workshop.

Install adjustable shelving against a wall. Use see-through plastic bins to store small items and keep them dust-free. Store fertilizers, bulb boosters, deicing chemicals, and other potentially hazardous items on top shelves.

Small Apartment or Condo

These efficient housing options often offer the amenities of convenient location and ready access to school, work, and cultural opportunities. Some units have extra storage in the basement or garage for out-of-season items. However, the downside can be small closets, minimum built-ins, no garages for extra storage, and little floor space for freestanding storage pieces.

DEFINING YOUR NEEDS

Whether you live alone or share your space is the first determinant of storage needs. If your household includes an infant or small child, you'll need more storage. Other factors to consider:

▶ How much cooking do you do?

▶ Do you entertain at home and need storage for dinnerware, glasses, and flatware?

▶ Do you work at home? Are you a collector?

▶ Do you ever have overnight guests?

Your answers will help you decide what kind of storage you need to make the most of your space.

SPACE SAVERS

Choose every piece of furniture for its storage possibilities. For dining, use a writing table with a drawer. Depending on your needs, it can contain everything from flatware and linens to office supplies. Use trunks wherever you can. For the most versatility, choose one with a flat top rather than a domed top so that it can easily double as a table or even a bench. Wicker trunks are readily available and are budget-priced.

In a small bath, think creatively. Extend the vanity top over the toilet for maximum shelf space. Use shaped, bracket-type display shelves from home furnishings stores and catalogs to keep the essentials at hand.

IDEAS THAT WORK

■ Take advantage of every square inch of available space with built-in shelves. Waste no window in a small apartment or condo. Seize the opportunity to design and construct a built-in shelving unit under a window for books, electronic equipment, and compact discs. Add a low freestanding storage unit or bench to hold books, plants, and favorite accessories. Have shelves built to flank a window or windows and to fit under the sills to maximize your storage. Include 24-inch-deep shelves for oversize books and electronic equipment.

■ Open shelving is accessible and economical. Because different shelf heights are more interesting than a uniform arrangement, design lower shelves for larger volumes, such as college yearbooks and art books. Use upper shelves for standard-size items. If you have a collection of paperbacks, fit shelves 8 to 10 inches apart.

In a one-room apartment or when your living room doubles as the guest suite, create a sleeping nook. Buy a daybed, or use pillows and a tailored coverlet to transform a standard twin bed. Hang operable draperies from a ceiling-mounted rod that can close as needed.

TIP TAG № 5
Office Space

IN THE CLOSET:

• Locate inside double bifold doors for accessibility.

• Outfit with a drawing board for a work surface, upper shelves, a lower bin with pullout baskets, a filing cabinet for papers and documents.

• Stock the upper shelves with see-through plastic boxes or bins so stored items are easy to find.

• Hang a bulletin board, pegboard, racks, or other wall-mounted storage on the side walls to organize tools or your office supplies.

ON WHEELS:

• If space is very tight, stock a small supply cart on wheels to roll in and out of the closet when needed.

QUICK FIXES

Choose handsome versions of necessary kitchen equipment, such as measuring spoons and cutting boards, so there's no need to store them out of sight.

Buy furniture that can serve dual functions. Substitute a small antique or vintage chest for a living room side table. As an alternative, shop thrift stores for 20th-century reproductions. Such pieces are good buys; they often emulate the lines and basic style of the original, without the price tags. If you use a chest to store silver, line with antitarnish cloth. Use dividers to keep items handy.

Sports and Outdoor Gear

Start with garage and basement walls for hooks, racks, and sport-specific organizers to get all your gear off the ground. A ski organizer, for example, may have slots for skis, boots, poles, goggles, and incidentals. An alternative that works well for basements with concrete-block walls is a sports bench or two. These are wire mesh boxes topped with a cushioned bench. They work well for items such as balls, helmets, and in-line skates.

OVERHEAD OPTIONS

A pulley-operated ceiling hoist is easy to use and lifts bikes, kayaks, surfboards, and sailboards up to overhead space, even above your car. Heavy-duty attachments allow a hoist to lift weightier items, such as canoes. You can also install simple ceiling-mounted racks and hooks to store gear, but you'll have to do your own hoisting. If space allows, a loft in the garage is an exceptional way to use often-wasted overhead space. A loft is ideal for sports gear as well as luggage, automobile roof boxes, and holiday ornaments.

Storage Safety

Unfortunately, the home environment can be a dangerous one. Never underestimate the importance of safe storage. When you bring home new fuels, oils, paints, and supplies, check to see if they're flammable or toxic or if they have special storage requirements. If they do, keep them away from children and pets and outside your home. Never store them them near the water heater or clothes dryer. Limit hazards by getting rid of excess. Call your city or county government to learn when and if hazardous waste disposal collections are held in your community. Here's how to handle a few dangerous materials:

GAS GRILLS

When the season is over, disconnect the propane cylinder from the grill, shut off the valve, and place the plug in the valve. Propane gas is volatile, and leaks are slow. Store outside in a protected area that is inaccessible to children, such as a toolshed near a rear fence.

SAFETY ALERT

Gun Safety

•

If you keep a firearm in your home, store it unloaded under lock and key in a secure, childproof place, such as in a metal lockbox or specially designed case. Store ammunition separately—also under lock and key. Trigger locks are available as an added precaution to prevent accidents.

Helpful Storage Shelving

Metal Wire Mesh:
Check the weight load. This style is easy to assemble and attractive enough to use in a storage-starved kitchen or bath.

Reinforced Metal:
These heavy-duty shelves are designed for utility rooms, workshops, or garages. Check stability and balance weights.

Lightweight Plastic:
Inexpensive and easy to assemble, these work best for light storage in a basement, laundry room, or garage.

Natural Wood:
These put-together shelves are strong enough for lightweight books or toys as well as basic kitchen or utility storage.

LAWN MOWERS

If gas-powered, drain the gas at season's end. For mowers powered by a combination of gas and oil, drain the fuel into a container, mark it clearly, and set aside for the next local hazardous waste collection. Keep the mixture away from children.

FUEL

Whether it is intended for a lawn mower, snowblower, or boat, store in a metal or plastic Canadian or U.L. Standards Approved container with a vapor-proof cap. Metal containers that don't meet approved standards can leak if exposed to heat or frost.

PAINT

You can store paint for two years or more. Seal cans tightly; then turn them upside down. The paint will form a seal against oxygen and stay fresh longer. Keep latex paints from freezing. Find out how unwanted paint is disposed of in your community. Some cities have special cleanup days to handle paint and items that cannot be disposed of in regular household trash.

PAINT SOLVENTS

Their vapors are a fire hazard. Keep caps tight on turpentine and solvents; store them outside, inaccessible to children or pets, in sealed containers.

PESTICIDES

Buy just enough for the season. Keep them away from children and pets and away from food supplies. For organic alternatives to avoid storage problems, check gardening books, magazines, and your county extension service.

Renting Space

Now and then your storage needs may exceed your living space. Check local directories to assess storage options. (Real estate agents may be sources too.) Boat dealers can direct you to unadvertised off-season storage.

Climate-controlled units are more expensive, but they are safer for clothing, books, fine furniture, musical instruments, and art.

Be cautious about leaving furniture, plush toys, or personal papers in an unconditioned unit for more than a month or two. In hot, humid climates, upholstery may mildew or absorb moisture. Temperature changes can cause damage to wood furniture. Even if they provide climate control, units are typically bare boxes.

Be prepared to provide shelving so you can arrange items for access. Find out if you rent by the month or season. Check into security, fencing, lighting, access, and responsibility for theft or damage as well as insurance coverage. Find out who rents nearby storage space. Check with the local Better Business Bureau to see if any complaints have been filed against storage companies.

BUDGET STRETCHER

Utilize Your Storage Unit

Before you rent a storage unit, prepare a list of questions: Is rental by the month? Are discounts offered for longer leases? How are units secured and lit? Who has access? Do you have 24-hour access? What is the policy for lost, damaged, or stolen items?

2

Setting Up Routines
- GETTING STARTED, 53
- YOUR OWN CARE STYLE, 53

Cleaning Frequency
- DAILY CHECKLIST, 53
- WEEKLY AND EVERY TWO WEEKS, 54
- MONTHLY CHECKLIST, 54

Cleaning Shortcuts
- KITCHEN, 54
- BATHROOM, 56
- HALL CLOSET, 56
- CENTRAL WORKSTATION, 56

Seasonal Cleaning
- SPRING INDOORS AND OUTDOORS, 57
- CLEANING CADDY, 59
- FALL INDOORS AND OUTDOORS, 60

Laundry Routine
- TWO-PERSON HOUSEHOLD, 60
- THREE OR MORE IN HOUSEHOLD, 61

Hiring Help
- HOUSEKEEPER RESPONSIBILITIES, 64
- FINDING THE HELP YOU NEED, 64
- HOUSEKEEPER CALENDAR, 65

Child-Care Options
- CHILD-CARE CENTERS, 65
- FAMILY DAY-CARE HOMES, 65
- SCREENING AND INTERVIEWS, 68
- LEGAL ISSUES AND INSURANCE, 69, 70

Elder Care
- FINDING HELP, 70
- RESOURCES AND REFERRALS, 70

Setting Up Routines

GETTING STARTED

You won't find a magic solution to maintaining a clean, well-maintained, and organized home. But if you create a routine that works for your lifestyle and cleanliness requirements, you can stay on top of cleaning. When you do, chores don't get out of hand. If you keep your residence reasonably decluttered, clean, and neat, you'll avoid the necessity of marathon cleaning sessions.

Depending on your lifestyle, you may find it easier to perform the basic chores on a daily basis (see the following suggested schedules) and relegate the big chores to a weekend morning or afternoon. If you enjoy free weekends, tackle one room or one big chore every day, in addition to daily chores, to allow time for leisure.

When your lifestyle is extremely busy with long work days and/or family obligations, it pays to plan your week and plot your course. Your week will go more smoothly if you start each Monday (or the first day of your work week) with a clean, neat home, clean clothes and other laundry, and a stocked pantry, refrigerator, and freezer. Your weekends (or days off) will be more enjoyable if you don't have rooms to declutter, piled-up dishes, and mounds of laundry.

YOUR OWN CARE STYLE

Determine your comfort level of neat and clean: Some things, such as a clean kitchen and bathroom, are nonnegotiable, but shelves or door frames that don't always pass the white glove test may be acceptable. Likewise, keeping public rooms—living and dining rooms—neat may be important to you, while you may be less vigilant about your bedroom or hobby space.

Read through the suggested daily, weekly, biweekly, monthly, and seasonal chores in this chapter. Establish your own routines. You may find it helpful to make your own filing system or notebook with a similarly organized chore list.

smart ideas

Living Room Neat

NO DUMPING ALLOWED

Refrain from dumping and piling. Your home will feel more orderly and function better if at least the living and dining areas aren't cluttered with the debris of everyday living. Never pile up mail or projects on the dining room table or entry table, coffee table, or shelf.

BEDTIME ROUTINES

Resolve to declutter the living and dining areas every night. If you have small children, teach them to return toys and books to their bedrooms. If you keep toys and children's books in the living area, buy baskets for attractive storage. Diligent decluttering works. Practice it every day.

Cleaning Frequency

DAILY

Perform these basic chores every day:
- Make the beds
- Put away clothes and children's toys
- Wash dishes, spray and wipe off counters and cooktop or range
- Take out trash and recycling

▪ Clean cat litter boxes

▪ Wipe out bathroom sinks and spray shower doors

If you work long days or have after-work pursuits, such as continuing education or children's activities, basic chores and meal preparation, and some laundry may be all you manage in one day.

WEEKLY

Weekly chores include the laundry, ironing, and dry-cleaning delivery and pickup. Also complete the following to stay on top of your housework:

▪ Clean the kitchen and bathrooms

▪ Dust furniture and shelves

▪ Shake or vacuum area rugs

▪ Vacuum living areas

▪ Mop hard surface (not wood) floors

▪ Change bed linens

▪ Sweep front entry and steps

▪ Buy groceries

Clean the kitchen first and the bathroom or bathrooms second to get the hardest jobs out of the way first.

EVERY TWO WEEKS

▪ Sweep the garage

▪ Shake out area rugs and doormats outdoors before vacuuming

▪ Vacuum furniture (underneath the cushions too)

MONTHLY

These are the chores to keep your home looking neat and clean. Block out time so they don't slip by.

▪ Clean inside window surfaces; clean decorative mirrors

▪ Wash out kitchen trash container and surrounding area (Stash three or four trash bags at the bottom of the container before putting in a fresh bag to make it convenient to replace a bag when the trash is taken out.)

▪ Clean the stove; wipe the interior of the refrigerator

▪ Clean baseboards, dust miniblinds, and vacuum curtains

▪ Dust, sweep, and vacuum before washing surfaces to rid rooms of as much loose dirt and debris as possible

▪ Change or clean filters on heating and cooling systems

Cleaning Shortcuts

PLACE FOR EVERYTHING

Create a place for everything throughout the house by following these suggestions:

Kitchen: Store cookware near the range or cooktop. Store utensils either in a drawer next to the range or cooktop or in an attractive container on the counter; store all wooden spoons in one container, and all stainless steel and plastic in another. Keep a spray

---

TIME SAVER

Clean Quick

•

In 30 minutes you can sweep the kitchen floor and wipe the cooktop; wipe the sink, mirror, and toilet in guest bath; and dust the dining or living room table. Two hours to clean: kitchen and bath basics; vacuum living area floors and dust major furniture; declutter throughout house.

Spring Cleaning Checklist

Bed Linens:

Pick a dry, warm day and treat your pillows (minus covers) and blankets to the warm spring sunshine. If that's impractical, check with cleaners that freshen pillows.

Chandeliers:

Remove the bulbs and glass base. Wash the base in warm soapy water. Dust the arms with soft cloth and clean feather duster. Wipe lightbulbs with damp cloth and dry.

Windows:

Choose a warm, dry day. Remove screens and storm windows and wash windows inside and out with a commercial cleaner or vinegar-and-water solution.

Upholstery:

Remove cushions and vacuum with the crevice and dusting attachments. Use a pet-hair tape if needed. If soiled, call a commercial upholstery cleaner for best results.

bottle with a solution of 1 part bleach to 4 parts water or an all-purpose spray cleaner in the kitchen for quick cleanup. Keep a broom and dustpan in the kitchen for sweeping after meals.

Bathroom: Stash a spray bottle with all-in-one window and surface cleaner and an extra roll of paper towels under each sink for surface cleanups.

Hall closet: Install storage bins with separate drawers for gloves, hats, scarves. Stock up on stackable see-through plastic containers to store lightbulbs, batteries, and emergency candles.

Laundry room: Hang the iron and ironing board on a wall caddy. Keep all laundry supplies together in a basket. Store sewing supplies in a container with multiple compartments. Find buttons quickly with a sewing center book: Fill a three-ring binder with blank pages, and staple on the little envelopes of extra buttons and thread that come with clothing purchases. Under each envelope note where the buttons belong.

Cleaning central: Store all cleaning implements and products in one place for easy retrieval. A closet works fine. If you have a laundry room or laundry corner, the space is ideal because soiled or used cloths can go directly into the washing machine. Wherever you store cleaning supplies, keep them out of the reach of small children, even if you have only an occasional young visitor. Post daily, weekly, and monthly chores on a small bulletin board in the cleaning center.

To make your cleaning center efficient, buy a wall rack to hang brooms, mops, and dustpans in one place. Use baskets, bins, and caddies to store products and supplies. Make sure all supplies are stored out of the reach of children. Create a customized, computer-generated supply checklist. Make photocopies on colored paper to post in the cleaning center. When a product is running low, note it on the list before the next shopping trip.

Seasonal Cleaning

Seasonal cleaning can be a daunting task: Projects seem to build up, even when you are persistent about daily, weekly, and monthly chores. To make the projects manageable, start with the right tools and products for the job. For general seasonal cleaning, you'll need:

▶ Broom, dustpan, scrub brush, mop, vacuum cleaner, supply of vacuum cleaner bags

▶ Cleaning rags (old white T-shirts work well)

▶ 2- or 3-gallon bucket, sponges, an extended duster (for cleaning blinds and ceiling fans)

▶ Stepladder, latex gloves, and paper towels

Rather than have a cleaning product for every task, select a product for multiple uses and use it for many cleaning projects.

Double Time

•

Minor chores to do while talking on a portable telephone:

• Unload the dishwasher

• Sweep the kitchen floor

• Fold or wash a load of laundry

• Pick up around the house

• Iron two or three garments

• Polish silver

• Clean out the catchall drawer

SPRING CLEANING

Be organized to save time and energy. Go through the inside and around the outside of the house to make a list of necessary projects. Prioritize the projects on three sheets of paper using these headings:

▶ Large projects (a half day or more)

▶ Medium projects (two to three hours)

▶ Small projects (chores that are easy to accomplish when you find yourself with a small block of time)

Map a cleaning route: Start with a room at the top corner of your home (two-story house) or a corner room (one-story house or apartment) and work inward and downward. Clean rooms from the top down (see Tab 3 for cleaning techniques and products). Completely clean each room before moving on to the next to save walking back and forth. Think about your own time and energy level, help from family members, and the state of your house before you start a cleaning marathon.

Instead of spending an entire day or weekend cleaning, clean half the house or one story of a two-story on one day or afternoon; clean the other half or other story on another weekend afternoon. Reserve a block of time for the attic, basement, or garage.

Some household projects are worth the exchange of money for time because professionals have the expertise and equipment to efficiently do the job. Consider hiring a professional window cleaner once a year, especially if you have a two-story house or storm windows. Hire a gutter- and/or roof-cleaning service in late fall. Choose services that are bonded and insured and get at least three references. Depending on your time and house size, rent the necessary carpet-cleaning equipment or hire a service. If you are renting equipment, steam-clean all carpets at the same time to save money. Some companies offer discounts to clean three or more rooms.

SPRING CLEANING: INDOORS

Chore list: Declutter, sort, and store before you start. (See Tab 1 for ideas on organizing and storing.) Pick up and eliminate clutter in each room before you start cleaning. Place a cardboard box and two or three garbage bags in each room that you are decluttering. Fill them as you sort through your shelves, cabinets, and clothes closets.

Donate old books, magazines, toys, and clothes that you don't wear to charity or fill a box for your next garage sale. (If you can't bear to give away old magazines and books, box them up and store them out of the way.) Have winter clothes cleaned.

TIPTAG No. 8

Calendar of Kitchen Chores

DAILY CLEANING:
- Spray and wipe countertops, range top, and vent hood.
- Sweep floor.
- Scrub sink with a general-purpose cleaner; wipe dry.

WEEKLY CLEANING:
- Mop floor (more often if young children or pets are in household).
- Clean exteriors of appliances.
- Wipe refrigerator door.
- Scour and polish sink.

MONTHLY CLEANING:
- Wipe off cabinet doors.
- Clean oven and refrigerator; sanitize refrigerator drip pan.

Consider storing them (a service offered by some dry cleaners) if space is tight. Put away gloves, winter clothing items, and boots. Bring out spring clothing.

Freshen all the bedrooms. Rotate and flip mattresses. Wash blankets or comforters or take them to be cleaned. Wash the mattress pad and bed skirt. Have pillows professionally cleaned or hang them outside in the fresh air, or freshen with the air (no heat) cycle of your clothes dryer. Wash or dry-clean rugs.

Wash and/or wax floors, depending on their material. Deep-clean rugs or have professionally cleaned. Wash baseboards. Vacuum upholstery and draperies. Dust and wax wood furniture. Flip sofa and chair cushions.

Clean light fixtures, ceiling fans, and mirrors. Dust or wash window blinds. Replace bent or worn miniblinds. Wash and iron curtains or have cleaned.

Clean heating and cooling vents. Change air filters in central units.

Thoroughly clean all bathrooms. Go through medicine cabinets and safely discard any outdated products. Replace worn bath mats, shower curtains, and liners. Or wash and dry shower curtains and liners.

Clear out pantry, kitchen cabinets, and drawers. Wipe out, and install fresh shelf paper. Store or donate equipment you don't use, such as small appliances or cookware. Discard stale spices or dated items such as baking powder. Clean the refrigerator and freezer. Vacuum the cooling coils under or behind the refrigerator.

Wash windows inside and outside, including storm windows and screens. Assess the state of your storage areas, whether you use an attic, basement, garage, carport, or storage shed. Add shelving units and containers to create order.

Bring out garden tools and potting supplies. Store shovels, salt, scrapers, and other winter items. Thoroughly sweep floors in storage areas to remove debris. Invest in pegboards, shelving units, and plastic storage bins to keep storage areas clean and organized.

Check the batteries in smoke and carbon monoxide detectors when the time switches to daylight saving time. Perform all required safety checks. If you don't own a fire extinguisher, purchase one and learn how to use it; keep it in the kitchen. If you use a humidifier during the winter, clean and store it. Make sure the dehumidifier is in working order.

SPRING CLEANING: OUTDOORS

Enjoy the first warm days of spring with a morning or afternoon of fresh-air chores. Chores vary with climate and locale, but in any location you'll need to determine how well exterior siding and

BUDGET STRETCHER

Cleaning On the Cheap

Hire a reliable neighborhood teenager, such as your regular baby-sitter, to come in and baby-sit for a whole day while you or you and your spouse clean the house. It's more economical to pay a baby-sitter than a housekeeper.

Stocked Cleaning Caddy

Window Cleaner:
Use for windows, glass tops, mirrors. Also use to polish chrome fixtures and to clean cooktops.

Floors and Walls:
Mop and scrub with nonsudsing household ammonia or formulated cleaners. Check if safe for sealed vinyl floors.

Cleanser:
Choose nonabrasive for general cleaning. Buy a heavy-duty cleanser for tough stains and rust.

General Purpose:
Buy a kitchen-and-bath spray product (and refills for spray bottles) or make your own with diluted vinegar.

Chlorine Bleach:
Dilute with 4 parts water to 1 part bleach for general cleaning and disinfecting (including toilet bowl).

Feather Duster:
Safely dust lampshades, light fixtures, art, and delicate collectibles with this handy tool.

Oil Soap:
Clean wood-stain cabinets, paneling, and other woods with this liquid soap made for use on wood; several brands on the market.

Latex Gloves:
Protect your hands from chemicals with household rubber gloves. Use for washing dishes too.

roofing survived the winter (use binoculars).

Clean out gutters and drainpipes before the spring rains. Wash windows and screens, replace storm windows with screens, and bring out, clean, and touch up or repair deck, porch, or patio furniture, if stored in winter. Use outdoor spray enamel to touch up chips on painted outdoor furniture.

Service the snowblower before you store it for spring. When the weather warms, scrub your deck or porch and decide if you'll need to reseal or paint it in summer.

FALL CLEANING: INDOORS

Life moves inside in the winter. Repeat the spring cleaning chores that your time and schedule allow. Light is precious in the winter months, so maximize it by washing interior windows and light fixtures. Clean chandeliers in preparation for holiday entertaining. Check the condition of lampshades, and update lamps with new shades if needed. Clean windowsills and window wells.

Bring your winter rugs out of storage and have sisal-type rugs cleaned before storing. Clean carpets or have them professionally cleaned. Replace doormats as needed to reduce tracked-in dirt and snow.

Flip and rotate mattresses and launder all bedding such as bed skirts, mattress pads, comforters, and quilts. Air and sun pillows and blankets. Clean out closets; launder all spring and summer clothing before storing. Bring out fall and winter clothing. Install pegs and racks for convenient back-door winter storage.

FALL CLEANING: OUTDOORS

Clean and store patio furniture, garden pots and planters, and tools. Clean outdoor furniture cushions before storing to prevent mildew. Drain and store garden hoses; store clay pots. Drain and service the lawn mower according to manufacturer's guidelines. Check caulk around doors and windows and recaulk as needed to help keep heat in and water and cold out.

For energy efficiency, install weatherstripping around outside doors. Check gutters and downspouts and clear debris, or hire a professional gutter service. Remove lint from outdoor dryer exhaust tubes. If you use a snow blowing service, schedule it in advance. If you remove snow yourself, check to see that your snowblower is in working order. Stock up on deicing products.

Laundry Routine

Gear your laundry routine to your lifestyle and family size. If you regularly use a professional laundry for dress shirts and dry cleaning, establish a regular day to drop off and pick up.

Two-person household: Doing the laundry once a week is generally sufficient unless you wash uniforms, work clothes, or gym

---

TIME SAVER

Winter Holidays

●

Spend an afternoon cleaning before you decorate. Vacuum living and dining room draperies and upholstery; dust and wax major furniture pieces. Clean light fixtures, including chandelier. Wash baseboards and indoor windows and polish mirrors.

clothes. If dress shirts and suits are part of your attire, add a weekly trip to the dry cleaners.

Three or more in household: Keep laundry from piling up by doing one load of laundry every morning (or every other morning) and folding clothes before or after dinner.

Train all family members to put dirty clothing in hampers. Place a basket or hamper in each bedroom closet and in each bath if space allows. Place three additional hampers in the laundry area—for dark clothes, light clothes, and special-care items. In households with teens, delegate a laundry responsibility to each family member. Delegate simple laundry chores, such as folding socks, to younger children.

Hiring Help

Hiring a housekeeper was once considered a luxury or solution for a difficult family situation. With changing family dynamics and fewer full-time homemakers, the decision to hire household help is a practical one based on cost versus time. Cleaning services that hire and manage professional house cleaners are proliferating.

Service personnel are normally bonded and insured, and the service firms handle the paperwork of Social Security and tax forms. However, don't automatically take the word of a cleaning service. To protect your possessions and to protect yourself from any potential liability, ask the cleaning service to provide written documentation of bonding and insurance.

Whether you hire an individual or a service, keep in mind that household help can be tailored to meet your needs, lifestyle, and budget. For example, you may only need a cleaning service every other week or only once a month to clean floors and surfaces. You may only need the service every other week and require extra help before the holidays or family visits.

Keep a notebook or file of monthly or occasional chores, such as cleaning the refrigerator, dusting and cleaning blinds, or changing shelf paper. Before you hire a housekeeper or cleaning service, discuss how to handle such occasional chores on a rotating basis.

If you plan to schedule extra services, particularly before major holidays, schedule the services at least two months in advance. Likewise, if you need extra help for a limited period, such as a new baby in the household, schedule well in advance.

HOUSEHOLD SITUATIONS

Here are examples of typical family situations with basic guidelines.

smart ideas

For Safety And Comfort

FURNACE AND FIREWOOD

Schedule your fall furnace inspection and servicing and chimney cleaning before cold weather sets in. If your furnace has a pilot light, check to see if it is in working order. Order firewood.

ENERGY AND SAFETY

Stock up on furnace filters. Clean the dehumidifier before storing; make sure the humidifier is clean and check to see it is working properly. Check caulking around windows and seals around doors. Do safety checks on smoke and carbon monoxide detectors and fire extinguisher.

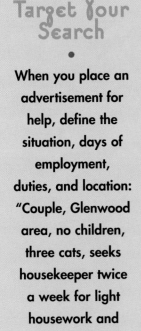

Single person, no children: When you aren't home during the day, the opportunities for creating messes are minimal. A cleaning service every other week or even once a month is usually workable. Basic laundry is minimal; you probably can handle it.

Housekeeper frequency: Twice a month.

Responsibilities: Cleaning kitchen and bathroom, dusting, vacuuming, ironing.

Two-career couple, no children: If both work, especially if you commute fairly long distances, you don't have the time or want to spend your days off cleaning the house.

Housekeeper frequency: Once a week.

Responsibilities: Basic weekly cleaning throughout the house, possibly grocery shopping or other similar errands.

Family with one or two preschool children and stay-at-home spouse: A stay-at-home spouse can take care of the basic laundry and cleaning chores, with help from the partner after work and on weekends. It may make sense to have a housekeeper or cleaning service come in once a month. Cleaning services are more likely than individuals to agree to contract for such an arrangement.

Housekeeper frequency: Once a month.

Responsibilities: Deep cleaning in bathrooms and kitchen, mopping floors, washing baseboards.

Family with three or more children, plus pets; one working spouse, one-stay-at-home spouse: The at-home spouse has more than a full-time job. If one or more of the children are preschoolers, it is worthwhile to hire a housekeeper to come in every two weeks to catch up on the cleaning and laundry.

Housekeeper frequency: Twice a month.

Responsibilities: Cleaning kitchen and bathrooms, laundry, ironing, general household assistance.

Family with school-age or teenage children, one working spouse, one spouse with part-time job: With children in school, the spouse with a part-time job will be busy with chauffeuring and after-school activities. Even when the children are part of the cleaning team, there are some household jobs, such as floor cleaning, that are more efficiently delegated to paid help. As the children grow up, household responsibilities, such as doing their laundry and cleaning their rooms, should be shifted to them.

Housekeeper frequency: Twice a month.

Responsibilities: Thorough kitchen and bathroom cleaning, ironing, and mending clothes.

Family with school-age or teenage children; two working spouses or single working parent: In addition to cleaning the house, the housekeeper can be responsible for family errands such as picking up dry cleaning and grocery shopping.

Tailor Help to Your Needs

Single

Unless you have several pets or entertain frequently, a cleaning service once or twice a month works. Key chores: kitchen, bathroom, dusting, vacuuming, ironing.

Couple

Hire a service or housekeeper for basic weekly cleaning, laundry, ironing, and possibly grocery shopping or errands. Clarify whether errands are part of the job.

Family: One Working Adult

If your family has infants or three or more children, hire cleaning help once a month for heavy-duty jobs, such as deep cleaning the kitchen and bathrooms, and mopping.

Family: Two Working Adults

If the budget allows, hire at least weekly help for cleaning, laundry, and errands. If school-age children need transportation, consider hiring help during the week.

Housekeeper frequency: Every week if budget allows or every other week for floors and kitchen and bath cleaning.

Responsibilities: Thorough kitchen and bathroom cleaning, ironing and mending clothes, grocery shopping and light errands.

HOUSEKEEPER RESPONSIBILITIES

Before hiring a professional housekeeper, make a list of specific household tasks that need to be accomplished. Housekeepers generally expect the homeowners to declutter the home prior to cleaning. Never assume that the housekeeper can take on extra tasks. It's unfair to expect a housekeeper to watch children and do housework while you run errands unless you have made arrangements in advance. Likewise, never ask a housekeeper to care for pets or do heavy lifting. For special jobs, such as walking dogs or washing the outside of windows, hire a service or a neighborhood teenager. If you hire a professional cleaning service, they may have set fees for services.

FINDING THE HELP YOU NEED

The most effective way to locate and hire a reliable housekeeper or cleaning service is through recommendations from family, friends, neighbors, or coworkers. Even with good references, keep in mind that what you want and need from a cleaning service may be different from what your friends want. Check newspaper classified advertising under "Services—Housekeeping." Look for phrases such as "excellent references" or "longtime experience," which suggests five years or more in the same household.

Key phrases to use in your classified advertisement are "excellent references required," "reliable," and "experienced." Define the position as clearly as possible. For example, "Professional couple, no children, two cats, seek experienced, detail-oriented housekeeper with impeccable references. Weekly." Or "Busy household of two adults, two teens seeks experienced housekeeper twice a month for housekeeping. Excellent references required."

When checking references, ask what the housekeeper's responsibilities were in the previous position. For example, was heavy cleaning involved or light cleaning plus child care? If a housekeeper with heavy-duty cleaning skills is required, someone who is experienced in doing light cleaning plus household errands would not be a good match. Before hiring a housekeeper, check with your insurance agent to see what liability coverage you have if someone is injured in your home.

Another alternative is to contact a franchise or local cleaning service. These housekeepers generally work in teams of two to four. With the team approach, if one person is sick or has an emergency, the rest of the crew can still get the job done. Although companies are set up to take care of paperwork associated with housekeeping,

SAFETY ALERT

Safe Care

Ask for references from a day-care center and check with your health department and licensing agency. Look for complaints filed against the center. The number of child-care workers per child is normally regulated by your state or county. Ask about the ratio of children to caregiver.

make sure the cleaning service provides workers who are bonded and insured and that the service assumes the responsibility for taxes and withholding.

Child-Care Options

Child care is an increasingly complex decision. When staying home isn't possible for financial, professional, or personal reasons—and using relatives isn't an option—hiring a care giver is a necessity. There are three main types of child care: child-care centers; family day-care homes where children are cared for in the provider's home; and in-home care, which involves hiring someone to provide care in your own home. Costs vary across the United States and Canada. However, in most cases, in-home care will be most expensive because you alone are paying for wages and benefits. Here's a look at the options.

CHILD-CARE CENTERS

Child-care centers are operated as for-profit centers or as part of a business, church, synagogue, educational institution, hospital, or government or social service agency. An increasing number of employers, such as hospitals and government agencies, offer child care as part of their employment packages. Finding out what is available through your employer, your spouse's employer, or in your community is the first step to finding quality child care.

As you investigate services, ask about waiting lists and enrollment criteria. Well-run centers often have high demand for services and long waiting lists. Centers may be structured for full-time care only, or they may allow part-time enrollment or offer drop-in or mother's morning out services. Some centers also have entrance requirements, such as potty training. Visit any center you are considering several times and discuss routines and programs with the director. Infants, for example, should be separated from older children to prevent mishaps. A key factor in opting to use a center is reliability. If you and your spouse have difficulty taking time off from work, the assurance of care is an important factor.

FAMILY DAY-CARE HOMES

Typically, home day cares are run by mothers of young or school-age children. They usually offer care for infants and preschool-age children, though some offer after-school care as well. This type of day care can work well, especially when you know the provider. As with child-care centers, check licensing and state and local regulations, including county health department standards. The

TIPTAG № 7

Housekeeper Calendar

WEEKLY CLEANING:
- Dusting furniture and lamp shades; vacuuming major upholstered pieces, such as sofa
- Cleaning switches and knobs
- Vacuuming carpets and area rugs
- Vacuuming wood floors
- Cleaning kitchen surfaces
- Stripping and making beds
- Cleaning bathrooms, including washing bath mats

MONTHLY CLEANING:
- Cleaning insides of kitchen cupboards and refrigerator
- Dusting window blinds
- Polishing copper, silver, and brass pieces as needed

number of children or infants that can be cared for in this type of facility may be regulated in your state or locality. As with child-care centers, the best family day-care homes may have waiting lists. Set up day care as early in pregnancy as possible. See the following section on in-home care for screening and references and advice.

IN HOME CARE OR NANNY

This can be the most convenient as well as the most costly child care. In-home or nanny care is ideal for infants and for households with two or three young children. However, because the provider will usually be alone in your home with your child or children, you'll need to be especially cautious and clear about your expectations.

Allow time. Unless you are in an emergency situation, take 60 to 90 days to hire. Whether you are developing prospects through classified advertisements, word-of-mouth references, or an agency, screening and interviewing applicants will take time.

Know what you want. Legally, there's a big difference between a friend or relative staying as a guest and helping out, a baby-sitter, a nanny, and an au pair. Here are helpful definitions:
■ Who is legally a baby-sitter? Generally, a person who performs child-care services is a baby-sitter. If the services are provided in your home, that person is a household employee. If the services are provided in the sitter's home, the sitter is not your employee. Whether the payments to a baby-sitter are subject to FICA tax depends on whether the sitter is related to you, whether the sitter is under age 18, and whether you pay more than the threshold amount. What is tricky is that the threshold requirement to pay taxes or file returns varies from year to year.
■ What is a nanny? As defined by the International Nanny Association, a nanny is a child-care professional working in a family's home, either full- or part-time, who has at least a high school diploma or equivalent, with proof of good health.

Hiring in-home child care: Some professional nanny organizations suggest placing advertisements, as well as hiring an agency, to ensure that you find the right care giver for your needs. If you live in a community near a college or university, working with a student-jobs registry or placing advertisements around campus may yield several candidates to interview. You may be more comfortable using a well-respected agency recommended by friends or coworkers. If you decide to use an agency, ask the following questions:
▸ How long has the agency been established? Is it a member of the International Nanny Association or other professional organization?
▸ Is the agency bonded? Some states require bonding, which means the agency can be held liable for a variety of damages or illegalities.
▸ How does the agency verify an applicant's identity? Does the agency do a criminal background investigation on applicants?

FAMILY FRIENDLY

Au Pairs

The host family receives 45 hours of child care a week in return for room, board, and cultural opportunities. Au pairs attend classes at accredited post-secondary institutions. Host families pay them a stipend based on the minimum wage, plus an education allowance.

Hiring Help for Chores

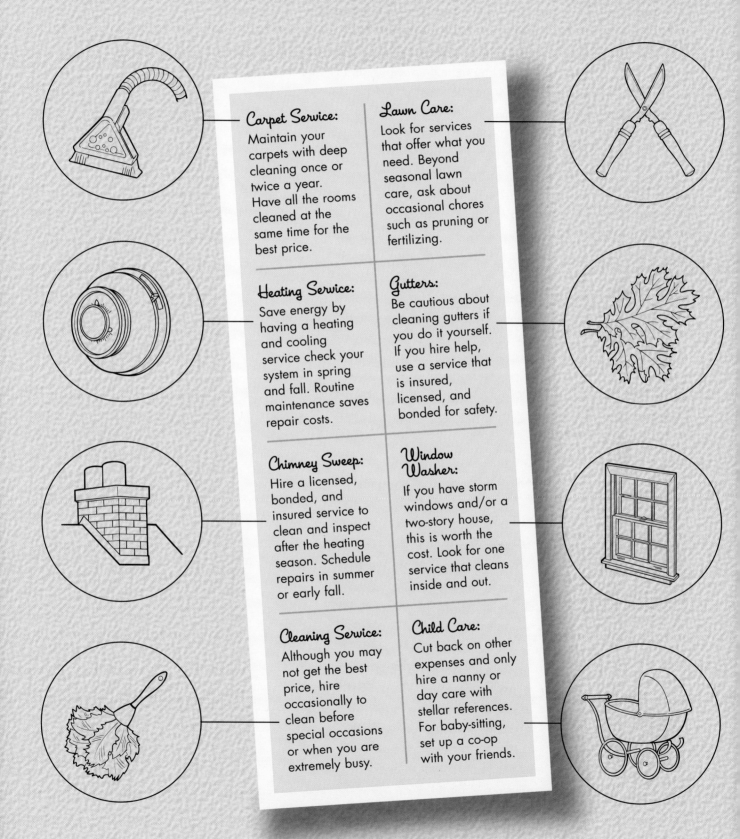

Carpet Service:
Maintain your carpets with deep cleaning once or twice a year. Have all the rooms cleaned at the same time for the best price.

Lawn Care:
Look for services that offer what you need. Beyond seasonal lawn care, ask about occasional chores such as pruning or fertilizing.

Heating Service:
Save energy by having a heating and cooling service check your system in spring and fall. Routine maintenance saves repair costs.

Gutters:
Be cautious about cleaning gutters if you do it yourself. If you hire help, use a service that is insured, licensed, and bonded for safety.

Chimney Sweep:
Hire a licensed, bonded, and insured service to clean and inspect after the heating season. Schedule repairs in summer or early fall.

Window Washer:
If you have storm windows and/or a two-story house, this is worth the cost. Look for one service that cleans inside and out.

Cleaning Service:
Although you may not get the best price, hire occasionally to clean before special occasions or when you are extremely busy.

Child Care:
Cut back on other expenses and only hire a nanny or day care with stellar references. For baby-sitting, set up a co-op with your friends.

FAMILY
FRIENDLY

Ad for
Nanny

Include:
• General area
where you live.
Don't give address.
• Phone number and
times to call.
• Experience and
references needed.
• Hours and days.
• Ages of children.
• Live-in or live-out
arrangements.
• Other duties.
• Automobile and
license required.
• Smoking policy.

▶ How does the agency check references?

▶ What training does the agency provide? Does it require CPR certification? (Also ask any potential care giver for children or for elderly to show proof of CPR certification.)

▶ Does the agency provide a contract or confirmation letter regarding terms of employment? Insist on full documentation.

▶ What are the agency fees and for what services?

▶ What follow-up does the agency provide? Is a replacement care giver guaranteed during a certain period if the care giver quits or you terminate his or her services?

▶ Does the agency inform employers about payroll taxes? Does it help calculate payroll taxes or refer you to a reputable tax professional versed in domestic employment regulations?

Screening and Interviews: If you use an agency (see the preceding section), set up your screening requirements and work with the agency to set up interviews. Ask for a minimum of three candidates as a starting point. If you are hiring by yourself, screen advertising replies or personal referrals by telephone before deciding whom to invite to your home. On the telephone, discuss salary up front. If your range is unacceptable, don't waste time. If the salary is acceptable, ask why the person is doing child care and ask about future plans. If driving is required, ask about license, vehicle reliability, and automobile insurance. Ask for at least three references and check them out before inviting anyone into your home. Set up your in-home interviews and consider the following:

▶ Background, health, education, experience, criminal convictions.

▶ Previous job and reason for leaving. Check and recheck references. Nothing is as important as the welfare of your children.

▶ Time commitments in relation to schedule requirements.

▶ Attitudes and experiences regarding discipline.

▶ Activities and hobbies. Discuss family rules about television and video viewing.

▶ Meals if applicable; cooking; and age-appropriate menu ideas.

▶ Child-related chores, such bathing a baby or laundry.

Pose a hypothetical situation involving child health, safety, or behavior, and see if you agree on how to handle the situation.

Salary and benefits: Because the cost of living varies significantly, there is no set rule on in-home care giver pay. It depends on the going rate where you live and your ability to offer other benefits, such as room and board. To get an idea of your area's pay scale, check with other families, read advertisements, and ask agencies. Benefits, except for legally required insurance, also depend on local practices and supply and demand. In tight labor markets, health insurance, paid holidays, and paid sick days are common perks to recruit and retain quality child care.

Taxes and withholding: Commonly called "The Nanny Tax," this law can be a tricky one. Under federal tax laws, a household employee is defined as any domestic worker whose work is subject to the employer's specifications. If a worker controls the work and the way it is done, provides his or her own tools, and offers services to the general public, the worker is considered self-employed. Workers provided through agencies are not household employees if the agency is responsible for who does the work and how it is done. If a one-time placement fee is paid to an agency, but the work thereafter is conducted between the employer and the worker, that worker is a household employee.

According to the Social Security Domestic Reform Act of 1994, household employers must withhold and pay FICA tax on wages of $1,300 or more in 2001. The amount can change yearly. Check annually. Federal income tax is withheld only if the household employee and employer agree. If you are unclear about your tax situation, ask your tax preparer or attorney for help in locating the appropriate expert advice. These taxes are required for full- and part-time employees:

▶ Social Security, Medicare, or RCA tax (6.2 percent each for employer and employee)
▶ Unemployment (or FUTA) tax (0.8 percent)
▶ Medicare tax (1.45 percent for each employer and employee, owed on all wages)
▶ As of 1995, household employers report household employees' FICA taxes and withheld income taxes (if there is an agreement to withhold income taxes) on a Schedule H with their Form 1040 tax return. Taxes due on Schedule H are paid by the due date for tax return filing, not including any extensions.

For further information on this topic:
▶ IRS Publication 926 "Employment Taxes for Household Employees"
▶ IRS Publication 937 "Employment Taxes and Information Returns"
▶ Social Security Administration at 800/772-1213 or www.ssa.gov
▶ I-9 Forms are available online at www.irs.gov

Green card issues: It is illegal to hire an undocumented noncitizen. Federal fines range from $1,000 to $3,000 per unauthorized employee. Employers are responsible for verifying the status of their employees by having them complete the Immigration and Naturalization Service Form I-9 and reviewing the identity documentation provided by the potential employee. Examples of

smart ideas

Know the Law

REQUIRED STEPS FOR HOUSEHOLD EMPLOYERS

Obtain a federal employer identification number (EIN) from the IRS.
• Complete Federal Form I-9 to verify an employee can legally work.
• Contact state unemployment tax agency to obtain a state EIN. Obtain a second state EIN if necessary for withholding state or local income taxes along with mandatory Social Security, Medicare, and unemployment taxes.
• Complete W-2 forms if withholding federal income taxes.
• The threshold to pay taxes varies from year to year. Contact the IRS, your accountant or your attorney.

legal documentation are an unexpired resident card (the green card) and a birth certificate.

Household employees are not exempt from federal minimum wage regulations. Other laws vary from state to state. Contact the appropriate tax, labor, or unemployment insurance agency for specifics. The U.S. Immigration and Naturalization Service can be contacted at 800/870-3676; www.ins.gov.

Insurance and liability: Domestic workers are usually defined by law as employees, not as independent contractors. Legally, independent contractors own or operate businesses, such as cleaning services, that hire workers to come to your home. Privately hiring nannies or housekeepers usually defines them as employees for tax and insurance purposes.

Mandatory insurance requirements vary from state to state. Contact your own agent or the state insurance commission for information applicable to your state. Although homeowner's insurance may cover accidental injury to a domestic worker, it may not cover lost wages or long-term disability. Discuss this with your insurance agent. Your state may require you to pay into a workers' compensation program that covers employees in case of job-related injury or illness. Check with your state's workers' compensation program or research online at insure.com for state guidelines.

ELDER CARE

As the population ages and life spans lengthen, many families face elder care issues. If you need to hire someone to care for an elderly relative in your home or your relative's home, it's important to be aware of the employment laws, tax and legal issues, and insurance concerns of domestic employment. The tax issues and your responsibility can be as involved as it is for child care. See information in the child-care section. Depending on your location, you may have the option of hiring an agency to provide some care or working with an agency to screen potential care givers. If you decide to use an agency, see the guidelines under in-home child care. Other sources to hire a care giver are recommendations from friends or family members or classified advertising. Get current references from agencies and from individuals and check them.

Elder care day-care centers, including those funded by large businesses, are available in some areas; they provide care while the family member is at work. If you have difficulty locating appropriate elder care, check with social service agencies under listings such as Council on Aging, Administration on Aging, or the Elder Care Locator Service (800/677-1116). Not-for-profit social agencies, such as the United Way and social services provided through religious organizations, may also have referral resources as well as information on nutritious meals for seniors.

SAFETY ALERT

Automobile Insurance

Be certain of coverage whether your nanny transports your child in your vehicle or hers. Check with your agent if your nanny drives your vehicle. If your children ride in her vehicle, ask the nanny to list your children under her policy and pay her premiums as a benefit.

3

Wood Floor Care
- REMOVING MARKS, 74
- WAXING, 74
- SEALING FLOORS, 76

Carpet Care & Cleaning
- VACUUMING TECHNIQUES, 77
- BUYING A VACUUM; OPTIONS, 77, 78
- STAIN REMOVAL GUIDE, 79, 80

Hard-Surface Care
- GLAZED AND UNGLAZED TILE, 81
- STONE, BRICK, AND CONCRETE, 84
- DRY AND WET MOPS, 84, 85
- RESILIENT FLOORING, 85
- VINYL, 85
- VINYL STAIN REMOVAL GUIDE, 86
- LAMINATE, 88
- CORK, 88
- LINOLEUM, 88

Walls
- PAINTED WALLS, 89
- PAPER AND VINYL COVERINGS, 90, 91
- WOOD PANELING, 92
- CERAMIC, STONE, AND BRICK, 92
- REMOVING CRAYON MARKS, 92

Ceilings & Moldings
- DECORATIVE MOLDINGS, 93
- LIGHT FIXTURES; CEILING FANS, 94

Windows
- WASHING TIPS, 94
- CLEAN SCREENS, 96

Cabinets
- PAINTED, 97
- METAL, 97
- LAMINATE, 97
- WOOD, 98

Countertops
- LAMINATE, 100
- TILE, 100
- WOOD AND BUTCHER BLOCK, 100
- STONE, GRANITE, SLATE, AND CONCRETE, 100

Cleaning Safely
- ITEMS TO STOCK, 101
- TECHNIQUES, 101

Caring for Surfaces

When you think of house cleaning, you likely think of floors, walls, windows, and ceilings. Although appliances such as vacuum cleaners have definitely made surface cleaning easier, this is still the time-consuming, down and dirty part of housework. Setting up your own daily and weekly routines for chores keeps cleaning manageable. See Tab 2 for time-stretching tips.

Getting Started

You will save time and money and avoid frustration if you buy the right supplies, keep them handy, and use them according to manufacturer's guidelines. The easiest method is to purchase a sturdy plastic cleaning caddy and stock it with the supplies and tools for your routine cleaning jobs. Use the same caddy for all your weekly cleaning chores, including care for furnishings (discussed in more detail in Tab 4, page 103). If you live in a two-story house or townhouse, you may find it convenient to stock a second caddy as well as brooms and mops on both levels and stock specific supplies in the bathroom and kitchen. Store all cleaning supplies on upper shelves behind locked cabinet doors out of the reach of children.

Wood Floor Care

Gleaming wood floors are an asset to a home. Although wood floors are a luxury in new construction, houses and apartments built before 1960 often have wood floors. If your residence has wood floors, enjoy the beauty by giving them proper care. Place mats both outside and inside exterior doors to lessen tracked-in dirt and slush. In snowy or rainy weather, include a boot removal area to avoid damage from water and deicers.

DEEPER CLEANING

Dirt, oil, and grime build up over time and aren't entirely removed by a weekly dust mopping. For occasional thorough cleaning, such as in the spring or before the winter holidays, use a wood-cleaning product, diluted according to label instructions. Saturate a sponge or rag mop in the water, then wring it almost dry so it feels only slightly damp to the touch. Damp mop, being careful not to allow water to stand on the floor. Rinse with a clean mop dampened in clear water only if the product requires it. Wipe up excess liquid. Standing water can damage wood surfaces. If the weather is humid, operate a ceiling fan or the air conditioner.

TIPTAG № 8
Wood Floor Care

MAKE IT EASY:

- Dust the floor with a dust mop that has been treated with a dusting agent to pick up dust, dirt, and pet hair that may cause scratches in the floor surface. Wash the mop head regularly.
- For weekly or bi-weekly cleaning, vacuum with a floor brush attachment on a vacuum cleaner or an electric broom. Do not use a vacuum with a beater bar attachment, which can scratch the finish of a wood floor.
- For quick dusting, use disposable electrostatic cloths that are sold at grocery and discount stores. Turn over and use both sides.

REMOVING MARKS

Prevent marks on the floor by using floor protectors under furniture and by making sure children's toys, such as cars and trucks, don't scratch the floor. When a scratch or mark occurs, consider the floor finish before attempting to remove the mark. If the scratch or stain is on the surface, your floor probably has a hard finish. (Widely used urethane-type finishes create a hard sealant on wood floors.) If the scratch or stain has penetrated the finish to the wood, the floor likely has a soft, oiled finish—common in older residences in which the floors have not been refinished and sealed. Most new construction finishes wood floors with urethane.

Hard finishes: Repair scratches with commercial touch-up kits from a wood flooring supplier. Never use sandpaper, steel wool, or harsh chemicals because they can permanently damage the finish.

Soft finishes: Use the following techniques to restore damaged spots. End each treatment by staining the wood (if necessary) and waxing and buffing the spot to match the rest of the floor. Choose the appropriate remedy for the mark or stain.

■ Dark spots and pet stains: Rub the spot with #000 steel wool and floor wax. If the area is still dark, apply bleach or vinegar and allow it to soak into the wood for about an hour. Rinse with a damp cloth.

■ Heel marks: Use fine steel wool to rub in floor wax.

■ Oil-based stains: Rub the area with a soft cloth and dish washing detergent to break down the grease, then rinse with clear water. If one or more applications doesn't work, repeat the procedure. (Keep children and pets out of the room.) Let the spot dry and then smooth raised grain with fine sandpaper.

■ Scratches: Repair deep scratches with a wood color stick or with a stain that matches the floor. Cover light scratches with floor wax. Let the wax dry; buff with a cotton cloth.

■ Water marks or white stains: Rub the spot with #000 steel wool and floor wax. If the stain goes deeper, lightly sand the floor and clean with fine steel wool and odorless mineral spirits.

WAXING

Wax is used to seal, protect, and beautify flooring. Choose water-based finishes in the correct type of wax for your floor and its finish. Follow wood manufacturer and finish label directions to protect your floor without having a dangerously slick surface. Use nonskid rug pads under all runners to avoid accidents. Wax and waxlike products also are used on linoleum (not resilient), unfinished cork, and some concrete floors. If in doubt about a product, don't use it.

Solid paste wax: Choose this old-fashioned wax in a can for unvarnished hardwood floors, true linoleum, unfinished cork, and concrete. Do NOT use paste wax on no-wax floors, vinyl, or urethane-finished floors. Apply by hand for a long-lasting shine.

Targeted Floor Protectors

Padded Rounds:

Sturdy plastic rounds securely cup furniture legs while the soft, textured side protects wood floors from scratches and dents. Use for heavy furniture.

Felt Circles:

Purchased in sheets, self-adhesive rounds attach to the feet of lightweight furniture pieces, such as dining chairs, that are used on wood floors. Replace when worn.

Color-Coded Plastic:

Plastic squares, designed to protect wood floors, are sold in dark and light tones to blend with the furniture or the wood floor. Sold at hardware stores and home centers.

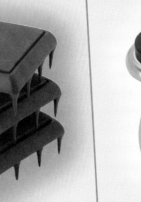

Clear for Carpet:

Spiked rounds and squares protect carpet from compression. Clear acrylic forms blend with carpet colors and furniture finishes. Choose shape to fit furniture legs.

Wood for Carpet:

Large furniture pieces need the support of heavy-duty spiked squares to reduce dents in plush carpet. Buy the size, shape, and color for your furniture piece.

Screw-In Protectors:

Attach these protectors to furniture pieces that are frequently moved, such as dining room chairs. Choose a smooth pad that won't scratch hard surface floors.

Wax Not Work Not

•

Avoid using excess wax, which attracts rather than repels dirt. When the floor is tacky or dull, remove the old wax finish and re-wax the floor, using light coats of wax. For a quick polish, dust mop and buff the floor with clean toweling.

Moisten a soft, lint-free, cotton cloth, such as an old T-shirt, and wring it almost dry to prevent the cloth from absorbing too much wax. Apply the wax lightly and evenly, working it into the surface, following product instructions. If you prefer soft wax, use the liquid equivalent of paste wax. As the waxed surface dries, it will appear cloudy. Buff to a shine with a clean towel, an electric polisher, or a terry cloth-covered sponge mop.

Liquid wax or oil: Use on unvarnished hardwood, linoleum, or unfinished cork. Follow label instructions. It is easier to apply than paste wax, but the finish doesn't last as long. Do NOT use on no-wax floors, vinyl, or urethane-finished floors. Dampen a soft lint-free cloth, a mop, or the pad of an electric floor polisher to prevent the wax from soaking in. Apply polish evenly and lightly. As it dries, the solvent evaporates, leaving the polish. When dry, buff the floor with a clean towel, an electric polisher, or a sponge mop covered with a terry cloth towel.

Water-based silicone polishes: Apply on all floors EXCEPT unsealed wood, cork, or linoleum. Use only this type of polish on urethane-finished surfaces. Apply these long-lasting polishes in several thin coats rather than one heavy coat, which is difficult to dry. To apply, dampen a clean mop head. Pour the polish onto the mop; pour some of the polish directly on the floor. Spread the polish evenly to avoid bubbles in the liquid. Allow the polish to dry and buff the floor with a clean towel, an electric polisher, or a terry cloth covered sponge mop. Apply second and third coats to high-traffic areas, buffing after each coat dries. Avoid splattering polish onto baseboards or walls because it stains wallcoverings and paint.

SEALING FLOORS

After several years of wear, cork and hardwood floor surfaces wear down and need to be refinished or resealed. Polyurethane finishes, both water- and oil-based, provide a hard and durable finish. Shellac, lacquer, and non-urethane varnish are less frequently used sealants. After these sealants are applied, they take several days to dry, and then provide a durable surface. Acrylic sealers, which are not as durable, are adequate finishes for low-traffic areas.

Brick, concrete, and unglazed tile require specially formulated sealants. Do not use polyurethane because it can cause discoloration. Before refinishing, thoroughly remove wax and residue with a product formulated for wax removal. Lightly sand any rough spots or dark stains. If more extensive sanding is needed, check with a professional refinisher or rent a vibrating sander. Schedule this chore on a warm, calm, dry day when windows can be open to avoid breathing fumes. Brush on the appropriate sealer with a foam pad, working from a corner to a doorway. Let the surface dry thoroughly before allowing traffic on the floor.

Carpet Care & Cleaning

HOW OFTEN SHOULD YOU VACUUM?

Regular vacuuming protects the life of carpeting and keeps it looking good longer. As dirt sifts between fibers, it causes carpet to wear. Frequent vacuuming, using quality filter bags, also reduces household allergens. Vacuum main living areas, stairs, and high-traffic areas of your home at least twice a week, more frequently if you have children or pets. Place door mats on both sides of each exterior door to trap dirt before it enters the house. Sweep and shake out rugs every day, particularly during inclement weather when more dirt can be tracked in.

VACUUMING TECHNIQUES

Before you vacuum, pick up debris, scraps of paper, buttons, and objects that may damage vacuum belts and hoses. Vacuum steadily and evenly in overlapping parallel patterns. Move dining chairs and side chairs each time you vacuum to clean thoroughly under them and to raise the nap under furniture feet. Move large pieces of furniture—especially those that sit close to the floor, such as heavy sofas and chests—less frequently. Use a crevice tool to vacuum along baseboards, along carpet creases on the stairs, and in narrow spaces where larger attachments do not reach. To vacuum stairs, start at the bottom and work up to avoid pressing dirt in the steps as you work.

DEEP CLEANING

Thoroughly clean your carpet every 12 to 18 months, more often in high-traffic areas. Also clean more frequently, such as two or three times a year, if you have children and pets that track in dirt or if you have light-colored carpet. Follow carpet manufacturer's cleaning guidelines. Remove furniture from the room and thoroughly vacuum the carpet. Use a rental cleaner (if recommended by the manufacturer), or have it professionally cleaned. Make sure the carpet dries completely within 24 hours to prevent mold or mildew growth in carpet or padding.

VACUUM OPTIONS

Vacuums are designed to meet specific needs, and generally come with a variety of attachments.

Upright: Although these models are comfortable to use in large areas because they require less bending, they may be clumsy to use on stairs and in tight spaces. Most models employ both suction and beater brushes. Uprights are heavy and awkward to carry.

Tank or canister: Portable, and lighter than uprights, large

Home Remedies

WAXING AWAY

Soft-Finish Floors

To remove wax buildup from wood floors that don't have a hard finish (such as polyurethane, varnish, or shellac), use a wax-removal product for wood, or a mixture of all-purpose cleaner and water. After the floor is dry, seal or wax it. If you decide to seal, consider polyurethane for a durable finish. Choose clear if you prefer the natural wood tone.

Hard-Finish Floors

These floors should NOT be waxed. But if they have been, remove the wax with a commercial wax stripper and a scrubbing pad made especially for urethane-finish floors. NEVER use mineral spirits or steel wool on a hard-finished floor.

tanks or canisters are awkward to carry. Some have beater brushes built into the carpet attachment. Canisters may not be as effective on carpet as upright models, but they perform well on smooth surfaces.

Wet/dry vacs: Heavy-duty units are ideal to vacuum water from basements, sawdust from the garage, and for removing excess moisture after spot cleaning.

Handheld vacuums: Available in both cordless and corded versions, these are best for light-duty cleaning, sucking up small dry spills, and getting into hard-to-reach areas. Powerful models (usually the corded ones) also work well on stairs and are helpful companions to upright models. Some have beater brushes.

Electric brooms: These are offshoots of hand-held vacuums and serve the same purpose. They're more comfortable to use on a daily basis because they are upright. A few models have detachable handles so you can use them as handheld vacuums.

Central (built-in system): Typically only seen in new construction or major remodeling, these vacuums are built into the house. A central motor and dirt canister are usually located in the basement, the garage, or a closet. A hose plugs into special outlets in each room. Most come with an upright beater brush attachment.

BUYING A VACUUM

Determine your needs and budget before choosing a model. A green CRI label on vacuums indicates that the brand has undergone voluntary testing by the Carpet and Rug Institute and meets performance and air-quality standards.

Look for a quiet model if you vacuum while children are napping or if you vacuum large areas.

Consider the power of the machine and match it to the type of cleaning you do. Instead of comparing motor size, check the cubic feet per minute, which is a measurement of the air movement through the vacuum. The higher the movement, the better the cleaning ability.

Check the weight so you will be able to move it easily up and down stairs and push it with ease. Some of the heavier models are self-propelled to make vacuuming easier.

Look at the dimensions to see how close to the wall the vacuum can move and whether it will fit under furniture.

Check the bag or collection canister to see if it is large, easy to remove, and easy to clean or replace. Bags can help keep the interior of the machine cleaner but add to housekeeping expenses and can be more difficult to handle than canisters. Bags that fill from the top are more efficient and less messy to change.

Look for variable speed and height adjustments if you have different styles of carpet or rugs.

Understand the importance of beater brushes. Brushes

BUDGET STRETCHER

Colorfast Carpet?

To test for colorfastness, use a carpet scrap or inconspicuous spot. Vacuum the carpet; dampen a cloth with a cleaner. Lay the cloth on the carpet for an hour; then blot the damp area with a white cloth. If the cloth is stained with carpet dyes, test another cleaning product.

Carpet Stain Removal

Rust:
Treat fresh spots with 1 cup of white vinegar to 2 cups water. If dry, have spots professionally treated and cleaned.

Pet Stains:
Apply an enzymatic cleaner, purchased from pet supply stores, that discourages repeat visits.

Wine and Juice:
Spritz with club soda. Blot. Repeat until the stain is gone. Use white vinegar to remove soft drink stains.

Blood:
Treat immediately. Apply cold water or club soda and blot with clean cloth. Repeat until stain no longer appears.

Tomato Stains:
Sponge with cool water. Dab with the detergent solution or citrus-oxygen cleaner. Rinse with cold water.

Grease and Oil:
Sprinkle with baking soda; let sit for at least six hours. Vacuum; apply spot cleaner. Rinse; blot or wet-vac dry.

Soft Drinks:
Try the detergent solution (page 80). If stain remains, mix 1 cup white vinegar to 2 cups of water. Sponge; blot.

Dirt:
Allow dirt to dry before treating. Scrape off as much as possible; vacuum. Apply the detergent solution (page 80).

gently pound out the dirt from deep within the carpet, elevating the dirt to the surface so that it can be vacuumed away. This feature is essential for cleaning large or high-traffic areas but may be wearing on delicate rugs, smooth floors, and antique carpets.

Know your attachments to get the most cleaning power. All vacuum cleaners, except hand-held models and electric brooms, should come with hoses; crevice tools for cleaning corners; dust brushes for draperies, lampshades, and walls; smooth floor brushes for wood and other surfaces; and upholstery attachments.

CARPET STAIN REMOVAL GUIDE

Time is of the essence when something stains your carpet. For liquids, blot—never rub—as much moisture from the carpet as possible. Use a white towel or plain white paper towels, working in from the outside edge. For solid spills, use a spoon or dull knife to remove any item that hasn't soaked into the carpet. Specific stain removal treatments appear in the following list. Take care when cleaning not to over-wet carpets, because excess moisture damages the backing. Citrus-based oxygen cleaners, mixed according to label directions, remove organic stains from carpets.

General stain-removal formula: Commercial spot carpet cleaners sold at grocery stores and home centers will remove many carpet stains. You also can make your own all-purpose cleaner with this basic formula: Stir 1 teaspoon of liquid dish detergent into a quart of warm water. Add ¼ teaspoon of white vinegar. Let solution sit on stain for 10 minutes before blotting.

White vinegar solution: This is another all-purpose do-it-yourself solution recommended by the Carpet and Rug Institute. Mix 1 cup of white vinegar with 2 cups of water.

Alcohol and soft drinks: Apply the detergent stain removal formula. Rinse; then blot or wet-vac dry.

Coffee or tea: Apply the detergent solution. Rinse and blot. If any stain remains, apply spot carpet cleaner. Blot or wet-vac dry.

Fat-based stains, such as butter, margarine, or gravy: Use a dry-solvent spot carpet cleaner according to label.

Gum: Peel away what you can. Harden gum by placing a zipper-lock bag of ice cubes over it; chip gum away with a spoon or dull knife. Vacuum. Spot-clean with a dry-solvent spot carpet cleaner.

Paint: Dry paint is hard to remove. For acrylic and latex, while wet, spot-clean with detergent solution. If color remains, dab with rubbing alcohol. For oil-based paint, while wet, sponge with odorless mineral spirits, being careful not to soak carpet backing.

Tar: Use a dry-solvent spot cleaner.

Tomato sauces: Sponge with cool water, dab with detergent solution or citrus-oxygen cleaner, rinse with solution of cold water with white vinegar, and blot or wet-vac until dry.

TIME SAVER

Quick Fixes For the Vacuum

•

Keep replacement belts and bags for your vacuum cleaner on hand. To unclog a blocked hose, straighten a wire hanger and slide it gently into the hose to snag or push the blockage. If you have reverse airflow on the vacuum, try to blow out the clogged item.

Urine, feces, and vomit: Apply the detergent solution or a citrus-oxygen cleaner. Rinse and blot or wet-vac dry.

Wax (melted): Harden, shatter, and remove as for gum. Dampen a clean white cloth or cotton ball with rubbing alcohol and blot remaining wax.

CARPET DESTROYERS

Some common household products permanently damage carpet. The best solution is to keep them away from carpet. Destructive products include acids (toilet bowl and grout cleaners), acne medications, bleaching solutions, insecticides, pet urine, and plant foods. Automatic dishwasher detergents as well as drain and oven cleaners can bleach carpet fibers.

Hard-Surface Care

Hard-surface floors are known for generally easy care and relatively low maintenance. For the best results in taking care of hard-surface flooring, find out whether it has been factory sealed or commercially sealed and find out what sealant was used. If you build or remodel, keep in mind that sealed tile, brick, concrete, and stone are easier to maintain than unsealed surfaces. If you replace vinyl flooring, discuss proper care of your new flooring material with the supplier. Manufacturers often sell cleaning and polishing products designed for their flooring, and these can be found at home centers.

TILE

Tile is made from nonmetallic substances and fired until it is hard. It may or may not have the shiny glazed finish typical of bathroom tile. Tile broadly includes terra-cotta, porcelain, quarry tile, and paver tiles, both glazed and unglazed. Each type has slightly different care requirements. Tile is manufactured in two categories—floor tiles and wall tiles. Floor tiles are generally thicker and larger. Walls tiles are usually glazed, such as for back splashes, and have a greater selection of texture and relief. Floor and wall tiles are made of the same basic materials, and care is similar.

GLAZED TILES

Glazed tiles are fairly impervious to stains, making them easy to maintain and practical for kitchens and baths. The grout between tiles may stain; it may also hold mildew and bacteria.

UNGLAZED TILES

Tiles without the glazed surface are more porous and tend to stain more easily than glazed tiles. If you have unglazed tiles on a floor or wall, wipe spills and splashes immediately to avoid permanent stains. Care depends to some extent on personal preference. If you want to keep unglazed tile, such as terra-cotta, pristine, vacuum or sweep frequently, daily or twice daily in a busy family living area. If you prefer a natural look, clean less frequently so small particles of dust can help age the surface. Sweep and wash with mild detergent or cleaner diluted in water.

Sealing unglazed tiles keeps them cleaner. Look for a sealer formulated for your tile type at flooring and tile stores. A penetrating sealer, which enters the pores of the tile, keeps the surface stain-resistant and should be applied before grouting. New quarry tile can be treated with linseed oil. Do not wash the tile for at least two weeks to allow the oil time to soak into the tile surface.

GROUT

Because it is more porous than the tile, grout often shows dirt and stains more than the tile itself does. Keep new or renewed grout looking good by using a grout sealer 10 to 14 days after grout cures.

To clean stained grout, use a strong bleach solution ($\frac{3}{4}$ cup of bleach to 1 gallon of water) and scrub with a small brush or toothbrush. Do not scrub too hard; otherwise you may damage the grout. Wear safety goggles to prevent the bleach from spattering in your eyes. Keep the work area ventilated. Or try a foaming grout cleaner that may need to soak for several minutes to be effective.

If grout is deeply stained and discolored, replace it. Tile stores sell or may rent tools for removing grout. Run the tool along the grout, taking care not to scratch the surrounding tile. Clean the space between the tiles with a strong bleach solution; then apply new grout and seal it. Do NOT spill bleach on porcelain, because it can cause pitting or yellow or pink stains.

TILE STAIN REMOVAL GUIDE

Test your stain removal technique on an inconspicuous spot of both tile and grout before cleaning. A nonabrasive all-purpose cleaner or a tub-tile-sink product removes most stains. Try the following techniques for common stains:

Blood: Dab with hydrogen peroxide or diluted bleach.

Coffee, tea, and juice: Wash with detergent and hot water; blot with hydrogen peroxide or diluted bleach.

Gum, wax, and tar: Place ice cubes in a zipper-type plastic bag and lay the bag over the material. Once the material has been solidified, use a crafts stick to gently scrape away as much of the substance as possible. Remove the remaining residue with nonflammable paint thinner.

Grease and fat-based stains: Wash with club soda and water or with a nonabrasive floor cleaner.

Ink and dye: Soak a clean cloth with diluted bleach and lay it

FAMILY FRIENDLY

Carpet vs. Teens

•

Light spots encircled by a halo on your carpeting may indicate spilled acne medication, which bleaches the dye. To test for the damage, apply lotion to a scrap of carpet and moisten with water. Place in the microwave for 10 seconds to speed up reaction time. If the same result occurs, avoid future spills.

Match Care to Tile Type

Laminate:
Versatile, easy-care, and made in a range of patterns. Damp mop with a mild detergent. Don't wax or polish.

Unglazed/Terra-Cotta:
Sweep to reduce dust before mopping with mild detergent and water. Rinse twice to avoid film buildup, and buff with a dry cloth.

Slate:
Vacuum this sturdy tile to pick up dust and grit. Mop with a slightly damp mop. Never let water pool on the floor.

Glazed Tile:
Wipe with mild detergent and clear water. Do not wax or polish; glazed tiles will become dangerously slippery, especially if wet.

Vinyl:
Use manufacturer's recommended cleaner or a mild vinegar and water solution. Use polish only if recommended.

Marble and Granite:
Vacuum and damp mop to remove dirt and grime. Do not wax or polish stone. Don't use acidic products as they may etch stone.

Tile Tips

Soapy reside on tile
surfaces causes
a hazy appearance.
Remove soap scum
with a nonabrasive
all-purpose cleaner
or a tub and tile
cleaner. Rinse with
clear water and buff
dry with a clean
lint-free cloth.
A mild acid (such as
fresh lemon juice)
may be used on
ceramic tiles but not
on marble.

over the stain. Let it stand until the stain disappears. Rinse well.

Iodine: Scrub with diluted ammonia and rinse well.

Mercurochrome: Scrub with diluted bleach.

Nail polish: Dissolve with nail polish remover. If a stain remains, dab it with hydrogen peroxide or diluted bleach.

STONE, BRICK, AND CONCRETE

Keep hard but porous surfaces—such as stone (marble, granite, slate, and others), brick, and concrete—looking good by sealing the surface before stains and dirt have a chance to penetrate. Check with flooring dealers and installers for products made specifically for your type of flooring and apply products according to the manufacturer's directions. The right sealer will enhance the look and depth of stone surfaces; the wrong sealer can dull the finish and wear poorly. Both matte and glossy finishes are available. Apply several thin coats to ensure proper drying and adhering. Reapply the sealer every few years or when the floor shows wear. If your floor has not been sealed, clean and dry before sealing.

Concrete floors also can be painted. Look for flooring paint made especially for concrete floors; regular porch paint will peel off. Crafts and decorating stores carry paints for concrete surfaces (often called patio paints). Some flooring paints are exceptionally durable and do not require a top coat. Others (often the decorative paints) must have a sealer to prevent wear.

Clean sealed stone, brick, and concrete floors with a vacuum, broom, or damp mop. For a deeper clean, use mild detergent diluted in water; rinse well. If a film develops after several washings, mop the floor with a weak solution of white vinegar and water. Never use abrasive powders or cleaners containing acids, oils, or organic solvents.

MOPS

This utilitarian tool is one of the cheapest and most effective ways to keep your home clean. Every residence needs both a dry and a wet mop. The dry version picks up dust, pet hair, and small amounts of dirt (common after sweeping or vacuuming). Wet mops are used for scrubbing and for applying sanitizing solutions to bath and kitchen floors. Both work when pressed firmly to the floor and moved in long, overlapping strokes. Dust mop with wood grain.

Dry mops (dust mops) have a shaggy cloth head. Spray the head with a cleaner made specifically for attracting dust. Purchase a mop with a removable cloth head that can be laundered. Shake the mop to remove dust particles. Some cities have ordinances against shaking dust mops outside, especially during times of high air pollution. If that's the case in your city or if you prefer not to shake the mop outside, tie a paper bag over the mop head and shake the mop vigorously. To wash the mop head, place in a mesh laundry bag and machine wash with detergent in cold water.

Some dust mops also have polishing heads that can be attached to lightly buff floors. A new version is the disposable-cover dust mop that attaches to a head. The cover is impregnated with dust-attracting agents. When the head is dirty, turn it over for another sweep; then replace it. Such products typically come in two sizes. Disposable covers are effective in picking up pet hairs; such mops are sold in grocery stores, discount retailers, and pet supply stores.

Wet mops come in sponge and rag (also called string) styles. Another practical style has removable terry cloth covers. All wet mops should be dampened well, then wrung almost dry before mopping. Sponge mops work well for homes with a relatively small area that requires mopping, such as a moderate-size kitchen and bathroom.

Sponge or terry cloth mops work well on smooth surfaces such as vinyl flooring. Some have pivot heads that make it easy to reach tight spaces, such as behind the toilet. Look for sponge mops with heads that are easy to replace and available. Check to see they wring out easily. Look for sturdy wringing hardware and a well-attached (not floppy) head.

String mops cover a large area faster than sponge mops and work well for uneven stone or brick areas. Select a removable head for washing; also test to see if it wrings out easily.

After mopping, rinse and wring the mop head until the water runs clear; then wring it well. (For terry cloth covers, attach a fresh cover and wash the dirty one in the washing machine.) Hang a mop or set it with the head up, so that the head dries completely, to avoid formation of mold or mildew. Proper storage also keeps the mop head from becoming misshapen.

RESILIENT FLOOR CARE

The term "resilient flooring" refers to floor products that have a slight softness and give. The comfortable cushioning makes a good choice for kitchens and workrooms. Although extra-cushion flooring is more comfortable, it is not as durable. Heavy furniture may cause dents. Chairs scooted across the floor may gouge the surface, and sharp objects that are dropped may make cuts.

Match your surface choice to its use—harder surfaces for high-traffic areas such as kitchens and softer surfaces for spots such as bathrooms where there is no sliding furniture.

VINYL

Vinyl sheeting and tiles are often considered the workhorses of flooring products—relatively inexpensive compared to other

TIP TAG № 9

Rating Tile

U.S. VERSUS EUROPE:

- American companies use a 1 to 5 rating scale for tile quality.
- European manufacturers typically use a 1 to 4 rating scale.
- Lower-rated (and cheaper) tiles are fired at lower temperatures, so the glaze is less durable.
- The rating is especially important for floor tiles because sand and gravel tracked across less durable surfaces may cause scratches and mar the appearance.
- High-quality tile are less likely to spot and streak because of their durable surfaces. If tiles streak after washing and rinsing, buff with a terry cloth towel.

products, easy to maintain, and available in an almost endless array of colors and patterns. Sheeting can be installed with few or no seams, depending on the size and configuration of your room. Vinyl tile floors have seams between each tile. Although seams are barely visible initially, they may collect dirt over time. Inexpensive, self-adhesive tiles may shrink and pull away from each other, leaving gaps. Vinyl composition tile (VCT) adhered to the floor with adhesive is a good longer-term choice.

Clean vinyl floors by removing dust and dirt with a broom, dust mop, or vacuum. Controlling grit and soil is crucial to prolonging the attractive appearance of any floor. A quick wipe with a damp mop works well between deep cleaning. Choose a nonabrasive all-purpose cleaning product or a product specifically formulated for the type of factory-applied sealant. Many products are no-rinse solutions. Purchase the cleaning product recommended by the flooring manufacturer. Rinse well. If you are unsure of the composition or coating, check with the previous owner, real estate or rental agent. If you are unable to find out the exact composition, a mild vinegar and water solution is probably safe. Water-based or acrylic-based floor polishes can be used on many resilient floors but may not be compatible with some no-wax floors.

VINYL STAIN REMOVAL GUIDE

Some stains may be permanent, particularly if your floor is old, but these techniques can at least lighten the discolorations. You may have to repeat the process several times. Some vinyl manufacturers make products for removing specific stains such as fruit juice, food dyes, and black heel marks. A nonabrasive all-purpose cleaning product often is enough for stain removal. Whatever products and techniques you try, test on a small inconspicuous spot first.

Black heel marks: Rub the area with an art gum eraser or a nonabrasive scrubbing pad and nonabrasive cleanser, or rub with regular toothpaste. If a stain remains, try using rubbing alcohol (91 percent isopropyl from the drug store).

Crayons: Rub with lighter fluid or odorless mineral spirits.

Fruit juice or wine: Wash the area with a mild bleach solution of ¼ cup bleach to 1 gallon of water. If a stain remains, try using rubbing alcohol.

Hair dye: Rub the area with rubbing alcohol. If the stain shows, scrub it with lighter fluid or odorless mineral spirits.

Ink: Wipe the spot with rubbing alcohol; repeat. If a stain is still visible, rub with lighter fluid or odorless mineral spirits.

Lipstick: Rub the stain with rubbing alcohol.

Paint and varnish: Immediately wipe up any wet spills. If the stain is dry, carefully scrape it with a plastic card, such as a credit card, or a thin spatula. Remove residue with rubbing alcohol. If a

TIME SAVER

Concrete Prep

Avoid having to repaint concrete floors by preparing the surface properly the first time. Scrape and wash the floor, and apply a commercial concrete etcher, following precautions and wearing eye protection. Let dry for 72 hours; apply paint or stain formulated for concrete floors.

The Right Vac Attachment

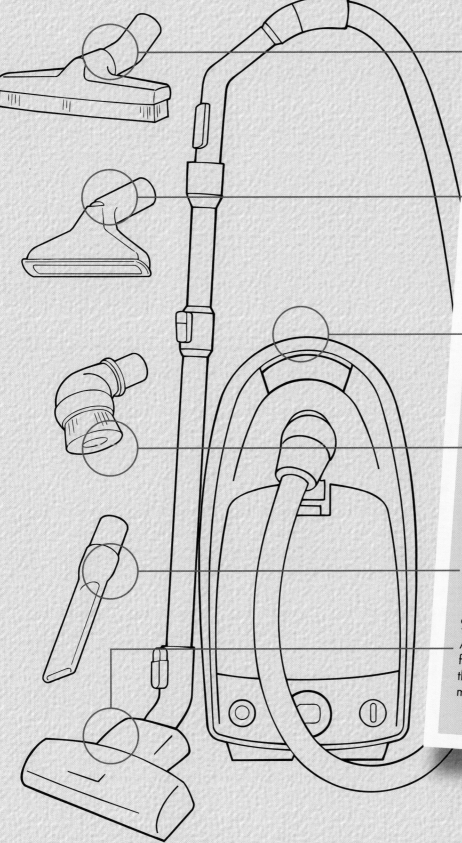

Smooth-Floor Brush:
For use on wood, vinyl, tile, and other smooth floorings, but not on carpeting. Pick up large objects before vacuuming.

Upholstery Nozzle:
Vacuum dirt and crumbs to prevent fiber damage. The nozzle may also be used on some draperies; adjust the suction control at the hose.

Canister: Bags or collection canisters store dirt until emptied. Empty either frequently for maximum vacuum efficiency.

Dusting Brush:
Dust baseboards, moldings, sills, wood trim, heating and cooling vents, and tops of doors with this attachment.

Crevice Tool:
Clean hard-to-reach places, such as narrow trim, stair treads, or upholstery with this narrow, angled tool.

Suction Setting:
Adjust settings based on flooring materials, lowering the beater bar brushes for maximum pick-up.

stain still shows, rub it with lighter fluid or odorless mineral spirits.

Permanent marker: Gently rub with lighter fluid or odorless mineral spirits. Rubbing alcohol may also remove marker stains.

Rust: Halve a lemon. Rub cut side over rust spot. If spot remains, pour on a small amount of salt-water solution and rub with lemon.

Shoe polish: Scrub the spot with lighter fluid or odorless mineral spirits. If a stain still shows, rub it with rubbing alcohol.

Tar: Scrub the spot with lighter fluid or odorless mineral spirits. If a stain still shows, rub it with rubbing alcohol.

LAMINATE

First available in Europe, laminate is now made in the United States by major flooring companies. Since the 1990s, this flooring has become increasingly popular. The laminate floor gets its appearance from a photographic reproduction, which is layered inside protective plastic coatings on a supporting core of wood-based material. Warranties typically range from 5 to 16 years. Laminate flooring can be installed on top of plywood subfloors, concrete slabs, or existing flooring. A foam underlay absorbs sound.

Follow care instructions if you have laminate installed. If you move into a residence with laminate flooring, the usual care is sweeping, dusting, or vacuuming, and then light damp mopping. Avoid wet mopping, which can result in seepage behind baseboards. Never use wax or acrylic products, because they can damage the finish. The flooring doesn't easily stain; however, if there is a problem, rubbing alcohol can be used on nail polish, cigarette burns, shoe polish, paint, ink, and crayon. Try mineral spirits for grease or tar. Dirt, grit, and scraping furniture can damage laminates, so use floor mats and casters to protect your flooring.

CORK

Cork is a soft surface that offers cushion and durability, thanks to pre-applied finishes. Typically, cork is finished with polyurethane, but a few manufacturers use acrylic. Cleaning cork means cleaning the surface finish. If the surface is sealed with polyurethane, clean with water and mild detergent or white vinegar; rinse well. If you install cork, check with the dealer about recommended products. Avoid polishes if you prefer a matte finish; expect to refinish every 8 to 10 years. If the cork is unfinished or waxed, follow the cleaning instructions for the polyurethane but apply solid or liquid wax.

LINOLEUM

Common in residences from the early 20th century to the 1960s, linoleum was the first sheet flooring in widespread use. Through the years, sheet flooring has been generically called linoleum; however, linoleum and vinyl are different products. Vinyl replaced linoleum for general use until the 1990s, when designers rediscovered linoleum's pattern potential.

BUDGET STRETCHER

Enjoy Your Cork

•

Get the most wear from this comfortable flooring by using common sense care. Avoid dropping sharp objects and sliding heavy furniture across the floor. Buy extra to replace damaged areas. Although the color may not match at first, it will blend as it ages.

The differences between vinyl and linoleum are significant. Vinyl, by far the most-used sheet flooring, is made from petroleum-based polyvinyl chloride. It's flexible and resilient and has a semisoft surface. Linoleum is composed of linseed oil, resin, cork, limestone, and wood flour that are mixed with pigments and then rolled onto a jute backing. Improved manufacturing procedures make linoleum a good choice for floors and countertops. Expect to pay more for linoleum than for typical sheet vinyls; the long wear and design possibilities can be worth the added expense.

Clean linoleum using the resilient-flooring instructions. Sweep the floor, wash with detergent or borax and water. Rinse clean and dry. Apply a coat of paste wax or liquid wax and buff to a shine.

Walls

Cut chore time with preventive maintenance. Keeping walls free of dust and spots means less scrubbing time. Vacuum walls with a soft brush attachment, wipe them down with a cloth-covered broom or mop (spray with a dusting agent for best results), or use an electrostatic dusting wipe. Wash away fingerprints and other marks soon after they appear. Avoid an excessive amount of water and never scrub plaster or drywall that hasn't been sealed or painted. Unsealed walls may take several days or weeks to dry.

PAINTED WALLS

Wash walls painted with latex paint with warm water and a nonabrasive all-purpose cleaner. Dip a clean sponge in the water, then wring it dry. Gently rub the wall; paying special attention to areas that get touched often, such as around doorknobs and light switches. Rinse with a second sponge and clear water. Take care not to wet areas around outlets, light switches, telephone jacks, and other electrical connections. When scrubbing becomes necessary, turn off electricity at the circuit breaker box.

For stubborn spots, such as fingerprints, newspaper smudges, or scuffs, make a paste of baking soda and water and rub the area with a nonabrasive pad. If cleaner (or white vinegar and water) doesn't remove the grime or stain on painted woodwork, wipe the woodwork with a rag dampened with rubbing alcohol.

Wash walls painted with oil-based paint in the same manner, substituting detergent solution (page 80) for the cleaner or white vinegar. Wring the sponge or cloth until only slightly damp. Texture-painted walls, such as those with a troweled finish, can be dust

TIPTAG № 10
Vinyl Facts

CARE DON'TS:
- Do not use abrasive cleaners, scrubbing tools, or beater-style vacuums to clean vinyl floors.
- Avoid harsh detergents and cleansers, paste wax, solvent-based polishes, and products that give a shiny look. For a dull no-wax vinyl floor, use only products made specifically for no-wax vinyl.

LABOR SAVER:
- Buff off a scuff mark with a tennis ball attached to a broom handle. Cut an X in the tennis ball and slide the broom handle into the hole. The texture of the ball removes surface marks from vinyl.

catchers and may require deeper cleaning. Add 1 ounce of borax to each pint of water to clean the wall.

PAPER AND VINYL WALL COVERINGS

Most wallpaper in general use is vinyl or vinyl-coated for durability and easy care. However, some imported, reproduction, embossed, flocked, custom-made, or older wallpapers are made of untreated or lightly treated paper. Some wallpaper companies also produce other paper-backed fabrics, most often silk. If you are in doubt about a paper or covering, treat it as plain paper. For general dusting and to remove cobwebs, tie a dust cloth or T-shirt sprayed with a dusting agent over your broom to wipe down the walls. Work from the top down. This doesn't work for flocked, grass cloth, or natural fiber papers, which need to be cleaned with a soft brush.

Vinyl wallpapers (also called washable) can be dusted or damp-wiped. Vacuum or wipe the wall with a soft rag. For deep cleaning, dip a sponge in warm water and all-purpose cleaner. Wring almost dry. Lightly scrub the wall in 3-foot sections, rinse with clear water, and pat dry with soft dry cloths. Do not allow the paper to remain wet and do not let water seep through the seams. For heavily soiled areas around light switches and other often-touched places, use detergent solution and a soft brush. Don't use abrasive cleanser, scrubbing pads, or solvent-based cleaners.

Plain uncoated wallpapers respond best to a dry wiping. If necessary, plain papers can be gently wiped with a damp cloth, then patted dry. Do not rub them dry. An art gum eraser may help remove dirt. Knead the eraser until it is soft; then gently wipe across the spot in a wide, sweeping downward motion. Do not rub upward or sideways, and avoid using pressure.

Specialty papers—heavy, durable papers, such as some grass or string cloths—can be cleaned with a soft, dry brush. Treat spots with a dusting of talcum powder. Leave the powder in place for several hours; then gently brush or vacuum it off. Clip any strings that come loose from the surface to prevent them from unraveling.

Whatever type of paper you choose, save and safely store scraps for future patching. Instead of rolling extra paper, tack it to the back of a closet with pushpins. The wallpaper will uncurl and age approximately the same as the hung paper, and matching will be easier if you have to patch. Tack a copy of the hanging instructions in the same place.

WALL FABRICS

Vacuum fabric-covered walls with a soft brush attachment. Spot clean by dampening a clean cotton rag with detergent solution (page 80) or an upholstery spot cleaner. Test in an inconspicuous spot to see if the colors run. Avoid stains by treating fabric wallcovering with a spray-on stain resister, such as Scotchgard.

Wallpaper Use and Care

Grass Cloth:
Textured coverings are used in living rooms and other adult areas. Vacuum with a soft brush attachment to remove dust that can damage fibers.

Vinyl-Coated:
The most frequently used type of wall covering is best for living areas. Wipe with a soft cloth. Damp wipe around light switches.

Backed Fabric:
Expensive, fragile fabric coverings are reserved for formal rooms or adult bedrooms. Lightly dust with a soft cloth, or vacuum with a soft brush. Do not use water.

Paper:
Reserve for formal rooms. Dust this paper lightly with a clean, soft cloth. Very lightly damp-wipe when grimy. Avoid candle wax.

Paper-Backed Vinyl:
The most durable general purpose wallcovering is ideal for kitchens, baths, and kids' rooms. Damp-wipe; gently scrub with mild detergent if grimy.

SPACE SAVER

Paper Protector

If your kitchen has a wallpapered backsplash, protect it with ¼-inch-thick acrylic sheeting. Measure and cut the sheeting to fit. Drill holes 1 inch from the edges, spaced 6 inches apart. Attach the acrylic to the wall with screws and cup-shape washers to prevent condensation and mildew.

CORK WALL COVERINGS

Clean cork walls by vacuuming them with a soft brush attachment. If the wall is sealed, wipe with a damp cloth. To keep the wall clean, seal unsealed cork with several light coats of polyurethane.

MIRRORED WALLS

Use commercial glass cleaner and soft, lint-free rags. For soiled or streaked areas, wipe the wall with a solution of 2 tablespoons of white vinegar, 2 tablespoons of ammonia, and 1 quart of water.

WOOD PANELING

Care for wood paneling using the wood floor cleaning instructions. In most cases, dusting or vacuuming with a soft brush attachment is sufficient for routine cleaning. For deep cleaning, use a commercial oil-soap wood cleaner diluted according to label directions. Wring the sponge until only slightly damp, wipe down the walls, and rinse with clear water and a clean sponge or cloth. If the paneling is in a kitchen where grease accumulates, use white vinegar and water instead of detergent. Deep cleaning, polishing, or waxing procedures are all determined by the surface finish of the paneling. See page 98 for tips and techniques on caring for untreated or polyurethane-coated wood surfaces.

CERAMIC, STONE, AND BRICK

Ceramic tile, brick, and stone are cared for in the same way as flooring made from the same materials. Sealing porous surfaces, such as brick, granite, marble, or grout, keeps these handsome walls stain- and bacteria-resistant. See the flooring section, pages 81–82, for tips and techniques on caring for and sealing tile, brick, and stone surfaces.

Ceramic tile used for bathrooms requires special care because it is prone to soap and mildew buildup. To remove scum, use a nonabrasive cleaner made for bathrooms, a daily shower cleaner, or a white vinegar and water solution. To keep soap scum and water spots from reappearing, wipe down the shower with a soft dry towel or squeegee after every use. Bath departments of some discount stores and home centers sell squeegees with suction-cup handles that can be attached to the shower wall for convenience. Daily shower cleaners for after-shower use also prevent soap buildup. Follow the directions. Using too much spray causes streaking. Some sprays also contain an oily ingredient designed to repel water and soap. If too much is used, drips and residue can make floor surfaces slippery and unsafe.

REMOVING CRAYON MARKS

If you have young children, purchase crayons designed for easy mark removals. If crayon mishaps do occur:

Brick and concrete: Spray with WD-40 from the hardware store or home center and brush with a stiff bristle brush. Respray and wipe with a cloth.

Carpet and upholstery: Scrape off excess crayon marks with a dull-edge knife or metal spoon. Use a spot carpet or upholstery cleaner or citrus-based oxygen cleaner, gently working into the spot. Blot. If stain remains, repeat.

Painted walls and wood, scrubbable wallcoverings: Spray the mark with a lubricant, such as WD-40, and wipe with a soft cloth. If residue remains, add liquid dish washing detergent to water. Wipe the surface with a sponge. Rinse with clear water.

Tile, laminate, metal, glass, porcelain, marble or other stone, vinyl flooring: Follow directions for painted walls. Specialty crayons and art materials may require other treatments. Visit www.crayola.com and key "stain" in the search box.

Ceilings and Moldings

Here's one job you don't have to add to your basic routine. Ceilings rarely need to be scrubbed unless your home suffers smoke, soot, or water damage. Occasionally, wipe down the ceiling using a broom covered with a soft, lint-free cloth or T-shirt. Or vacuum with a soft brush attachment. If the ceiling does need washing, use an all-purpose cleaner, or dilute 2 tablespoons of white vinegar or ammonia in a quart of water and scrub one small section at a time. After you've washed the ceiling, rinse with clear water and a clean sponge or rag. If the stains remain, apply a stain-resistant sealer, such as Kilz, and repaint.

DECORATIVE MOLDINGS

The grooves and raised surfaces in decorative molding trap dust, grease, and soot. Clean dusty trim with a vacuum brush attachment, a feather duster, or a soft paint brush. Clean dirty molding with an all-purpose cleaner; test cleaner first in an inconspicuous spot. Mix a solution of 1 cup ammonia, ½ cup white vinegar, ¼ cup baking soda, and 1 gallon warm water. Pour part of the solution into a spray bottle to spray and wipe small sections of molding at a time. Rinse with clear water, and wipe the molding dry with a soft clean cloth.

For picture molding that has spaces for picture hooks, located below the crown molding, use a new soft paintbrush or cotton swabs to remove the dust. If the space is grimy, dip a cotton swab in the cleaning solution used for molding, follow with a swab dipped in clear water, and finish with dry swabs. As houses settle and gaps appear between the crown molding and the ceiling, fill the space

Home Remedies

WALL SCRUBS

Top or Bottom?

Cleaning experts disagree on whether to start at the top or bottom when scrubbing a wall. For dusting, the consensus is to start at the ceiling and work down toward the baseboard. Then clean the baseboard and floor as needed. For scrubbing, some cleaning experts theorize you should work from top to bottom to move the dirt downward and prevent drips. Others say to work from the bottom to the top to catch any drips of cleaning solution that could stain walls. Bottom line: As long as you keep your oversize sponge or rag wrung to slightly damp and rinse it often in clear water, the matter comes down to personal preference.

with a bead of paintable caulk. If you have picture rails below the crown molding that you don't plan to use to hang pictures, fill the spaces with paintable caulk and paint to match the trim or the walls.

CEILING TILES

Vacuum regularly with the brush attachment to remove dust. Because of texture and color variations, spots and dirt aren't normally major problems. Streaks and spots from water damage do show and are difficult to remove. Replace the tile if possible. Or seal it with a stain-resistant sealer, such as Kilz, and paint the tile.

CEILING FANS

Blades and even the housing collect large amounts of dust and grease because they often draw air upward. (This is especially true if you have a fan in or near your kitchen.) Dust ceiling fans monthly with a long-handled feather duster or one of the new electrostatic dust cloths, or use a specially designed ceiling fan blade cleaner. These long-handled brushes have a narrow U-shape head that slips over the blade and wipes away the dust. They are available at many home supply and lighting stores.

LIGHT FIXTURES

Regularly dust ceiling and other light fixtures with a feather duster or soft cloth. Turn off the light before dusting and wait until the bulb and shade are cool. If lights hang from the ceiling pendant-style, dust the entire fixture. Take extra care when you dust halogen bulbs. Use a clean feather duster, and don't touch the bulb with your fingers or cleaning product because this shortens its life.

Before the holidays or special occasions, give chandeliers and other decorative fixtures extra attention. Dust with a feather duster and wipe the entire fixture with a soft, clean cloth. Be especially careful with cut-glass or crystal chandeliers. If you use a commercial spray designed for chandeliers, read and follow the directions to avoid damaging the arms and housing. The safest method is to dilute white vinegar in warm water. Dip a clean, soft cotton cloth in the solution and wipe each crystal. Wipe a second time with a slightly damp rag and polish with a third cloth. Although this is more time consuming than the spray method, it's safer for fragile fixtures.

Windows

Clean windows make a home look warmer and more welcoming, and they let in more and clearer light than dirty ones. Before you start cleaning, remove or pull back draperies, curtains, blinds, surface trims, or other window treatments. Use lint-free cloths, strong paper towels, or chamois cloth to clean small windows or those with small panes. Save work with a squeegee for large windows. If windows are only slightly dirty, use only clear water.

For dirty windows, use a commercial glass spray. If you prefer to

Protect Your Counters

Food or Wine Stains:
Wipe immediately, especially on porous materials such as butcher block. Use an all-purpose cleaner with bleach. Rinse well.

Package Ink Stains:
Ink from damp household packaging can stain; be particularly cautious with laminate or solid-surface materials.

Rust Stains:
Cans and damp spots are culprits. When you cook, wipe up as you spill. Use an all-purpose cleaner with bleach, and rinse well.

Cleansers:
Abrasive cleansers scratch. Use baking soda or a non-abrasive all-purpose cleaner applied with a sponge or cloth.

Newspaper Ink:
Keep newspapers and ad supplements off counters. A hint of dampness transfers the ink to the countertop.

Knife Cuts:
Use wood or acrylic cutting boards on countertops, especially laminates. Keep one on the counter for easy access.

Water Damage:
Wipe up spills immediately. Laminates and glue can loosen, especially around seams and back splashes.

Scorches from Pans:
Use trivets or hot pads, especially for laminates. Wood cutting boards and heavy-duty tea towels protect in a pinch.

use a homemade solution, add 2 tablespoons of ammonia or white vinegar to a quart of water to make your basic cleaning solution.

Start at the top and work first across and then down. Wash the window in small sections. If using a homemade solution, rinse with clear water. Polish the glass with a clean cotton cloth, paper towels, or chamois. Gently clean corners with an old toothbrush or cotton swabs. Rub away streaks with crumpled newspapers. If you use the commercial spray, skip the rinsing step. If you clean both the inside and outside of a window, wash one side horizontally and the other vertically so that it is easier to see and wipe away streaks.

CLEAN SCREENS

Dirty screens block light and airflow, can harbor allergens, and may cause spots on windows when it rains. If you don't have time to remove screens, vacuum with a soft brush attachment for a quick dusting. For a thorough job, remove the screens. Place the screen on a flat, cloth-covered surface, such as a picnic table. Gently scrub with a soft brush dipped in sudsy water. Rinse with a garden hose. Shake off water; dry in the sunlight.

REMOVING PAINT, VARNISH, PUTTY

Wipe away fresh latex paint with warm soapy water; use odorless mineral spirits on fresh oil-based paint or varnish. For dried-on paint, varnish, or putty, soften the material with odorless mineral spirits; then scrape it away by sliding a razor blade along the surface of the glass. For safety, look for a tool that holds and retracts the razor blade, making it less likely that you'll cut your fingers when working. Remove residue left by labels, stickers, or tape by spritzing them with water and keeping them wet until the adhesive softens. Scrape away with a razor blade.

For tough residue, try odorless mineral spirits or fingernail polish remover. Commercial residue-removers are available but may leave an oily coating behind which can be removed with diluted ammonia.

STAINED GLASS

Care for stained glass in the same manner as regular glass. Avoid washing on extremely hot or cold days, because the temperature affects both the lead and the solder. Pieced windows are less stable than solid sheets of glass. Use only gentle pressure to clean. Have a window professionally repaired if you notice slight bowing.

If your stained glass shows signs of scratching or if clear spots show, the glass is painted instead of stained. Do not wash. Wipe with a soft paintbrush or cloth.

Cabinets

Cabinet care is the same whether you clean a kitchen, bath, or storage area. Use the following information to keep cabinets looking good. Kitchen cabinets require the most cleaning time because the

TIME SAVER

Window Washing

If you must do this chore on a cold day, add ¼ cup rubbing alcohol or 1 tablespoon glycerin (from drug, health, or crafts stores) to keep the water from freezing on the glass. Wash on an overcast day. You'll have less eye strain from reduced glare and be able to detect streaks.

kitchen faces the constant challenges from dirt, grease, bacteria, and fingerprints. Grease from cooking or cooking sprays, condensation from temperature changes and steam, and dirt and bacteria from hands and food can damage and stain cabinet exteriors.

If you have a busy kitchen, some cabinets may need to be wiped once a day; others need a weekly cleaning. Clean around handles and close to appliances.

PAINTED CABINETS

Painted cabinets that are sealed with one or more coats of oil-based paint are more durable and scrubbable than latex-painted wood. Wash painted cabinets with warm water and diluted all-purpose cleaner, wood cleaner, or white vinegar. Do not get the wood excessively wet. Rinse the surface with a second cloth and clear water.

Wipe areas that may be contaminated with food-borne bacteria with an antibacterial kitchen cleaner or a solution of 1 tablespoon bleach to 1 quart water.

If grease builds up, wipe the cabinets with ammonia and water; rinse with clear water. For stubborn stains, loosen dirt with a paste of baking soda and water. Don't use abrasive cleaners or scouring pads because they can scratch the surface.

METAL CABINETS

Metal cabinets usually have an enamel finish, so they are cared for in the same way as other painted cabinets. Avoid soaking with water because prolonged dampness can lead to rust along seams or cracks. Check for spots of rust and touch up with paint for metal surfaces.

LAMINATE CABINETS

Wipe the surfaces with all-purpose cleaner or white vinegar diluted in water, rinse, and dry with a clean cloth. Disinfect surfaces with an antibacterial kitchen cleaner or a solution of 1 tablespoon bleach to 1 quart of water. Pay close attention to seams between cabinet surfaces, such as where the door meets the edge of the frame. Use a soft brush to clean these areas. Do not use abrasive cleaners or cleaning pads. To clean a stain, rub with a paste of baking soda and water; alternatively, lay a cloth or hold a cloth or paper towel soaked in lemon juice over the spot.

Laminate surfaces occasionally pop loose, especially along narrow edges. Repair these spots immediately. Glue the laminate to the wood and hold in place with clamps, clothespins, or painter's tape. Don't let glue ooze out at the joint or drip onto the cabinet. For best results, use glue made for laminate surfaces available at hardware stores and home improvement centers.

WOOD CABINETS

Cabinets may be solid wood, veneer over wood, or vinyl-coated wood. The wood may be sealed with polyurethane, wax, or varnish or left natural. Care depends on the surface treatment. See wood flooring care, pages 73–74 for details. General purpose oil-soap wood cleaners work well for general care. Whatever the sealant, frequently clean and polish or wax your wood cabinets. Heat and temperature changes can dry wood. Wood cabinets are also victims of the opposite damage—condensation caused by steam from cooking and dishwashers. Wipe dry. Do not get wood excessively wet. Occasionally disinfect all surfaces with a diluted antibacterial cleaner without bleach. Wipe on; rinse with a clean, damp cloth. Dry with a third cloth. Work with the grain of the wood when cleaning and polishing.

When the hinges become loose and wobbly, remove the screw and lightly pack the hole with a mixture of sawdust and wood glue. (Lumber yards are a source of sawdust.) Put the screw back in place and let the glue dry overnight or until the hinge is solid.

BEHIND CLOSED DOORS

Wipe the inside of the cabinets and drawers with all-purpose cleaner or white vinegar diluted in water. Rinse and dry. Use a toothbrush to clean along the edges and cracks. Let the surface dry completely before placing any item back in the cabinets or drawers. Seal unfinished wood or metal surfaces for easier cleaning and to avoid bacterial buildup. Sand lightly and apply a coat of polyurethane (wood) or an appropriate paint.

Install shelf paper to help preserve the surface and for easier cleaning. Shelf paper comes in several forms: paper that is cut and laid in place, vinyl or rubber cut to fit, self-adhesive vinyl, and low-tack self-adhesive vinyl. Paper is inexpensive but cannot be washed and needs to be replaced frequently. Vinyl is inexpensive and is washable but may slide and bunch up in high-use areas. Rubber slides less and offers some cushioning and is washable. It's a good choice in areas prone to earthquakes. Self-adhesive vinyl is washable and stays in place but can be difficult to remove if worn. A low-tack self-adhesive vinyl can be repositioned but is washable and durable.

Measure carefully before cutting shelf paper. Cut the piece slightly larger than your measurement and lay the shelf paper in place. Run the blade of a dull knife along the edge to score the exact lines of the shelves and drawers; cut along these lines.

Countertops

Countertops are one of the most easily damaged areas in the kitchen—and an area of prime concern for contamination. Protect

Choose for the Chore

Rag or String Mop:
This classic mop works well for large areas and tight corners. Rinse well after use and let it dry upright to retain its shape.

Sponge Mop:
The best models have easy-to-replace sponge heads. They are easy to use and work well for smaller kitchens and for baths.

Utility Broom:
These brooms are for large areas that require heavy-duty sweeping, such as decks, patios, garages, or driveways.

Dust Mop:
These mops pick up particles vacuums miss; ideal for quick touch-ups. Spray with a dusting agent for better results.

Angled Bristles:
This lightweight broom fits into tight corners and around and behind furniture. It also works well for baseboards and trim.

Natural Bristles:
This classic is fine for general sweeping with a dustpan. Choose the best quality to avoid bristles that shed when you sweep.

countertops with trivets or hot pads, use cutting boards, and avoid abrasive cleaners and scrubbers. Wash countertops immediately after food preparation. A general cleaner is warm, soapy water, but an antibacterial kitchen cleaner or a mild bleach solution (1 tablespoon bleach to 1 quart water) is more effective at bacteria control. Use a separate cloth for cleaning and rinsing and a third cloth for drying. Do not use a dishcloth that has been used on food, dishes, or hands to dry the countertop.

LAMINATE AND SYNTHETIC

These versatile surfaces include everything from linoleum or vinyl sheeting to surface-applied laminates to solid surfaces. Use warm, soapy water, a mild bleach solution, or a nonabrasive kitchen cleaner to clean these surfaces. Don't use abrasive cleaning pads. Use a soft toothbrush along seams or in the case of linoleum countertops, along metal edging. For greasy buildup, use a kitchen cleaner or white vinegar and water. If the surface is tacky, rub with a paste of baking soda and water and rinse. Take care when using bleach solutions: They may alter the countertop color or cause other surface damage. Test first on an inconspicuous spot.

TILE

Unless tiles are rinsed thoroughly, soap may leave a film on the surface. Adding white vinegar to the rinse water may alleviate this. Do not use abrasive cleaners or pads. Although tile doesn't stain easily, grout does. It's also the area most likely to harbor bacteria. Scrub the grout with a mild bleach solution and a toothbrush; then seal it with a commercial grout sealer.

WOOD AND BUTCHER BLOCK

Countertops can take more punishment than many other surfaces, but they can be damaged by hot pans, pooling water, deep cuts and gouges, and food stains. When the surface is damaged, it may be possible to sand it for restoration. Oiling wood countertops keeps the wood from drying out, helps seal the surface, and gives a sheen. Wipe the wood with a light coat of mineral oil, letting the oil soak into the surface. Sop up oil that does not soak in. Do not use excess oil because the surface may become tacky and attract dirt. Don't use linseed or vegetable oil because they can become rancid.

STONE, GRANITE, SLATE, CONCRETE

Although these surfaces appear hard, they are porous and prone to stains. Sealing with an appropriate sealer formulated for the material helps prevent stains and makes everyday cleaning easy. Wipe the surface with warm, soapy water and rinse thoroughly. A mild bleach solution may be used. Don't use abrasive cleanser or scrub pads because they scratch.

If a stone surface stains, make a paste of baking soda and water or talc mixed with a diluted solution of either ammonia, bleach, or

BUDGET STRETCHER

Metal Restoration

•

Remove as much of the cabinet as possible (perhaps only the doors and drawers) and have pieces sandblasted and repainted at an automobile body shop. For a temporary fix, remove doors and sand them. Prime and paint with products formulated for metal.

hydrogen peroxide. Gently scrub the spot with the paste and a soft brush. Rinse thoroughly. Several applications may be necessary to lift the stain.

Slight scratches and cuts may heal over time, especially in slate. If superficial damage remains, gently buff the area with a dry #0000 steel wool pad. Do not do this on highly polished surfaces.

Cleaning Safely

Chemical allergies and economics have convinced many people to use common household products such as baking soda, salt, lemons, soap, bleach, and white vinegar to clean their homes. Repeated applications may be necessary to remove stains and heavy dirt or grime. NEVER MIX BLEACH AND AMMONIA. The mixture releases toxic gases. Shop for commercial products that are neutral pH, nonirritating, nonhazardous, biodegradable, and low VOC (volatile organic compound).

Baking soda: As a natural deodorizer, sprinkle or place containers of baking soda in refrigerators, suitcases, closets, dresser drawers, and drains. For extra effectiveness, pour into a larger container so the exposed surface area is larger, or sprinkle it directly over a smelly area. Use the abrasive quality of baking soda to clean sinks, bathtubs, and countertops by sprinkling on a damp surface and scrubbing with a damp sponge or cloth. Make it into a paste the consistency of peanut butter for added scrubbing power. Sprinkle it onto damp spots, small spills, or greasy spots on carpets and rugs, let it dry, and vacuum away the residue.

To clear slow drains, pour 1 cup of baking soda down the drain. Slowly add 1 cup of white vinegar. (Reduce proportions to one half cup for small sinks.) Cover with a stopper, let the mixture fizz for five minutes, and flush with a gallon of hot, not boiling water if your pipes are PVC. This also works well for cleaning scorched pots and for removing baked-on foods from oven-safe dishes.

Salt: Slightly more abrasive than baking soda, salt will scratch only the most delicate surfaces. Sprinkle salt on the area to be cleaned and rub gently with a damp cloth. Remove hard-water spots from vases with a paste of ⅓ cup salt and 2 tablespoons of white vinegar. Apply it to the film, let set for 20 minutes, scrub to loosen the residue, and rinse. To remove rust from metal, make a paste of ¼ cup salt and 1 tablespoon of lemon juice, scrub, rinse, and buff dry. Because salt is absorbent, use it to clean spills by sprinkling it

TIPTAG No 11
Naturally Clean

ROUTINES WORK:
- Be aware of the strength and capabilities of natural cleaning products, such as baking soda, salt, and vinegar. They work best for routine, daily, and weekly cleaning, rather than grimy surfaces.
- Don't over-do antibacterial soaps, but consider using them to wash your hands before and after handling raw meat, poultry, and eggs—or when someone in your household is ill.
- Treat natural cleaning products with the same cautions as commercial products. Keep out of the reach of children.
- NEVER mix bleach and ammonia.

No Vinegar Smell

For a fresh scent when you clean with vinegar, add a few drops of an essential oil from a health food or crafts store to your vinegar and water solution. Lemon, lavender, pine, and mint are pleasing fragrances.

on the spot. Let stand for one hour, and vacuum to remove it.

Lemons: The natural acid cuts through mineral buildup and tarnish but not grease. Fresh lemons or freshly squeezed lemon juice is more effective than bottled lemon juice. After cleaning with lemons, cut the rind into small chunks to run them through the garbage disposal—freshening the disposal. On bathroom surfaces, dip a half lemon in borax, scrub, and rinse. To remove tarnish from copper, dip a half lemon in salt, rub it on the surface, rinse, and dry.

Ammonia: Household ammonia is a strong grease and dirt cutter (followed by soap, then borax). Always dilute ammonia by at least 4 parts water to 1 part ammonia. Breathing ammonia fumes can cause lung damage; open windows for fresh air movement before using ammonia solutions. Use diluted ammonia to clean windows, glass surfaces, appliances, range hoods, filters, and greasy surfaces. NEVER mix ammonia or products containing ammonia with bleach or bleach-containing products. Mixtures of ammonia and bleach release deadly gases.

Detergent: Liquid hand dishwashing detergent dissolved in warm water is a good all-purpose cleaner. After washing with the cleaner, rinse well to avoid dulling films that attract dirt. To avoid suds, fill a cleaning bucket with water, then stir in the detergent. Combine detergent and white vinegar to clean and cut grease.

Bleach: A mild bleach solution (1 tablespoon to 1 quart water) will kill bacteria; stronger solutions can be used for whitening. Test areas for color fastness for applying bleach solutions. Regular liquid chlorine bleach has the best disinfecting qualities. Bleach and water solutions that are stored for more than 24 hours lose effectiveness.

White vinegar: The acid in vinegar cuts through soap film and mineral deposits, making it an excellent rinse for other cleaning products. Use vinegar to dissolve light surface grease, sticky dirt, soap film, and hard-water stains. Add vinegar to water used for scrubbing or rinsing. For mineral buildup on faucets and around drains, soak a cloth in vinegar, wrap or lay the cloth over the stained spot, and let it work for at least an hour. Scrub away the deposits with a soft brush and rinse thoroughly.

Concerns: Keep in mind that a number of oxygen-based and sulfite-based products, when used correctly, can be safer to use and friendlier to the environment than chlorine bleach and ammonia. Also note that products designed to clean food-contact surfaces must undergo safety and efficacy testing for their intended uses. Read labels to make sure you are purchasing cleaning and disinfecting products for their intended use. Most hard-surface cleaning can be accomplished with mild products, such as vinegar, baking soda, or the correct commercial product. Save ammonia and bleach for tough jobs where they are needed.

Upholstery

- DEEP CLEANING, 105
- PREVENTING STAINS, 105
- SLIPCOVERS, 106
- BASIC FIBERS AND FABRICS, 108
- LEATHER AND SUEDE CARE, 108, 109

Wood Care

- DUSTING TOOLS AND TECHNIQUES, 109
- WOOD CLEANERS, 109
- APPLYING PASTE WAX, 110
- EXPERT TIPS AND TECHNIQUES, 112

Furniture Surfaces

- GLASS, 114
- AGED, 114
- METALS, 114

Window Treatments

- DRAPERIES, 116
- CURTAINS, 116, 117
- LACE AND SHEERS, 117
- BLINDS AND SHADES, 117, 119
- SHUTTERS, 119
- BAMBOO, PAPER, AND PARCHMENT SHADES, 121

Rugs

- BASIC CARE, 118
- PET CONCERNS, 118
- NATURAL FIBERS, 118
- ORIENTAL AND HAND-TIED, 120
- FUR AND SHEEPSKIN; HIDES, 120
- WOVEN AND BRAIDED, 120

Accessories

- LAMPS AND SHADES, 120
- CEILING AND WALL LIGHTS, 121
- CRYSTAL CHANDELIERS, 121
- ART AND COLLECTIONS, 122
- CLOCKS, 122
- CANDLESTICKS, 122
- HOUSEPLANTS, 123
- DECORATIVE TASSELS AND TRIMS, 124
- UPDATING LAMPS, 124
- QUILTS, 124
- PILLOWS, 124

Taking Care

Furnishings turn rooms into a comfortable home. With timely care and cleaning, furniture and accessories can last for years—or even for generations. Proper care will also keep your furnishings looking good while they add enjoyment to your home. Although families with young children and house pets often have extra work to maintain furnishings, prudent care is worth the effort.

Upholstery

Prevent dust, dirt, and stains from embedding in the fibers of your upholstered pieces to keep them looking new. Frequent vacuuming is the best way to clean and maintain upholstery. Before vacuuming, check for loose buttons and threads, weak spots in the fabric, or debris that could clog the vacuum. Clip threads and repair or tighten buttons before vacuuming. Use a vacuum and a soft brush attachment. Keep the attachment clean and free of oily residue. Use a crevice tool for corners and tight spots.

If the fabric has a nap (such as velvet, corduroy, or plush fabrics), vacuum in the direction of the nap. Use your hands to determine the direction of the nap: Running your hand with the nap feels soft; running your hand against the nap feels rough.

DEEP CLEANING

Deep-clean upholstered furniture every year or two, depending on the use, color, and pattern. Commercial cleaning, do-it-yourself cleaning, and foam cleaners all work. Do not soak the fabric or furniture structure with upholstery cleaners. Use a cleaning product that contains a soil retardant to prevent future staining. Remove all soap residue to avoid attracting dirt to the cleaned upholstery. Check label directions or consult a professional cleaner about soil retardants.

If frequent soiling is a problem, use a spray-silicon soil retardant to prevent dirt and stains from setting. If your fabric was treated at the time of manufacture or purchase, it is important that you use compatible products: Read and carefully follow furniture manufacturer's and cleaner label directions to apply the recommended finish.

AN OUNCE OF PREVENTION

Before buying new upholstered furniture or having an old piece re-covered, ask about stain-resistant fabric finishes. Fabrics treated at the mill normally perform well for typical residential use; however,

TIPTAG No.12

Quick Fabric Care

SMOOTH NAPS:
- If a napped fabric looks streaked after vacuuming, run your hand or a dry towel over the fabric to smooth the nap in one direction.

REMOVE PET HAIR:
- Use a clothes brush with either a bristle head or napped fabric head to collect pet hair.
- Use a clothes lint remover with a refillable sticky tape to pick up pet hair. Similar brushes are sold in pet stores or pet care sections of discount and drugstores.
- In a pinch, wrap masking tape around your hand, sticky side out, to pick up loose hair and fuzz.

untreated fabrics will stay fresh-looking longer when surface finishes such as Teflon or Scotchgard are applied to the surface. These protectants work best on cotton, linen, rayon, and nylon fibers. If you have a commercial finish applied, ask about the finish warranty and special care instructions. Some companies provide toll-free numbers to guide you.

SLIPCOVERS WORK

Slipcovers are fashionable and have the practical function of protecting upholstered pieces. Traditionally, slipcovers were used during the summer, especially in hot climates, to freshen, protect, and relax upholstered pieces. Slipcovers also offer a way to update or revive worn upholstery without reupholstering. Custom-made slipcovers, sewn locally, vary in costs. For a polished look, choose fashionable fabrics in inexpensive and washable cotton ticking or cotton duck. When children and pets are in the household, choose washable, bleachable fabric to save the expense of frequent dry cleanings.

Economical, loose-fitting furniture covers are held in place with elastic ties. They are sold in linen outlets, home furnishings stores, and home furnishing catalogs. Choose slipcovers that are machine-washable, preshrunk, and close to the size of your furniture. If the slipcover is lightweight and your furniture takes abuse, provide extra protection by first covering the seat and back with a lightweight and light-color blanket. Slip on the cover as usual.

Wash and dry slipcovers according to the manufacturer's directions. If in doubt, wash in cold water with a mild detergent formulated for hand washables. Remove from the dryer while slightly damp and allow to dry on the upholstered piece. (However, this isn't advised in humid climates.) If you iron a slipcover, press it on the wrong side to avoid damaging the surface. After the slipcover is in place, treat in place with a stain-resistant finish, if desired.

To keep slipcovers from slipping, cut pieces of ½-inch diameter PVC (polyvinyl chloride) pipe slightly shorter than the seat back and side measurements of the cushions. After tucking the slipcover into place, slide the pipe pieces into the crevices as far as you can to hold the fabric in place.

GO, SPOT, GO

Spills are inevitable, especially when there are children in the house. Gently blot spills—don't rub—as quickly as possible with a white towel or paper towel. Don't use colored towels or printed paper towels because they may transfer dye or ink to the upholstery. If a large amount is spilled, remove as much as possible with a spoon; blot up the rest. Remove loose slipcovers to spot-clean, but leave fitted covers in place for spot treatment. For more on treating specific stains, see page 80. Always test your cleaning method first

BUDGET STRETCHER

Instant Slipcover

•

Convert a canvas painter's drop cloth into a slipcover for heavily used sofas. These drop cloths are washable, prehemmed, and available in a variety of sizes. Purchase a cloth slightly larger than overall dimensions. Tuck excess between cushions and allow to pool on the floor.

Upholstery Fabric Basics

Linen:
This fiber is best suited for formal living rooms or adult areas. Have soiled pieces professionally cleaned.

Leather:
This tough material can be gently vacuumed, damp-wiped as needed, and cleaned with leather conditioner or saddle soap.

Cotton:
Durability and use depend on the weave and finish. Damask weaves are formal; canvas works for family rooms.

Wool:
Wools and wool blends are sturdy and durable to use for sofas and chairs. Blends can be spot cleaned when necessary.

Cotton Blend:
Depending on the weave, this can be a sturdy, family-friendly product. A stain-resistant finish should be applied for everyday use.

Vinyl:
Easy-care and less expensive than leather, vinyls are ideal for busy family living and dining areas. Durability depends on quality.

Silk:
This delicate fabric is only suitable for adult areas, such as formal living rooms, and must be professionally cleaned if soiled.

Laminated Fabrics

•

Spills wipe off laminated (coated) fabrics, a plus for family dining and play areas. For information about lamination, check with a fabric store that carries upholstery fabrics. Choose a matte, not glazed, finish for the most natural appearance.

on an inconspicuous spot. If a ring remains around the stain after cleaning, deep clean the entire seat cushion, chair, or ottoman.

BASIC FIBERS AND FABRICS

Manufacturer's labels are required to show fiber content. Some fabric stores, outlets, and manufacturers provide brochures to help you compare fabrics. Consider the following information before purchasing upholstered furniture or fabrics:

Synthetics: This general category includes nylon, rayon, polyester, acrylic, and other materials. These fibers wear well and tend to be naturally stain-resistant. Lower-quality fabrics may pill.

Natural fibers: Cotton, silk, wool, and linen are used alone or, for improved durability, blended with synthetics. Blends of natural fibers, particularly cotton and linen, are often used for upholstery. Tightness of weave and weight of fabric determine strength and wear. Natural fibers are comfortable in hot weather because they "breathe;" however, they may not wear as well as synthetics. They are unlikely to pill unless blended with a synthetic fiber.

Brocade: The weaving process creates a high-low pattern similar to sculpted carpeting. Depending on the fabric color and the room lighting, this pattern may either hide minor amounts of dirt or have a permanently shadowy look.

Canvas or sailcloth: These heavy cotton fabrics are especially durable. The flat surface shows grime, and the heavy weave may hold dirt particles. Frequent vacuuming is a must.

Chintz or glazed chintz: This lighter-weight cotton may not wear as well as canvas, but the shine and tight weave resist soil. Generally chintz is patterned, hiding small stains or dust. Tightly woven chintz may help spills bead up so they don't soak into the fabric. Do not iron chintz—the heat damages the surface.

Damask: Typically used for formal interiors, this firm, lustrous fabric is woven into distinct patterns. The pattern reverses from front to back, shiny to matte finish. Choose tightly woven fabric without loose threads that may snag. Brush and vacuum gently to avoid breaking threads. Clip any broken threads close to the surface when necessary.

Velvet and velveteen: Rayon, cotton, or blends are used in velvet and velveteen fabrics. Avoid cleaners on this highly napped fabric because it may be difficult to remove all of the detergent residue. Many napped fabrics crush, making them a poor choice for furniture that receives active wear. To raise nap, brush with a clothes brush or lint-free towel, or steam with a clothes steamer.

Leather: Furniture upholstered in leather has several advantages: Spills don't permeate unless allowed to pool for an extended period, dust doesn't settle in deeply, and pet hair and surface dirt brush off. Although commercial conditioners are easy to use for large pieces such as sofas, homemade leather reconditioners work well for smaller pieces, such as footstools or side chair seats. To make leather reconditioner, add 1 teaspoon of household ammonia and 4 teaspoons of white vinegar to 2 cups of water. Apply the mixture, dry with a soft cloth, and then wipe on castor oil, using a soft cloth. Rub on leather shoe cream in the appropriate color. Buff well.

Suede: Handsome and more durable than it appears, rugged suede is the rough undersurface of leather. Vacuum with a soft brush attachment or use a soft clothes brush. Use only made-for-suede leather cleaners. Freshen and restore with suede brushes and soapstones (the kind used for suede shoes). Remove small spots with art gum erasers. To lighten pale suede that has darkened, purchase a resin bag from a sporting goods store and pat the bag over the suede. Brush away excess resin with a suede brush followed by a clothes brush. Keep suede away from sunlight and heat. If you live in a dry climate, make sure your indoor air is not excessively dry, which can damage suede.

Wood Care

Don't avoid dusting wood furniture. Frequent dusting removes airborne deposits that build up in a filmy layer and scratch the surfaces. Clean, dry, soft cloths or feather dusters effectively remove dust; however, both tend to scatter dust into the air, where it floats until landing back on furniture surfaces. As a solution, dampen the cloth very slightly. Lamb's-wool dusters contain lanolin, which attracts dust and makes it cling to the cleaning tool. They're also effective for dusting carved or turned areas that cloths can't reach.

A STEP DEEPER

Eventually, wood furniture will need deep cleaning. Avoid soap and water and all-purpose cleaning sprays unless your furniture has a plastic coating, such as the kind used on kitchen tables and children's furniture. Sticky spots on tables, however, may need to be treated with soap and water. Dip the cloth in mild soap or detergent dissolved in water, wring the cloth nearly dry, and wipe the area. Rinse with a second cloth; immediately dry with a clean, soft cloth.

CLEANING A FOUND TREASURE

To clean an old table that has been stored or purchased from a thrift store, you may need to deep-clean to remove layers of grime. As a first step, use an oil soap and water to remove grime. Rinse and dry well. If the finish still seems dirty, clean with #0000 steel wool dipped in naphtha. Or instead of naphtha, use a commercial wood

Home Remedies

LEATHER CARE

Leather Dye

Don't sweat small scratches. They often heal over time, becoming less conspicuous. But take care of noticeable deep scratches in leather upholstery with commercial leather dye. Manufacturers sell touch-up kits in the same color as the furniture. Consider buying one or two kits when you purchase the piece, in case the color is discontinued. If you have several leather pieces, label the kits to avoid confusion.

Other Options

If a touch-up kit isn't available or if you acquire a previously owned or vintage piece, check with a shoe and leather repair shop for the closest match.

cleaning product. Some products with a milky appearance are formulated to dissolve both solvent-based and oil-based residues. Do not use mixtures containing boiled linseed oil, turpentine, or white vinegars. Museum conservators say these things darken wood and attract dust and lint. Instead, apply clear paste wax.

TO WAX OR NOT TO WAX

Experts from museums, antiques stores, and auction houses have varying opinions on the care of fine wood furniture. Wood furniture care depends in part on the finish of the piece, or in the case of stripped pine, whether it has been sealed. When you purchase new furnishings, ask for guidelines concerning finish.

Typically during manufacture, varnish, polyurethane, or shellac is applied to wood to protect the surface. Applying wax or polish simply protects the protectant. Although this may seem redundant, polishing reduces scratches and shines the finish. Highly polished or mellow finishes are matters of personal preference.

Oil polishes, cleaners, and furniture oils protect the wood by making the surface more slippery; they do not offer a hard protective layer. Those that contain a high percentage of oil make the surface smear, showing fingerprints. Avoid polishing with pure olive oil, which smears and attracts dust.

Most commercial spray and liquid furniture polishes contain silicone oil, which provides some protection. If you have used sprays and polishes in the past or suspect that furniture has been polished with them, be aware that residues interfere with refinishing. If you plan to refinish a piece, first check with a professional refinisher about removing the polish.

Waxes are more durable than sprays or polishes. Wax provides a hard finish and long-lasting protection, and it doesn't smear. Use paste wax or liquid wax made specifically for furniture. Liquid wax is easier to apply but leaves a thinner coating; it may need to be applied more frequently than paste wax. Depending on use, paste wax finishes may last as long as two years.

APPLYING PASTE WAX

Put a spoonful of wax, about the size of a golf ball, in a square of 100-percent-cotton fabric. Wrap the fabric around the wax ball and knead it until soft. Rub in a circular motion, one small area at a time, until the waxing is complete.

When the surface dulls, wipe off the excess wax. Use a clean, soft cotton cloth and turn it frequently. Repeat waxing and wiping until the entire piece is waxed. If you notice a streak, keep wiping to remove excess wax.

Polish the wood with a soft cloth or a lamb's-wool pad attached to an electric drill or power buffer. If the wax smears, wipe with a soft cloth and continue buffing.

BUDGET STRETCHER

Wood Cleaners

Revive grimy wood furniture with a mixture of equal parts olive oil, denatured alcohol, gum turpentine, and strained lemon juice. Apply with a soft cloth and buff with a clean cloth. Another method: rub on mechanic's hand cream; then follow with buffing.

Unusual Chair Materials

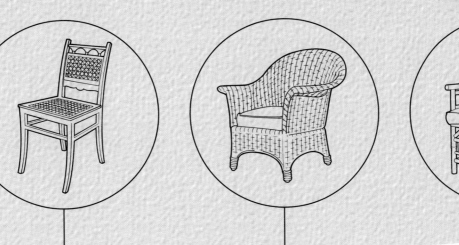

Caning:
Wipe gently with a soft, dry cloth. Inspect for damage. Tack loose corners. Have tears professionally repaired by a furniture restorer.

Wicker:
Vacuum with a soft brush attachment. Wash with a brush dipped in soapy water or spray with a garden hose. Dry in a shaded, breezy area.

Bamboo:
Wipe with a slightly damp, soft, clean cloth. Be especially gentle with older burnt bamboo pieces, prized for their dark colorations.

Rattan:
Gently scrub this tropical material or douse it with the garden hose. Let it dry in a sheltered area away from direct sun. Rub with a clean cloth.

Chrome:
Spray a glass cleaner onto a soft lint-free towel and rub gently. Check for tiny rust spots. Treat spots with a metal polish formulated for chrome.

Rush Seat:
Vacuum with a soft brush attachment, or gently brush with a soft, wide brush. Don't wet or dampen. Spot-clean spills with a clean damp cloth.

Freshen Finds

•

If a vintage piece has a lingering smell, air outside on a warm, dry day. Shade from direct sunlight. Pour talcum powder or baking soda over the surface to absorb odors. Place a shallow pan of charcoal briquettes inside drawers. Rub the upper edge of sticking drawers with a white candle.

For a deep shine, apply a second coat of wax in the same manner; to maintain waxed furniture, dust with a lamb's-wool duster. Don't use liquid or aerosol furniture polishes, which dissolve the wax and leave a hazy film.

WHAT THE EXPERTS SAY

For fine furniture or treasured family heirlooms, use this three-step cleaning and care routine recommended by Gracious Home, the New York City home furnishings and products store.

Clean: Approximately every year, apply Formby's Deep Cleaning Build-up Remover. Use fine-grain, #0000 steel wool, working with the grain. Read and carefully follow product directions.

Restore: Every year to year-and-a-half, or as needed, apply Howard Restor-A-Finish. Choose a shade closest to the wood stain. To restore original color from sun fading, apply the finish with #0000 steel wool to a small section of the piece at a time. Work with the grain of the wood and use moderate pressure. Immediately wipe with a soft, lint-free cloth, such as cheesecloth.

Feed: As a monthly routine, apply Howard Orange Oil or Feed-N-Wax beeswax to prevent drying and cracking.

Additional treatments: To clean a grimy or heavily soiled piece of wood furniture, use Lakeone Heavy Duty Deep Cleaner. Remove old wax and dirt in sections with clean, soft, dry cloths. If you suspect insect infestation, apply Liberone Fongix SE, then apply a thin later of buffing wax over the cleaned surface. Let dry and buff to desired sheen. To revive faded or discolored hard lacquered or varnished finishes, apply Liberone Burnishing Cream Hard Finish Reviver to a clean, wax-free surface. Soak a lint-free cloth with the burnishing cream and rub vigorously with the grain. Allow to dry to a milky white powder; buff with a clean, soft cloth.

SCRATCHING THE SURFACE

If the top surface of wood furniture is slightly scratched, apply paste wax or use a felt-tip touch-up pen. To treat deeper scratches that gouge into the wood, use wood filler or a colored filler wax stick available at hardware and home improvement stores. Match as closely as possible to the color of your furniture, applying in several thin layers rather than in one thick layer.

SOTHEBY'S ADVICE

Restoration experts at Sotheby's, the well-known fine furniture and art auction house, advocate the less-is-best approach for antique and vintage wood furniture of all eras and origins. Their recommendations include the following:

Get professional advice from a restorer and have fine or old pieces, such as family heirlooms, cleaned if dirty or grimy.

Wax approximately every year. Prepare furniture for waxing by first dusting with dusting cloth or static cloth.

Apply Sotheby's Restoration professional furniture wax, formulated from beeswax and carnauba wax, with a clean, soft, dry cotton cloth. See source on page 360. Allow to dry.

Buff in a circular motion with rolled up cheesecloth. Purchase cheesecloth at supermarkets and hardware stores.

To polish hardware, remove it from the furniture piece. Clean with a brass cleaner and buff dry. When hardware is cleaned on the furniture, the cleaner may leave a halo effect on the hardware.

SOTHEBY'S SUGGESTIONS

▸Keep furniture out of the sun.

▸Maintain humidity at 45 to 50 percent and the temperature at a constant 65 to 68 degrees F.

▸Dust weekly.

▸Don't clean with a solvent or water: Both remove finish and alter the patina. Don't use lemon oil or products that contain silicon or synthetic materials. Read labels.

▸Don't apply oil, because it imparts a grayish or yellowish tinge to wood.

OTHER FURNITURE SURFACES

New paint: Wipe the surface with a clean, slightly damp cloth dipped into warm water mixed with either all-purpose cleaner or vinegar. Rinse with a second cloth and clear water. For stubborn soiling, make a paste of baking soda and water, rubbing in the paste with a nonabrasive pad. As an alternative, dampen a cloth with rubbing alcohol and wipe the wood. Rinse with clear water and dry immediately. Clean decoratively painted and sealed new furniture as you would plain painted pieces. For unsealed decorated furniture, use only warm water and diluted vinegar.

Old paint: Unless the piece has a delicate painted finish, use a whisk broom to clean it with the grain. Vacuum with a soft brush attachment. Do not scrub if the paint is loose.

Veneer: Periodically check to see if the veneer is tight. If there is a bubble in the veneer, use a crafts knife to make a small slit that follows the wood grain. Work in a small amount of polyvinyl resin glue (generally labeled for veneers) with a knife. Cover the patched bubble with aluminum foil and several layers of kraft paper or fabric. Press with a dry, hot iron. After one minute, turn off the iron and leave it in place for several minutes.

Inlays: Before cleaning, check that all the pieces are tightly adhered to the frame of the furniture. Use a feather duster to clean the surface. Unless you are confident that all the pieces are tight or

smart ideas
Tabletop Tips

AVOID SCRATCHES
Cloths between wood table tops and lamps, vases, and accessories prevent scratches and the leaching of moisture. As an alternative, apply self-adhesive felt dots or glue a felt round to the bottoms of tabletop objects. Use water-tight coasters that don't wick moisture from the glass to the wood.

NO WAXY BUILD-UP
Properly apply paste wax or liquid wax to eliminate streaks and a cloudy appearance: Apply wax or polish in light coats, multiple coats if needed, and rub into the surface with the grain. Allow to dry and buff to a clear shine.

have a durable seal over them, do not vacuum. Do not dust with a cloth because it may catch in small edges and chip the pattern. Because materials other than wood, such as ivory or mother-of-pearl, may be inlaid, clean inlay designs with mild soap and water. Wring the cloth almost dry and carefully wipe over the surface. Dry immediately with a second cloth. Seal with clear paste wax.

Laminates: Wash with warm soapy water and rinse thoroughly. Dry immediately, taking care that water does not seep between joints. Do not use abrasive cleaners or pads. Periodically check for loosening laminate. If it starts to loosen, work in a small amount of wood glue or laminate glue between the laminate and wood base. Wipe off excess glue. Place a soft cloth over the laminate and, if possible, clamp it until the glue dries.

Glass: Dissolve 2 tablespoons of vinegar in a quart of water. Moisten paper towels or lint-free cotton cloths with the solution, and wipe the glass surface. Rinse with clear water and wipe with a dry cloth. Or use commercial glass cleaners. For sticky deposits, dip a cloth in the vinegar solution and lay it over the spot until the residue dissolves. Paint, glue, and other household products that can't be dissolved with vinegar, soap and water, or commercial cleaners can be gently and carefully scraped with a razor blade. Take care not to scratch the glass. Do not slide objects across glass.

Gilded finishes: Dust with a feather duster or soft paintbrush. For deep cleaning, use a soft cloth dipped in odorless paint thinner that has been warmed by placing the sealed bottle in a bucket of warm water. Gently dab or pat gilded areas; do not rub, especially if it is flaking. Never use water to clean. Do not attempt to touch up with gold gilt paint; the color and finish won't match. Leave restoration to professionals. Papier-mâché tables found at thrift stores or flea markets may have gilded finishes.

Aged metals: Take note of pieces sold in import or home furnishing stores. Some reproduction rusty pieces continue to rust or leave powdery rusty flakes on clothes or textiles. To solve this, wipe the metal with tack cloths to remove powdery rust; then wire-brush rough spots. Seal with matte-finish polyurethane, or prime and spray-paint with products formulated for metals. Put floor protectors under furniture legs to avoid damaging the floor.

Other metals: Wipe wrought iron, steel, and aluminum with a cloth to prevent dust from accumulating. If excess dirt or airborne grease makes the surface tacky, wipe with a vinegar and water solution of 2 tablespoons of vinegar to 1 cup of water. Rinse with clear water and dry immediately. Put furniture protectors under legs to avoid rust spots on carpet or scratches on wood or tile. Choose a protector sized to fit the legs of your piece.

Help with Dusting Chores

Lamb's-Wool Duster:

The long wand on this duster makes it ideal for hard-to-reach areas, including light fixtures and ceiling fans. Dense fibers attract, rather than scatter, dust and dirt.

Treated Cloths:

For dusting, soft, nonscratching cloths pick up and hold dirt. Use them in place of silicon sprays, which are not recommended for fine wood furniture.

Duster for Blinds:

The soft-fiber fingers of this tool slide between blinds to trap and remove dust. The duster works best when used frequently—before heavy dust and dirt build up.

Classic Feather Duster:

An ostrich-feather duster removes dust from easily damaged, delicate surfaces, such as silk lampshades, mirrors, picture frames and art, and fragile collectibles.

BUDGET STRETCHER

"Aged" Metals

•

Wire-brush new rusted or painted metal to avoid flaking. Use a soft brush for vintage or fragile metal pieces. To prevent new or "aged" metal furniture from causing rust spots on flooring, seal with a clear matte-finish polyurethane.

Window Treatments

Care depends on construction and fabric. Sun, as well as dust and grime, is destructive to fabrics. If your windows face west or south, particularly if you live in a warm climate, consider professionally installed window film to diminish the damaging effects of ultraviolet rays. Light color fabrics generally reflect sunlight and resist fading. Dark colors absorb light and fade. Use lined window treatments, blinds, or shades to protect fabrics from the sun. Acrylic and polyester stands up to sunlight better than other textile fibers and will retain color over time. Cotton, rayon, and acetate offer slightly less sun resistance. Acetate often is blended with silk or cotton to make it more sun-resistant.

DRAPERIES AND CURTAINS

Although the terms drapery and curtain are often used interchangeably, there is a technical difference. Curtains are made of lightweight fabrics and most often are unlined and operable. Draperies extend to the floor, tend to be lined, and are sewn of heavier fabric. Daily care of lined draperies or drapery panels is simple: Give them a gentle shaking as they are drawn closed at night; this will prevent dust and dirt from lodging in the fibers. Every month or so, vacuum with a handheld vacuum and soft brush attachment. Use the low-suction setting if your vacuum has one. Always check that trims, buttons, and other embellishments are secure before vacuuming. Do not wash draperies under the following circumstances:

▶ The drapery or lining isn't washable.

▶ The drapery and lining are made of different fibers. One may shrink, causing the other to pucker and hang poorly.

▶ Sunlight has weakened the fabric.

▶ The draperies are constructed with pleats, which may not hold their shape during machine washing.

▶ The draperies are too voluminous for the washing machine.

▶ Trims and embellishments aren't washable or colorfast.

GENERAL CARE

Wash plain-panel or simply constructed draperies that are labeled washable. Hand or machine wash on gentle cycle, using cool water and mild detergent. Don't overload the washing machine. Rinse gently and thoroughly. Tumble dry on the low or air setting, or line dry. Press on the wrong side.

Although fiberglass draperies are rarely sold, they still exist in some homes and are sometimes sold in stores that feature vintage or mid-20th century textiles. Hand wash fiberglass draperies wearing rubber gloves; never machine wash or dry-clean. Glass fibers that break away during machine agitation will be picked up in the next few laundry loads and cause itching and discomfort. Launder panels in a large laundry tub—not a bath tub—filled with water and detergent. Allow them to soak; then swish gently until the dirt is removed. Rinse thoroughly. Press out excess water; do not wring. Line-dry, hanging from the top of the panel. Do not fold over the clothesline. Rinse the laundry tub and your gloves several times to remove residue.

CURTAINS

Check the label before laundering ready-made curtains. If your curtains are washable, remove hooks, rings, and hardware. Check that trims are tightly attached. Unless the directions instruct otherwise, machine wash on a short gentle cycle, using cool water and mild detergent. Tumble dry on low and remove immediately, or line-dry. If necessary, iron on the reverse side. If seams have puckered, spritz lightly with plain water. Pull the seams to stretch back to size, taking care not to break the stitching. Reattach metal hardware only after the curtains are dry.

LACE AND SHEERS

Remove dust from lace curtains by tumbling in the dryer on the air cycle. Many new lace curtains are hand- or machine-washable. Follow the label directions or gently wash in cool water. Use the gentle cycle to machine wash. Use detergent made for fine washables. For extra body, dip freshly washed lace curtains in a light starch solution. For a soft look, rehang the curtains without starching while they are slightly damp. If you use metal hooks, temporarily place a piece of tissue paper under each hook where it comes in contact with the damp lace. This will prevent the hook from rusting onto the fabric. Most sheers are washable synthetics; unless the label states otherwise, wash in the same manner as lace curtains. Dry-clean organdy sheers, which are fragile and prone to sun damage.

Rugs

Rugs warm and add color, pattern, and texture to a room. Easily change a room from winter to spring by replacing a wool or heavy cotton rug with a lighter natural sisal rug. Have the winter rug professionally cleaned and wrapped before storing it. Store in a climate-controlled area to avoid damage. When you purchase a new rug, keep the care tag intact. If you must remove the tag, file it with your household maintenance and furnishings files. Purchase a pad sized to your rug dimensions or one that can be cut to fit.

TIPTAG No 13
Metal or Vinyl

REALLY CLEAN BLINDS:
- Remove from the window.
- Hang from the shower rod or lay in the tub. Wash each slat with warm soapy water or ammonia and water, and a clean sponge. Rinse with clear water and a new sponge.
- Alternatives: Hang from a clothes line and wash as above, or hang outside and wash with a gentle spray from the garden hose.

CLEAN AND QUICK:
- Put on a pair of rubber gloves; top with cotton gloves. Mix 1 teaspoon of ammonia to 1 quart of water. Dip into the solution. Run your fingers along the top and your thumb underneath each slat.

BUDGET STRETCHER

Curtain Care

•

Avoid shrinkage by prewashing fabric and trims before sewing curtains or having them custom-made. Hand-sew or fabric-glue loose trims with fabric-tacking product from a fabric or crafts store. Don't use hot glue, which can soften in the sun.

BASIC CARE

Rug care is determined by size, construction, and material. Care for large size room rugs as you would wall-to-wall carpet. Fine Oriental rugs and other unusual materials, however, require special care.

Small rugs, such as those used at entrances, are difficult to vacuum. Take them outside and shake them vigorously until dust and dirt are no longer evident. (Some cities have ordinances against this once common practice.) You can also hang rugs over a clothesline or sturdy outdoor furniture and beat them with a broom to remove dust and dirt.

Consult care labels for small rugs, determining whether they should be dry-cleaned, spot-cleaned, or laundered. If a rug, even a cotton one that appears washable, is labeled dry-clean only, it may not be colorfast. Imported rugs tend to require dry cleaning; colors may bleed otherwise. Test before spot cleaning.

When you determine that a rug, such as a small cotton rug, is washable, machine wash on delicate. To lessen the problem of long rug fringes becoming tangled and knotted in the washing machine, divide the fringe into several hanks, wrapping each hank with white string. Place the rug in a mesh laundry bag or zippered pillowcase and wash in cold water on the gentle cycle.

Hang wet rugs over a clothes-drying rack, a slatted picnic table, or several bricks stacked on a porch, patio, or breezeway. Hanging a wet rug over a single clothesline will distort the shape of the rug as it dries. Small rugs that are made from synthetic fibers similar to carpeting can be laid to dry on a small worktable or counter that is protected by a drop cloth, old sheets, or towels.

PET CONCERNS

When pet hair accumulates in a rug, brush the rug vigorously with a stiff clothes brush or utility brush. Brush with the nap until dirt and hair cease to come out. Attack urine and fecal stains with an enzymatic cleaner such as Nature's Miracle, available at pet supply stores. The enzymes break down stain and odor.

SPECIAL CASES

Many different materials and methods are used to create rugs. If you purchase a rug at an antiques show, flea market, or garage sale, find out all you can about the material composition and recommended care. Follow these instructions to care for some of the favorite rugs used in decorating:

Coir (coconut), sisal, rush, grass, and other natural materials: These rugs tend to have an open weave, allowing dirt to sift through to the floor beneath. Vacuum often, removing the rug occasionally to vacuum the floor. If possible, take the rug outside and gently beat it to loosen dirt trapped between the fibers. Many of these rugs are reversible; flip rugs over each time you vacuum for

Blinds and Shutters

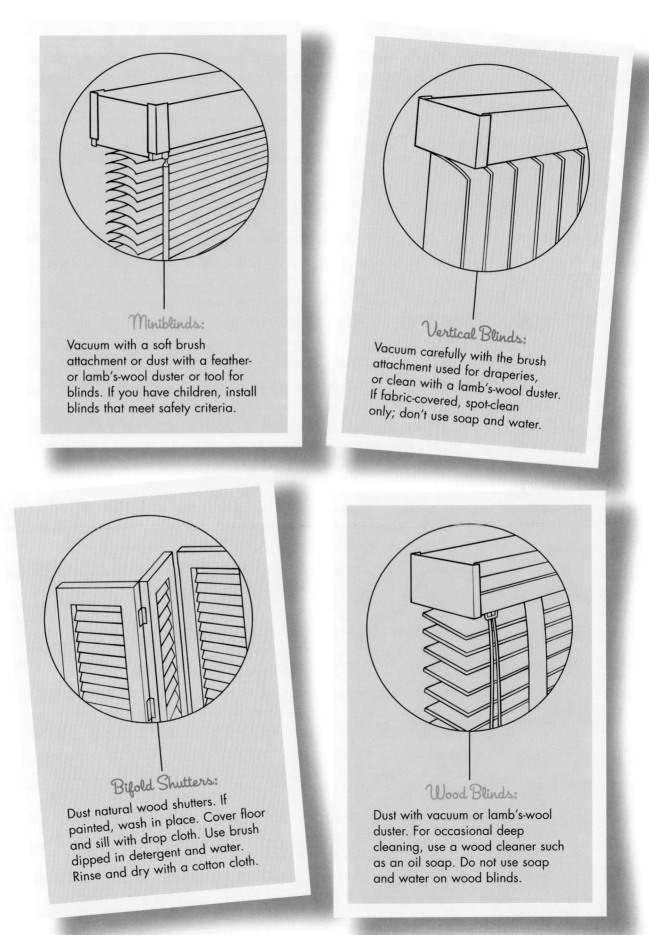

Miniblinds:
Vacuum with a soft brush attachment or dust with a feather- or lamb's-wool duster or tool for blinds. If you have children, install blinds that meet safety criteria.

Vertical Blinds:
Vacuum carefully with the brush attachment used for draperies, or clean with a lamb's-wool duster. If fabric-covered, spot-clean only; don't use soap and water.

Bifold Shutters:
Dust natural wood shutters. If painted, wash in place. Cover floor and sill with drop cloth. Use brush dipped in detergent and water. Rinse and dry with a cotton cloth.

Wood Blinds:
Dust with vacuum or lamb's-wool duster. For occasional deep cleaning, use a wood cleaner such as an oil soap. Do not use soap and water on wood blinds.

even wear. To clean stains or discolorations on a room-size natural fiber rug, leave the rug in place, protecting the floor beneath with a plastic drop cloth and towel. Scrub the stains with a soft brush dipped in soapy water. Rinse with clear water. Place a towel over the wet area. Blot the cleaned spot as dry as possible. Use a portable fan or hair dryer to speed drying. Move small rugs to a protected counter or table to clean. Water weakens the fibers, so work quickly and dry thoroughly to extend the life of these natural rugs.

Handmade, hand-knotted, antique, and Oriental rugs: Vacuum a new Oriental rug as you would carpet and wool area rugs. Use special care with delicate vintage or antique rugs. Protect delicate, antique, or hand-knotted rugs from the vacuum by laying a piece of nylon screen over the rug and weighting it around the edges with books or bricks. Vacuum over the screen. The dirt will be removed while the screen protects the rug from the vacuum. Alternatively, tie nylon mesh over the vacuum attachment and change the mesh frequently as dirt accumulates. Immediately treat wine and other beverage spills with club soda; use baking soda to soak up gravy, sauces, and liquid foods. Once a year, have these rugs professionally cleaned by a rug cleaner or a laundry that cleans rugs. Rug dealers may offer cleaning service or referrals. Rotate rugs to ensure even wear; direct exposure to sun will cause fading.

Fur, sheepskin, hair-on hides: Shake unscented talcum powder over the rug and leave for several hours. Brush the talcum powder through the hair; then shake it out. Repeat the process several times, depending on the length of the fur. Dip a clean cotton cloth in lukewarm soapy water and wipe off the back. Rinse with a cloth dipped in clean water. Allow to dry before replacing.

Woven or braided rugs: Check for stitching breaks before and after cleaning. Check labels to determine whether small rugs are washable. Place washable rugs in a zippered pillow case or mesh laundry bag. Wash in cool water on a gentle cycle, rinsing thoroughly. Tumble dry on low setting. Place large rugs on a vinyl or concrete floor or place an old blanket beneath them. Sponge commercial carpet cleaning foam over the surface and rub it in according to the product directions. Finish by rinsing or vacuuming. Dry thoroughly before replacing the rug on the floor.

Accessories

Accessories, lamps, and collections stamp your personality on your home and add important finishing touches if they are neat and sparkling clean. If you can't keep up with dusting and maintaining your treasures, put away a few and rotate collections.

LAMPS, LIGHTS, AND SHADES

Regular cleaning will keep your lighting sparkling, making your home appear even cleaner.

Table and floor lamps: Unplug the lamp and remove the shade and bulb. Dust the bulb. Wipe glass, ceramic, marble, stoneware, china, or plastic lamps with a damp cloth and warm soapy water. Rinse with clear water and another cloth. Dry thoroughly, replace the bulb and shade, and plug in the lamp. If your lamp is brass, nickel, or chrome, dust with a soft dust cloth and polish with a cleaner formulated for the specific metal.

Lampshades: Remove the lampshade and place it on a solid surface. Most lampshades are assembled with glue that is easily damaged by water. Vacuum the shade with a handheld vacuum and a soft brush attachment, or use a feather duster or soft, clean paintbrush. Do not use a lamb's-wool duster, because the lanolin may stain the fabric. Wipe metal and plastic shades with a slightly damp cloth. Dry immediately. Metal shades may rust, especially at rivet points, and plastic shades may water-spot. Dry-clean silk shades, antique shades, or those with delicate trims.

Ceiling and wall lights: Regularly dust ceiling lights, track lights, canister lights, and sconces with a feather duster. Removable shades usually can be washed in warm soapy water. Rinse and dry thoroughly before replacing them. For fixtures such as sconces and track lights, turn off the electricity at the breaker box. Wipe the fixtures with a slightly damp cloth. Dry thoroughly before turning on the power.

Crystal chandeliers: Use a feather duster to regularly dust chandeliers. For deep cleaning, turn off the power at the breaker box. Remove and wipe the bulbs. Move the dining table or other furniture from beneath the chandelier if possible, and protect the floor with heavy-duty plastic drop cloths. Mix a solution of 1 part rubbing alcohol to 3 parts water OR 1 part nonsudsing ammonia to 3 parts water. Use distilled water if your tap water is hard. Thoroughly dust the entire fixture with a clean cloth or duster. Do not use commercial dusting agents because they may leave a residue. Inspect for problems such as loose wiring. Gently wipe with a barely damp soft cloth or sponge. Cover sockets with plastic sandwich bags held in place with rubber bands. Hang a lightweight oversize umbrella, such as a golf umbrella, upside down under the fixture to catch dripping. Spray one crystal with the solution of your choice, avoiding wires, hangers, and electrical components. Allow to drip-dry. Rinse crystal with a spray of distilled water, avoiding wires. If you are satisfied, spray the remaining crystals. Allow fixture to air-dry overnight. Remove the

TIP TAG No. 14
Window Shades.

VINYL OR COATED:
- Remove from window. Unroll and lay flat. To flatten, place a small weight, such as a mug, at each end.
- Wash one side with a sponge dipped in mild soap and water. Rinse with a clean, damp rag and dry with a cloth. Turn over and weight corners. Repeat other side.

BAMBOO:
- Follow vinyl directions but use as little water as possible. Hang outside in a protected area to dry on a warm, breezy day.

PAPER OR PARCHMENT:
- Don't attempt washing. Gently brush with a clean feather duster. Never use dust sprays.

bags from sockets. Wipe with a soft dry cloth to ensure that there is no seeping moisture before turning on the power.

Brass, metal, and other chandeliers: Dust with a feather duster or lamb's-wool duster. Turn off the power at the breaker box and remove the bulbs. Clean the chandelier following the instructions given for table and floor lamps. Replace the bulbs and restore the power.

ART AND COLLECTIONS

Take care of your prized collections and you'll have family heirlooms to pass down for generations. Sentimental value is as important as monetary value, and meaningful objects deserve the best care.

Paintings, prints, and drawings: Leave deep cleaning and restoration to professionals. Dust artwork with a soft, dry paint brush. Keep away from direct sun, heat, cooking, and smoke.

Picture frames: Dust picture frames with a soft, dry paint brush. Frequently dust the tops of frames, being careful that dust doesn't fall onto the art. Clean ornate frames with pure canned air that contains no cleaners or lubricants. It is available at computer and art supply stores. Use the attachable straw-like nozzle to reach small cracks and crevices.

Ceramics: Wash glazed ceramics in lukewarm soapy water. Rinse and dry thoroughly. Wipe unglazed ceramics with a damp cloth, avoiding immersing into water.

Brass: A gentle patina is desirable; tarnish is not. If you prefer shiny brass, use brass polish that contains wax to seal the surface and prevent the brass from acquiring an aged look. If you like patina, use brass polish without wax. The brass will initially look shiny, then mellow. Keep brass away from humidity and handle as little as possible.

Antique ivory, horn, and bone: To keep the desirable warm white color, expose to natural light but keep away from intense sunlight and heat. Dust with a soft, dry cloth. Do not expose antique ivory, horn, or bone to water or cleansers. Wipe ivory piano keys with a soft, damp cloth. If the keys are soiled, swipe the cloth over a cake of Ivory soap and rub the key in a lengthwise motion until the stain disappears. Dry the keys with a soft cloth. Do not use solvents or chemicals.

Clocks: Follow the care instructions that you would for furniture made from the same material. Keep clocks on level surfaces, away from temperature changes, direct sunlight, and heat vents. Place tall case clocks—such as grandfather clocks—in stable corners where they are least likely to be tipped over or knocked into. Clock repair and sales shops sell devices to secure clocks to the wall.

Candlesticks: Polish brass, silver, or other metal candlesticks with a cream metal polish formulated for the specific metal and a

Treat Houseplants Right

Croton:

To keep the color, place in a window with bright light. Crotons like warm, moist conditions and thrive in steamy bathrooms. Leaves are toxic to kids and pets if chewed.

Cactus:

This heavy-duty plant survives in less than ideal conditions: cool foyer, or cool or warm sunrooms. Pot in a cactus soil mix and allow soil to almost dry before watering.

Pothos:

Easy to maintain but can be toxic if chewed. Allow soil to dry 2 inches below surface before watering. Can live in low light; needs bright filtered light for color variations.

Fiddle-Leaf Fig:

This classic floor plant is easy to grow but can be toxic if chewed. It grows large and can be pruned to shape. Repot as it grows and wipe leaves with a soft, damp cloth.

clean, soft cotton cloth. Never use paper towel as it can scratch the metal surface. Take care to remove polish from the crevices. Wipe glass and crystal candlesticks with a mild vinegar-and-water solution or with a clean, soft cotton rag moistened with commercial glass cleaner. Soak grimy candlesticks in a vinegar-and-water bath. Rinse, dry, and polish with a lint-free cloth.

TEXTILES

Soft accent pieces, such as pillows, textiles, tassels, and trims, collect as much dust as upholstered furniture—and may be too fragile to withstand vacuuming or beating. Clean them safely.

Decorative tassels and trims: To remove accumulated dust and dirt, remove the trim from upholstery, pillows, or window treatments. Place the trim in a mesh laundry bag. Fluff in the dryer on air cycle. Reattach by hand-stitching into place. Note: This works best for trims that have been hand stitched. Do not remove trims that are securely attached or have been glued.

Quilts: Launder as little as possible. When they require washing, check with quilting or fabric shops to purchase laundry soap formulated for washing quilts. Wash in cool water on the gentle cycle. Dry on low temperature. Do not dry-clean quilts. To display a stack of folded quilts and textiles, occasionally rearrange and refold the pieces to prevent a permanent crease and to avoid light damage along the folded edges. If you use a quilt as coverlet or folded on a bed, turn and rotate it for even wear. If you hang a quilt as art, keep it out of direct light and turn it for even wear.

Throws and afghans: Consult manufacturer's directions for laundry or dry cleaning instructions. Fibers and construction vary widely, preventing set rules. Recently made throws and afghans are likely to have acrylic yarns and can be laundered by machine using a gentle cycle, cool water, and mild detergent. Tumble dry on low until completely dry. Do not line dry afghans; the weight of the wet yarns may distort the shape.

Pillows: Take off removable outer shells. Most fabrics require dry cleaning; however, some cotton fabrics, such as bedspread chenille, chintz, and other plain weaves can be gently machine-washed in cool water and then dried on low heat. Spot-clean with a commercial stain remover to eliminate small amounts of soil. Follow the manufacturer's directions and always test the cleaner on an inconspicuous area. Embellishments such as fringe, trims, buttons, and other decorations are often the most fragile and least colorfast parts of pillows. Let professionals deal with heavily accented pillows. For washable fringed pieces or those with sturdy button or stud trims, place the pillow cover inside a pillow protector to machine wash on gentle cycle in cool water. Remove the pillow immediately to prevent trims from rusting or bleeding. Dry in a cool dryer.

BUDGET STRETCHER

Shade Update

Refresh an old lamp with a new shade in an interesting shape or texture. For the correct shade height, have a lamp shop fit the new shade and replace the harp, which attaches the shade, if necessary. Add a new finial for a decorative touch.

5

Basic Equipment
- STARTER KITCHEN, 127
- STARTER KITCHEN WITH EXTRAS, 128
- BUSY FAMILY KITCHEN, 128
- KITCHEN FOR ENTERTAINING, 128

Stocking the Pantry
- BASIC PANTRY, 130
- BASIC PLUS OR FAMILY KITCHEN, 130
- EXTRAS FOR ENTERTAINING, 131

Cookware
- CHOOSING WHAT WORKS, 132

Small Appliances
- BREAD MACHINE, 136
- COFFEEMAKER, 136
- CROCKERY COOKER, 138
- FOOD PROCESSOR, 138
- SPECIALTY APPLIANCES, 139

Large Appliances
- RANGE AND COOKTOP, 140, 142
- OVEN, 142
- VENTILATION SYSTEMS, 143
- REFRIGERATOR AND FREEZER, 144
- DISHWASHER, 146

Sinks
- MATERIALS, 148
- BOWLS AND MOUNTING, 150
- FAUCETS, 150

Lighting
- AMBIENT AND TASK LIGHTING, 150
- BULBS, 151

Accessibility
- UNIVERSAL DESIGN, 151

Purchasing Guidelines
- ENERGY SAVING, 152
- WARRANTIES, 152

Garbage & Trash
- GARBAGE DISPOSALS, 154
- TRASH COMPACTORS, 155
- HOME RECYCLING CENTER, 156

Fighting Kitchen Germs
- CONTROLLING BACTERIA, 158
- SAFETY TIPS, 158

After nearly a century of changes in housing, lifestyles, and family roles, the kitchen remains the heart of the home. Use this chapter to stock and organize yours to fit your lifestyle and life stage. Begin with the basic equipment section, which is organized into the following categories: starter, starter with extras, busy family, and entertaining kitchens. Read through the equipment supply lists, adding necessary items to create a kitchen that works for you. The busy family kitchen is an expansion of both the starter and the starter-with-extras equipment lists. The kitchen for entertaining boasts several amenities that help a creative host.

Basic Equipment

You don't need a large number of bowls, utensils, and small appliances to cook well, but you do need the correct tools for the task. Well-made equipment will last for years, even for a lifetime. Although small appliances don't have the longevity of quality knives and cookware, they can provide years of trouble-free service if you buy high-quality items and follow the warranties.

STARTER KITCHEN

Note the difference between baking pans and baking dishes. A baking pan refers to a metal pan, and a baking dish refers to an oven-safe glass container. When you use glass or ceramic cookware in the oven, reduce the recommended baking temperature by about 25 degrees for best results. An easy way to begin setting up a kitchen is to buy one piece of cookware, preparation tools, or necessary small appliance every payday. If you have a shortage of helpful gadgets, pick up one or two with your weekly grocery shopping or when you shop at discount stores.

Small appliances: coffeemaker, handheld portable electric mixer, two-slice toaster

Range-top cookware: 1-quart covered saucepan, 2-quart covered saucepan, 4- or 6-quart Dutch oven, 10-inch ovenproof skillet with cover

Bakeware: 2-quart rectangular baking dish (12×7½×2-inch), 2-quart square baking dish (8×8×2-inch), 15×10×1-inch baking (jelly roll) pan, 8×1½-inch round baking pan, baking sheet (2), 8×4×2-inch loaf pan or dish

Preparation and cooking gadgets: bottle opener, can opener, chef's knife, clear glass measuring cup (for liquids), colander, corkscrew, instant-read thermometer (for meat), kitchen timer, ladle, long-handle fork, pancake turner, paring knife, pasta

TIPTAG № 15

Make-Do Cookware

IF YOU NEED:

- Covered casserole: Cover a baking dish with foil.
- Double boiler: Place a metal or heat-resistant glass bowl in a saucepan. The bowl should be wide enough to avoid touching the bottom of the pan.
- Pastry bag: Snip the corner off a heavy plastic bag.
- Sifter: Pour flour or powdered sugar into a sieve set over a bowl; then stir it with a spoon to force grains through the holes.
- Soufflé dish: Substitute a straight-sided casserole with same volume.
- Pizza pan: Use a baking sheet, building up crust to hold toppings.

server, plastic cutting board, potato masher, rubber spatulas, serrated knife, set of dry measuring cups, set of measuring spoons, set of mixing bowls, knife sharpener, slotted spoon, tongs, utility knife, vegetable peeler, wire cooling racks, wooden spoons

STARTER KITCHEN WITH EXTRAS

As you discover new recipes and techniques, you'll acquire more small appliances, cookware, and convenience tools. Time-crunched households often rely on crockery cookers and microwave ovens.

Small appliances: blender; 3½- to 4-quart crockery cooker; small, basic countertop microwave; steamer

Range-top cookware: 3-quart covered saucepan, 6- or 8-inch skillet, double boiler

Bakeware: muffin pan, 9-inch pie plate, pizza pan, 9×9×2-inch baking pan, roasting pan with rack

Preparation and cooking gadgets: basting brush, flexible metal spatula, grater, kitchen shears, pizza cutter, oven thermometer, rolling pin, small and large strainers, wooden cutting board

BUSY FAMILY KITCHEN

Rely on small appliances to prepare food while the family is at work or school. Appliances and cookware, such as bread machines, crockery cookers, Dutch ovens, and roasting pans, will help you get meals on the table quickly.

Small appliances: bread machine, food processor, four-slice toaster, 6-quart crockery cooker, microwave oven, mixer with stand, pressure cooker, programmable coffeemaker

Range-top cookware: griddle

Bakeware: large Dutch oven or stockpot, 3-quart rectangular baking dish (13×9×2 inch), 9×1½-inch round baking pans, fluted cake pan, various sizes of casserole dishes, 6-ounce custard cups, 9×5×3-inch loaf pan or dish, 10-inch tube pan

Preparation and cooking gadgets: additional vegetable peelers, extra utility and paring knives, cutter shapes, four-egg poacher, hand juicer, pastry blender, meat mallet, rotary eggbeater, ruler (to measure dough thickness, width, and length), sifter, whisk

KITCHEN FOR ENTERTAINING

Add a few small appliances and gadgets to set up your kitchen for entertaining.

Small appliances: 12-cup coffeemaker or urn, deep fryer, electric wok, 12-cup food processor, tabletop grill, rice steamer

Range-top cookware: grill pan, wok pan

Bakeware: mini-muffin pans, quiche plates, soufflé dishes, tart pans

Preparation and serving accessories: 12-cup carafe, cookie press, cheese slicer, garlic press, bulb baster, pastry bag and

Baking Pans Basics

Baking Sheet:
Shiny surface reflects heat for softer-set, not crisper cookies. Also use for pizza and frozen entrées.

Bundt Pan:
Darker bakeware gives heavier cake crusts. Bundt pans turn cake-mix cakes into festive desserts. Some are glazed in pan.

Rectangular:
Use this 13×9×2 for brownies, bar cookies, as well as lasagna and casseroles. Check recipe or mix box for pan size.

Square Pan:
Use this 9×9×2 square for brownies, bar cookies, coffee cakes, corn bread, and small casseroles.

Pie Pan:
Pie pans are metal for basic baking. Pie plates are glass or ceramic. Use either for quiches and quick potpies.

Tube Pan:
Recipes for light, spongy cakes will specify this type of two-piece cake pan. The pan is inverted to neatly remove the cake.

Jelly-Roll Pan:
This 15×10×1 pan also can be used for cookies, pizza, and bread. The dark finish gives even browning and crisp crusts.

Loaf Pan:
These pans are 8×4×2 or 9×5×3. They are used for quick breads as well as meat loaf or even frozen desserts.

Muffin Tin:
This handy pan is ideal for muffins, corn bread, or cupcakes. Tins are also sold with six cups and with mini cups.

Cake Pan:
Sizes are 8×1½ or 9×1½. Buy at least two for layer cakes. If using dark finish pans, reduce oven temperature by 25 degrees.

tips, pastry blender, pepper grinder, salt grinder

Stocking the Pantry

A well-stocked pantry saves money and time. Although a traditional pantry is a convenient luxury, any cool and dry space will work. Plan to have the basics for meals and cleaning supplies on hand. Avoid unplanned trips to the grocery store for missing items by stocking staples, such as flour, sugar, and canned tomatoes, along with such items as paper towels purchased on sale. Build your pantry slowly. If you shop weekly, add one or two seldom-used items to your list to make stocking the pantry easy on your budget. Because spices lose flavor over time, buy only small quantities of those used regularly.

BASIC PANTRY

The following items are a good start to a well-stocked pantry.

Baking: baking powder, baking soda, cornmeal, flour (all-purpose), sugar (white and brown)

Beverages: coffee, tea (bags or instant)

Canned goods: beans (one or two kinds, such as black or chili), canned soups (cream of tomato and chicken broth), corn (whole-kernel, creamed), spaghetti sauce, canned tomatoes (pasta sauce, whole, Italian-style stewed, or diced), tuna

Cereals, pastas, starches: Breakfast cereals (one or two you eat regularly), grits (quick-cooking), instant mashed potatoes, oats (quick-cooking, rolled), pasta (spaghetti or angel hair and macaroni), rice (regular or instant)

Condiments: ketchup (refrigerate after opening), dressings (one or two; refrigerate after opening), mayonnaise (refrigerate after opening), mustard, preserves or jelly, salsa

Snacks: crackers, peanut butter

Seasonings and spices: chili powder, cinnamon, garlic (instant minced, garlic salt, and garlic powder), hot-pepper sauce, Italian seasonings, paprika, black pepper, salt, soy sauce, vanilla

Staples for meal preparation: bread crumbs (fine dry), evaporated milk, nonstick cooking spray, oils (olive and vegetable), onions, potatoes (baking, red, instant), vinegar (balsamic and white)

Kitchen care: all-purpose cleaner, aluminum foil, waxed paper, plastic wrap, automatic dishwasher detergent, dishwashing liquid, kitchen trash bags, paper towels, storage bags and containers.

BASIC PLUS OR FAMILY KITCHEN

This list is designed to add to the basic list for families, singles, or couples who do more than basic cooking. What items you add to your pantry depends on what and how often you cook, the ages of any children in the household, and your family's food preferences and lifestyle. Because many people like occasional treats and sweets, storable items—such as graham crackers—are included. If

TIME SAVER

Fridge Basics Plus Extras

•

Life is easier with the basics on hand. Fresh: milk, fruit juice, butter or margarine, eggs, apples, lemons, Parmesan cheese, carrots, celery. Frozen: peas, corn, green beans, pie and puff pastry (quick desserts), and phyllo and hors d'oeuvres if you entertain.

you prefer to limit sweets, stock up on dried fruits, whole wheat crackers, raisins, dry roasted nuts, and unsweetened fruit juices. Avoid giving nuts and nut butters to very young children, who may have or develop allergies to them.

Baking: biscuit or baking mix, cake and brownie mixes, chocolate (semisweet chips, plain candy bars to add to desserts), cocoa, flour (wheat and self-rising), molasses, pancake mix, pie filling (cherry, apple), yeast (active, dry)

Beverages and sweeteners: chocolate-flavored syrup, fruit juice, honey, hot chocolate mix

Canned goods: fruit (water packed pears, peaches, or pineapple; applesauce), green chiles, salmon

Cereals, pastas, and starches: add fettuccine, shells, bow tie, and assorted pasta shapes to basic list; assorted rice and bean mixes, such as seasoned dry black or red beans with rice

Condiments: pickles (sweet and dill)

Snacks: dried fruit (apricots, peaches, figs, mixed fruits, raisins), graham crackers, marshmallows, microwave popcorn, tortilla chips, vanilla wafers, whole wheat crackers

Seasonings and spices: almond extract, basil leaves, bay leaves, cloves (ground), cumin (ground), curry powder, garlic (minced, bottle), marjoram leaves, dry mustard, nutmeg (ground), onion powder, oregano leaves, rosemary leaves, sage leaves, seasoning mixes, tarragon leaves, thyme leaves

Kitchen care: Cleaning wipes; brown paper sandwich bags; disposable plates, cups, and utensils for emergencies; freezer bags; sandwich bags

EXTRAS FOR ENTERTAINING
Stock a few extras if you entertain or create special spur-of-the-moment meals and snacks. For ethnic cooking, stock up on items found in ethnic markets.

Beverages and sweeteners: canned tomato juice, flavored coffees and assorted teas, ginger ale, soft drinks (including soda and tonic water), lemonade mixes

Canned goods: anchovies, artichokes (in water and in oil), plum tomatoes (Italian), capers, caviar, chile peppers (pickled; chipotle in adobo), garbanzo beans, pickled vegetables (including pickled okra), roasted red peppers, sardines

Cereals and pastas: arborio rice, couscous, soba noodles (Asian), wild rice

Condiments: pickles (sweet and dill), mustard (Dijon-style, stone-ground, honey mustard)

Snacks: crackers (assorted), honey-roasted nuts, kalamata olives, olives (stuffed and ripe, whole and sliced), pepper jelly

Seasonings and spices: bean sauce, Cajun seasonings, cilantro, Asian fermented fish sauce (nam pla or nuoc nam), Jamaican jerk seasonings, red pepper flakes

Staples for meal preparation: bouillon cubes, Asian chili oil (wok oil), dried tomatoes (dry in package and in oil), extra-virgin olive oil, pine nuts, port wine, red wine vinegar, Asian rice vinegar, sherry, tamari sauce and tamarind paste, toasted sesame oil

Cookware

With the growing interest in culinary arts, choosing and caring for cookware has become a major decision and investment. If you shop garage sales or antiques fairs, you've probably seen cast-iron cookware, evidence that quality cookware does indeed last for generations. Before shopping for cookware, assess your cooking needs and make a realistic budget. If you want to acquire quality cookware for both the service and good looks it provides, consider purchasing open stock cookware individually until you accumulate the pieces you want. Restaurant supply houses in large cities often sell to the public.

CHOOSING WHAT WORKS

It's tempting to choose cookware by price and appearance; however, weight, quality construction, and material composition are far better criteria. Heavy is better. Thick cookware bottoms that make a piece feel heavy absorb and evenly distribute heat from the stove—avoiding hot spots that impair your best cooking efforts. Heavy cookware lasts longer, won't dent, and resists warping caused by raising and lowering cooking temperatures. When you buy heavy cookware, select pieces with all-metal, rather than plastic, handles. Handles should be sturdy and comfortable, even when the cookware is full. On ovenproof cookware, select metal handles that are also safe to the touch during range-top cooking. If you prefer plastic handles, look for handles that withstand temperatures of up to 400 degrees. Lids should be heavy and tight-fitting to match the heft of the cookware. Helpful cookware extras include pouring spouts, tempered-glass lids, built-in strainers, and hanging rings.

Aluminum: This cookware heats quickly and uniformly so that foods brown and cook evenly. Because the material is durable and relatively lightweight, aluminum cookware is sturdy and easy to handle. It is relatively inexpensive compared to other cookware; however, aluminum reacts chemically with acidic foods such as tomato sauce. Most new aluminum cookware, however, is now manufactured with a nonstick coating, which alleviates oxidizing.

Care: Generally, hot soapy water is suggested for washing most

Useful Measuring Tools

Meat Thermometer:
For food safety and accuracy, use a meat thermometer. Gauge notes temperatures for specific meats. Always use for pork and for poultry such as turkey.

Kitchen Scale:
This accurate tool is indispensable if you are dieting and need precise weights. Some European-style cuisines also call for measured ingredients. Useful for produce too.

Nesting Cups:
Use for dry ingredients such as flour. Choose metal cups for durability. Better-quality cups don't easily dent or become misshapen. If you bake frequently, stock two sets.

Measuring Spoons:
Use metal spoons to accurately measure ingredients. Buy metal. Painted measurements on cheap plastic can flake off after repeated use.

Cooking Timer:
If your stove doesn't have a timer, buy one where kitchen gadgets are sold. Accurate timing is essential to cooking, particularly for baking cookies, cakes, bread.

Measuring Cups:
Buy easy-to-read glass or plastic for liquids. Most cooks find it helpful to stock 2-cup (1-pint) and 1-cup sizes. One-pint cups can be used for mixing bowls.

aluminum cookware. Check manufacturer's instructions. Also check the advice for using the dishwasher; often the handles should not be subjected to the temperature changes in a machine. For brightening the interior of an aluminum pan, fill the pan with water and add 1 tablespoon cream of tartar per 1 quart of water. Boil for 5 to 10 minutes; then wash as usual.

Anodized aluminum: Anodized aluminum cookware has a hard, smooth oxide film that doesn't corrode or react with foods. The dark gray surface is integral to the cookware and doesn't chip or peel. If bottoms of metal pans are no longer flat, they do not conduct heat well on smooth glass ceramic cooktops. To reduce chances of warping, do not heat empty aluminum cookware or place hot cookware in water.

Care: Do not wash anodized aluminum cookware or bakeware in the dishwasher.

Stainless-steel-lined aluminum: The aluminum base or core conducts heat quickly and evenly, and the stainless-steel liner doesn't react chemically with foods. One manufacturer offers a quality three-ply design that bonds an aluminum core to stainless-steel layers inside and out.

Care: Check manufacturer's instructions. Dishwasher recommendations often are determined by the handle material.

Cast iron: Cast iron absorbs heat slowly and evenly. Because it stays hot after being removed from the heat, cast iron is ideal for keeping foods hot at the table. It works well for foods that cook slowly over a long time, such as stews and casseroles. Traditionally, cast iron has been used to bake corn bread and other quick breads. The weight of cast iron makes it warp-proof. Because it heats slowly, cast iron is not the optimum choice for quick cooking, such as sautéing. The cookware is heavy to handle, may discolor, and imparts a metallic flavor when used to cook acidic foods if seasoning is not renewed from time to time.

Care: Wash cast iron by hand and dry it completely to protect it against rust. Season regularly with vegetable oil.

Lined Copper: This beautiful cookware is a top-notch heat conductor. With proper care, this investment will last for generations. Because copper reacts with many foods, the cookware is usually lined—exceptions include some special purpose pieces, such as bowls that enable the cook to beat higher and lighter egg whites and saucepans for candymaking. The lining process bonds stainless steel inside the copper, forming a nonreactive and easy-to-clean interior. Cookware is manufactured by weights or gauges: Lower numbers represent thicker metal and better-quality cookware.

Care: Wash by hand, not in the dishwasher. Rinse and towel dry.

TIME SAVER

Boil Out Burned on Food

Instead of scrubbing, immerse a burned pan in a larger, water-filled pot. Add at least 1 tablespoon of baking soda and boil for several minutes. Allow the pan to cool before scrubbing loosened food particles.

Enameled cast iron: This cookware is manufactured with an even-heating cast-iron interior fused to an enamel exterior that prevents the iron from affecting food flavor. Enameled cast iron doesn't allow quick browning, and the enamel may darken and stain with use.

Care: Use wood or plastic utensils to avoid scratching.

Enameled steel: This cookware blends the best of two materials. The enamel surface is dishwasher safe, stick-resistant, and chemically nonreactive. Because the cookware is lightweight, enameled-steel roasters and stockpots are easy to handle. Enameled steel is a good choice for cooking flour-based sauces, soups, stews, and casseroles slowly and evenly. Enamel may crack if subjected to prolonged high heat. Some coatings scratch, chip, or stain with heavy use. Look for metal rims to protect enameled-steel cookware from chipping and for heavy-gauge metal cores to prevent buckling.

Care: Wash with mild soap and sponge or in dishwasher.

Stainless steel: This material resists scratches, dents, corrosion, and tarnishing, and tolerates extreme temperature changes. Stainless steel is nonporous, so it does not react with foods. Stainless steel performs best when bonded with aluminum and copper for even heat transference. To prevent the aluminum disk bottoms from separating, do not leave empty stainless-steel saucepans on a hot burner.

Care: Check manufacturer's guidelines. Many stainless-steel pieces with metal handles are considered dishwasher-safe, although some manufacturers suggest washing by hand.

Rolled steel: The forging process of rolled steel creates an excellent heat conductor, ideally suited for quality range-top woks and omelet pans. Choose rolled steel for cookware that will be exposed to high heat.

Care: Follow manufacturer's instructions; season to prevent rust.

Glass and ceramic: Glass cookware is no longer manufactured for range top cooking. It is, however, still available at flea markets and thrift stores. If you have any of this cookware, use it for baking, serving, or display. It is not considered safe for range tops.

Care: To maintain appearance, wash by hand. Generally glass and ceramic are considered dishwasher-safe, although they may develop a dull surface after repeated machine washings.

Glass and ceramic baking dishes: When you use these popular baking dishes, keep in mind that they are a combination of

smart ideas

Cast Iron

SEASON CORRECTLY

New or old, cast-iron cookware needs care to avoid rust and corrosion. Before first use, and periodically, season your cookware. Preheat the oven to 250 degrees, oil the pot with vegetable oil, and heat in the oven for 20 minutes. Remove and wipe with paper towels. Repeat. Don't burn yourself with warm oil. Don't wash cast iron with detergent, don't submerge in water, and don't wash in dishwasher.

SELF-CLEANING PANS

When food or carbon builds up, put the cast-iron pan in the oven on the self-cleaning cycle for two hours. Remove with a pot holder and wipe with paper towels.

glass-ceramic and ceramic. The chemical formulations allow them to be used in ovens and microwaves—and to go directly from the refrigerator to the heating unit. If you happen to have an old glass baking dish that could possibly be pure glass, it isn't safe for such drastic temperature changes and should be allowed to reach room temperature before baking or washing.

Care: If food is baked on, soak first with warm water and dishwashing liquid to loosen. Clean with nonabrasive, self-polishing cleanser or baking soda. Use nylon or plastic, never scouring pads.

Small Appliances

The microwave, blender, coffeemaker, and toaster are among the most popular kitchen appliances, according to industry surveys. Continuous slow cookers are highly rated by working parents.

BLENDER

Purchase: Versatile enough for foods from soups to nuts, blenders are available in 32- to 42-ounce sizes. Blenders are frequently used to make drinks and shakes, as well as to blend, chop, and puree foods. Units are two-speed, two-speed plus pulse, or 5-, 10-, and 15-speed. Blender containers can be plastic, which is lightweight and safe for kids to use; glass, which is heavier and may present safety issues; and stainless steel.

Care and maintenance: Choose a model with a removable bottom for easy cleaning. Separate the blade, gasket, and container to wash them by hand. Never immerse the motorized base in water. To get the best results from a blender, don't overload it. Cut fresh fruits and vegetables, cooked meats, fish, and seafood into ½- to 1-inch pieces before adding them to the blender. Cube cheese before blending and add one cube at a time. Add ice cubes one at a time.

BREAD MACHINE

Purchase: This appliance is a boon to bakers who love the smell and taste of home-baked bread without all the work. Standard sizes are 1½- and 2-pound bread machines.

Care and maintenance: To make cleanup easier, spray the bread pan and kneading paddle with nonstick coating before adding the ingredients. After baking, allow the bread pan to cool; then fill it with hot, soapy water. Soak the kneading paddle separately.

COFFEEMAKER

Purchase: There are many options beyond making basic coffee: coffee-espresso makers, espresso-cappuccino makers, and coffeemakers with built-in coffee-bean grinders. Consider how much counter space you have, because the coffeemaker is likely to be out much of the time. Units brew from two to 20 cups at a time.

Care and maintenance: Many coffee carafes and filter holders

TIME SAVER

Sharpen Your Knives

With handheld sharpening steel or stone in one hand, hold the knife in your other at a 20-degree angle to the sharpener. Draw the blade across and down. Turn the blade over and reverse directions. Or invest in a knife sharpener.

A Well-Stocked Pantry

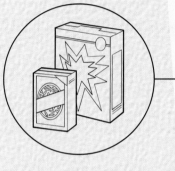

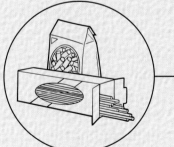

Beverages:
Stock coffee (and filters) and tea bags. Hot chocolate mixes and honey are handy to have.

Snacks:
Buy saltines and wheat crackers and peanut butter. Add pretzels or cookies and dried fruit if you snack.

Cereals and Grains:
Store your favorite cereal. Instant rice and cornmeal are helpful for last-minute meals.

Canned Goods:
Include diced tomatoes, tomato paste and sauce. Tins of tuna and juices are staples.

Condiments:
Store extra jars of mustard, mayonnaise, ketchup, dressings. Refrigerate after opening.

Oils and Vinegars:
Start with basic vegetable oil and olive oil and white and balsamic vinegars.

Pastas:
Make quick meals from the pantry if you keep bags of spaghetti, macaroni, and angel hair pastas.

Baking Products:
Include all-purpose flour, baking powder, baking soda, salt, and sugar for basics.

Cooking Flavorings:
Add nonstick coating and baking sprays. Keep vanilla for basic baking.

Spices:
Buy small jars for freshness. Basics include black pepper, garlic and chili powders, cinnamon, thyme.

can be washed in the dishwasher, but other parts should be cleaned with a sponge or cloth. Check manufacturer's guidelines.

CROCKERY COOKER

Purchase: Crockery cookers include two types of cookers: continuous slow cookers and intermittent cookers. Continuous slow cookers cook foods slowly at a very low wattage. The heating coils wrap around the sides of the cooker and remain on continuously. This type of cooker has fixed settings: low (about 200 degrees), high (about 300 degrees), and in some models, automatic (shifts from high to low heat automatically). The ceramic liner may or may not be removable. For foods that cook all day, use the low-heat setting of this cooker. For shorter cooking time, use high heat and cook foods in three to six hours (depending on the recipe). Intermittent cookers have heating elements or coils that are located below the food container. These cookers have temperature dials to indicate degrees. They cycle on and off during operation and are useful for keeping dips and sauces warm during parties. Recipes that require continuous slow cooking will not cook properly in intermittent cookers. Recipes are designed for either one or the other type of cooker, so determine which cooker to use before preparing a recipe. Crockery cookers range in size from mini 1-quart models to large 6-quart models. Midsize crockery cookers—3½-, 4-, and 5-quart models—are the most popular.

Care and maintenance: Turn off the cooker and allow the unit to cool. Carefully follow manufacturer's guidelines to clean and store. Some crockery cookers and lids can be washed in the dishwasher. Wipe the base of the unit with a damp clean cloth. Do not use abrasive cleaners or immerse in water.

ELECTRIC MIXER

Purchase: Determine your needs and price range. Economical handheld mixers work well for most recipes. They are easy to use for cakes, cookies, and icing, and they are easy to store.

Care and maintenance: Basic care for handheld mixers involves washing the beaters by hand or in the dishwasher (read manufacturer's instructions). Wipe the exterior with a hot, soapy cloth. Mixer life is shortened by prolonged use with stiff dough or heavy batters.

FOOD PROCESSOR

Purchase: With the variety of models and price ranges, food processors have become the small appliance of choice for many cooks. Capable of both mixing and shredding, food processors integrate many of the jobs of blenders and electric mixers. The two basic types are belt driven and direct power driven; the latter is more durable and powerful.

Care and maintenance: Bowls are dishwasher-safe. Stainless

BUDGET STRETCHER

Good Coffee

•

Get the most taste from your coffee. Every two months, drip white vinegar through your automatic coffeemaker; follow with two to three dripped pots of clear water. Scrub the pot with baking soda paste and rinse thoroughly.

steel blades and disks should be hand washed; don't submerge base.

TOASTER

Purchase: In addition to toasting bread, wide-slot units also warm bagels and breakfast pastries.

SPECIALTY APPLIANCES

Deep-fat fryer: To make homemade french fries, onion rings, and fried chicken, electric fryers are available in several sizes. They maintain a set temperature and are equipped with slotted scoops for easy food removal. Nonstick surfaces aid in cooking and cleanup, and most have lids to store oil in the fryer. Choose a fryer with a capacity that matches your needs—from the most basic 2-cup mini fryers to 8-cup fryers with convenient, generously sized dividers for cooking two foods at once. Do not immerse the base in water.

Tabletop grill: Choose from covered or uncovered models. Foods cook quickly on covered grills, which heat from both the top and bottom. Cook foods that are 1 inch thick or less, such as hamburgers, skinless boneless chicken breasts, fish fillets, and steaks. Read manufacturer's directions to clean. Uncovered grills include those that are part of the range and have special grates and fans. They heat from the bottom only, increasing cooking time. Remove grill racks and drip pans to wash in hot, sudsy water; follow manufacturer's directions to clean the nonremovable parts of the grill.

Pressure cooker: Around for decades, the pressure cooker continues to attract new converts. The speedy cooking and juicy results fit well with busy lifestyles. Lightweight aluminum cookers are less expensive than stainless-steel cookers and are good heat conductors, but they do not have nonstick coatings. Heavier stainless-steel cookers must have bimetal bases. Choose a 4-, 6- or 8-quart pressure cooker. The 4-quart is adequate for making whole meals for singles or couples or for preparing one course for a large family. Use the 6-quart capacity for more than two people, and the 8-quart for families or pressure canning in pint or half-pint jars. Choose a pressure cooker with a removable pressure regulator, which allows the vent pipe to be examined before each use. Some regulators jiggle and allow steam to escape constantly; others release excess steam in short bursts. Select a regulator that has a maximum operating pressure of 15 pounds. The cover interlock prevents the lid from blowing off with high pressure inside the cooker. Check the Underwriters Laboratories (UL) listing as well as the handle construction for

TIPTAG No 16

Kid-Proofing

COOKING:
- When possible, cook on back burners. Turn pot handles in.
- Keep children out of range when you carry and pour hot liquids. Keep hot coffee and other hot liquids out of reach.
- If you store medicines, vitamins, or wines for cooking in the kitchen, store on upper shelves, out of reach.

CLEANING/STORAGE:
- DO NOT store cleaning supplies, including dishwashing liquids and plastic bags, under the sink.
- Install safety locks on reachable cabinet doors. Use a child-safety gate to keep a young child out of the kitchen while you are elsewhere.

comfort in lifting. An optional cooking rack or basket allows several foods to cook at one time. Follow the manufacturer's instructions for proper use and cleaning.

Rice cooker or steamer: Most rice cookers or steamers hold 2 to 12 cups of cooked rice (1 to 6 cups of raw rice). Features to look for are automatic signals to indicate that rice is finished cooking, automatic shutoff, stay-warm features, and trays for steaming vegetables. Look for a rice cooker with a nonstick removable pan. The removable chamber is usually dishwasher-safe; do not immerse the heating unit in water.

Waffle iron: This familiar appliance bakes classic comfort food, such as Belgian waffles or crispy cookies. Choose from a variety of sizes and shapes. Select an iron that signals when it is hot and when the baking is complete. Nonstick grids can be wiped clean, as can the exterior.

Electric wok: Use a wok to stir-fry foods quickly and flavorfully or use in place of a deep-fat fryer. Select nonstick surfaces for easy cleanup, a heat-resistant base and handles, and a steaming rack to keep foods warm while others are being prepared. Most wok bowls are cleaned with hot, soapy water, rinsed, and toweled dry. Keep the electrical components away from water.

Also handy: Depending on your interests and household, you may also want to consider other specialty appliances such as ice cream/yogurt makers, espresso or cappuccino makers, or vacuum package sealers to store food.

Large Appliances

Even basic value-priced large appliances are expensive. Shop around and check energy ratings and warranties before making such a major purchase. It pays to be informed.

RANGE

With burners on the top and an oven below, the range is the most common cooking appliance. New bargain-priced basic ranges are 30-inch white or almond freestanding or drop-in models, which include either electric coil or standard 9,000-Btu gas burners with oven. Better-quality ranges are marketed with ceramic-top electric burners, self-cleaning ovens, dual-fuel options, and convection ovens. Top-of-the-line residential models have professional styling with stainless-steel or anodized finishes, widths from 30 to 60 inches, downdraft or restaurant-style hood venting, high-performance Btu burners, and continuous grates, along with built-in grill or griddle and double-convection oven options.

Freestanding ranges rest on the floor as self-contained units and are normally 30 inches wide. Models that are 24 and 36 inches wide are also available. Wider models usually have a fifth burner and

Cookware Comparisons

Enameled Cast Iron:
Handsome pieces can be used for baking, range-top cooking, and serving. The material is ideal for long, slow cooking with even heat.

Stainless Steel:
Preferred stainless-steel cookware is labeled 18/10, which means the metal contains 18 parts chromium and 10 parts nickel.

Copper:
Professional-quality, well-maintained pieces last for generations. Pots heat quickly and cool quickly. Copper is expensive and requires polishing to look good.

Anodized Aluminum:
This well-made cookware is often the choice of serious cooks because it doesn't chip or peel. It heats quickly and evenly.

an extra-wide oven.

High-low ranges include built-in microwave ovens near eye level as well as conventional ovens and burners.

Slide-in ranges are freestanding ranges without side panels. Slide-in ranges fit into 30-inch openings between base cabinets. For exposed sides, cabinet side panels can be installed.

Drop-in ranges are similar to slide-in ranges, but they must be permanently fastened to base cabinets. They usually rest on built-up wood bases. Broilers are located in the oven. Some drop-in and slide-in units are well-suited for island or peninsula installation, because controls are on the top or at the front. No raised control back panel interrupts the counter.

COOKTOP

With the advent of peninsulas and islands, cooktops joined ranges as cooking options. Basic cooktops are 30 or 36 inches wide and have four electric-coil or gas burners. These cooktops have top-mounted controls and no ventilation system. Midquality cooktops are 30 or 37 inches wide and usually have smooth-glass electric burners or higher Btu gas burners and downdraft vents.

If you have a choice between gas and electric, keep in mind that gas burners heat and cool more quickly than electric burners. Cooks can easily see and adjust the height of the gas flame. Electric burners don't have flames or the possible gas fumes. Magnetic induction and halogen cooktops are less common. Consider a cooktop with interchangeable components—such as electric coils, sealed gas burners, grill, wok, fryer, griddle, or downdraft ventilator.

OVEN

For use with a cooktop or as an addition to a range, budget ovens are 27-inch wall models. Budget-priced ovens are black or white and typically have plastic handles. Better quality ovens are usually 30 inches wide with self-cleaning features. Convection ovens may be an option. Top-of-the-line ovens include luxury features, such as larger interior space, convection and finish options, heavier racks, precision temperature controls, and double units.

Conventional ovens are also called radiant or thermal ovens. Design is based on two heating elements, one for baking and roasting and the other for broiling. Heat radiates up and pushes cold air down, creating a potential for uneven heating.

Convection ovens circulate heated air for faster, more even cooking than conventional ovens can offer. A fan installed in the back wall of the oven circulates the hot air. Even heat distribution allows for more of the oven space to be used. Convection ovens also warm faster than conventional ovens and may reduce cooking time for some foods. Disadvantages include noise from fans on some models and drying or overbrowning caused by the forced air.

Microwave ovens have become standard kitchen features. Microwave recipes are usually designed for the typical microwave cooking power of 600 to 700 watts. If you own a lower-wattage (under 600) microwave, adjust cooking times.

Combination ovens combine convection with microwave heat, convection with conventional heat, or microwave with conventional heat. Double wall ovens that use all three heat sources are available. Combination ovens are often used to save space.

VENTILATION SYSTEMS

Delicious aromas may be an enticing part of good cooking, but moisture, grease, odors, and heat from stove-top food preparation will damage the surrounding areas. Steam from cooking condenses on windows and walls, and carbon monoxide from gas-range combustion can build up. Mechanical ventilation from a range hood or vent—which removes stale, odorous, steamy air through ducts— eliminates or lessens these problems.

General Types: Choose from basic ductless wall-mount units or more-versatile systems with multiple lights, timers, and easy-clean surfaces. Some slim hood designs hide under over-stove cabinets, then slide out for use; others serve as shelves for microwaves with venting fans beneath. Elaborate vent systems integrate a wall-mount microwave conveniently set over the range. Because a vent functions by capturing air and steam, its hood or canopy should be as wide as the range top.

Range hood fans with ductwork: A hollow sump area under the hood holds stale air until a fan moves it outdoors through ducts; the deeper the sump, the more it holds. The fan plays a crucial role: A powerful unit keeps the air fresher. Axial fans have blades similar to ordinary fans. Centrifugal fans resemble a wheel and move more air for longer ducts. Filters trap grease and particles, preventing entry into ductwork and potential clogs that can be a fire hazard. Filters should fit snugly yet remove easily for cleaning or replacement.

Room and stove size determine the required rate of air removed, which is measured in cubic feet per minute (cfm). According to the Home Ventilating Institute, the general recommendation is a minimum of 40 cfm for every linear foot of a range. Usually, an average-size range requires air removal at 120 cfm when using an overhead range vent hood.

Recirculating range hoods: This is the most basic but least efficient system. These hoods attach to the wall above the cooktop

---

Home Remedies

CLEAN COOKTOP

Burner Grates

Wait until the stove is cool. Remove drip pans and soak in warm, soap water. Spray surface with all-purpose cleaner or vinegar-and-water solution. Wipe with a sponge or clean cloth. Wipe excess with paper towel. Use a baking soda paste on tough spots. Wipe with a damp sponge. Scour pans with a nylon-type, nonscratching pad if necessary. Dry with towel and replace.

Sealed Range Tops

Wait until the stove is cool. Spray with a general-purpose cleaner or vinegar-and-water solution. Wipe with a sponge or clean cloth. Apply a baking soda paste, scrub gently, and rinse.

and pull air through a filter, recirculating it back into the room, often including odors or gases. Filters do absorb grease and require frequent cleaning or replacement. These hoods are easy to install because they don't require ductwork.

Downdraft systems: Such systems are typically part of the range, often on the stove top near the burners. Some stove designs can be retrofitted for venting from underneath. "Hidden" styles remain flush with the cooking surface until necessary; then with the push of a button, they rise 8 to 10 inches above the cooking surface. These are best for island or peninsula cooktops where hood installation may be awkward or impossible.

Downdraft units use one or more fans, pulling air through a filter into ductwork (usually beneath the floor or above cabinets, and sometimes out the wall). Downdraft units need a minimum of 150 cfm. Stove placement is also a factor: Wall units need up to 400 cfm; an island cooktop needs up to 600 cfm.

Decorative hoods or canopies: These are used to dress up a range or cooktop hood in stainless steel, tile, or paneling that matches the cabinetry. Hoods can be semicustom or custom.

Maintenance: Because their purpose includes removing grease and moisture from cooking, these systems quickly collect dirt and require regular cleaning. Always check the manufacturer's specific cleaning instructions if available. The usual routine includes washing external surfaces often—even daily—with a solution of warm water, detergent, and ammonia. Rinse well with clear water. Don't use abrasive or scouring pads because they scratch surfaces. Sponge cool lightbulbs with the solution, rinse, and thoroughly dry. If the blades are accessible, wipe frequently with the washing solution. If inaccessible, schedule annual professional maintenance. Remove metal mesh filters; soak in solution for a few minutes. Sponge off dirt as necessary, rinse, and air dry before replacing in the hood. Charcoal filters are not cleanable; replace them once a year.

REFRIGERATOR AND FREEZER

Evaluate features and extras before you buy a refrigerator. Some rental properties do not include refrigerators, so this may be a young consumer's first major appliance purchase. With proper care and maintenance, refrigerators can operate for 15 years or more, so plan for changes in family size.

Configuration: The most popular is the two-door, top-freezer design. Bottom-freezer units put fresh food at eye level and frozen items below. Side-by-side models have narrow doors that open at the center. They generally offer more storage capacity and easy access for children or people in wheelchairs.

Space available: Refrigerators vary in size and required clearance space. Measure the height, width, and depth of the space

Efficient Kitchen Helpers

Microwave:

Budget ones are used for heating, reheating, boiling water, and for defrosting frozen food. More expensive ones include turntables and browning functions.

Stand Mixer:

Stand mixers can knead bread dough and mix large amounts of thick batter. They are ideal for serious bakers. Handheld mixers work for basic baking.

Toaster:

Quality models have cool-touch exteriors and controls to adjust browning. Families may prefer the four-slot model. Remove crumbs from the bottom crumb plate.

Coffeemaker:

Selling features include number of cups brewed at a time, programmable timers, filtration for better taste, temperature controls, and brewing cycles for strength.

for your refrigerator, and take those dimensions with you when you shop. Shallow models that extend from the wall about as far as standard cabinet fronts look better than models that extend beyond countertops, blocking traffic flow or a doorway.

Capacity: Sizes range between 9 and 30 cubic feet. A family of two needs 8 to 10 cubic feet of fresh-food space. Add an extra cubic foot for each additional family member.

Freezer space: A family of two needs 4 cubic feet of freezer space. Add 2 cubic feet for each additional person. Increase the freezer space if you stock frozen products or shop infrequently. Top and bottom freezers offer the most storage flexibility. Side-by-side models may offer more total storage space, but sometimes it's difficult to store large items in them.

Interior features: Adjustable-height shelves make room for foods of any size and shape. Spillproof shelves help reduce cleanup time. Look for shelves that lift all the way out for washing in the sink and that are adjustable for easy access to gallon-size milk, juice, and soft drinks. Spacious crispers with clear fronts and adjustable humidity controls help you keep track of fresh produce. In the freezer, side and tilt-out baskets are handy.

Icemaker and water dispenser: Some models are manufactured with icemakers, and other models are designed so that icemakers can be installed. Ice and water dispensers are useful for children or for people who frequently get cold drinks. These devices also save energy because the door is opened less frequently. High-end refrigerators may include built-in water filters that help dispensed ice and water look and taste better.

Color and finish: White and almond are popular choices. Black is striking and can be ideal if you want to match other appliances. Options include stainless-steel exteriors, restaurant-style glass doors, and trim panels to match cabinets.

Noise and energy: When you shop, ask to turn on a model so you can listen as it operates. The noise will be quieter in your kitchen than on a concrete sales floor. Check the yellow Energy Guide label to determine the average energy use. Compare models that have the same capacity.

DISHWASHER

Dishwashers are classified as compact or standard. Although compact models use less energy, they also hold fewer dishes. If you must run the dishwasher frequently because of the number of dishes you use, you may be using more energy. Look for a dishwasher with different cycle selections. For dishes that are not heavily soiled, select energy-saving or light-wash cycles. These save energy by using less water and operating for a shorter time. Consider drying and air-drying options. The first method draws

SAFETY ALERT

Freezer Outage

Never refreeze frozen food that has thawed completely, or ice cream or creamed foods that are partially thawed. Foods that still have ice crystals, bread, cake, cookies, and plain doughnuts can be refrozen. Never refreeze raw meat or poultry; if in doubt, throw out food items.

electricity; the latter method relies on evaporation.

Size and type: If you replace a dishwasher, you may choose the same size and type; measure your space before you shop. For a new installation, measure the space available in your kitchen and take the dimensions with you to the dealer. Choose between built-in and portable, full-size or compact models.

Noise level: If family activities and conversations take place in or near the kitchen, a noisy dishwasher is irritating. Reduce sound by adding or improving insulation around the washing tub, door, toe panel, and access panels. Some models offer extra-quiet motors and vibration-absorbing materials.

Energy: If you always choose the highest wash cycle, you'll use more hot water and energy. Consider cycles that use less energy and water—as little as 4 gallons—when dishes are less soiled. A delayed-start control lets you wash during less costly off-peak hours. Read the Energy Guide label for operating costs.

Special features: Angled control panels, large digital displays, wide push buttons, and soft-touch electronic controls are among the design elements to consider before you select a dishwasher. You may also want to elevate the dishwasher 12 to 18 inches to minimize bending. Look at models with sensors to measure the soil content of the water and adjust wash cycles to fit. Check that detergent and rinse additive dispensers are large enough and conveniently located.

Racks: Dish and glass racks are usually nylon or vinyl coated wires. (However, one manufacturer offers a model with stainless-steel racks.) The tops of tines wear first; check those areas. Adjustable-height racks add flexibility when you need to load large items or serving pieces. If you entertain frequently, consider models that hold 12 place settings instead of the standard 10. Also compare baskets, hooks, and trays for knives, cooking utensils, and small, lightweight plastic items.

Performance comparisons: When you shop, compare the number and types of wash cycles among models and brands. High-performance dishwashers have two or three spray arms that soak dishes with water from several levels and angles. In the spray arms, smaller holes emit a more forceful spray. A central wash tower may improve washing performance, but you'll lose rack space. A twin-pump system drains dirty water faster than a standard single pump. Wash-water filters and internal food disposals are common on many models. Less common is a booster that heats rinse water to help sanitize dishes without elevating the water heater temperature.

Exterior: Higher-end models are available in the restaurant-style look. If you want your dishwasher to "disappear," look for a built-in model with the option of adding trim panels to match your cabinets. Some manufacturers have moved controls from the front to the top of the door to further disguise the appliance.

Longevity: Dishwasher tubs are made from plastic, porcelain-enameled metal, or stainless steel. Plastic resists chipping and rusting better than enameled metal, but it can discolor. Stainless steel stands up to abuse, so it looks new for a longer time. Its natural sheeting action saves drying time.

Sinks

Choose from a variety of styles, sizes, and materials for a sink that fits your kitchen needs.

MATERIALS

Cast iron: This sturdy material is enamel fired on an iron form. These durable sinks lessen noise and vibration more than other materials but can be heavy for installation.

Composite: Whether these sinks are made of quartz, granite, or other materials mixed with an acrylic- or polyester-resin base, they usually feature speckled color, resistance to stains and scratches, and easy care. They also can be expensive.

Fireclay: The clay base is fired at intense heat to produce a durable, glossy finish. The glazed surface resists scratches and abrasion and won't rust, fade, or discolor. Some manufacturers offer sinks with painted designs fired onto the surface.

Vitreous china: Originally made for bathrooms, vitreous china is now also used for kitchen sinks. The glazed clay material is hard and nonporous with a glasslike shine. Similar to fireclay in construction, durability, and cost, vitreous china is less porous because of the nature of the construction process. It is easier to mold double bowl sinks from vitreous china than from fireclay.

Solid-surfacing: Chosen for its stonelike appearance and easy care, solid-surfacing is made from a polyester or acrylic base. The material can be colored or patterned to resemble stone and resists scratches and chips. Because the color runs through the entire material, minor burns or scrapes can be sanded out.

Stainless steel: Stainless steel continues to be improved and upgraded. The newer 16- and 18-gauge sinks are thicker and less noisy than their less-expensive predecessors. Stainless-steel sinks contain a percentage of chromium and nickel, which is indicated by numbers such as 18/10 (18 percent chromium and 10 percent nickel). The metal imparts a rich glow and adds corrosion

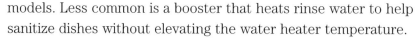

TIME
SAVER

Clean Stove Overnight

•

Soak grates, knobs, and drip pans in hot, soapy water. If the oven isn't self-cleaning, loosen grime: Make sure the oven is off and inaccessible to children. Fill a small bowl with ammonia and place inside the oven overnight. In the morning, open windows for air. Wipe out oven with paper towels.

Anatomy of Refrigerator

Icemaker:
May be added to some models. If problems arise, check hoses before calling the repair person.

Freezer Compartment:
Wipe with a solution of 2 tablespoons of baking soda and 1 quart warm water.

Door Handle:
Wipe smudges at least weekly. Use a baking soda paste on tougher grime.

Shelves:
Wash in the sink with warm water and mild soap or detergent. Rinse and dry before replacing.

Door Compartments:
Wash removable parts in sink; wipe supports with baking soda solution. Wipe and dry jars and bottles.

Door Seal:
Wash with water and mild detergent. Rinse and dry. Apply petroleum jelly.

Produce Drawers:
Remove and wash in sink with mild soapy warm. Wipe walls with baking soda solution. Rinse; dry.

Coils and Vents:
Vacuum condenser coils two to six times a year (more if you have pets). Remove drip pan if possible; wash.

resistance. Finishes range from a mirrorlike shine to a satin luster.

BOWLS AND MOUNTING

Double-bowl sinks offer many options in size, depth, and bowl placement. Study your kitchen needs to determine what works for you. Triple-bowl sinks usually have two large bowls with a smaller bowl centered between for food preparation. Standard 33-inch double-bowl sinks provide 13-inch-wide basins and don't accommodate large cookware. Standard depth is 8 inches; budget-model sinks often measure only 6 or 7 inches deep. If you use large or awkward cookware, select a sink to fit your needs.

Sink mounting affects the appearance of the sink as much as sink configuration does. Easy-to-install top-mount sinks have a ridge that fits over the countertop. Flush-mount sinks, which are level with the countertop, provide a neat look but don't catch splashes as well as the top-mount. Under-mount sinks are recessed below the countertop and work especially well with solid-surface countertop materials. Integral sinks—sink and countertop fused as one—are made of solid-surface material or stainless steel.

FAUCETS

The right kitchen faucet makes cooking and cleaning easier while enhancing the room with an attractive but practical fixture. Chrome, easy-care brass, and other decorative finishes are options. Special features—including tall gooseneck faucets that swivel out of the way, detachable hose-type faucets, and traditional-looking faucets that appear to be set flush but pull upward for additional height—allow versatility.

Purchase and installation: Account for such tasks as filling and cleaning tall stockpots, as well as the style, depth, and finish of the sink and surrounding hardware. Make a list of preferences—for example, for a single handle or separate hot and cold controls. Keep in mind that some sinks are sold with predrilled holes for faucets and handles, which can affect faucet selection. Comparison shop. Visit several plumbing supply stores or home centers to compare prices, installation, and faucet styles. Find out whether your choices meet local codes. Faucets have an average life span of 8 to 12 years with proper maintenance. Chrome faucets, most commonly used in kitchens, are the easiest to maintain.

Lighting

Effective lighting makes your kitchen efficient, attractive, and safe. If you build or remodel, take a look at how to illuminate task areas.

AMBIENT LIGHTING

Provided by windows or skylights, central ceiling fixtures, or perimeter soffit lights that direct light up to reflect off the ceiling, this soft, general light spans a whole room. Determine how much

BUDGET STRETCHER

Kitchen Cover-Ups

Save money with paint. Hire a professional to electrostatically paint old appliances in fresh colors, listed as "Appliances—Major Refinishing" in the Yellow Pages. To re-enamel sinks, look under "Bathtubs and Sinks—Repairs and Refinishing."

light is adequate by measuring room height and considering room color. Dark tones absorb light and require more lighting; bright tones reflect light and require less lighting. In kitchens, upper cabinets may cut into window space and prevent light from entering. Although arched windows or skylights may provide adequate light during the day, indirect lighting provides essential supplemental illumination on overcast days and at night.

TASK LIGHTING

Over sinks, food preparation sites, and cleanup centers, task lighting is usually in the form of a beam focused on specific locations. Specialty areas, such as desks or baking centers, call for bright but not harsh task lighting. Install task lighting in a position that will allow you to work without casting shadows over the area. Select from recessed downlights, track lights, pendent lights, or undercabinet strip lights. Light each work center with a minimum of 100 to 150 watts of incandescent light or 40 to 50 watts of fluorescent light. For convenience, specify a wall switch to control the light for each area.

BULBS

Each type of bulb has advantages. Incandescent light has a warm glow and is available in many styles. Bulbs are inexpensive and easy to change and can be used with a dimmer switch or rheostat to vary the brightness of the light. Fluorescent lights are energy-efficient and last up to 20 times longer than incandescent bulbs. They produce up to 4 times as much light as incandescent bulbs of the same wattage, so fewer fixtures are required. The light from warm white fluorescent bulbs resembles incandescent tones. Halogen lights provide powerful illumination despite their small size, producing up to 3 times as much light as comparable incandescent bulbs and lasting twice as long. The compact design allows for installation in tiny unobtrusive fixtures. Halogen bulbs burn at high temperatures, and they can be damaged by contact with oily substances. For safety reasons, install them only as ceiling-mounted task lights.

Accessibility

The trend toward large open kitchens in homes and apartments is helpful for people with limited mobility.

UNIVERSAL DESIGN

For the most ease and safety, follow the accepted standards for kitchen design and modification. Allow a 5-foot turnaround for wheelchairs. Install electrical switches at seated height. If new construction or remodeling is an option, choose a shallow sink. Models that are 6½ inches deep and have a drain toward the rear of the bowl are available. Insulate exposed pipes to protect knees.

Think beyond the standard 36-inch counter height. For a shared family kitchen, lower some countertops to 30 to 32 inches, with at least 27 inches below for knee clearance. Such lowered work surfaces should be at least 30 inches wide for best use. Place a low countertop by the sink, the most-used kitchen component. Consider which appliances to elevate, such as the dishwasher.

Purchasing Guidelines

Major kitchen appliances are long-term investments. To get the most from your money, consider the years of use along with the energy consumption. As with all major consumer purchases, it benefits you to comparison shop. Beyond initial cost and features, factor financing charges (if purchasing on credit) as well as energy consumption and standard and extended warranties.

ENERGY SAVINGS

Look for Energy Guide efficiency labels, which are required by the Federal Trade Commission, on refrigerators, freezers, and dishwashers. These federally mandated labels report the capacity of particular models, the estimated annual energy consumption, and the range of consumption or efficiency ratings of comparable appliances. Some appliances feature an Energy Star logo, indicating that the appliance has been rated by the Environmental Protection Agency as significantly more energy-efficient than other appliances. Finally, a notation indicates the energy efficiency of the appliance. Even though two appliances look similar, one may be better engineered on the inside.

Although all manufacturers use standard test procedures, not all use the equivalent independent testers. Even if they did, there are significant differences in each household's use of appliances and the energy costs for each region.

WARRANTIES

Appliance warranties generally fall into two contrasting categories. The law recognizes implied warranties as unspoken, unwritten promises made by the seller to the consumer—an application of the old common law principle of "fair value for money spent." The general promises are that the appliance is worthy of merchantability (being sold) and that it is fit for a particular, clearly expressed purpose. Even though implied warranties are overseen by state law, the federal government states that merchants cannot sidestep responsibility for injuries caused by a defective product.

Under current law, the Magnuson-Moss Act covers only written

FAMILY FRIENDLY

Quickly Accessible

•

Replace standard door hinges with swing-clear hinges for wider access. Add roll-out shelves for dishes and a large lazy Susan for spices and staples. Replace faucet knobs with levers and cooktop controls with easy-grip modifications.

Dishwasher Loading Tips

Light Plastic Items:
Place containers and utensils on upper rack to avoid melting. Use silverware basket for small plastic items that can slip through racks.

Pots and Pans:
Use the lower rack. Fill the dishwasher for efficiency, but don't crowd. Use rinse and hold if not full. When full, choose pot scrubbing cycle.

Cups and Glasses:
Load on prongs to avoid breaking. Don't wedge in small glasses. Don't machine wash fragile stemware or delicate bone china cups.

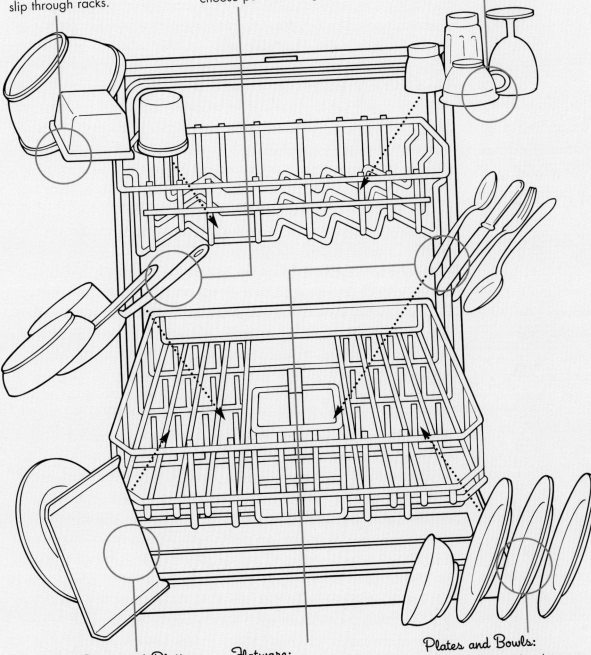

Cookie Sheets and Platters:
Load vertically on the sides of the dishwashers. These can normally be loaded on the upper and lower racks. Don't wedge in over other items.

Flatware:
Sort by type in divided basket for easy unloading. Alternate flatware up and down, except for sharp knives, which should be turned down.

Plates and Bowls:
Add along the sides, between holders. Plates and bowls aren't cleaned properly when they are crammed in or wedged over the top.

warranties, reflecting the purpose of making the warranties as competitive as possible. The act encourages manufacturers to create warranties that cover more possible problems with more clearly expressed promises for longer periods of time. Manufacturers and retailers may also offer service contracts and extended warranties at a cost to consumers. Compare the costs of such features as you shop and consider what is and is not covered. File major appliance warranties and service contracts (along with repair contacts) with household papers for easy reference.

Garbage and Trash

Whether buying for the first time or replacing aging units, keep the following in mind to make the best purchase for your needs.

GARBAGE DISPOSALS

Garbage disposals come in two types. Batch feeders turn themselves on only when special locking covers get set in place, activating a magnetic switch. This is safer for households with children. Continuous feed units turn on and off with a wall switch and allow quicker disposal of larger quantities.

Purchase and installation: Some plumbing codes forbid induction of foreign material, including food, into waste lines, making disposals illegal. If waste goes into a septic tank instead of a sewer, do not install a disposal before checking with code-enforcement agencies. InSinkErator manufactures septic-compatible disposals, which use enzyme additives. Always follow code requirements.

Installation requires plumbing and electrical work, so hiring a professional plumber is often best. Before new installation, have a plumber check the kitchen plumbing for compatibility with sewer and other plumbing hookups; then determine the horsepower requirements. Disposals usually have ½- or 1-horsepower motors. The smaller motor works for moderate use. Busier kitchens may require the larger motor. Choose a disposal that has a dishwasher drain connection so that ground food from wash cycles can be flushed through the system. Features such as sound and antisplash baffles and manual reset make units quieter and easier to use.

Care and maintenance: Follow manufacturer's directions. In general, less powerful units can't handle highly fibrous materials, such as corn husks. Take care with any fibrous food, such as artichoke leaves or celery stalks; put in small amounts at a time under flowing water. Standard units can't handle large bones, yet smaller bones, such as poultry bones, help scour the grinding chamber. Overloading causes clogs. For full flushing, run a strong flow of cold water for at least 10 seconds after the grinding stops. Run the disposal every time you add food. Allowing food to build up may result in corrosion from acids that form from rotting waste.

BUDGET STRETCHER

Disposal Alert

•

Use the overload protectors to avoid motor damage. If a disposal stalls, turn it off. Remove the object. Press the reset button on the base under the sink. If it doesn't start, wait a few minutes and push reset again. If it still doesn't start, check the electric panel.

Check manual before disposing of cooking grease.

Cover continuous-feed disposals for protection against small particles that might be ejected from the force of the grinding. Avoid leaning over a running disposal when feeding waste into it. When using a sink that contains a garbage disposal, remove small objects from the water and sink edge before draining, to avoid knocking anything into the grinder.

Garbage disposals are self-cleaning with proper use. Never use corrosives, such as lye or drain cleaners, or acidic household remedies, such as lemon juice or vinegar. These may damage plumbing and cause splash-backs. Some manufacturers recommend enzyme products for clearing clogged drains. Avoid problems by correctly dealing with fibrous items. Follow up the disposal of these items by filling the sink with 2 to 3 inches of cold water. Turn on the disposal and allow the water to run through. As an occasional routine to scour cutting blades, fill the disposal with ice; turn on at first without running water; then as the ice crushes, turn on hot water full force, with the disposal running, until the ice melts and the water drains. Turn off the water first, then the disposal. Meanwhile, heat about 6 quarts of water until very hot but not boiling. Add a cup of chlorine bleach and pour the solution down the disposal. Do not rinse. Diluted bleach won't hurt plumbing but will kill fungus, mold, mildew, and bacteria. Leave disposal and drain unused for several hours or overnight.

TRASH COMPACTORS

A compactor can reduce the kitchen garbage for a family of four to about one bag per week.

Purchase: Freestanding compactors have finished sides and a cabinet top. Built-in models have raw sides; they are made to fit under a counter between cabinets. Most include an air-freshening device, usually a deodorizing spray canister or a charcoal-filter chamber. Freestanding units plug into standard receptacles. Built-ins require carpentry and electrical work. When selecting a unit, consider safety features. Some models may have key locks to keep children out. Check the amount of ram pressure in compacting. A ram or tamp presses down inside the container, compressing the trash. The more it compresses, the heavier the bag gets. If lifting heavy sacks is a problem, check into a bag caddy for lifting compact trash out of the machine.

Care and maintenance: Always read the operating instructions before first use. Never compact containers of poisons, flammable or explosive chemicals, aerosols, or spray paints. Never

TIPTAG № 17
Butcher Block
SAFETY FIRST

- Use separate cutting boards for produce, meats, poultry, and fish to avoid cross-contamination.
- Clean wooden surfaces with warm soapy water, a mild bleach solution, or cleaner for food-prep surfaces.
- If possible, avoid placing raw meat, poultry, or fish on butcher block. If meat, fish, or poultry are cut on butcher block, disinfect immediately. Wash your hands at the same time with hot, soapy water.
- Use cutting boards on top of the butcher block when working with meat, fish, or poultry.
- Sanitize an acrylic cutting board by washing in the dishwasher.

push items into the compactor with your hands or feet. Place trash in the compartment, but don't try to compact the trash yourself.

Regularly clean the exterior with a cloth or sponge dipped in warm, sudsy water. Rinse and dry. Before cleaning inside, turn off the compacting controls and remove the key on locking models. Remove the bag and follow the manufacturer's cleaning instructions. These usually include a reminder about wearing sturdy gloves when cleaning the ram and the inside of the container drawer. Most compactors have a drawer with a slide that tilts and lifts for easy reaching and cleaning. Remove the drawer and vacuum inside the cabinet. Clean the drawer, reusable bin, bag caddy, and ram with a sponge or cloth, using warm, sudsy water. Rinse and dry, replace drawer or reusable bin, and install a new bag. Check air freshener or charcoal filter and replace as necessary.

HOME RECYCLING CENTER

Learn the local regulations for what and how to recycle; then make it as easy as you can to get into the habit of recycling—by considering your space and household routine. Designate a convenient area near the kitchen, where most solid waste is generated, to temporarily collect recyclables. Collect larger amounts of recyclables in a garage or basement area away from household traffic. You will either be carrying bins to the curbside for pickup or loading your car for trips to the recycling center. Make recycling a family activity and encourage everyone to participate. Teach small children about recycling by asking them to carry empty plastic milk jugs to the collection bin. Older children can be responsible for gathering newspapers, cleaning and disposing of cans, and flattening boxes for the collection bin. Provide incentives for recycling by allowing the person who collects the recyclables or carries them to the recycling center to keep any profits—or donate them to a charity.

Kitchen Safety

Safety begins with accident prevention. If you build or remodel, or replace worn-out vinyl, choose slip-resistant flooring. Never use small throw or scatter rugs in the kitchen. If you prefer small rugs or mats at work areas, use only mats and rugs with nonslip backing. If possible, select counters, island, and kitchen table with rounded corners. Do not hang curtains or towels near a range or cooktop.

Have all electrical outlets connected to ground-fault circuit interrupters. Set the water heater temperature at 120 degrees F or less to reduce the risk of scalding. Keep an ABC-rated, 5-pound fire extinguisher in the kitchen (see pages 238–239).

Use proper storage for small appliances, equipment, and household cleaners. If you keep small appliances such as a coffeemaker on the countertop, push them back toward the wall

SAFETY ALERT

Safe on the Range

•

In a household with young children, select a model with controls on the top rather than the front. Never use a stove as a substitute heat source—burners are too hot. Store a full, opened baking soda box in a nearby cabinet to pour on grease fires.

Know Your Kitchen Knives

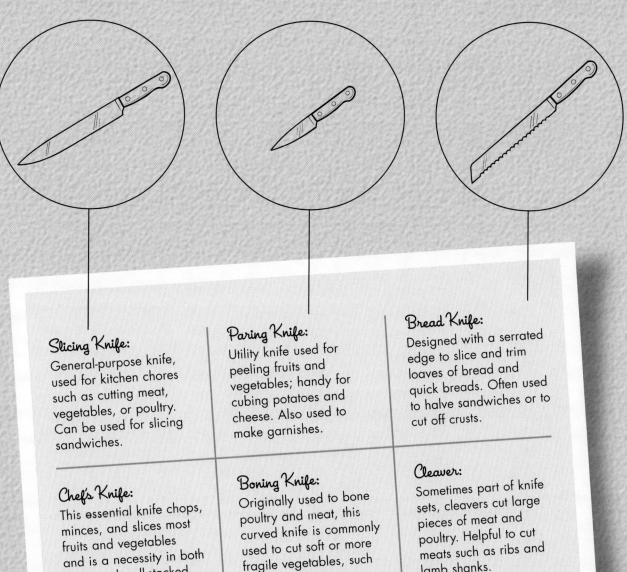

Slicing Knife:
General-purpose knife, used for kitchen chores such as cutting meat, vegetables, or poultry. Can be used for slicing sandwiches.

Paring Knife:
Utility knife used for peeling fruits and vegetables; handy for cubing potatoes and cheese. Also used to make garnishes.

Bread Knife:
Designed with a serrated edge to slice and trim loaves of bread and quick breads. Often used to halve sandwiches or to cut off crusts.

Chef's Knife:
This essential knife chops, minces, and slices most fruits and vegetables and is a necessity in both basic and well-stocked kitchens.

Boning Knife:
Originally used to bone poultry and meat, this curved knife is commonly used to cut soft or more fragile vegetables, such as ripe tomatoes.

Cleaver:
Sometimes part of knife sets, cleavers cut large pieces of meat and poultry. Helpful to cut meats such as ribs and lamb shanks.

with the cords behind them. Never let cords dangle over the countertop. Store infrequently used small appliances in cabinets. Pay particular attention to knives. If you use a knife box, place it out of the reach of small children. As an alternative, install a knife rack safely above the reach of children. Do not store sharp knives in drawers; besides being accessible to little hands, they will be dulled by scraping against gadgets.

Never store cleaners, detergents, insecticides, or other toxic substances in lower cabinets that are accessible to children. Install childproof latches on lower cabinets to keep little hands away from cookware and glass dishes. If vitamins, medications, and alcohol are stored in the kitchen, store them in upper cabinets.

Fighting Kitchen Germs

Sad but true: Even the cleanest looking kitchen may be full of bacteria. Dishcloths and sponges may spread rather than remove bacteria. Two types of bacteria of concern are staphylococcus, which is spread by hand contact, and salmonella, which can be spread from contact with undercooked meat or poultry. Wash your hands thoroughly before and after handling food—particularly when handling raw meat, poultry, or eggs.

CONTROL BACTERIA

To minimize kitchen germs, be vigilant in your storage, cleaning, preparation, and shopping practices. Here's how to be safe.

■ Shop at the supermarket last when running errands. In the store, collect refrigerated and frozen foods last. (In summer, keep an ice chest or cooler in the car if you drive more than 30 minutes.)

■ Do not buy expired food or food in dented or bulging cans. Select frozen foods from below the frost line or load line of the display case (a line is marked on freezers to indicate safety level).

■ Set refrigerator at 40 degrees F or lower and freezer at 0 degrees F.

■ Securely wrap or cover foods to prevent cross-contamination.

■ Thaw frozen foods in covered containers in the refrigerator, in a sink filled with cold water that's replaced every 30 minutes, or in a microwave set to defrost—never at room temperature.

■ Sanitize cutting boards with fresh bleach. If you use wood, purchase hard maple, not soft wood. Sand wood to remove scratches that harbor bacteria; oil according to directions to seal.

■ Refrigerate leftovers immediately. Use containers that provide a large flat surface to allow foods to chill quickly.

■ Use paper towels, not cloths or sponges, to wipe meat juices.

■ Clean preparation surfaces with hot soapy water; rinse thoroughly; sanitize with a solution of 1 tablespoon of chlorine bleach to 1 quart of cold water. Or use a commercial product tested and formulated for food-contact surfaces; check labels to follow correct use.

Sponge vs. Cloth

•

Dishcloths that are reused for kitchen chores carry more germs than sponges do. If cloths are machine-washed and dried after every use, they are cleaner than sponges. Replace sponges frequently—odor is a sign of bacteria.

Buying Upholstered Pieces

- FRAME,161
- SEATS AND CUSHIONS,162
- SHOPPING FOR FABRIC,164
- FIBER AND WEAVES,165,168
- FINISHES,168

Buying Wood Furniture

- WOOD TYPES,169
- DINING TABLE SIZES AND SEATING,169
- CHILDPROOFING FURNITURE,170
- STORAGE UNITS,172
- FINISHES,173
- UNFINISHED FURNITURE,173
- READY-TO-ASSEMBLE FURNITURE,173
- DINING CHAIR STYLES,175
- TELEVISION CABINETS,177

Lighting

- INCANDESCENT,174
- FLUORESCENT,176
- HALOGEN,176
- READING,176
- OVERHEAD AND WALL LIGHTING,176,177
- TASK,178
- CHANDELIER SIZE AND HEIGHT,178
- SPECIALTY LIGHTING,178
- DIMMERS,178
- TYPES OF LIGHTBULBS,179

Carpet & Rugs

- CARPET CONSTRUCTION,180
- CARPET FIBERS,181
- PADDING,182
- ORIENTAL RUGS AND SPECIAL CASES,182
- NATURAL FIBER RUGS,182

Buying Upholstered Furniture

Whether you buy new, vintage, or antique furniture, quality construction and materials are the key concerns. The old adage about people applies equally to furniture: Beauty is often skin deep. Unless good structure and real value lie underneath, the relationship won't last. To make the best choice for a long-term commitment, follow these guidelines:

Start with the two most important factors, comfort and style. As you shop, spend time sitting on each piece you are considering. Move around. Try different positions. Do the height and depth of the seat fit the length of your legs? Can you lean back comfortably? Can you easily get in and out of the seat? Are the arms at a comfortable height?

If you custom-order a piece, ask to sit in one that has the exact same frame and structure. Most stores have an example of each piece on the floor. As you start narrowing down your selection, compare construction and quality. Use the following sections to learn how to choose quality pieces that fit your budget.

THE FRAME

No matter how pretty the piece, unless the frame is strong and well-made, the furniture won't wear well. This may not be critical for an entryway console table, a bedroom slipper chair, or other pieces that are basically decorative accessories, but sturdy construction is vital for pieces meant for daily use. Before you purchase upholstered furniture, consider the following buying points for frames:

■ Kiln-dried hardwood, such as birch, maple, ash, or gum, is more durable than soft woods, such as pine, poplar, or fir. Particleboard is strong but prone to splitting and chipping.

■ Wood joints should be mortise-and-tenon (one piece slides into the other, as Tab A fits into Slot B for a toy or model) or dovetail (finger-like projections that fit together like gears do) and secured with glue. They're much stronger than butted and screwed joints or glued joints. The joints should fit tightly with no gaps.

■ The piece should not feel light or flimsy. If it does, it may tip easily. This can be a problem for families with children or for people with impaired movement who need support to get up or down. A family member with impaired movement, for example, may need to use the arms and back of a chair or sofa for leverage when standing or sitting, and the less sturdy piece may topple.

■ Larger pieces, such as sofas or love seats, should not sag in the

smart ideas

Upholstery Buys

CHECK CONSTRUCTION

Wood should be smooth, evenly colored, and blemish-free. Check that frame pieces fit together tightly with no gaps. Avoid furniture that shows buckling between parts—cushions and frame, fitted pillow and arm, or wooden and upholstered parts. Squeeze padded areas to be sure that they are adequate; you shouldn't be able to feel the frame. Test buttons, tassels, and trim to see if they are firmly attached. Check piping construction.

BE A SAVVY CONSUMER

Read warranties on frame, fabric, cushions, and fabric finish. Ask how the store deals with problems and defective products.

middle. Sagging indicates a lack of proper support and bracing. The sofa may eventually sag more or even break at that weak point.

■ The coils in the seat (and sometimes back) of an upholstered piece act much as the box spring in a mattress does. They give the piece firmness and stability and determine how long it will last. Zigzag, wave-shaped, or interwoven bands are more likely to sag and lose their shape than regular spring-shaped coils. Steel coil springs that are hand-tied where they meet the adjoining coils and frame offer the best stability.

SEATS AND CUSHIONS

Most larger pieces have removable seat and back cushions. As you shop for chairs and sofas, evaluate what will wear best, the look you like, and the degree of firmness you prefer. Decide which of these factors are most important to you. The highest quality upholstery cushions have an inner core of springs similar to the springs in a bed mattress. The springs are generally covered with plain fabric, then wrapped with polyester batting, a layer of polyurethane foam, and a plain muslin cover. The decorative cover zips over all of this. These cushions are extremely durable and unlikely to lose their shape. However, they tend to be firm, so the snuggle-down factor may be low. Unless cushions are wrapped in down, they won't have a soft, cushy, fashionably slouchy look.

Although down-filled cushions look and feel plush, they aren't practical for everyday use. Down, which is not as durable as synthetic materials, flattens and mats down, even before the down wears out.

More common (and more affordable) are cushions made of a solid piece of polyurethane foam covered in polyester batting. A muslin cover is sewn over the cushion; then the decorative cover is zipped in place. As long as high-quality materials are used, these cushions will last for years under normal conditions. The density of the foam and the amount of batting determine how firm the seating is.

Lower on the quality scale are cushions made from a single piece of polyurethane foam with the decorative cover sewn permanently in place. This type of cushion isn't as comfortable as cushions with batting. The cushions may shift within the cover, giving your furniture a slightly askew look that's hard to remedy. The cover cannot be removed for washing or dry cleaning. However, this construction has its place: It is generally economical and makes fine short-term investments for children's room, college dorm rooms, first apartments, or guest rooms. Don't expect long wear.

At the bottom of the quality chain are cushions filled with shredded foam or pellets. The covers are permanently sewn in place. If the seams break, expect a snowstorm of messy little cushion innards.

BUDGET STRETCHER

Durable Seating

•

Shop for chairs and sofas with hand-tied coils, not crimped springs. For long wear and comfort, look for coils that are tied in as many as eight places. Those tied in only four won't last as long, and the springs may pop loose.

Living Room Table Styles

Pedestal:
Available in a range of styles (traditional shown), round pedestal tables work well for lamps, accessories, and beverages. A drawer offers convenient storage.

Nesting:
When space is tight, nesting tables pull out as needed for beverages, snacks, and reading material. Pairs or trios are common and come in a variety of styles and materials.

Demilune:
These half-round tables work well in foyers or entries. Painted or stained, traditional or contemporary, many styles are on the market.

Drop-leaf:
When space is limited, a drop-leaf table is a classic solution that adds extra dining space when needed. Vintage tables, new reproductions, and antiques are readily available.

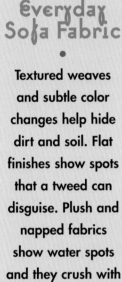

Everyday Sofa Fabric

Textured weaves and subtle color changes help hide dirt and soil. Flat finishes show spots that a tweed can disguise. Plush and napped fabrics show water spots and they crush with wear, resulting in a mottled, discolored appearance.

SOFA AND CHAIR BACKS

Sofa and chair backs may be of the same construction as the seat cushion, or they may be constructed of completely different materials. Like seat cushions, they may be loose or permanently attached. Those with firm construction will not shift or sag, but the look can be stiff. Loose, pillowlike cushions have a softer, more comfy look but will often sag and move around, flopping out of place. They need more fluffing, primping, and straightening. If you purchase a piece with loose cushions, check the construction to see if the sofa back is solid and firm so that the cushions will stay put as much as possible. Some sofa styles have soft floppy cushions that are tacked in place toward the middle. Although the concept sounds promising, it is hard to clean behind these cushions. It's much easier to remove the whole cushion for vacuuming than to try to maneuver a nozzle around a partially attached pillow.

Shopping for fabric: The fabric of an upholstered piece is the most visible sign of quality and also the part most likely to show premature wear or become quickly outdated. When choosing a fabric, consider the following:

■ Neutral colors and patterns will stay in style longer than trendy prints. You'll be less likely to tire of something that doesn't catch your eye the moment you walk into a room. Neutrals also take the backseat and let your accessories shine. If you do want bold pattern in your upholstered pieces, keep it on the smaller ones.

■ Reputable stores show you how a custom-ordered piece will look. If you are shopping at a store where you pick the frame and fabric separately and have the piece custom-made, ask to see a computer image of what the finished piece will look like. The stripe or floral that looks demure on a little swatch may be overpowering on a 5-foot-long sofa. If the store cannot show you a picture or computer image, go elsewhere.

■ Patterned fabric should line up throughout the piece. This is especially important on large pieces such as sofas, where the pattern should be unbroken from top to floor and from side to side. Even though the furniture is made of separate pieces, from a distance it should look as though one piece of fabrics drapes the entire piece.

■ Stores that sell quality upholstered pieces normally allow swatches to be checked out. If possible, keep the swatch several days so you can "live" with it and also see how it looks in different kinds of light. Some stores may ask for a deposit on the swatch, but they should refund it when you return the fabric.

Quality counts: When choosing fabric, consider how your upholstered piece will be used in your home. Sofas, chairs, and ottomans receiving only moderate amounts of wear will do fine with a less durable fabric. However, pieces subjected to daily heavy wear need to be covered in tough, durable, tightly woven fabrics.

■ Fabric cost and grade do not necessarily reflect quality. A lower-cost and lower-grade canvas may be more durable than a more expensive and higher-grade damask because the canvas is cheaper and less complex to produce. The maker may produce more yards of the canvas than the damask, further holding down the cost.

■ Heavy fabrics, such as tapestry, canvas (duck and sailcloth), woven wool, and leather, are generally more durable than lightweight fabrics, such as satin, taffeta, chintz, and linen.

■ Thread count refers to the number of threads per square inch of fabric. For example, a fabric with a 300 thread count has 300 threads per square inch; one with a thread count of 150 has 150 threads per square inch. Generally, the higher the thread count, the more tightly woven the fabric is. The exception is when the threads are especially thick. A heavy wool thread cannot be packed as tightly as a fine cotton thread. When comparing thread counts, compare similar fabrics. The fabric with the higher thread count will wear better, and it is more likely to resist dirt and stains. Open weaves allow both dirt and liquids to penetrate into the fibers and through to the cushion below. Tightly woven fabrics help keep liquid spills on the surface and make cleanup easier.

Fiber and fabric basics: Both fiber and fabric affect the appearance and performance of upholstery. Fiber is the raw material (either natural, synthetic, or a blend) used to make the finished product. When the fiber is woven or knitted, it becomes fabric. Natural fibers come from plants or animals, including cotton, linen, silk, and wool. Other fibers are manufactured and come in two types: regenerated and synthetic. Regenerated fibers are derived from cellulose in cotton and wood pulp, such as rayon and acetate. Synthetic fibers are made entirely from chemicals, such as nylon, polyester, acrylic, and olefin.

Natural fibers often are more luxurious and accept dyes better than synthetics; they may not be as strong or as easy to care for, however. Synthetic and man-made fibers may be stronger, but they may not be as comfortable or as attractive as naturals. Blends can be less expensive than 100-percent-natural fabrics. To significantly affect the appearance and performance of the finished product, a fiber must typically make up at least 20 percent of the blend.

Common upholstery fabrics: Read about the characteristics of commonly used upholstery fabrics to decide what works best for

Home Remedies

BUYING VINTAGE

Check Construction

Furniture purchased at tag sales or thrift stores can be a bargain, but the seller may not know about the construction. Gently lean on the piece in different directions to see if it is sturdy. Check for sagging spots and run your hand over the surface to check for rough areas. Tip the piece over to look for maker and material labels. If the cloth covering the underside is loose, peek at the construction.

Note Smells or Stains

Soil is often only surface-deep. If you reupholster, old fabric won't be a problem. If smells and stains permeate the entire under-construction, the piece will need to be completely rebuilt, especially if it is water damaged.

your style, lifestyle, and budget.

■ Acetate: Regenerated. Developed as an imitation silk. Good resistance to fire, mildew, pilling, and shrinking. Fair resistance to soil. Poor resistance to wear, wrinkling, and fading. Not a good choice for furniture that will receive rough wear or be placed in direct sunlight.

■ Acrylic: Synthetic. Developed as an imitation wool. Good resistance to fire, wear, wrinkling, soiling, and fading. Poor resistance to pilling. Low-quality acrylics may pill excessively in areas that receive high degrees of abrasion. High-quality acrylics are manufactured to pill significantly less.

■ Cotton: Natural. Good resistance to wear, fading, and pilling. Poor resistance to soil, wrinkling, and fire. Surface treatments and blending with other fibers often make up for the weaknesses.

■ Linen: Natural. Good resistance to pilling and fading. Fair resistance to wear. Poor resistance to soiling, wrinkling, and fire. To avoid shrinkage during cleaning, have the fabric treated with a shrink-resistant product.

■ Nylon: Synthetic. Developed as an imitation silk. Good resistance to fire, wrinkling, wear, and soiling. Poor resistance to fading and pilling. Rarely used alone but often blended with other fibers. Nylon is very resilient; in a blend it helps eliminate the crushing of napped fabrics such as velvet. Nylon is one of the strongest fibers.

■ Olefin: Synthetic. Developed as an imitation wool. Good resistance to fire, fading, soil, wear, wrinkling, and pilling. No pronounced weaknesses. A good choice for furniture that will get heavy wear.

■ Polyester: Synthetic. Good resistance to fire, fading, mildew, and wrinkling. Poor resistance to pilling, soiling, and wear. May actually add to the pilling when blended with a low-quality wool. Rarely used by itself in upholstery, but commonly blended to add wrinkle resistance, eliminate crushing of napped fabrics, or reduce fading. More commonly used for the inner materials, cushions, and batting.

■ Rayon: Regenerated. Developed as an imitation silk, linen, or cotton. Good resistance to wear. Poor resistance to fire and wrinkling. Recent developments have made rayon much more practical, although the quality varies widely.

■ Wool: Natural. Good resistance to fire, wear, pilling, fading, wrinkling, and soil. Generally blended with a synthetic fiber to make it easier to clean and to reduce the possibility of felting the fibers (causing them to bond together until they resemble felt) when spot-cleaning. Wet abrasion (scrubbing) or improper steam cleaning may felt pure wool; this process cannot be reversed.

Common upholstery fabrics: Upholstery fabrics are labeled by the type (such as chintz) as well as the fiber (such as cotton). If you have doubts about the durability and weight of a fabric for an

Common Carpet Weaves

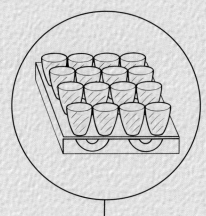

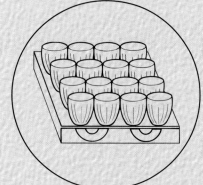

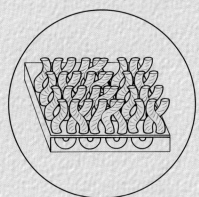

Cut-Pile Saxony:
Many popular berber styles are level-loop with color flecks on a lighter background. Durable for playrooms, family rooms, entries, stairs, and halls.

Cut-Pile Plush:
Two or three loop heights give a multidimensional effect that wears well. Considered a casual look that is ideal for playrooms and dens.

Cut-Pile Frieze:
Often used for adult bedrooms and formal living areas, the deep pile of the cut loops imparts a rich, luxurious feel to a room.

Level Loop:
Twists of pile yarn result in visible ends that create a less formal look. Ideal for casual areas because footprints are minimized.

Multi-Level Loop:
Twisted yarns create an informal look. The curly textured surface minimizes footprints in traffic areas as well as vacuum marks.

Cut and Loop Pile:
Cut and loop yarns give a variety of surface options, including sculptured. Crisp definition helps hide wear and footprints.

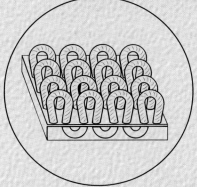

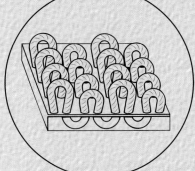

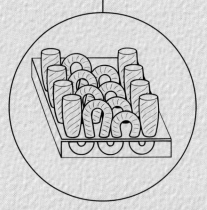

SPACE SAVER

Furniture That Fits

•

Measure the space for your piece and the areas it must pass through. Know the width of doorways, stairs, and halls. If you have tight corners, cut plastic pipe and connect to create the base size. Walk through to be sure furniture can pass snug spaces.

upholstered piece, ask whether it is upholstery weight.

Upholstery Weaves

Product literature and salespeople sometimes refer to how fabrics are woven. Basic weave patterns for fabrics are single horizontal threads that are woven over and under single vertical threads—one by one, alternating an over-under-over-under pattern with each row. This weave produces many variations, as follows:

▶ Close weave: The threads are tightly woven with virtually no space between them; also called tight weave.

▶ Open weave: Threads are loosely woven with space between them.

▶ Jacquard weave: Horizontal and vertical threads are interwoven into a complex design in which threads "float" over others or retreat to the back to create large surface designs. Brocade and damask are examples of this handsome weave.

▶ Pile weave: A plain woven background has loops of fabric added to the top surface. They may be left as loops, or the loops may be cut. Velvet is an example of cut pile.

▶ Rib weave: Two or more vertical threads go over each horizontal thread, creating a raised stripe design.

▶ Twill weave: Similar to a rib weave, twill weave has a diagonal ribbed design. Denim is an example of twill weave.

▶ Sateen weave: Each vertical thread floats over four to eight horizontal threads, goes under one thread, and floats over another set of threads. The spans of unattached threads give a shiny look.

▶ Satin weave: This is the same as sateen weave, except the horizontal threads float over the vertical threads.

Upholstery Finishes

Chemical finishes are commonly applied to fabrics and fibers to enhance their durability. Ask at which point during the manufacturing process the finish is applied, what the finish repels, whether the finish is guaranteed (and for what), whether the finish can be reapplied, and whether the finish affects the cleaning of the fabrics. Typical finishes include the following:

▶ Antibacterial: Resists bacterial growth, including mold and mildew. This is used mainly in bathroom and outdoor fabrics. Mildew-resistant is a related term.

▶ Fireproofing: Makes the fabric less likely to burn.

▶ Fire-retardant: Helps the fabric resist igniting and slows burning.

▶ Flame-resistant: Aids in resisting ignition. This is worth consideration in homes where people smoke or small children may play with matches.

▶ Glazing: Gives a high-gloss finish to fabrics such as chintz.

▶ Mercerization: Improves the strength and luster of cotton.

▶ Sanforized: Limits shrinkage to 1 percent or less; important for furniture with slipcovers.

◗ Stain-resistant or soil-release: Keeps stains and soil from penetrating the surface. Products each have their own process; check the guarantee, life span, and cleaning instructions of these finishes before applying them to upholstery fabrics.

◗ Soil-repellent: Coats the fibers to make easier to remove dirt.

◗ Water-repellent: Helps water bead up on the surface so it will not quickly soak in.

◗ Waterproof: Water will not penetrate the surface.

Buying Wood Furniture

The quality of wood furniture depends on the material, construction techniques, and the type of finish. Hardwood, soft wood, or composite wood is used in furniture construction. Some furniture is constructed from solid wood, but a large percentage of new pieces are manufactured from veneers, which are thin sheets of decorative wood laid over another material.

WOOD TYPES

Hardwoods are more durable than soft woods and typically more expensive. Colors range widely among woods—even those of the same type—and various woods can be stained or bleached to alter their original color. Composite woods are used for shelving, on the back of furniture pieces, and for some modern styles of furniture.

Hardwoods: Among all the hardwoods, cherry, maple, mahogany, oak, teak, and walnut are prized for quality furniture. However, cherry and maple are considered more difficult to craft than the other widely used hardwoods. Hardwood choices are generally a matter of appearance, furniture style, budget, and personal preference.

◗ Birch: Light tan to almost white. Good resistance to shrinking, swelling, and warping. Takes stains well and is often stained to resemble mahogany, walnut, or cherry. Hard to work with for intricate details; it is commonly used in furniture with simple lines, including some contemporary styles.

◗ Ebony: Brown to near black. Often stained black, emphasizing its distinct grain pattern. Very strong but rare. Used mostly in inlays.

◗ Poplar: Light tan often with pink- and green-tinted streaks. One of the weaker hardwoods, but has the same shrinkage rating as teak. Easy to work with; best for interior furniture parts.

◗ Rosewood: Deep red with black graining. Good resistance to shrinking, swelling, warping, and wear. Easy to work with. Quite rare and expensive. Often used as a veneer.

▶Teak: Often used outdoors; extractions, such as silica, make it resistant to rotting. Also used for indoor furniture.

Soft woods: More available than hardwoods, these woods are typically less expensive. They can be a good choice, depending on use and preference. Because surfaces are generally softer than hardwoods, they require extra care to avoid marring or denting.

▶Cedar: Brown to white. Often used for drawer lining or for decorative panels. Only eastern red cedar is naturally moth-repellent. Commonly used for outdoor furniture.

▶Pine (white): Because it was readily available and easy to work with, white pine was used for many primitive pieces. The softness of the wood is why many of these old pieces show traces of wear. Vintage pieces are valued for the patina and reasonable cost; vintage pieces are also frequently painted.

▶Pine (yellow): Tan, orange, yellow. Grainy, and does not finish well. Not a good choice for exposed wood.

Composites: These are manufactured wood products. Prices and performance vary.

▪Plywood: Usually white to tan. Multiple layers of thin sheets of wood are glued and pressed together. Strong and resistant to warping, shrinking, and swelling. Most often used as support. Some contemporary furniture is manufactured from plywood, which can be shaped and bent into permanent contours.

▪Particleboard: Usually light to medium brown. Made of sawdust, small wood chips, and glue or resin that have been mixed together and pressure-treated. It is a common component of inexpensive furniture that is covered with laminates or veneers. It splits easily and often the veneer or laminate pops loose when the particleboard swells and shrinks with moisture changes. A similar product called hardboard is made under higher pressure, which creates an improved product.

VENEERS

Veneers sometimes evoke negative connotations of being inferior to solid wood; in reality they are commonly used on high-quality furniture as well as budget pieces. Veneer is a thin sliver (about 1/28 inch) of wood applied to a wood or plywood base.

A single large slab of wood, such as a tabletop, can warp and split over time. For a tabletop made of a secondary (cheaper) wood, several boards are edge-joined, the covered with a veneer of a finer wood. A veneer can also be applied over plywood. Veneers add interest by making the most of the grain-lines in the wood. Grain-lines can be matched to look like one solid piece, or they can be arranged in diamond, radiating, checkerboard, or other patterns.

When buying veneer furniture, inquire about the base material as well as the face veneer. If the base is of inferior material, a veneer

Common Furniture Woods

Cherry:
Reddish-brown. Good resistance to shrinking, swelling, and warping; dyes well. Easy to detail for decorative carving.

Pine:
Clear, near white. Poor resistance to shrinking, swelling, and warping. Soft grain; easy to work with but not always durable.

Walnut:
Dark grayish-brown. Often stained darker. Good resistance to swelling and warping. Takes stains evenly and carves well.

Maple:
Light beige to tan. Good resistance to shrinking, warping, and wear. Very hard. Difficult to detail; sometimes dyed.

Mahogany:
Reddish-brown to red. Good resistance to shrinking and warping. Softer hardwood, easy to detail for carving. Takes rich, dark stains.

Oak:
Light pinkish-brown. Good resistance to shrinking and warping. Takes stains evenly, generally available, carves well for detailing.

will not solve all the potential problems. Check the underside of tables; pull out drawers or slide out shelves and check areas that are not covered by the veneer. If the base material is particleboard or a soft, open-grained wood, it may still warp and split. Run your fingernail along the edge of the veneer to see if it is tightly attached to the base material. If there are gaps and loose spots right after manufacturing, the veneer will pop loose eventually.

LAMINATES

Laminates cover a base material. Most laminate is glued to a medium-density fiberboard or particleboard, but some office and kitchen pieces have laminates applied to wood to make the furniture more durable, more practical, smoother, and easier to clean. Such laminates generally mimic the wood used for table legs, chairs, and other exposed surfaces. Check the match between the laminate and wood as well as the composition of the core wood.

Commonly, laminates are solid colors that are used in children's, contemporary, or casual furniture. The core material is usually particleboard or medium-density fiberboard. Particleboard may split or warp, and screws work loose, resulting in unstable furniture. Fiberboard is more stable, and the furniture is likely to be of higher quality and a better investment. When considering laminate furniture, check quality, using the methods for veneer furniture.

CONSTRUCTION TECHNIQUES

The methods used to assemble furniture determine its durability. Joints should be mortise-and-tenon or dowel and should be stable and secure. Butted and mitered joints are weaker and won't stand up to heavy wear unless reinforced. Table legs and chair legs should be reinforced with triangular or diagonal blocks of wood that will keep the joints square and help stabilize the furniture when it is moved or when pressure is applied to the surface. To check for stability, apply pressure at the diagonals.

BUYING STORAGE UNITS

Shelving units and armoires: Check tall pieces for stability. If a unit is top-heavy, it is more likely to topple over when filled with books and heavy objects. Some shelves and armoires have adjustable feet to compensate for uneven floors. You can adjust the feet with shims. Some large pieces have hidden casters.

Movable shelves should be tight and secure but still slide in and out with ease. Thin wires or tiny plastic clips will not support the weight of books for long. For stability, the back of a storage unit should be tightly attached and not bowed. Thin wood or cardboard backing is a sign of lesser quality.

Drawers in storage units should slide in and out evenly and easily. Drawers with rollers and glides on each side are best, but one center bottom roller and glide is satisfactory if the drawer won't get heavy

SPACE SAVER

Right Size Tables

The standard proportion for a coffee table is one-half to two-thirds the length of the sofa it will accompany. Leave enough space between for passage and leg room; keep it close enough so the table isn't floating.

use. A pull on each side of the drawer front (as opposed to a single center pull) also helps drawers slide evenly. All drawers should have a stop so they cannot be accidentally pulled all the way out. Dust liners that form a divider between each drawer are usually found on only the highest quality furniture. Drawers are often finished only on the front or for a few inches on the sides. This is not necessarily a sign of poor quality, although the highest quality drawers will be completely finished. Even unfinished wood should be smooth.

DINING TABLE AND CHAIRS

Tables for a formal dining room, informal dining room, or kitchen need to be large enough to allow adequate "elbow-room" for comfort without crowding. Allow 24 to 30 inches per person and at least 30 inches across the table. Standard dining height is 29 to 30 inches.

Check leg placement on any table that will be used for seating. A leg at or near each corner, a center pedestal, multiple pedestals, or trestles are stable and common. Complex and artful shapes also work well, as long as the leg placement doesn't interfere with comfortable seating. Lean on the table from all angles to see whether it tips or wobbles.

Dining chairs should have fairly upright backs, so that diners can sit comfortably close to the table and still have the support of the chair back. Avoid chairs with legs that splay out widely. They fit awkwardly at the table and are easy to trip over, and they may be weaker than other chairs. Slide chairs up to the table. Chairs and table should fit easily. Arms should be low enough so that the chair seats slide under the table. For passage and serving while people are seated at the dining table, allow 24 inches behind each chair.

Before you purchase a dining table and chairs, sit at the table. Determine whether there is adequate space between the apron (the skirtlike extension around the underside of the table) and your thighs. If you decide to use lower chairs because of the apron depth, check that the chairs are still high enough for dining.

FINISHES

The finish on wood furniture is often the first thing to show wear. Manufacturers use the following terms to describe treatments applied to wood:

Bleach: Lightens the color of the wood. Some woods will become almost white while still showing grain. A clear coating, usually lacquer, is applied over bleached wood.

Enamel: Gloss or semigloss paint is applied over one or more primer coats of paint, hiding the wood color and grain. It gives the furniture a tough, cleanable surface that resists scratches.

Lacquer: Generic term for quick-drying synthetic finishes that are brushed or sprayed on, usually in multiple layers. Lacquers may be clear to show grain or colored to change natural color and grain.

Oil: Linseed, tung, or other oils are rubbed into the wood surface in several coats, with the excess wiped from the surface after each application. The result is a natural appearance with enhanced color and grain. Oil finishes are delicate but easily restored.

Paint: Gloss or semigloss paint is often applied to inferior woods to hide imperfections; however, painted furniture in all styles is always popular and easy to achieve. Paint can be applied in a variety of techniques and finishes.

Shellac: A gum dissolved in alcohol leaves a clear coat after the alcohol evaporates. Shellac is easily damaged and will show water spots and other marks. It is often used as a sealer.

Stain: The colored pigment penetrates the wood surface to alter the color. Stain used in combination with a wood type generally indicates that the appearance differs from the actual wood type. For example, mahogany-stained furniture is often made of birch that is stained to resemble mahogany. A clear finish is applied over the stained wood.

Varnish: A gum dissolved in a solvent. As the solvent evaporates, it leaves a transparent coating with a brownish tone. Varnish may be matte, satin, or glossy. Varnish is used on many antiques and reproduction pieces.

Wax: Provides a protective surface for a finish while maintaining a natural appearance. Wax may darken the wood slightly and needs to be reapplied periodically. The amount of buffing determines the sheen. Wax is also used over shellac, varnish, or an oiled finish to add protection and sheen.

Lighting
INCANDESCENT

This is the original filament-style lightbulb that has been around for decades and is readily available at retail stores. The color of the emitted light is warm and flattering, mimicking natural light. The light level is easily controlled with a variety of different wattages.

Incandescent bulbs are available in decorative shapes (candle flame for chandeliers, oversize globe for exposed downlights, or tubular for modern styles) and clear, white, and colored styles. Clear bulbs give a bright, harsh light and are often used in high-tech styles, where the bulb and its workings are part of the design, or in fixtures with clear glass shades. White bulbs are the most common. They soften the light to help prevent eyestrain when reading.

Popular Dining Chair Styles

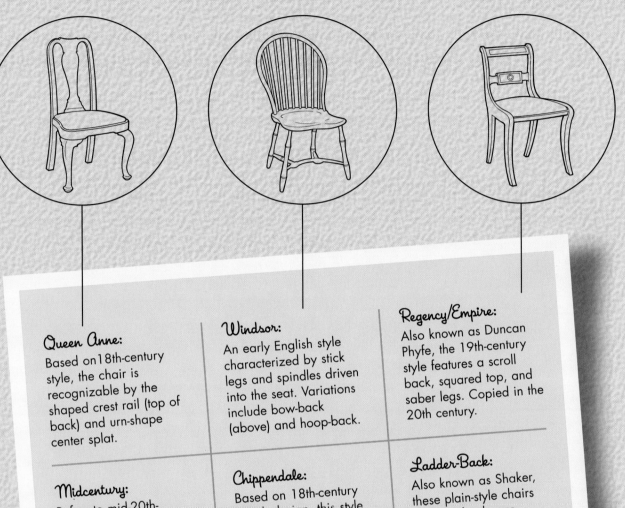

Queen Anne:
Based on 18th-century style, the chair is recognizable by the shaped crest rail (top of back) and urn-shape center splat.

Windsor:
An early English style characterized by stick legs and spindles driven into the seat. Variations include bow-back (above) and hoop-back.

Regency/Empire:
Also known as Duncan Phyfe, the 19th-century style features a scroll back, squared top, and saber legs. Copied in the 20th century.

Midcentury:
Refers to mid 20th-century designs for the modern house styles of the period. This chair is by Heywood-Wakefield, a well-known company.

Chippendale:
Based on 18th-century British design, this style is noted for elaborate splats (center back support). May include ball-and-claw feet.

Ladder-Back:
Also known as Shaker, these plain-style chairs with slat backs are associated with country furniture. Seats may be woven from rush or tape.

Colored bulbs are used for mood lighting. The most common color is pink, which yields a softer glow than white bulbs.

Incandescent bulbs also come in special-use varieties, such as spotlight, long-life, and anti-vibration (sometimes called overhead garage door) bulbs. Anti-vibration bulbs are a good choice for high-traffic areas in multistory homes, where the bulb on one level is jarred by people walking above.

FLUORESCENT

Fluorescent bulbs offer true light, although the light is not as pure and friendly as incandescent. Fluorescent bulbs are more expensive than incandescent but last much longer and are more energy efficient. Over time, they generally save money. The long tubes make them ideal for recessed ceilings in basements and other low-ceiling areas. The original ring-shape fluorescent bulbs are still available. Fluorescents are also available as screw-in bulbs that fit many lamp and ceiling fixtures. Before purchasing a fluorescent bulb for a light fixture, check that it fits the socket and does not extend beyond the shade. Because fluorescent bulbs are long-lasting (some last up to seven years), they are ideal for hard-to-reach areas.

HALOGEN

The newer bulbs on the block boast a crisp white light that intensifies the colors of the room. Halogen bulbs are more common and less expensive than they were in the early 1990s, but they are still pricey compared to incandescent bulbs. They are designed to be long-lasting, but common variables can shorten their life considerably. Contact with any type of oil can drastically reduce their life span. Oil from fingerprints left during installation of the bulb can cut the bulb's duration by up to half. Airborne oils from cooking, fireplaces, and perfumed sprays have a less drastic impact but still shorten the longevity of the bulb. Accumulated dust has a similar effect on the bulb. To help the bulbs last longer, wear disposable plastic gloves or a plastic sandwich bag over your hand whenever handling a new bulb. Dust the bulb frequently with an untreated feather duster (carefully remove stray feathers afterward) or use canned air (formulated to clean computer keyboards and cameras) that has no additives.

A halogen bulb gets very hot; let it cool completely before removing it. Halogen ceiling lamps should hang far enough from the ceiling that they do not scorch the ceiling, and those hanging over a table should be high enough that they cannot come in contact with centerpieces or overheat persons sitting below them. Halogen bulbs provide an exceptionally strong light from a small bulb, allowing for many design possibilities. They also work well with dimmers.

OVERHEAD LIGHTING

Ambient lighting may not dispense enough light for individual tasks,

FAMILY FRIENDLY

Reading Light

Bedside lighting should be in the 60- to 100-watt range for incandescent bulbs. The standard bedside lamp height is 28 to 32 inches. The incandescent bulb of a desk lamp should be about 15 inches above the surface and 60 to 100 watts.

but it should have sufficient brightness to support the room's basic activities—playing games, watching television, reading, or dining, for example. Install fixtures high enough so that even your tallest friends won't bump their heads.

Match the style of the fixture to the room's architectural style rather than the furniture style. With the exception of the dining room and entryway, the central light in a room should not be a major focal point. When purchasing a new overhead light, check the total wattage of the current light. If it provides adequate light, pick a replacement fixture that uses about the same total wattage. If the room has always seemed dark, use a higher-wattage light and install a dimmer switch. In large or long rooms, more than one ceiling light may be needed.

WALL LIGHTING

The two types of electric sconces (wall lamps) are direct-wire and plug-in. Direct-wire sconces have no exposed cords and are permanently wired into an outlet in the wall. An electrician is needed to install direct-wire sconces. Some direct-wire sconces operate from light switches in the room and turn on and off with the ceiling lights or from a separate switch. Others have a switch attached to the sconce and are turned on independently. Determine your needs before purchasing a direct-wire sconce. If it is to be a part of the room's total lighting, select one that turns on at the switch. If you want to use it independently, such as for bedside reading after the main light is turned out, choose the kind with its own switch.

Plug-in sconces hook to the wall with brackets and are plugged into an existing outlet. Although these are easier and less expensive to install than direct-wire sconces, the exposed cord from the fixture to the outlet can be unsightly. Cord strips that are available at home improvement and lighting centers attach to the wall to encase the wire. They often match the metal in the lamp (brass, silver) or can be painted to match the painted wall color. Plug-in sconces are operated by a switch on the lamp. To turn the sconce on and off at the wall, plug the cord into an outlet controlled by a wall switch.

Most sconces fit close to the wall and direct light up or down. Up-lighting enhances the room; down-lighting brightens specific areas. The hinged arm on swing-arm wall lamps allows them to be positioned against the wall or to extend away from the wall. These work well when there is no room for a side table and lamp but additional light is needed for tasks such as reading or needlework.

smart ideas

Electronics

STASH THE TELEVISION

If you plan to place your television in a storage unit, take the TV measurements (height, width, and depth) with you when you shop. Check that the storage unit outlet holes are large enough to accommodate a plug. If you find a wardrobe without holes that otherwise fits your TV, drill holes and reinforce or add a shelf for the TV.

PLAN FOR VIEWING

Consider seating before you buy a unit. If you won't have a straight-on view of the screen, invest in a reinforced television shelf that swivels or pulls out and swivels. If you collect videos, look for a unit with extra storage space.

SPACE SAVER

Chandelier Height

Before hanging a chandelier, determine the dining table location. Use a less obvious fixture if the table is moved frequently. Standard distance between the bottom of the chandelier and the tabletop is 30 to 36 inches. The chandelier should be 2 feet narrower than the table.

Swing-arm lamps come in both direct-wire and plug-in styles.

TASK LIGHTING

Because ambient lighting doesn't cover the entire room, table and floor lamps usually provide additional light. Task lighting casts light in specific areas for certain jobs. For task lighting, soft white bulbs are better than the clear or colored variety. If you experience glare, the wattage is too high. Three-way bulbs or a light controlled by a dimmer switch can adjust the light level.

For the most comfort, place a table lamp so that the bottom of the shade is approximately at eye level. When the shade is higher, the glare from the bulb causes eyestrain; lower lamp light sheds the light onto the table instead of the work. Keep table lamp in proportion to the table. As a general rule, the shade should be approximately two-thirds the height of the lamp base, deep enough so that a small portion of the neck (the fitting between the lamp and socket) is visible, and about one-and-a-half times the width of the lamp base. Some retailers code lamps and shades to make it easy to mix and match shades and bases successfully. Rules and proportions vary with each lamp base and shade shape.

SPECIALTY LIGHTING

Accent lighting draws attention to an aspect of the room, such as art. Recessed spotlights and track lights are the most common accent lights, but sconces, uplights, decorative spotlights, and some table and floor lamps also can provide accent light.

Spotlighting: To draw attention to a specific item, such as artwork, place an accent light at a 30-degree angle and focus its beam on the object. Approximately three times the room's normal light level is required to create a spotlighted focal point.

Wall washing: This works well when a wall or multiple objects on the wall are the focal point. A row of accent lights that evenly brightens the entire area should be placed on the ceiling 2 to 3 feet from the wall. On an especially high ceiling, this lighting should be 3 to 4 feet from the wall.

Wall grazing: Stone or brick walls, fireplaces, and textural areas can be emphasized by skimming a row of lights down the surface. Track or recessed lights should be placed 6 to 12 inches from the wall and aimed down and across the wall.

DIMMERS

Varying light levels can enhance almost any room of the house. Dimmers are commonly used in the dining room; however, kitchens, bathrooms, bedrooms, and entryways can benefit from bright light, which is needed for everyday tasks, and softer light that creates an intimate mood.

Before purchasing a dimmer switch, check to see whether your overhead light can be dimmed. If it can, buy the switch to match

Right Bulb for the Job

Fluorescent Bulbs: Chosen for long life and energy efficiency, the bulbs are manufactured for newer lamps designed for fluorescents.

Tubular Bulbs: With a candelabra base, these are used to highlight art and sheet music. They also are used in some small accent lamps.

Reflector: Designed for ceiling or wall track lighting and recessed fixtures, these coated bulbs provide directional light.

Three-Way: Used for lamps with three-way switches, these bulbs are an easy way to create mood lighting without dimmers.

Halogen: In fixtures and lamps, these bulbs provide clear white light. Do not use in homes with small children; the bulbs get quite hot.

Fluorescent Tubes: Cool, long-lasting, and energy-efficient, these tubes are practical for overhead lighting in utility areas.

Compact Fluorescent: Designed for undercounter spaces and tight spaces, these generate less heat and last longer than incandescent bulbs.

Globes: Clear or white, these round bulbs are sized for lighted vanities as well as decorative indoor and outdoor lantern-type lighting.

Incandescent: Classic for warm, soft light or for light tinted by colored bulbs, the easy-to-find bulbs are used for lamps and overhead fixtures.

Chandelier: These candle-shape bulbs, which may be displayed without a shade, are made for chandeliers and some sconces and lamps.

your light style. Unless equipped with a special dimmer at installation, most fluorescent lights and bulbs cannot be dimmed. Some halogen lights also require special dimming switches. Dimmers are available in toggle, rotary dial, or touch-sensitive styles.

Some dimmers have two components: One automatically turns the light to full power or a preset power; the other adjusts the light. Deluxe models automatically adjust lighting to preset positions or control multiple lights from a single switch. Occasionally, a dimmer interferes with cordless telephones or stereo equipment. Ask for a dimmer with a noise filter and check that the outlet is grounded.

Dimmer attachments also are available for floor and table lamps at hardware, home improvement, and lighting centers. If a lamp with a dimmer control occasionally buzzes, the noise is usually caused by bulb filaments that vibrate when the power cycles on and off at the lower settings. Switch to lower wattage bulbs to solve the problem.

On-line dimmers: These slider devices fit into the cord of the lamp. Splice the cord apart, then clamp the cord into the dimmer attachment. The teeth in the attachment will pierce the cord and work in the same manner as an on-line switch. For simplicity, place the dimmer about 6 inches from the base of the lamp.

Socket dimmers: A socket with a rotary dimmer switch can be purchased and used to replace the lamp's existing socket.

Plug-in dimmers: These separate dimmers often operate by a remote control plugged into the wall, then into the lamp plug. No wiring is involved.

Carpet and Rugs

For both wall-to-wall carpet and area rugs, quality of materials and construction is important to how well the flooring will wear. Over 90 percent of the carpet sold today is synthetic and made to resemble wool. Synthetic carpet is practical for most families because synthetics are stain-repellent and colorfast and the fibers can be altered to create special effects. Each synthetic has its own properties, and often fibers are blended to take advantage of the strengths of each fiber. With the exception of some cotton carpeting, wool is the only natural fiber used in home carpeting. Wool carpet is durable, static-resistant, resilient, comfortable, lustrous, and attractive. Although harder to clean than synthetics, it is still the standard for good-quality carpet.

QUALITY CONSTRUCTION

Before purchasing carpet, consider how it will be used. For high-traffic areas, buy the best quality you can afford. Comparison shop among brands by looking at the performance rating guidelines. When you shop for carpet, you may notice that some, but not all, carpet is rated on a scale for use. The No. 4- and No. 5-rated carpets are best for high-traffic areas. No. 2 and No. 3 are acceptable for low traffic areas, such as formal living rooms and adult bedrooms. Some rating systems use a 10-point scale with No. 8 through No. 10 as the top-rated carpets.

When purchasing carpet, check the density, twist, and thickness of the yarns. The more closely packed the loops or piles, the longer the carpet will last. With the sample face up, bend the sample over your hand. If a great deal of backing shows, it is not a dense weave or tuft. The less backing that is visible when the carpet is bent or ruffled, the better. Tightly twisted yarns also wear longer. Rub a single fiber between your fingers in both directions; if the fiber easily untwists or becomes fuzzy, the carpet will wear quickly from traffic and moving furniture across it.

Tufting is the most common construction method. Yarns are pushed up through backing to leave a loop on the surface of the carpet. Loops vary from standard length to flat cuts that resemble velvet pile to loop-and-pile patterns. A second backing is applied to hold the tufts in place. Woven carpets are constructed so that the pile is part of the fabric, and there is no separate backing.

Dyeing and finishing are also important in how your carpet will look and wear. Carpet can be colored before construction when fibers are made (solution dyeing) or after the fibers are made into yarns. Most rugs are constructed from dyed yarns. The finishing process gives the carpet its final appearance; it involves vacuuming to remove lint, removing loose carpet fibers, and shearing the tips of the fibers for cut-pile styles.

When measuring and purchasing carpet, keep in mind that most carpet is produced in 12- or 15-foot widths. To estimate how much you will need, multiply the length (feet) by width (feet) of the room for square footage. Add about 10 percent to account for the room shape and pattern matches. Have the installer make final measurements before purchasing to ensure accuracy. Before you finalize a purchase, ask the retailer to give you a complete cost estimate in writing that includes the cushion, installation, moving furniture, and disposing of old floor coverings. (If you are replacing carpet that is in reasonably good condition, find out if a nonprofit agency or charity in your area can use it.)

SPECIAL CASES

Woven, tied, and imitations: Handmade carpets and rugs are often expensive and intended for decorative, rather than daily, use. Hand-knotted or hand-tied rugs have individual yarns that are

TIPTAG № 19
Carpet Fibers
COMPARE QUALITIES:
- Acrylic is warm, soft, and resists soil and wear. Color and texture may be glossy, and it is prone to crushing. Moderately priced.
- Nylon takes dyes well for good color range. The dull to glossy finish resists mildew. Static-resistant treatments available.
- Olefin is durable but limited in color and pattern. Excellent water resistance; glossy, wavy fibers.
- Polyester resembles wool in texture and wide range of colors. Crushing is possible.
- Wool has excellent texture, resists soil and wear. Takes dye well; may fade in strong sunlight. Expensive.

tied onto the background fabric. Handwoven rugs are made in a similar method, but the yarns are not tied in place. Hooked rugs are made by hand using a similar process to tufted rugs. Braided rugs have fabric strips braided together and handsewn into spiral-shape design. Loom-woven rugs have strips or small bundles of fabric trapped between the warp and weft threads of a hand loom. Imitations of the latter two styles are also commercially produced and generally less expensive.

Oriental and Oriental-style: Area and throw rugs are made with the same basic techniques as wall-to-wall carpets. Some room-size rugs are crafted from bound carpet pieces; others have specialized designs. The broad term "Oriental rugs" usually refers to an area rug with a very short dense pile, brilliant colors, and detailed pattern. Antique Oriental rugs and high-quality new rugs are hand-knotted. They are investment pieces and should be purchased from reputable dealers, not from traveling sales.

Many less expensive Oriental-style rugs on the market are machine-made using a similar process as carpet. Always check fiber content, tightness of the weave, and strength of the backing. Inexpensive Oriental-style rugs may not be colorfast. Flat woven wool kilim rugs or wool dhurrie rugs are typically sold by reputable dealers who also sell Oriental rugs. Kilim and dhurrie rugs made of wool are durable and budget-stretching alternatives to Oriental rugs.

Natural fibers: Rugs made from grasses and other natural materials add texture but not much softness. Sisal, coir, and rush are the most common, but other exotic materials make their way into stores periodically. Reserve these rugs for special uses, such as for summer in your living room or a porch or sunporch. Avoid damp areas (including under floor plants) because these materials tend to hold moisture and grow mildew. Some are rougher and more uncomfortable than others, making them a poor choice for areas where people will sit on the floor or walk barefoot. Coir, which is made from coconuts, can be especially bristly. This rough texture also holds pet hair, sewing threads, and other small particles.

Check to see that the construction is tight and that any stitching is secure. If the rug is bound, it is better to have the binding sewn rather than glued in place. Natural rugs are sometimes dyed or painted with designs. Paint may eventually wear off the surface, leaving the design much fainter than when purchased. Dyed designs will fade more gradually and evenly over time.

Use pads to protect the floor and your rug when placing the rug on carpet, tile, or wood. Pads help to hold the rugs in place and prevent rugs from slipping and wadding as they are trod upon; they also protect the floor beneath in case the rug is not colorfast. Replace worns pads to ensure the floor is protected.

BUDGET STRETCHER

Long Life For Carpet
•

A quality pad extends the life of carpet. Choose a thin and firm pad. For cut-pile carpet, use a pad with a maximum thickness of $7/16$ inch. A berber carpet pad should be no more than $3/8$ inch thick.

7

Choosing Furniture

- CHEST OF DRAWERS, 185
- BED FRAME, 186
- MATTRESS AND BOX SPRINGS, 186
- BED ALTERNATIVES, 188
- NIGHTSTAND, 189

Comfortable Environment

- LIGHTING; BEDSIDE LIGHTING, 189
- CEILING FANS, 190
- WINDOW COVERINGS, 192

Making the Bed

- PILLOWS; MATERIALS; CARE, 193, 194, 195
- COMFORTER AND DUVET, 194
- BED COVERINGS, 196
- ELECTRIC BLANKETS, 197
- ALLERGY CONTROL, 197

Kids' Rooms

- CRIB SAFETY, 198
- WINDOW TREATMENT SAFETY, 198
- BUNK BED SAFETY, 200

Bathrooms

- CLEANING TIPS, 199
- LOW-FLOW TOILETS, 201
- VENT FANS, 201
- SINK STYLES AND MATERIALS, 201
- TUBS AND SHOWERS, 202
- ACCESSIBILITY, 202
- LIGHTING, 202

Choosing Furniture

Before buying bedroom furniture, evaluate your needs. Other than the bed, most bedroom furniture is designed for storage. Rooms with ample closet space will benefit from drawer units in varying sizes. In rooms that have skimpy closet hanging space, consider an armoire or furniture unit that combines hanging rods and a few drawers. Some units with door-covered shelves can have a hanging rod substituted for the shelves. If you have a television and stereo equipment in the bedroom, consider an armoire that is designed for electronics.

CHEST OF DRAWERS

Deep drawers work well for large items; however, socks, jewelry, and small items tend to get lost or jumbled when stacked deeply. Look for units that feature both shallow and deep drawers for the most practical storage. If your wardrobe includes many folded items, consider using shelves instead of drawers. It's easier to find what you are looking for when you scan shelves rather than dig through drawers.

Drawer construction is one of the most essential elements of bedroom furniture. Drawers should be made of solid wood and the surfaces should be smooth to the touch, whether finished or unfinished. Finished drawers are less likely to swell and stick in humid climates. To inspect, remove one or more of the drawers and check corners for squareness. Joints at the back of the drawer should be dovetail. The sides and front should be attached with a grooved dovetail joint where the sides slip into a wedge-shape cutout in the drawer front. The bottom of the drawer should sit in a groove in the front and sides of the drawer. Inferior drawers have the sides, front, back, and bottom nailed and glued together. As the drawers wear and swell with temperature and humidity changes, the joints may loosen.

Drawers that don't operate easily or evenly are frustrating, so check for smooth movement when the drawers are opened and closed. Drawers should sit on a single center rail or double side rails that have rollers similar to those in kitchen drawers—making the drawers stable and easy to operate. Drawers should have a stop at the end so that they can be removed when necessary, but so that they do not pull all the way out when opened daily. High-quality drawers have dust panels between them made of thin wooden sheets used as dividers to prevent items from falling out the back and into a

smart ideas

Fit Tight Spaces

BIG BED UPSTAIRS

Larger mattresses and box springs often won't fit around tight corners, up stairways, or into elevators. If you have that situation, shop for split box springs or even a split-spring mattress. King-size box springs often come in two pieces. Other sizes have hinges in the middle so they bend.

SEATING AND SLEEPING TOO

Futons double as sofas by day and beds by night. The futon, which is the mattress, is typically made of cotton batting or a foam core covered with muslin or mattress ticking. It should be at least 8 inches thick for comfort and to fit sheets. The frame should fold out smoothly.

drawer below. They also help to keep the drawer contents cleaner.

Determine whether drawer pulls are comfortable to use and securely attached. Two small pulls or one long pull contributes to easy opening and closing. Check the inside of the drawer to see how the handles are attached. Pulls that work loose can be tightened with a screw or with a nut and bolt (screws are superior because they don't protrude, snag clothing, or scratch your hand). Methods of attachment vary with the pull style. Bolts should not protrude more than one-half inch. Check the construction of the furniture case or frame in the same manner as you would check drawers.

BED FRAME

The first decision to make when buying a bed is size. Headboards and footboards will add 3 to 4 inches to each end. Bed coverings also add about 3 inches to the sides. Standard bed sizes are

▸ Twin: 38–39×75 inches
▸ Extra-long twin: 38–39×80 inches
▸ Double/Standard: 54×75 inches
▸ Queen: 60×80 inches
▸ King: 76–78×80 inches
▸ California King: 72×84 inches

Draw your room dimensions on graph paper and sketch in the furniture and various bed sizes to determine what bed size will work best. Allow 36 inches of clear space on at least one side of the bed for movement and changing bed linens. To get an idea of which bed size works for you, lay newspapers, towels, or rugs in the room and walk around the space. As you shop for bed frames, look for adequate slats for supporting the box spring and mattress and determine that the slats fit tightly into the frame. For beds designed to be used without box springs, a solid base provides support and even wear.

MATTRESS AND BOX SPRING

Industry officials and salespeople recommend "test driving" a mattress before making a final decision. If you will share the bed with someone, take him or her along. Wear comfortable clothing and easy-to-remove shoes and leave your dignity behind. Lie on the bed, move around, bounce a little, and sit on the edge. If you sit in bed to read or work, sit in the position you are likely to use. Firm does not always mean better; it comes down to personal preference and body shape. The mattress should support your spine and have a bit of give at the pressure points where your body sinks deeper into the mattress. No mattress is right for everyone.

Check labels and cutaway samples to see how the mattress is constructed. The most common type of mattress is innerspring, which is made of tempered spring coils covered with layers of padding and upholstery. Compare the number of coils and their

BUDGET STRETCHER

Need New Pillows?

•

Place the pillow on the floor and fold it in half. For down or feather pillows, squeeze out the air. When you release it, the pillow should return to normal shape. For synthetic pillows, place a medium-size tennis shoe on the pillow. The pillow should spill the shoe and return to shape.

How to Make Your Bed

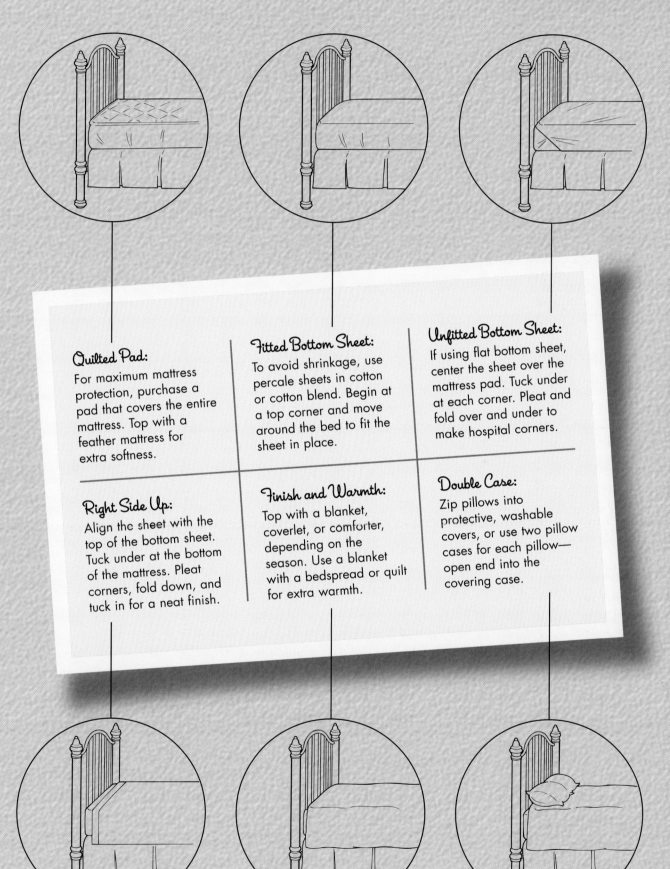

Quilted Pad:
For maximum mattress protection, purchase a pad that covers the entire mattress. Top with a feather mattress for extra softness.

Fitted Bottom Sheet:
To avoid shrinkage, use percale sheets in cotton or cotton blend. Begin at a top corner and move around the bed to fit the sheet in place.

Unfitted Bottom Sheet:
If using flat bottom sheet, center the sheet over the mattress pad. Tuck under at each corner. Pleat and fold over and under to make hospital corners.

Right Side Up:
Align the sheet with the top of the bottom sheet. Tuck under at the bottom of the mattress. Pleat corners, fold down, and tuck in for a neat finish.

Finish and Warmth:
Top with a blanket, coverlet, or comforter, depending on the season. Use a blanket with a bedspread or quilt for extra warmth.

Double Case:
Zip pillows into protective, washable covers, or use two pillow cases for each pillow—open end into the covering case.

construction, the number of padding layers and their materials, and special features. The higher the number of coils, the better the bed will wear. A guideline is 300 coils for a double, 375 for a queen, and 450–600 for a king, each side topped with several layers of upholstery, one or more layers of foam, and a quilted pillow top.

Check the warranty. Some manufacturers and stores offer a "sleep guarantee" or test period. If after buying the mattress, you find it's not the right one for you, they will swap it for a different style. Check on delivery costs: If they charge for each change, it can get costly. Don't base the useful life of your mattress on the warranty, which is protection against defects and faulty workmanship, not loss of comfort. Test your old mattress twice a year as you would a new one to be sure it is still comfortable and offers adequate support.

Most mattresses are about 9 inches thick; some manufacturers offer "extra deep" mattresses, which may or may not mean more comfort. Comparison shop before assuming that deeper is better, and be aware that your choices in bedding may be limited—contour sheets will need to be deep enough to accommodate a deep mattress or they won't stay in place.

ALTERNATIVES

Water beds: Soft-side water beds have a shell similar to an innerspring mattress, a quilted cover, and they look like innerspring mattresses. The center usually consists of water-filled cylinders. Hard-side water beds rely on the bed frame to keep the bladder-style mattress in shape. There is no padded cover on these traditional water beds, and they must be used with a heater because the cool room temperature water will draw heat from your body, causing a chilly sensation. The vinyl covering should be at least 20 millimeters thick; check to see if sturdy patch kits are available. The bed should also have a liner in case of rupture. Baffles, cylinders, and antiwave devices control the amount of movement.

Sofa beds: Today's sleeper sofas are improved over older versions. The sofa is more comfortable and often not recognizable as a foldout unit; the bed is less cotlike and usually has a sturdy mattress that offers support, and the folding mechanisms work easily. Sofa beds range in size from twin (a large chair) to queen (a large sofa), but are sometimes shorter than a conventional bed.

Determine your priority when purchasing a sofa bed. Will it be used as a sofa daily? If so, the comfort of the sofa takes the front seat. If it will be primarily used as a bed, either for you or a guest, the comfort of the bed is of utmost importance. When planning a room arrangement around a sofa bed, allow at least 4 feet for folding out the sofa. Furniture placed in front of the sofa bed should be lightweight or easily movable.

BUDGET STRETCHER

Sets Make Sense

Make your new mattress wear longer by buying the accompanying box spring. Box springs in good condition take the brunt of the wear. The exception: bunk beds with padded bunk boards that don't need to be replaced.

Daybeds: A daybed typically consists of a three-sided decorative frame with a link-spring platform forming the base. Daybeds use standard-size twin mattresses and no box spring. Backed with bolsters or piles of pillows, daybeds double as sofas. Some styles have collapsible trundles that slide out of sight to be pulled out when needed. Because daybeds have a link-spring platform with few or no slats and no box spring, mattress quality is critical. Standard twin sheets fit daybeds; look for dust ruffles and comforters designed especially for daybeds.

NIGHTSTANDS

Nightstands are necessary with many bed styles and are most convenient when they stand just a few inches taller than the height of the mattress—about 27 to 33 inches high. Evaluate how you'll use the nightstand and what you will store. Tissues, eyeglasses, and books are simpler to reach in nightstands that have shelves rather than all drawers.

If you use medications or items that you would like to keep out of sight, choose a nightstand with at least one drawer. The top should be large enough to accommodate an alarm clock, a photograph, a decorative item, and perhaps a telephone. If the room has no fixed lighting beside the bed, you will need space for a small table lamp. Nightstands should complement the bed size and style but do not have to match the bed exactly. Small chests work well beside twin beds but look out of place next to king-size beds.

Guest room nightstands don't require drawers and shelves that everyday nightstands need because visitors aren't likely to store items in them. Put to use a vintage table or small chest that doesn't work elsewhere in your home.

Comfortable Environment

Create a bedroom that is a haven for quiet and relaxation—the room where you refresh yourself as you sleep. The quality and quantity of sleep is critical to how you feel and function. Proper lighting and light control contribute to an atmosphere that is conducive to rest.

LIGHTING

Bedrooms are frequently used for more than sleeping, and lighting is important. Most homes with bedroom overhead lighting have a single light fixture located in the center of the ceiling. For ceilings that are high enough, single-light fixtures can be replaced with octopus-style lights that have canisters that direct light in several directions—toward dressing areas, reading areas, or closets. Ceiling

TIPTAG № 20

Bedroom Storage

THE SMALL STUFF:
- For maximum drawer organization, purchase honeycomb-style dividers.
- Look for dividers that expand to create bins in each drawer. Reserve one space for socks; arrange other items in the remaining spaces. Most dividers expand to fit drawers and are easily installed.

EXTRA SHELF PAYS OFF:
- Inside the closet, add a shelf above the door to use wasted space for out-of-season items.
- Buy easy-to-attach stock wood or wire shelves with the appropriate hardware to save shopping and installation time.

SPACE SAVER

Bedside Shelf

•

If you have no space for a nightstand on one side of the bed, install a narrow wall shelf on decorative wall brackets to place an alarm clock, lamp, and other items. Be sure the shelf allows adequate space to access the bed.

fans also have this adjustable style of lighting. Placing the light on a dimmer switch can control the brightness to create mood or function.

Bedside lighting on each side of the bed makes it convenient to read or work in bed. Nightstand lights need to be shorter than traditional table lamps to allow for lower seating and reclining. The bottom of the shade should be at about cheek height so the glare of the bulb does not cause eyestrain. Flared shades help to direct light toward the bed and working or reading material.

Sconces that cast light downward are alternatives to nightstand lamps and require no nightstand space. (Up-cast sconces provide good mood lighting but provide poor reading light.)

Pendants hung close to the wall serve the same purpose as sconces. The disadvantage of using sconces and pendants near the bed is that they dictate the placement of the bed. They may be in an awkward position for rearranging furniture. If you use sconces and pendants, position them so that the shade is above your head and the light cascades over your shoulder.

Track or recessed lighting can be used for reading light or as accent lighting for areas of the room. A row of lights over the head of the bed provides reading light; a span elsewhere may emphasize artwork or a piece of furniture.

Vanity lights, also known as dressing lights, offer flattering illumination when located at face height. The height varies depending on whether the mirror is intended for seating or standing illumination. Provide balanced lighting on both sides of the mirror.

Soft-white lightbulbs provide the best light for bedrooms. Colored bulbs may make matching clothes or applying makeup difficult. Use 60-watt bulbs at the bedside, always consulting the fixture label for recommended wattage. Never use a higher-wattage bulb than the fixture recommends.

CEILING FANS

In warm climates or climates with hot summers, ceiling fans add comfort to the bedroom and conserve energy for cooling. Match the fan to the room size: Standard fan sizes are 36–54 inches in diameter (blade tip to blade tip). A 42-inch-diameter fan is usually sufficient for smaller bedrooms, such as a 12×12-foot children's room. Medium-size bedrooms require a 44-inch fan; a 52-inch fan works well for spacious master bedrooms.

Whichever size you choose, keep safety standards in mind, particularly for children's rooms. Standard mounts fit 8- to 9-foot ceilings. Fan blades should be at least 7 feet above the floor; however, 8 to 9 feet above the floor allows for optimum circulation. For higher master bedroom ceilings, you may need to install a downrod extension. For low ceilings, select flush-mounted low-

Bedside Lamp Options

Candlestick:
Narrow lamps fit on bedside tables, allowing space for an alarm clock and a book. Lighting should be in the 60- to 100-watt range for incandescent bulbs.

Swing-Arm:
When the bedside table is tiny or nonexistent, opt for a wall-mounted swing-arm lamp. Consider three-way switches or dimmers if you like soft mood lighting.

Ginger Jar:
The pleasing rounded shape is a classic that can easily move to the living or family room. Choose a smaller style to fit the scale of your room and bedside table.

Pharmacy:
The adjustable arm and head make it easy to find the most comfortable lighting height and angle. The standard bedside lamp height is 28 to 32 inches.

profile (hugger) models.

WINDOW COVERINGS

Keeping light out of the bedroom is as important as letting in and controlling light. Heavy draperies are seldom appropriate for the scale and style of bedrooms, so a combination of light draperies and shades or blinds is often used. Common bedroom window coverings are roller shades, venetian blinds, miniblinds, pleated or cellular shades, and decorative Roman shades.

Roller shades vary widely in price and quality. Covering material should be at least 6 millimeters thick, or they are likely to tear when pulled down or released. Vinyl covering or fabric-and-vinyl laminated combinations are commonly used. Fabric stores carry kits and materials for fusing decorator fabric to roller shades to coordinate fabrics within the bedroom. Extra-heavy room-darkening shades muffle light and sound, and they are a worthwhile investment for people who sleep during the day and for napping children. Fit the roller shades snugly, leaving little space between the shade edge and the inside of the window frame.

Venetian blinds and miniblinds offer more options in light control than roller shades. Although they operate the same, venetian blind slats measure about 2 inches wide and miniblind slats generally are 1 inch wide. Measure the depth of your window to determine which will fit. Blinds can be raised to let in the light and view or lowered partially or fully for privacy. Lowered slats can be tilted to control the light.

Slats turned upward direct light toward the ceiling; slats turned downward direct light toward the floor. Look for blinds with slats that have little or no space between them when they are closed. Blinds do not offer as much noise control as heavy shades, and they offer privacy only when tilted all the way closed. If the slats don't fit tightly and are turned downward, upstairs neighbors may be able to see through the slats. The same goes for slats that are turned upward—downstairs neighbors may be able to peer in.

Pleated and cellular shades are made of fabrics with degrees of translucency. Both raise and lower similar to blinds without pivoting slats for light control. Pleated shades fold accordion-style. The honeycomb construction of cellular shades offers insulation against light and sound. Some cellular shades have an extra fabric panel that provides additional light and sound control. Check the fabric to determine how much privacy and light control it offers; some shades are quite sheer.

Decorative shades made with heavy fabrics offer the most sound and light control. Custom-made decorative shades that match fabrics in the room are frequently expensive. Sewing centers offer patterns, instructions, kits, and hardware for making affordable

SAFETY ALERT

Cut Your Blind Cord

Cord loops can strangle your child. Buy blinds with safety-wand devices. To retrofit old blinds, cut the cords above the tassel (or untie the knot) and remove the equalizer buckle. Put a tassel on the end of each cord and knot it.

decorative shades. Home sewers with good skills can save money by making their own shades. For added light and noise control, line the shades. Use sheer fabrics, if desired, when privacy and noise control are not concerns.

Valances and swags soften the look and control the light when used with shades and blinds by filling in the space between the window treatment and the window.

Making the Bed
PILLOWS

Pillow selection is a matter of personal preference. Look for pillows that can be fluffed and squashed and that have the thickness and firmness you find comfortable. Natural-fill pillows, such as feather and down, offer the most comfort, longest wear, and most adjustability; however, they are not suitable for people who are allergic to feathers. Although feather pillows offer support and resilience, down has more softness. Combination feather and down pillows have feathers on one side, a fabric divider through the center, and down on the opposite side.

Synthetic and polyester pillows are generally solid but may be textured, shaped, or wrapped in batting for added softness. A wedge-shape pillow can elevate the head of someone who suffers from breathing difficulties or congestion. Other shapes claim to offer shoulder, neck, and back support. Consult a doctor before investing in specialty pillows.

Pillow materials:

■ Down: Filled with tiny goose or duck feathers, down pillows are soft and plush. White goose down is considered the best quality natural fill for bed pillows. Down pillows are expensive and require frequent fluffing, but they adjust to sleeping positions.

■ Down-and-feather mixture: This mix is soft but not as plush as pure down. This fill combines the softness and resilience of down with firm support of feathers. It is an affordable alternative to down.

■ Feather: Goose feathers are best quality; duck feathers are second. Feather pillows are more flexible than down, although they can be problematic for allergy sufferers. Fluff the pillows occasionally in a dryer set at the hottest setting for dust mite control.

■ Synthetic fiber: This is a good choice for people who are allergic to down. Quality synthetic fills are durable and inexpensive. Polyester puffs mimic the performance and resiliency of down.

■ Latex: These economical pillows are resistant to dust mites and

smart ideas
Roller Shades

KITS FOR DRESS UP

Create custom fabric-covered shades with a fusible shade kit purchased from a fabric store. Kits are sold in 42-inch widths and can be cut to fit most windows. Typically, 2½ yards of 45-inch-wide fabric are needed. Follow directions for fusing the fabric to the shade. For added weight, attach tabs and a wooden rod to the shade bottom.

RESCUE THE ROLLER

Tighten a shade that has lost its spring by unrolling it almost all the way. Leave the pin end in place and lift out the flat end. Roll the shade by hand and put the flat end back in place to tighten the spring and help the shade snap in place.

mildew but less comfortable than down or synthetic pillows.

■ Buckwheat hulls: This fill, which has been used abroad for centuries, is relatively new to the United States. The pillows are generally smaller than standard pillows, they mold easily to form, and they are not conducive to dust mites, making them a good choice for allergy sufferers. Some people find them annoying and noisy to sleep on. Before buying one, ask if it is returnable.

■ Foam rubber: This inexpensive pillow is considered hypoallergenic and can be sculpted for specific sleep style support. Foam rubber wears out quickly. If you like soft, plush pillows, the extra firmness will likely be uncomfortable.

Pillow care:

Down and down-and-feather pillows should be dry-cleaned once or twice a year. Some cleaners promote pillow cleaning service periodically. Synthetic pillows generally can be machine washed; check the care labels. If you use pillow protectors, which are sold with bed linens, wash synthetic pillows annually.

Pillow sizes

▶ Standard (20×26 inches)
▶ Queen (20×30 inches)
▶ King (20×36 inches)
▶ European square (26×26 inches)

Decorative bed pillows:

▶ European pillows are large, 26-inch-square pillows. They can be propped up against a headboard for support and used decoratively with a European sham or pillow cover.

▶ Boudoir pillows are used for accents and for traveling.

▶ Neck rolls or bolsters are tube-shape pillows designed to support the head and neck while resting or reading. They can be custom-made in varying thicknesses and diameters for specific needs.

COMFORTERS AND DUVETS

Comforter and duvet are both terms for lush bedding. Comforters and duvets are filled with down, feathers, cotton, wool, silk, or hypoallergenic synthetics. Washable comforters, often sold as complete bed sets, do not have removable covers. Duvets are made to be encased in a duvet cover—a giant pillowcase—to protect the duvet shell.

Down comforters used daily should be dry-cleaned every three to four months. Synthetics generally can be machine washed following manufacturer's directions. If you own another type of natural-filled comforter, such as wool or cotton, check the label or check with a professional laundry before attempting to wash it.

Fill and weight: Unless you are allergic to down, consider a quality down-filled comforter. With proper care, a down comforter will last 8 to 10 years. Goose down is best because the large clusters

---

HEALTHY HOME

Stay Warm With Down

•

Down or down-and-feather comforters are insulators. They keep out cold air and keep in the warmth. For people with allergies, look for cotton-, silk-, wool-, cashmere-, or synthetic-filled duvets.

Dress Your Bed With Style

Pillow Shams:
Square shams that open at the back dress oversize 26-inch-square pillows. Chic, and comfortable for reading.

Accent Pillow:
Don't overpillow your bed. One accent pillow in an interesting shape and color makes a design statement.

Colorful Cases:
Contemporary patterns make it easy to update your bed. Match to your comforter or duvet cover for a unified look.

Turned Down:
Make the bed with the wrong side of the top sheet up; fold over the right side to cover the top of the comforter.

Pleated Bed Skirt:
Unless you have an antique bed, hide the metal supports and rails with a bed skirt or dust ruffle.

Matching Comforter:
Line up the bottom of the comforter with the footboard rail for a neat look. Shake often to keep the look puffy.

have better loft (fluffing) than duck down. Although white and gray goose down give the same service, gray may show through a duvet. When you shop, look for the amount of fill, which is the number of cubic inches per ounce of down. The higher the fill, the better the quality. Standard fill is 500 to 550; high-quality is 600 to 700. Above 700 is unusually high and expensive.

Comforters are manufactured in weights by season and region. The lightest weight, called southern weight, is 26 ounces for a queen size; a winter or mountain weight queen size is 54 ounces.

Shell construction: Even though duvets are encased in duvet covers, the shell should be a lightweight, downproof fabric, also known as ticking. Stitching is important and depends on the size and weight of the duvet. Down needs room to loft; if the down moves around too much and bunches up at one end of the duvet, it isn't warm and comfortable. All comforters should be shaken frequently to fluff and even out the filling.

BED COVERINGS

Blankets: Blankets are sized to drop over the sides and bottom end of the mattress, extending slightly beyond the mattress depth. Blanket covers are versatile and can serve as a lightweight blankets or be used with a heavier blanket.

■ Cotton (honeycomb, herringbone, or waffle weave) is a good choice for a light blanket between the top sheet and comforter.

■ Quilted cotton, matelassé, and piqué fabrics are also called coverlets. A coverlet, which is often used with pillow shams, combines the dressiness of a bedspread with the practicality of a top blanket. These fabrics usually can be laundered in cool water; some shrinkage is possible.

■ Cotton fleece provides medium warmth and is machine-washable.

■ Wool is quite warm and is either dry-cleanable or cold-water washable. The fabric is extremely durable as well.

■ Wool-silk blends provide warmth without weight. These silky soft blankets are usually dry-cleaned.

■ Acrylics, as warm or warmer than wool, are machine-washable.

Quilts: Quilts are used in place of coverlets, as blankets, or as extra bedding folded at the foot of the bed. Handmade and heirloom quilts deserve careful treatment. Special washing solutions are sold at quilt supply shops. Quilts can also be professionally dry-cleaned by a laundry that specializes in fine linens. Older quilts should not be exposed to direct sunlight and should be refolded frequently, using new folds, to avoid creasing the fabrics. Durable machine-made quilts, appropriate for everyday use, are widely available.

Bedspreads: Classic bedspreads cover the entire bed, including the mattress, box springs, and pillows. Shams are typically not used when a bedspread covers bed pillows, but decorative pillows may be added. The top spread may be folded down to expose the pillows.

Electric blankets: No longer bulky and limited in heating options, electric blankets offer individual heat zones—allowing feet to be warmer than shoulders, for example. With careful attention, they can be machine washed; gentle laundering extends the life of the blanket while keeping it fresh.

Follow these steps to gently wash electric blankets:

▶ Disconnect electrical cord.

▶ Check the care label.

▶ Pretreat soiled areas.

▶ Fill washer with warm water to high water level.

▶ Add liquid laundry detergent; agitate briefly to mix.

▶ Stop washer.

▶ Load blanket evenly; soak for 15 minutes—do not agitate.

▶ Set dial for 2 minutes of gentle agitation; start washer.

▶ Put three or four clean, dry bath towels into dryer; preheat for 10 minutes on high.

▶ Load blanket into dryer with warm towels.

▶ Set timed drying cycle for 20 minutes; start dryer.

▶ Check after 10 minutes. Continue only if wet, not simply damp.

▶ Remove slightly damp blanket (overdrying damages wiring and causes shrinkage).

▶ Hang blanket over two lines, or lay flat, until dry.

Health concerns have arisen about the safety of electric blankets in recent years. The blankets are now generally considered safe, but people with poor circulation in their legs and feet (including diabetics), who might not be aware of temperature changes, need to take care to select appropriate temperature settings and use only well-maintained blankets to avoid overheating or burns. Proper maintenance of electric blankets reduces hazards of electric shock or fires caused by worn wiring. Watch for worn or frayed fabric; signs of scorching; worn, damaged, or missing wiring, tapes, or cords; or loose connections. If any damage appears, discard the blanket.

Kids' Rooms

Many parents dream of making one initial investment in their children's furniture and having those pieces last from infancy to adulthood. Rarely does that dream come true. With good planning and wise shopping, however, you can come close. Select neutral styles and colors and invest in good-quality multiple use pieces that can be modified. Basic styles and finishes will blend with additional

Home Remedies

ALLERGY CONTROL

Cover Control

Encase bedding in allergen-impermeable covers that zipper around pillows, comforters, mattress, and box springs. Vacuum the mattress and box springs before covering. These don't work on products containing down. Some bedding is made with allergy-resistant fibers that are washable and mimic the feel and fullness of down.

Hot Water Helps

Wash bed coverings not encased in the zippered covering every two weeks in hot water. Wash covers twice a year in warm water. If you don't like the feel of nonallergenic covers, encase in a washable cotton cover. Wash all bedding weekly to control allergies.

furniture pieces through childhood.

THE NURSERY

A crib, changing area, and minor storage may be all you need for furniture when you first bring your child home; that will change, however. Storage space for clothing and toys will soon be inevitable. Look for pieces that convert as the child grows, such as changing tables that can be transformed into dressers or armoires.

Crib safety: Be wary of using antique, tag sale, or handed down cribs; many do not meet current Consumer Product Safety Commission standards and may result in infant injury or death. All new cribs sold in the United States must meet safety standards. If you choose to use an old crib, observe the following:

▪ Drop-side catches should not accidentally release when the crib is moved, bumped, or jostled; nor should they be easily released by a small child. A two-stage catch is best; stationary sides will prevent the baby from rolling out.

▪ Crib cutouts should be small enough that they won't allow head entrapment, which can be fatal to an infant.

▪ The mattress should fit snugly into the crib to prevent a child's arms, legs, or head from getting caught. Measure both the crib and the mattress, allowing no more than two fingers' widths of space on all sides.

▪ Look for cracks, shaky construction, unstable wheels or legs, loose hardware, missing slats, rough or splintered spots (including the plastic strip covering the top rail), removable decorations, cracked or flaking finishes, or exposed bolts. If the crib is older and painted, test it for lead paint using a kit available at hardware stores.

Safe furniture and furnishings:

Follow these guideline to ensure your child's safety:

▪ Choose stable furniture that will not tip.

▪ Place the crib away from windows, drapery and blind cords, electrical outlets and light switches, wall shelves, lamps, wall-hung pictures, and dangerous items that children could reach. Do not pile the crib with pillows, stuffed animals, or overly fluffy comforters. Use tightly fitted bottom contour sheets.

▪ Changing tables should have straps to hold the infant in place and nearby drawers so the child does not have to be left unattended while you reach for supplies.

▪ Toy chests should not have lid latches that can trap a child inside. They should be equipped with a completely removable lid or a hinged lid with spring-loaded lid support that will hold the lid in position without closing. All toy chests should have ventilation holes or spaces in the front, sides, or lid in case a child gets inside.

▪ Blinds and draw-style draperies should have breakaway cords joined by a plastic barrel, or two separate cords. Either style will

Cleaning Bathroom Fixtures

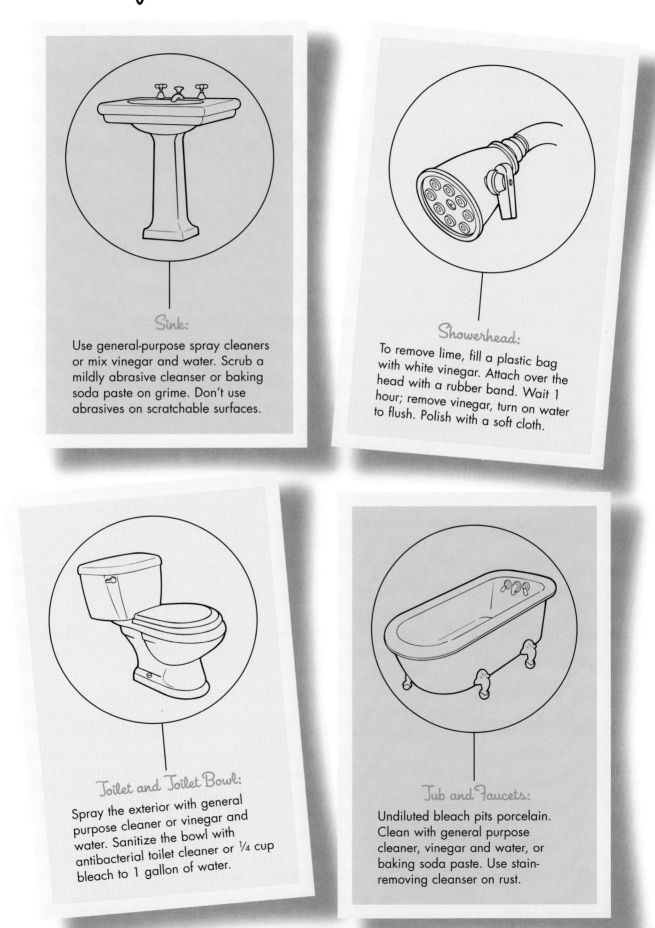

Sink:
Use general-purpose spray cleaners or mix vinegar and water. Scrub a mildly abrasive cleanser or baking soda paste on grime. Don't use abrasives on scratchable surfaces.

Showerhead:
To remove lime, fill a plastic bag with white vinegar. Attach over the head with a rubber band. Wait 1 hour; remove vinegar, turn on water to flush. Polish with a soft cloth.

Toilet and Toilet Bowl:
Spray the exterior with general purpose cleaner or vinegar and water. Sanitize the bowl with antibacterial toilet cleaner or ¼ cup bleach to 1 gallon of water.

Tub and Faucets:
Undiluted bleach pits porcelain. Clean with general purpose cleaner, vinegar and water, or baking soda paste. Use stain-removing cleanser on rust.

prevent accidental strangulation. Older loop cords can be cut to form two cords; window-treatment retailers can provide adaptations.

FIRST REAL FURNITURE

A grown-up bed, more storage, and perhaps a desk are the items needed next. Consider using plastic rolling drawers or bins that can slide into the closet under hanging clothes for additional storage. Low open shelves are ideal for books, games, and puzzles, and often fit under windows where other furniture won't work; the tops can be used for display.

Bunk-bed safety: Guardrails should surround the top bunk, except for the small ladder area on some styles. Guardrails should be spaced less than 3½ inches from the mattress so that children cannot slip their head or body between the mattress and the rail. The rail should rise at least 5 inches above the mattress, high enough to prevent rolling out of bed. The top mattress foundation should be supported by several slats to prevent it from becoming dislodged by movement or pushing from beneath.

The ladder should be secured to the frame. Removable ladders should have long hooks to secure them in place. If the bunk bed consists of two separate beds that can be unstacked and used independently, they should be bolted securely when bunked. Simple pegs will not hold the beds in place under stress.

TWEENS AND TEENS

Preteens and teens have their own sets of special needs and enjoy spaces to call their own. If you make additions to their furniture, choose furniture that they can use later in life, or that you can live with after they leave home. If they choose to express their decorating creativity, provide sturdy old furniture from tag sales and flea markets, and let them paint or decorate it with their choices of paint, motifs, and finishes.

Special-use furniture includes computer desks, tilt-top drawing tables, large desks, and shelves for stereos, televisions, and videocassette recorders. Adequate lighting is needed for each task. Up to five light sources (including windows) may be needed, depending on how the room is used. A chair and plenty of pillows make lounging comfortable.

Organization and display are more important than ever. Shaker pegs hold backpacks and clothing. Bookshelves, additional storage bins and baskets, and wall-hung shelving or plate rails store, organize, display, and keep teens' possessions in order.

Bathrooms

Although bathroom fixtures aren't the most glamorous items to buy, they are a daily necessity. Poor quality fixtures can be more than an inconvenience. Look for these qualities in bathroom necessities:

FAMILY FRIENDLY

Shopping For a Bed

•

Know the detriments of owning a metal bed. Bolts often work loose and enlarge the bolt holes. Wooden beds tend to be more stable, and holes can be redrilled or filled with sawdust and glue to securely hold bolts in place.

FIXTURES

Toilets: Federal law prohibits the manufacture of toilets that use more than 1.6 gallons of water per flush. Unfortunately, some of the models don't flush as completely as older toilets. Toilets that operate by gravity alone may need two flushes, especially in areas with naturally low water pressure. Toilets with pressure-assisted flushing mechanisms are more effective; however, they may make more noise and are almost twice the cost of gravity models. A rare version uses a small electric pump to push through water and waste; the newer variety employs the vacuum method of flushing used on airplanes.

Toilets are available in standard two-piece styles, sleek one-piece models, and designer shapes. One-piece units are easy to clean because there are no crevices between the tank and toilet where urine, dirt, and bacteria can collect. Some two-piece toilets have a "sanitary dam" that bridges this spot to prevent bacteria buildup. Two-piece units are available in several styles.

Sinks: Vanity, wall-hung, and pedestal sinks are affordable varieties of bathroom sinks. Reproductions of antiques and designer styles are available from bathroom fixture designers and contractors.

Whichever style you choose, look for a model with few crevices and seams that will attract soap scum and dirt. All-in-one sink and countertop units or sinks that are undermounted (positioned just below the vanity top) are the easiest to keep clean. Also measure the space between the faucet and handles and the back of the sink to determine whether you can easily clean that area. Select a sink or countertop with a rim to keep splashed water from running onto the floor. The remaining area (with the exception of built-in soap dishes on some models) should be flat so that water doesn't puddle.

■ Vanities offer counter space for grooming tools, soap, water glasses, toothbrush holders, and regularly used bathroom items. They also offer the bonus of under-sink storage. Determine whether the base of the unit has been treated to withstand moisture.

■ Pedestal sinks take up less space than vanities and make a small bathroom appear larger. Although they lack the storage space of a vanity, the open space beneath the sink can accommodate a wastebasket or bathroom scale. Baskets of towels, bandboxes to hold extra tissue paper, and other creative storage solutions can fit under pedestal sinks. When purchasing a pedestal sink, consider which items you want it to hold: soap, water glass, cosmetics, or

TIP TAG № 21
Time to Vent

CEILING-MOUNT FANS:
- Install a vent fan to prevent moisture buildup in the bath. Look for quiet units that move the air at least 8 times per hour.
- Figure the required cubic-feet-per-minute (cfm) air movement rate.
- Calculate the cubic feet of the room by multiplying the length by the width by the height. Multiply this figure by 8, divide by 60, for the exchanges per minute.

FOR EXAMPLE:
- 8×10×8 is 640 cubic feet
- 640×8 is 5,120 exchanges
- 5,120 divided by 60 is 85.3 exchanges per minute and a required cfm rating of 85.

grooming aids that you use while at the sink.

■ Wall-mounted sinks take up less space than a vanity but more than a pedestal sink. Old versions with chrome legs can be made more fashionable by attaching a skirt with double-stick hook-and-loop tape to hide the legs and provide concealed storage.

■ Vitreous china is the most common sink material because it is inexpensive, can be molded into a variety of shapes, has attractive sheen, and cleans easily. Vitreous china can chip or scratch.

■ Other common sink materials include porcelain-glazed cast iron, such as that used in bathtubs; cast polymer, which is often used for large all-in-one vanity top and sink units; enameled steel; glass; plastic; pottery; and stone.

■ Faucets and handles are sold by style, material, and quality. Look for smooth operation and ease of cleaning. Before purchasing faucet units, measure your sink for fit. See page 150 ("Kitchens") for more on sink hardware.

Tubs and Showers: Tubs are commonly manufactured in porcelain-coated cast iron, enameled steel, and fiberglass.

■ Cast iron holds heat for long baths, has a lustrous finish, and often feels more substantial than other tubs. Cast iron is heavy and requires sufficient support below. It also requires that the surrounding walls be covered with a waterproof material, such as tile or a fiberglass shower enclosure.

■ Enameled steel is similar to cast iron in its advantages and disadvantages; it is not as durable, nor does it hold the heat as well.

■ Fiberglass is frequently used as it is lightweight, inexpensive, and easy to install and clean.

■ Most spa tubs are made of acrylic or fiberglass to reduce their weight. The weight of the tub is reduced to accommodate the large amount of water that creates heavy weight. Avoid too-thin plastics, however, and spa tubs with uneven thicknesses or blemishes. Before you purchase, check the number and locations of the jets, the noise and power level of the motor, and special effects. If the tub is part of a remodeling, extra support structure may be needed.

■ Showerheads massage, pulse, are used as handheld units, and are adjustable for different heights. Water-efficient showerheads reduce water use. Oversize shower heads often measure up to 5 inches in diameter and offer a gentle cascade of water over a large area. Many extend on a long arm and adjust at several pivot points.

■ Shower-curtain rods come in straight bar, L-shape, and ring or oval shapes. Tub styles determine which shape is installed. Round and oval rods are suspended from the ceiling; L-shape rods have both wall and ceiling support. Most rods are adjustable. Fit them directly over the tub, making the shower space as large as possible to help keep the shower curtain liner at a distance while you shower.

FAMILY FRIENDLY

Accessible Fixtures

•

If you retrofit a bath, install grab bars into wall studs at the toilet, tub, and shower stall. Wall-mounted sinks work best for wheelchair users; and levers are easier to manipulate than faucets. See pages 357-368 for resources.

Bathroom Brushes at Work

Long-Handled Sponge:
Use to clean hard-to-reach areas, such as inside shower and tub enclosures and behind or around toilets.

Toilet Bowl Brush:
Round shapes are most efficient for the job. Use to reach under the rim and scour the bowl.

Cellulose Sponges:
Wipe and clean countertops, fixtures, and other surfaces. Change frequently for cleanliness.

Handled Brushes:
Scrub tile floor and around fixtures. Soft brushes can be used to scour the tub and shower enclosure.

Special-Grip:
For nooks and tight areas, such as around built-in soap dishes that accumulate gunk. Note easy-to-hold handle.

Grout Brushes:
Use with grout cleaner, baking soda, or a mild bleach solution to scrub mildew and stains; also use around faucets.

Heavy-Duty:
Best brushes for scouring a floor, old cast-iron tub, or stained sink. Do not use on scratchable surfaces.

Tub and Tile Cleaner:
If similar to a scouring pad, don't use on fiberglass, laminate countertops, or other scratchable surfaces.

TIME SAVER

Curtains Return

•

If you opt for a shower curtain (less to clean than doors), add a heavy vinyl liner. Make sure the liner has weights or magnets at the bottom so it stays in place during the shower. Buy rings that slide easily. Read the label for care instructions.

LIGHTING

Warm, white incandescent bulbs provide true and flattering light in bathrooms. Depending on the size and shape of a room, one or more overhead fixtures provide the main light. Combination vents and lights are often installed in the ceiling above the toilet or near the shower. Shower, bathtub, and toilet alcoves need their own overhead light sources. Additional light around mirrors aids grooming. Identical lights on each side of the vanity mirror provide even light. Place the lights about 60 inches up from the floor and 28 to 36 inches apart. For mirrors wider than 36 inches, choose an overhead strip with three or more separate lights. Place the strip 78 inches off the floor or higher for higher mirrors.

KIDS' BATH

Avoid carpet and hardwood floors and choose a surface such as vinyl or ceramic tile. Choose a flooring with texture. If the existing floor is smooth, add washable, rubber-backed rugs. Avoid rugs or covers around the toilet; these are messy and trap dirt, odors, and bacteria. Choose a scrubbable paint. Easy-care gloss or semi-gloss paint, ceramic tile, or scrubbable wall coverings are good choices. Consider hooks or Shaker pegs as an option to towel racks—it's easier for young children to toss a towel over a hook than fold it over a bar. Provide a nonskid stepping stool for small children. A second mirror, hung at their height, is a handy grooming aid as they learn to brush their own teeth and comb their own hair. Keep medications, sharp objects, and other dangerous items locked in a separate area.

Essential standards: Keep the following in mind as you plan a shared or children's bath:

■ Standard tubs are 5 feet long and 30 inches wide. A comfy minimum for shower stalls is 36 inches square, although they commonly range from 32 to 48 inches.

■ Vanities range from 31 to 34 inches tall, but 36 inches can be easier on the back for adults.

■ Large bowls minimize splashing. Space twin sinks at least 12 inches apart, leaving 8 inches at the end of the vanity countertop.

■ In a shower-tub combination, mount a faucet 30 to 34 inches above the bottom of the tub. Set a shower faucet 48 to 52 inches from the bottom for ease when standing. Mount a showerhead 69 to 72 inches from the bottom.

■ Toilet-tank widths vary from about 17 to 23¼ inches. Toilets extend from the wall 25 to 30 inches. Toilet seats are usually 14 inches high.

■ Allow at least 36 inches of towel-bar space for each person using the bath. Hand towels fit on 18-inch bars; bath towels need at least 24 inches. Set towel bars 26 to 42 inches from the floor.

■ Lower the temperature of the water heater to 105 degrees.

8

Linen Closet Organization
- STORAGE, 207
- IN APARTMENTS, 207
- MONOGRAMMED LINENS, 207

Sheets
- BASIC SIZES, 208
- SHEET FABRICS, 208
- LINENS FOR MASTER BEDROOM, 210
- CRIB BEDDING, 210
- FOLDING FITTED SHEET, 213
- FOLDING FLAT SHEET, 213

Bath Linens
- TOWEL SIZES, 209
- TOWEL FABRICS, 211
- TOWEL CARE, 212
- FLUFFING TOWELS, 214

Laundry Room
- SAFE PRODUCT STORAGE, 214
- BUYING A WASHER, 215
- TIPS FOR BEST RESULTS, 215, 221
- BUYING A DRYER, 216
- ENERGY EFFICIENCY, 216
- LOADING WASHER AND DRYER, 218, 219
- HAND LAUNDRY, 219
- FOLDING CLOTHING, 220
- FABRIC CARE, 225

Ironing
- HELPFUL EXTRAS, 217
- BUYING AN IRON, 220
- IRONING BOARD, 222
- HOW TO IRON CLOTHES, 223
- IRONING A TABLECLOTH, 223

Stain Removal
- COMMON STAINS, 224
- HELPFUL TIPS, 227
- PRODUCTS TO STOCK, 228
- COMMON PROBLEMS, 228
- CHILDREN'S SLEEPWEAR CARE, 230

Setting up a Linen Closet

The old-fashioned idea of a well-stocked linen closet is again in vogue. Who can resist sweet-smelling sheets and fluffy towels? With minimal organizing, you can enjoy this simple home pleasure. If you have a designated linen closet near the bath or master bedroom, recognize its potential. If your home doesn't have a designated linen closet, store linens in satellite locations throughout the house.

ORGANIZING STORAGE

■ Add built-in shelves or a free-standing storage unit to stock extra towels in the bath.

■ Create extra bed linen storage on a closet shelf or in under-the-bed storage boxes.

■ Dust and wipe shelves. Freshen with a coat of paint or cover with shelf paper, if desired.

■ Divide linens into categories. Separate bed linens by size and style or by sheet sets. Tie sheet sets together with ribbon for easy retrieval or encase them in a matching pillow cover. Rotate sheets for even wear by putting freshly washed linens at the bottom of the stack and using sheets from the top of the stack. Organize towels by type (bath, hand, fingertip) or by type and color for easy identification.

■ Group table linens by type, such as tablecloths and runners. Install door racks for convenient tablecloth storage, or hang tablecloths on quality wood or plastic hangers—do not use metal hangers for linens. Store napkins together, separated by set for easy identification. If the linen closet isn't convenient to the kitchen or dining area, store napkins in a sideboard or chest of drawers close to the kitchen or dining room.

■ When fine linens include matching place mats and napkins, sandwich each pressed set between cardboard. Tie with ribbon to hold securely.

■ Use baskets, bins, or plastic-coated wire shelving to divide spaces. When space allows, store extra or out-of-season comforters, blankets, and coverlets on separate shelves. Add cedar block or fragrant sachets made for linen closets to scent your linens.

■ If you use your linen closet to store extra toiletries, such as shampoo and soap, use plastic or woven storage bins to keep like items together. Label the bins for easy identification.

FOR APARTMENT DWELLERS

Finding room for linen storage can be a challenge in an apartment, especially older apartments with minimal closet space. For a solution

TIP TAG No. 22

Monograms

WHAT TO MONOGRAM:
• Pillowcases, towels, hand towels, top sheets, and napkins.

RULES:
• Place the initial of the last name in the middle. It is larger than the two side initials—first name initial on the left, middle name initial on the right.
• For a couple, use shared last name initial in the center with the husband's first name initial to the left and the wife's to the right.

STYLES AND TYPES:
• Block and script lettering or diamond pattern.
• Initials monogrammed as first letter of first or last name; or first letters of first, middle, and last names.

that serves now and later, purchase a piece of furniture that can serve more than one purpose, such as a chest of drawers or an armoire. The chest will work well as a hall or lamp table in a small apartment or as a bedside table in a guest or child's room in a larger residence. A vintage or reproduction armoire, outfitted with shelves and racks, can hold linens as well as clothing. To save valuable storage space, stash extra comforters in zippered bags (to prevent dust buildup) and store beneath the bed.

Sheets

Combined with pillows and top coverings, practical and pretty sheets refresh a room for an easy makeover. Crisp white sheets never go out of style. Sheets in colors, prints, plaids, and patterns are easy to find in all sizes and price ranges. Frequent washing tends to fade colors on budget-priced sheets. Here are some additional sheet terms and facts to keep in mind:

Thread count refers to the number of threads woven into one square inch of fabric. The higher the thread count, the softer and smoother the bed linens. Thread count also determines whether a sheet is muslin or percale. Sheets with a thread count of 140 to 180 are muslin; everything higher is percale. The most common percale have thread counts of 180 to 200. Higher-quality sheets have a 250 to 300 thread count and feel silky to the touch. Look for a minimum thread count of 200 when selecting sheets (for cotton/polyester sheets, 220 or more is a good choice). Sheets with a high thread count (300 to 400) are considered luxury quality.

BASIC SHEET SIZES

Check package labeling to be certain that you are buying the correct size for your bed. If you buy European brands, read the measurements as well as the labeled sized names. Standard sizes are listed in inches; see page 382 for the metric conversion chart.

▶ Twin flat: 66×96
▶ Twin fitted: 39×75
▶ Full flat: 81×96 (to 100)
▶ Full fitted: 54×75
▶ Queen flat: 90×102 (to 106)
▶ Queen fitted: 60×80
▶ King flat: 108×102 (to 106)
▶ King fitted: 78×80
▶ California king flat: 102×110
▶ California king fitted: 72×84

SHEET MATERIALS

For comfort and durability, cotton is still king. One-hundred-percent cotton is a natural, breathable fabric. If you are allergic to dyes and chemicals, look for sheets made from organically grown, natural,

Make Your Set
•

For the most savings on quality sheets, look for sales of marked-down individual sheets instead of sets. Mix and match fitted and flat sheets with pillow cases and shams. For mixing, choose white or a solid pastel for one of the sheets or for the pillowcases.

Bathroom Towel Sizes

Fingertip Towels:
Standard size is 11×18 inches. Sometimes used with decorative guest towels in powder rooms or placed by the sink when guests visit.

Face Cloths:
Also called washcloths, the standard size is 12 inches square. Stock extras, especially when infants and young children are in your household.

Bath Sheets:
Sizes from 30×60 inches to 40×72 inches add a luxurious touch to your bath. Not included in standard bathroom towel sets.

Hand Towels:
Sizes range from 16×26 inches to 18×32 inches. Buy extra to keep fresh ones out for family and guests. Freely mix colors and trims.

Bath Towels:
Standard sizes start at 22×44 inches. Quality towels start at 27×50 inches. Luxury towels are sized 30×54 inches (also called French size).

undyed cotton fibers. About 90 percent of all sheets in the United States are woven from American upland cotton, which is grown in the southern tier of states from Virginia to California. However, higher-thread-count sheets (and clothing) are also woven from extra-long staple cottons, such as Egyptian.

Flannel, muslin, oxford, percale, and sateen weaves are most commonly used for cotton sheets. Percale, which is tightly woven, is a basic weave for sheeting, as is sateen. Muslin sheets are at a lower price point than percale; prices are based on the thread counts. Flannel sheets are typically used in cold climates or in winter because the napped finish provides warmth. Oxford cloth, similar to the dress shirting fabric, translates into a soft but heavy sheet.

Look for wrinkle-resistant cotton sheets as an alternative to stiff cotton-polyester blends. Machine-washable, combed cotton percale with a thread count of 200–250 will provide long wear. Select from these choices for sheeting fabrics:

■ 50-percent cotton/50-percent polyester sheets resist wrinkling but can be stiff. The 60-percent cotton/40-polyester blend is another option. Look for a high thread count (above 220) to ensure quality in cotton-polyester blends.

■ Silk satin sheets are ideal for cold climates because the material traps warmth. These sheets feel smooth and luxurious, but they are expensive and must be dry-cleaned. Avoid satin-style sheets made of polyester; they feel scratchy against the skin.

■ Cotton jersey knit is made from the same breathable fabric as cotton T-shirts and is comfortable year-round; dark colors and patterns tend to fade.

■ Linen is considered the finest sheet fabric, and it is ideal for hot climates. Fine linen sheets last for decades, making them a worthwhile investment.

LINENS FOR THE MASTER BEDROOM

Traditional January white sales are the ideal time to purchase bargains. Linen outlets are year-round destinations for bargain hunters. Stock these items to dress the bed in comfort and style:

▶ Two mattress pads—one in the linen closet, one on the bed; wash every two to four weeks

▶ Two or three sheet sets—top and bottom sheets, with pillowcases for each pillow

▶ Two pillowcase protectors per pillow

▶ One duvet and duvet cover or one comforter, if using

▶ One coverlet, quilt, or spread

▶ One summer blanket

▶ One winter blanket

▶ One bed skirt, if using

LINENS FOR THE GUEST ROOM

SAFETY ALERT

Crib Bedding

A fitted bottom sheet and a light- or medium-weight blanket are all the covers your baby needs. Don't fill the crib with heavy bedding, and don't add toys or pillows. *Never* hang fabric over the bed. All have the potential to smother an infant.

For guests, wash linens and remake the bed after each visit so the room will always be ready. Suggested linens include:

▶ One mattress pad—or two for twin beds in the room
▶ Two sets of sheets per bed
▶ Two pillows per twin bed; four pillows for a full-size bed
▶ Two pillowcase protectors per pillow
▶ Two pillowcases per pillow
▶ One duvet or comforter per bed, if using
▶ One duvet cover per bed, if using
▶ One summer blanket per bed
▶ One winter blanket per bed
▶ One bed skirt per bed, if using

Bath Linens

Towels, face cloths, and bath mats are as much home fashion accessories as necessities. As with sheets, you have the choice of ever-popular classic white or an array of fashion colors, trims, and patterns. Fluffy white towels give a clean, spa-like feel to a master, guest, or shared family bath. White and ecru coordinate with any bathroom color and have longevity; colors tend to fade over time.

If you like color in the bath, choose light colors that don't show fading as much as dark colors. Mint green, fresh pink, and light blue are good choices, or combine two colors, mixing shades such as green with gold, or wheat with white or cream. If you use two colors for towels, choose a bath mat in one of the colors. For a clean look, use only washable cotton bath mats. Avoid using top or seat covers on the toilet and don't use a rug around the base; they all trap moisture and are dust and bacteria catchers.

FABRICS

Along with bedding linen, towels also are traditionally discounted during January white sales. At linen outlets and home discount stores, you can find good buys year-round on fashionable towels. Don't use softness alone as the barometer to measure towel quality. Manufacturers sometimes add fabric softeners to towels to create a silky feel; these silicone-base additives coat the towel fibers so a soft towel can actually be less effective than its coarser cousin. When selecting towels, use weight as an indicator of durability.

To get the most for your money, keep in mind that towels are differentiated on the basis of material and method of manufacture. Because of its absorbency and strength, cotton is the fabric of choice. Longer-staple varieties, such as those grown in the delta

Home Remedies

BED CARE

Wash Gently

Change and launder sheets and pillowcases once a week. Protect pillows with washable zip-on covers. For even wear, rotate sheets, storing fresh sheets at the bottom of the stack. Wash sheets in warm water, and use nonchlorine bleach when needed. Wash all-cotton spreads, blankets, and coverlets in cold water to avoid shrinkage.

Air Frequently

Naturally refresh pillows, comforters, and duvets by airing them outside on a sunny, breezy day. Even in large dryers, only twin comforters can fit for a fresh tumbling. Set the dryer on the lowest setting and add clean tennis balls to increase loft.

regions of the United States, are stronger and softer than shorter-staple versions. As the staple length increases, the individual loop gets softer and more supple, for better wear and less lint. Combed cotton is considered a top-quality fiber for toweling because only the best grades of cotton can be combed.

Weaving determines towel appearance. The least expensive products are woven on cam looms that move only horizontally or vertically, creating flat surfaces with no decoration. More common for general use, towels woven on dobby looms have decorative borders. Jacquard looms take dobby capabilities a step further, making sculptured designs possible. Texture also can be added by shearing the closed terry loop to create a smooth velour surface.

The manufacturing process and the material affect towel absorbency. Although sheared towels are the most absorbent, they aren't necessarily the best dryers. Towels don't dry simply by absorbing moisture; the fiber loops also brush water off the body. Bottom line: The number of loops per square inch is the most important indicator of performance.

TOWEL ENSEMBLES

Towels are usually sold individually but in matching colors and style. The minimum ensemble is a bath towel, hand towel, and face cloth. However, fingertip towels are often added in powder rooms or bathrooms used by guests. Oversize bath towels or bath sheets are luxurious additions to the family bath.

To outfit a standard bathroom, stock four complete sets of towels to allow two sets in the wash and two sets in use. Each basic set includes a bath towel, hand towel, and washcloth. Stock two complete sets, with the addition of fingertip towels, in guest baths or extra sets for guests if they share the family bath. Bath mats and shower curtains are also considered part of the basic bath ensemble. Neutral colors and patterns are tasteful for both mats and curtains. Install a plastic liner to protect a fabric shower curtain. Buy extra washcloths during January white sales or at outlets to have plenty for removing makeup and helping children to clean up before meals.

TOWEL CARE

Good-quality bath towels can last for 10 years with proper care. To get the most from your towels:

Wash and dry new towels before use to remove finishes and excess dyes.

Launder on a normal wash cycle. Wash separately, not with clothes, for sanitary reasons. Use warm water (not hot) to wash towels and do not overdry; overdrying destroys the integrity of the individual cotton fibers. Use softeners according to directions; don't overuse. Do not use softeners (liquid or softener sheets) every time towels are laundered. To prevent waxy softener buildup, use

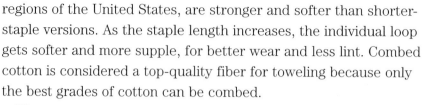

TIME SAVER

Towel Styling

Update towels with new display techniques. Fold bath towels to the same width as hand towels and layer both sizes for a tiered look. Fold towels lengthwise; then roll them. Cluster the rolled towels in natural or wire baskets or crates, or stack them in pyramids.

How to Fold Sheets Neatly

Fitted: Corners:

Fold on counter or bed. Neaten corners and fold crosswise, right sides together. The job is easier with two people.

Four to Two:

Tuck the fitted corners from bottom to top. Queen- or king-size sheets are much easier to fold on a flat surface.

Two to One:

Fold in half lengthwise so that three of the fitted corners fit into one. Neaten and smooth sheet as you work.

Final Fold:

For closet stacking, fold sheet in half lengthwise and again crosswise. If you prefer, fold in thirds as towel folds.

Flat: Hem to Hem:

With right side out, fold crosswise (bottom to top). Easier on a bed, a clean countertop, or with help.

Second Fold:

Fold again, carefully aligning hems. Smooth with your hands as you work to avoid wrinkles.

Smaller Size:

Make a crosswise fold so the sheet can be neatly stacked on a shelf. Twin sheets can be stacked at this folded size.

Final Fold:

Conserve the linen closet or shelf space with the final fold. Stack as as part of a set or with other flat sheets on the shelf.

once every three or four washings.

Wash dark-color towels separately for the first few washings because colors may bleed. Then, wash similar colors together.

Use color-safe bleach for color towels. Wash white towels separately or with other white items to avoid subtle discoloration over time. Occasionally bleach white towels if needed.

If you hang-dry towels, shake them while wet and again when dry to fluff the terry loops. Don't iron terry towels; this will reduce absorbency. Linen hand towels should be ironed.

Outfitting the Laundry Room

If you have a choice, deciding on location is the first step to planning a laundry center. Kitchen installation, for example, makes sense if you do laundry along with other chores. Instead of the traditional laundry room, a washer, dryer, and utility supply closet near the bedrooms may save steps for you.

PLANNING AND PURCHASING

When you move into an apartment or house, keep the following in mind before you purchase a washer or dryer:

Location, location: Locating the washer and dryer in the basement means extra steps, but this arrangement frees up valuable upstairs space. Spills, splashes, or an overflow normally do less damage in a basement location. Upstairs, a leak could damage walls, flooring, and the ceiling below. If you install a washing machine in your main living area, add an emergency shut-off valve and regularly check hose connections.

Plumbing and wiring: Washers require drains and hot and cold water lines. Gas dryers need a gas supply line and not more than 50 feet of venting to the outside. Electric dryers require 120-volt circuits. Some models condense moisture into a drip pan without venting. Washers and gas dryers require 20-amp small-appliance circuits. Units must be on independent, grounded circuits.

Storage: Install shelving near the washer to keep supplies handy. Bleach and other laundry products are dangerous to young children, so place them on shelves well out of the reach of children. If possible, install a childproof lockable cabinet. Install a rack to hang clothes that drip-dry, or buy a double-tier clothes rack on wheels or casters. For close spaces, use wooden, metal, or plastic drying racks. Purchase drying racks for sweaters and knits that must be air-dried while flat, and place them on the top of the washing machine, dryer, or a bathtub if drying space is limited.

Lighting: Uniform, glare-free lighting is important to thoroughly inspect, sort, and fold clothes. Compact fluorescent bulbs illuminate without adding heat. Some wall-mounted ironing boards include a built-in task light.

BUDGET STRETCHER

Sort and Save

•

Avoid ruining clothing in careless sorting.
New garments can bleed and stain other clothing. Wash colors, especially red, by themselves the first time, first in cold or cool water with detergent. For stains, use a bleach alternative formulated for colorfastness.

WASHERS AND DRYERS

Size and style: Washers and dryers measure from 24 to 33 inches wide. For loading and unloading, allow 36 inches in front of a washer, 42 inches for a dryer. Measurements differ for front-loading models. Stacked units occupy less than 33 square inches of floor space and are accessible to people who have difficulty bending or stooping; front-loaders are more accessible to wheelchair users. Install a dryer about 15 inches off the floor to make loading and unloading more comfortable.

Selecting a washer: Consider both capacity and loading type. Capacity depends on the size of the wash basket. Compact capacity runs 1.7 to 2.3 cubic feet; medium is 2.1 to 2.5 cubic feet; large is 2.7 to 3 cubic feet; and extra large is 3.1 or more cubic feet. Families with children and several loads daily may like the convenience of a large-capacity washer. Smaller-capacity models, which use less water and energy, can be economical for singles and couples. Front-load washers use less water, making them energy and environmentally friendly.

Wash and rinse speeds, temperatures, and cycles: Basic washers have between one and four agitation and spin speeds. Some top-of-the-line models offer additional options. Preset wash cycles combine differing speeds, temperatures, and levels of agitation to clean specific types of clothing. An average washer may have regular, permanent press, and delicate cycles. High-end models may offer additional cycles, such as a heavy-duty cycle for work clothes, jeans, and towels, as well as presoak and prewash cycles for dealing with difficult stains.

Water temperature options usually include hot/cold, warm/cold, and cold/cold. Some more expensive models may feature additional temperature combinations to suit more fabrics. Controls are mechanical, with rotary knobs and push buttons, or electronic with conveniences such as digital displays and more custom cycles. Water-saver options recycle water from lightly soiled loads.

High-efficiency (water- and energy-saving) washers: Save energy and extend the life of your clothes and linens with a well-designed washing machine. Look for horizontal-axis, front-loading washers or top loading washers with the energy star, which tumble instead of twist or rub clothes. These models, which don't have agitators, use less water and energy than top-loaders of the

smart ideas

Laundry Tips

MORE FROM TOWELS

To maximize the absorbency of your towels, add a cup of white vinegar to the rinse water once a month when washing a load of towels. When the cycle is complete, dry as usual. The vinegar removes excess detergent that can decrease absorbency.

PET HAIR REMOVAL

To remove pet hairs from dry-clean-only bedcovers and throws (or those you don't wash frequently), place the item in your dryer along with an anti-static dryer sheet. Run the dryer on low or no heat for 20 to 30 minutes. Clean the lint trap after each load. Repeat if necessary.

TIME SAVER

Manage Laundry

•

Laundry is often accomplished while doing other household chores. Allow 5 minutes to sort into white, light, and dark loads. Plan for 25 to 35 minutes per wash load and 30 to 50 minutes per dry load. Allow 5 to 10 minutes to fold or hang laundry, depending on items.

same size. They use the same amount of detergent as regular washers. The amount of detergent needed depends on the load size, not on the amount of water used. Front-loading washers are ideal for washing linens without going out of balance. Consider the following additional features:

■ Delay-starts, common on dishwashers, allow you to turn on the washing machine when utility rates are lower.

■ Automatic water level control selects the right amount of water for each load to prevent overfilling.

■ Internal water heaters reduce demand on your home water heater. The heater also improves cleaning performance.

■ Polypropylene and stainless-steel washtubs don't chip or rust as enameled steel can. Smooth interior surfaces are easier on clothes.

■ Spin speeds of 700 to 1,600 revolutions per minute mean that clothes are almost dry when they leave the washer. Drying gets done in less time and at lower temperatures.

Selecting a dryer: Consider energy costs as well as basic and special features when you purchase a clothes dryer.

■ Capacity: The size of the dryer drum determines capacity, which is measured in cubic feet. A larger capacity means the dryer is capable of drying more clothes. Descriptive terminology varies according to manufacturer, so check the actual cubic-foot capacity when shopping for a dryer. In general, dryer capacity ranges include compact (2 to 4 cubic feet), medium (4 to 5.8 cubic feet), large (5.9 to 6.9 cubic feet), and extra-large (7 or more cubic feet).

■ Cycles, temperatures, and controls: Basic dryers include delicate, permanent-press, and regular cycles. Expensive models offer more options for fabric care. Some models include a cycle for home dry-cleaning products. Standard temperature settings are hot, warm, and cool; some moderately priced dryers include timers and settings for specific fabric types.

■ Labor-saving dryers: Minimum drying times save energy and reduce wrinkling. To iron as little as possible, use the lowest dryer setting and do not overdry. Remove laundry as soon as the dryer stops. Take out all-cotton and permanent-press clothing when slightly damp and hang to dry. Consider other dryer options:

▶ Electronic moisture control detects moisture content to prevent overdrying and shrinking.

▶ Dryness monitor indicates a nearly dry load; minimizes ironing.

▶ A damp-dry cycle shortens drying time; garments can be ironed while damp or finish drying naturally, which is better for knits.

▶ Two-direction tumbling keeps clothes from clumping as they dry.

▶ An interior dryer-drum light helps to locate small items.

▶ A stationary rack allows shoes to be dried without tumbling.

■ Time-remainder indicators give read outs of the time left in cycle.

Ironing Tools of the Trade

Steam Iron:

Use an iron for last-minute touch-ups and unexpected wrinkles as well as basic ironing. Invest in a steam iron with permanent-press settings for the most versatility.

Board with Cover:

A full-size ironing board with a clean, well-fitting cover ensures the best results. Choose an easy-to-fold model to make it easy to set up and store away as needed.

Sleeve Board:

If you frequently iron garments with puffed sleeves or special detailing, or if you sew, a sleeve board is a helpful tool that folds away when not in use.

Scented Ironing Water:

If you enjoy sweet-smelling sheets or garments, spray with scented water made for ironing. Use in place of tap water in your steam iron. Buy only ironing water.

WASHER-DRYER COMBINATIONS

These efficient appliances, designed for small spaces, are available in stacked, side-by-side, or all-in-one units. Before selecting one of these styles, consider where the combo will be located, such as in a closet or in an upstairs bedroom or bath. Selection criteria are the same as for standard washers and dryers.

LAUNDRY LESSONS

A few techniques will make a cleaner wash and save money. Most important, sort light colors from dark colors. If you have doubts about the colorfastness of an item, wash it separately in a low-water setting, or a minibasket if your machine has one. To check for colorfastness, mix a small amount of detergent with a cup of water. Moisten a seam or inconspicuous spot. Rub with a clean, dry white towel. If color comes off, the garment should be laundered separately. Follow these tips for wash-day success:

Check pockets for pens, crayons, coins, tissues, and whatever you and your family put into pockets. Be especially vigilant if you have young children who put crayons in their pockets. If the crayons survive the wash, they will surely melt in the dryer.

Treat stains and heavy soiling before washing. Pretreat shirt collars and cuffs that are heavily soiled using a prewash stain removal product or liquid laundry detergent. Never dry stained items. If the stain remains after laundering, re-treat with the stain removal product and rewash. For very tough stains, try Zout, developed for hospital use. In addition to removing bloodstains, its intended use, the product has been formulated to remove grease, ink, grass, red wine, crayon, oil, olive oil, ketchup, and pet stains. If you can't find it in your area, call 800/548-9770 for information.

Use the recommended detergent amount. For heavily soiled garments, large loads, or hard water, use a little extra.

Check the water temperature, especially in the winter. Detergents work best in warm or hot water. Use cold water only for washing clothes that might fade or clothes that are lightly soiled.

Use automatic temperature control if your model has it to sense and adjust temperatures for maximum efficiency. For example, warming cold water to dissolve detergents.

Wash delicates in mild, gentle detergents made for fine washables, such as knits and sweaters. Turn delicates inside out and use the delicate or knit setting on your washer. If you wash delicate blouses, panty hose, tights, or lingerie in the washing machine, place them in zippered net bags.

LOADING THE WASHER AND DRYER

Never overload the washer or the dryer. In the washing machine, tub capacity and load weight determine wash-cycle water levels. Putting too many items in the machine leaves less room for water, so circulation decreases, limiting effective cleaning. A too-heavy load can also damage fabrics as they rub against the agitator. "Walking" washing machines that shift out of position and go noisily off balance during spin cycles are often caused by overloading. Consistent overloading can bend the washer's frame or damage the motor, which will eventually require repair or replacement. The consequences of overloading the dryer are equally dire. Overloading results in poor air flow so it takes more time and energy to dry clothing and linens. Too many overweight loads can result in misalignments of the drying drum, necessitating repair.

Proper washing machine loading: Check the loading instructions on the machine's lid. If these are not available, the most common order is detergent, laundry items, then water. This prevents excessive sudsing and minimizes the risk of fabric damage from full-strength detergents directly in contact with clothing.

Dryer loading: Underloading can be as wasteful and inefficient as overloading. Overloading prolongs drying time and can result in uneven drying; too few items in the load doesn't use heat efficiently. Either use a short cycle to avoid overheating a light load or wait until you can dry more items. Avoid putting heavy, hard-to-dry items in the same load with lightweight items.

Drying times depend on load size, garment weight, and fiber content. Six cotton bath towels that weigh 5 pounds will dry in 40 to 50 minutes, for example. A permanent-press load of 12 items—slacks, shirts, shorts, and dresses—also weighing 5 pounds, will dry in 30 to 40 minutes. As load size increases, so does drying time.

If the dryer seems to run for a long time, it may be the final cool-down cycle, which minimizes wrinkling. Some dryers offer extra tumbling without heat.

HAND LAUNDRY

Read care labels for instructions and water temperature. Some clothing, such as cotton knits and sweaters, retains color and shape best when hand laundered.

For best results, use a mild laundry detergent or product made for hand-washables. Products with high alkaline content are not recommended for cotton hand-washables. Read the label to be sure.

Fill a sink or small tub with water and detergent. Soak the garment; never scrub or twist. Rinse with clear water. Gently squeeze out excess water. Don't wring. Roll heavy garments in clean cotton towels to remove water. Use a towel that has been laundered

TIP TAG № 23

Iron a Shirt

FOR A LAUNDRY LOOK:
• Start with the underside of the collar, working toward the end and back to the center.
• Smooth shoulder yoke by slipping one shoulder over the narrow end of the board, ironing from shoulder to the center back. Repeat on the other side of the shirt.
• Iron cuffs inside, then outside. Iron body of each sleeve, beginning at the cuff; then do the reverse side. For a French cuff, use a sleeve board or roll a towel up into the sleeve and iron directly on the cuff.
• Iron shirt body, doing one front panel at a time. Re-press collar top.

several times so there's no chance of lint clinging to the newly washed garment. Follow label directions for reshaping and drying.

FOLDING CLOTHING AND LINENS

Create a sense of order in your closets and drawers with neatly folded everyday clothing and linens:

Casual shirts or T-shirts: Fasten buttons and closures. Hold the shirt by the shoulder seams near the neck seam, with the front facing you. Fold sleeve and sides back so the sleeves meet in the middle of the back. Drape the sleeves so they lie flat along folded edges. Fold the garment from the top to bottom either in half or thirds, according to preference or storage needs.

Alternatively, place the shirt front side down on a bed or tabletop. Smooth wrinkles by gently pulling at the seams, making the shirt slightly taut. Fold both sides in along the line of the outer edge of the collar or neck band, toward the center. Smooth the sleeves. Fold in half by bringing the bottom edge to the neck or collar.

Slacks: Line up seams and hems to keep creases crisp. Hold upside-down by bottom hems; match inseams to the outer seams, keeping the crease sharp. Fold in half onto a pants hanger or in thirds to place in a drawer.

Another method involves holding pants by the waistband and flapping them several times to smooth large folds. Lay on a flat surface with seams from each leg parallel, pulling seams gently until slightly taut. Fold one pant leg over the other, matching and smoothing the outside seams. Fold in thirds lengthwise to place in a drawer or fold in half for a hanger.

Towels: Folding style is a matter of preference. If you prefer to fold towels so they are ready for placement on towel bars, fold to half their width, then fold into thirds to stack. If you want to avoid extra wear along towel-bar crease, fold in half widthwise with short ends together. Fold in half again, short ends together, then in half again for storage.

Ironing

Even with the rise of cotton-blend and synthetic fabrics, typical households still have ironing chores. If you or your family members wear dress shirts or uniforms to work or to school, ironing them yourself, at least some of the time, is a money saver.

IRONS AND IRONING BOARDS

Irons and ironing boards come in many styles for a variety of needs. Irons range from under $10 upward to $100 for top of the line, hand-held cordless steam irons. European manufacturers design and market specialty irons, including moderately-priced models in discount and home furnishing stores. Ironing boards also are available in several styles and range from $15 up to $800 for

---

BUDGET STRETCHER

Fabric Care

•

Proper pressing extends the wear of your garments. To avoid a shiny look when pressing wool or dark fabric slacks or shirts, use a press cloth or clean cotton dish towel or a soleplate attachment for the iron.

Laundry Advice and Tips

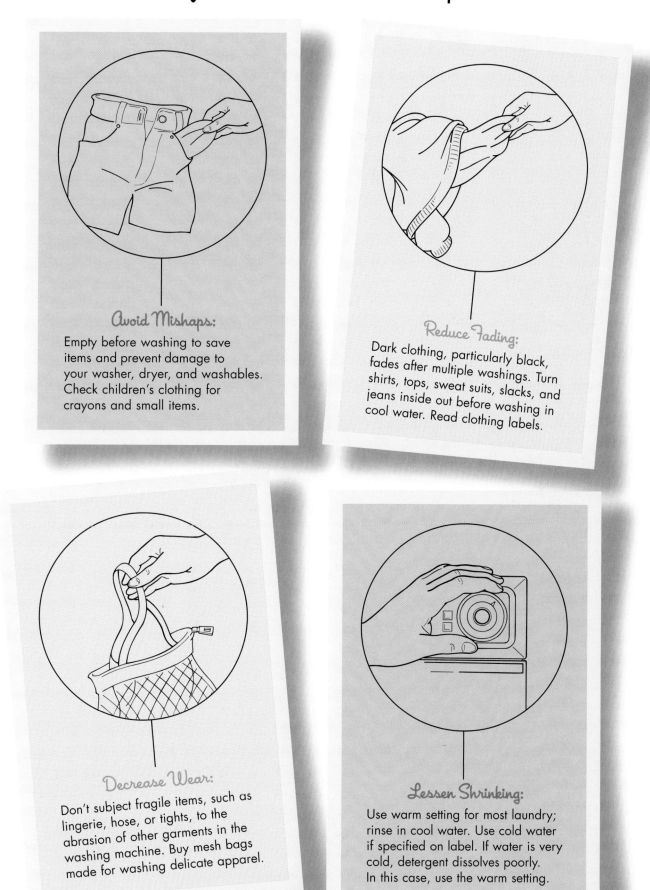

Avoid Mishaps:

Empty before washing to save items and prevent damage to your washer, dryer, and washables. Check children's clothing for crayons and small items.

Reduce Fading:

Dark clothing, particularly black, fades after multiple washings. Turn shirts, tops, sweat suits, slacks, and jeans inside out before washing in cool water. Read clothing labels.

Decrease Wear:

Don't subject fragile items, such as lingerie, hose, or tights, to the abrasion of other garments in the washing machine. Buy mesh bags made for washing delicate apparel.

Lessen Shrinking:

Use warm setting for most laundry; rinse in cool water. Use cold water if specified on label. If water is very cold, detergent dissolves poorly. In this case, use the warm setting.

professional-quality models that are marketed through specialty home stores and catalogs.

Dry iron: The most basic iron has a flat soleplate with a heat-generating electrical element.

Steam iron: This is the most common and versatile iron. Features vary by price and manufacturer. Features include

▶Spray: Mists clothes with a fine water spray.

▶Automatic shutoff: Some units have timers that turn off the iron when it remains horizontal for a specified period.

▶Variable steam: Adjusts the amount of steam released.

▶Burst/surge of steam: Produces a concentrated outflow.

▶Nonstick soleplate: This has little to do with how smoothly the iron glides over fabrics; a clean stainless-steel soleplate glides just as easily. A nonstick surface makes cleaning starch buildup easier.

▶Vertical steam: Some models produce steam while the iron is upright, allowing use as a steamer for clothes on hangers.

▶Variable heat settings: Top-of-the-line irons include more temperature settings for a wide variety of fabrics.

▶Cord swivel: Some units have a mechanism that allow cord movement in any position, reducing wire stress within the cord and the nuisance of the cord getting in the way.

▶Cordless: Some cordless irons warm on heat plates, allowing free movement while ironing. They retain heat levels for about five minutes, then need to be returned to a hot plate for reheating.

Steam iron care: If you have a care booklet with your iron, read it carefully. Unless stated otherwise, use ordinary tap water rather than distilled water in steam irons. If you live in an area with extremely hard water caused by mineral deposits, use bottled spring water or a half-and-half mix of untreated tap water and distilled water. Never use 100-percent distilled water unless the care label recommends otherwise. Don't use household water softeners in the iron; they may cause the iron to leak or spit. Commercially available scented linen water is safe, but test it first to be sure it doesn't stain.

Before using a new steam iron, clean the vents according to the care booklet. This usually involves filling the water well, plugging in the iron, setting it on the highest temperature (typically linen), and allowing it to sit upright for about three minutes to build up steam. Turn off the iron, unplug it, and drain the reservoir by pouring the water down the sink drain. If your iron has a "self-clean" setting, switch to it after unplugging and before draining. During regular use of your iron, drain well after each use.

Ironing boards: The most common and easiest to use ironing boards are the adjustable metal X-leg types readily available at retailers. Look for adjustable models that allow comfortable use either when sitting or standing. Ideally, the ironing surface should

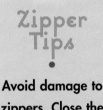

TIME SAVER

Zipper Tips

Avoid damage to zippers. Close the zipper and press the inside flaps with the iron tip. Unzip and iron lightly along the surrounding fabric. Close the zipper and iron covering fabric. Be cautious of ironing over the teeth of plastic, nylon, and polyester zippers, which melt easily.

be at hip level for ease of use. Some affordable boards provide cord holders that prevent tangles, iron rests that prevent scorching the cover, and racks for hanging clothes.

Depending on the size and location of the home laundry area, a built-in with a pull-down board may be a convenient feature, easily hidden in a wall cabinet when not in use.

When you buy pads and covers, select thick cotton padding to reduce overheating from beneath and to reduce wrinkling. Pad covers come in many colors and patterns, in plain cotton, and with nonstick coatings to make starch or sizing cleanup easy.

IRONING CLOTHING

Clothing constitutes the bulk of home ironing for the typical household. In most cases, garments worn to work or school or for special occasions are ironed. (See the tip tag on page 219 for instructions on how to iron a shirt.) For tips on ironing table linens, often a job before special meals, see "Ironing a Tablecloth," the following section.

Slacks: Lay pockets on the ironing board and press flat. Fit the waistband around the end of the ironing board, and rotate slacks as you press waistband and pants top. Lay the pants flat, one leg atop the other. Align inseams with outer seams. Iron the inside of the bottom leg by folding back the top leg. Flip and repeat to iron the other side. With inseams aligned, press the outside of each leg. If using a steam iron, use a burst of steam to set creases. If not, cover the creases with a press cloth or towels to press.

Dresses: Follow the instructions for shirts. (See tip tag on page 219.) Large items require the wide end of the ironing board. To iron a long skirt, place a plastic tablecloth or sheet on the floor beneath the board to protect fabric that drapes to the floor. Iron embroidered designs by laying the garment face down on a terry cloth towel and pressing with a burst of steam. Cover delicate buttons by placing the bowl of a spoon over each one and ironing the surrounding area.

For gathers and ruffles, iron on the inside, moving from the outer edge toward the gathers. If the material is difficult to maneuver, hang the garment and use a vertical burst of steam. For pleats, start at the bottom with the inside of the pleat and then move to the outside. Set pleats by applying a burst of steam.

IRONING A TABLECLOTH

This can be an unwieldy chore, given the size and length of most tablecloths. Iron tablecloths when they are slightly damp. Place a clean sheet on the floor underneath the ironing board to protect the

smart ideas
Dryer Efficiency

BE SAFE

Always check the lint trap before each load. (Make it habit to check before starting the dryer.) A full lint trap is a fire hazard and reduces efficiency.

PREHEAT

Do lightweight, quick-drying items first in a separate load. Placing these in a cold dryer to start reduces shrinkage risk while preheating the dryer for later, heavier loads.

AVOID WRINKLING

Do several small loads rather than one large, crammed load. You'll save energy with the shorter drying times and make use of the residual heat.

ends of the tablecloth. Use a steam iron and choose the heat setting appropriate for the fabric type. If desired, lightly apply a spray starch to the back side. Work in small sections holding the can 6 inches from the fabric. Press in a fluid motion to prevent creases.

Round or oval: Carefully lay the tablecloth across the ironing board and press the center area of the tablecloth. Working outward, iron the edges one section at a time. Visualize the cloth as a large pie and iron in pie-slice sections.

Fold round or oval: Fold the cloth in half (wrong sides together) to make a half circle. Fold in half again. Lay the tablecloth across the ironing board and bring the edges together to fold crosswise two more times until you have a small "pie-slice" triangle. Store flat in a drawer or linen closet.

Rectangular: Iron wrong side first. To reduce sheen, press the wrong side on a lower heat setting. Iron unfolded to avoid creases. To iron very large tablecloths, fold in half lengthwise, right sides together, and press. Refold the tablecloth with wrong sides together and iron until dry. To erase a center crease, fold the tablecloth loosely into thirds and iron down the middle.

Fold Rectangular: Fold the cloth in half lengthwise with wrong sides together. Fold the top and bottom ends together and fold in half crosswise. Fold the bottom end of the tablecloth, meeting in the center. Fold one more time and store flat.

Stain Removal

Protect your investment in washable clothing and linens by promptly and correctly treating stains. If a fabric is dry-clean-only, blot off excess stain and take the garment to the cleaners as soon as possible. Always point out stains and spots so they can be marked for special professional cleaning. The following tips are for general home laundry.

FABRIC GUIDE

Photocopy this list and post it in your laundry room or near your washing machine and dryer. As a general rule, inspect all clothing and linens. Treat stains as soon as possible and pretreat before washing. If a stained item goes through the drying cycle, the stain will be harder to remove.

Baby formula: Pretreat or soak stains with a product containing enzymes. Soak dried stains for at least 30 minutes. Launder normally. (Always launder infants' clothing in mild detergent formulated for baby clothes.)

Blood: For fresh stains, soak in cold water (hot water sets stains). Launder. For dried stains, pretreat or soak in warm water with a product containing enzymes (read the label). Launder. If stain remains, use a bleach safe for the fabric.

Care for Common Fabrics

Cotton:
Holds up well to home laundering. Remove from dryer promptly to reduce wrinkling. Press with spray starch for the crispness of a laundered shirt.

Acrylic Knit:
Normally can be machine-washed. Read label and check for proper drying. Some knits retain their shape best if reshaped and dried flat.

Wool Knit:
Typically wool can be dry-cleaned, but check the label. If hand-washable, use cool water and detergent for fine washables. Dry clean to retain shape.

Linen:
Typically may be dry-cleaned or hand-washed. Read care labels. If touching up or pressing, use a steam iron for a crisp look.

Polyester:
Read label. Normally machine-washed (cool) and dried (low). Read to see if air-drying is recommended. Touch up with cool iron—never hot—if necessary.

Silk:
Dry cleaning may be required. Some silks are hand or machine washable (not dried). Usually looks best when professionally dry-cleaned.

Cotton Blend:
Dry on permanent-press or low cycle and remove immediately to reduce wrinkling. Touch up with a steam iron; starch for professionally laundered look.

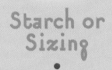

TIME SAVER

Starch or Sizing

Get the most for your money with the right product. Use starch for natural fabrics such as cotton; use sizing for synthetics. Spray lightly from several inches away before ironing. For a soft finish, spritz with plain water; then iron lightly.

Chocolate: Pretreat or prewash in warm water with a product containing enzymes. Or treat with a prewash stain remover. Launder. If stain remains, rewash with bleach safe for the fabric.

Collar and cuff soil: Pretreat with a prewash stain remover, liquid laundry detergent, or a paste of granular detergent and water.

Crayon: For a few spots, scrape off the surface with a dull knife. Place the stained area between clean paper towels and press with a warm iron. Replace paper towels as the crayon is absorbed. Place stained area face down on several layers of clean paper towels. Sponge with a prewash stain remover or cleaning fluid. Blot with paper towels. Allow to dry before laundering. If color remains, rewash with a chlorine bleach, if safe for fabrics. Otherwise, use a color-safe bleach. For an entire load of clothes affected by crayons loose in the dryer, wash with hot water using laundry detergent and 1 cup of baking soda. If color remains, launder with chlorine bleach, if safe for fabrics. Otherwise, pretreat or soak in a product containing enzymes or a color-safe bleach. Use the hottest water safe for the fabric and rewash.

Diesel fuel or gasoline: Use extra caution when treating these stains—they can make clothing flammable. When washing fuel- or gasoline-soaked fabrics, use only detergent-based stain removers, not solvent-based ones. Air clothing and other items thoroughly and do not place in the dryer if fuel smell is detected.

Fruit juices: Soak in cold water (hot water sets the stain). Wash with bleach safe for the fabric.

Grass: If lightly stained, pretreat with stain remover or liquid laundry detergent. Launder using hottest water safe for fabric. For heavy grass stains, place face down on several layers of paper towels. Apply cleaning fluid to the back of the stain. Replace paper towels as the stain is absorbed. Let dry; rinse. Launder using hottest water safe for fabric.

Ink: Some common inks are extremely difficult or impossible to remove. Common inks include ballpoint, felt-tip, and liquid. Try one of these three pretreatments before giving up. As the easiest first step, pretreat with a prewash stain remover and launder as usual. Don't put in dryer if stain remains. Instead, try another method.

Using denatured alcohol or cleaning fluid is a method worth trying. Sponge the area around the stain with either before applying the solvent to the stain. Place the stain face down on clean paper towels. Apply alcohol or cleaning fluid to the back of the stain, frequently replacing the paper towels. Rinse thoroughly; launder.

As an alternative method, place the stained fabric over the mouth of a jar or glass. Hold the fabric taut so the ink spot doesn't spread. Drip the alcohol or cleaning fluid through the stained fabric; as it leaves the fabric, the ink will drop into the container. Rinse thoroughly with cool water; launder as usual.

Mustard: Pretreat with stain remover. Launder with chlorine bleach, if safe for the fabric or with color-safe bleach.

Nail polish: This may be impossible to remove. Try this method using nail polish remover, but don't use on acetate or triacetate fabric. Place stain face down on several layers of clean paper towels. Apply remover to the back of stain. Replace towels as they accept polish. Repeat if stain begins to lift. Rinse and launder.

Paint (water-based): Rinse fabric in warm water while stains are wet. Launder. For dried paint, take the article to a dry cleaner, who may be able to remove the paint. Removal depends on the paint formulation and the fabric.

Paint (oil-based paint and varnish): If the label on the paint can recommends a thinner, use that solvent for stain removal. If label is not available, try turpentine. Rinse. Pretreat with a prewash stain remover, bar soap, or laundry detergent. Rinse, launder, or take to a dry cleaner. Oil paint is harder to remove than latex.

Perspiration: If perspiration changes fabric color, apply ammonia to fresh stains or white vinegar to old stains; rinse. Launder using hottest water safe for fabric or wash with an enzyme product or color-safe bleach in the hottest water safe for the fabric.

Scorch: Fabric may be beyond repair. Launder using chlorine bleach, if safe for fabric. Otherwise, soak in color-safe bleach and hottest water safe for fabric, then launder.

Urine, vomit, mucous, feces: Pretreat or soak in a product containing enzymes. Launder using chlorine bleach (which also disinfects), if safe for fabric. Otherwise, use color-safe bleach.

STAIN REMOVAL TIPS

■ Blot rather than rub to treat a stain. Blotting draws the stain away from the fabric; rubbing pushes the stain into the fabric and damages the fiber, finish, and color of the fabric. Use a gentle rubbing motion under running water to help remove dried food, protein, or oil stains from denim-weight fabrics of cotton or cotton/polyester blends.

■ Do not use terry-cloth towels or dark-color cloths when blotting stains; lint and dark colors may worsen the problem.

■ Before doing laundry, check for stains. Pretreat before washing.

■ Check wet laundry before putting it into the dryer to see if the stain is gone. If the stain persists, do not put the item in the dryer. The heat of the dryer can make a stain permanent.

■ Wash heavily stained items separately to avoid transferring stains.

smart ideas

Paper to Cloth Napkins
GOOD FOR ENVIRONMENT

Cloth napkins aren't just for special occasions. In the long run, you'll save money and help save trees too. To make the transition from paper to cloth, purchase two or three colorful cotton napkins for each member of your family. Look for sales at linen outlets. Mixing and matching colors and patterns (including washable place mats) is fine for everyday use. Napkins should be laundered after every use; launder with your regular wash. Remove from the dryer and fold; it is unnecessary to iron cloth napkins for everyday use.

■Do not use hot water on stains of unknown origin. Hot water can set protein stains in the fabric.

■Never wash pesticide-soiled clothes with other laundry.

Products to stock: Keep the following products on hand in the laundry area. Brand name examples are given when available. Note that all products should be kept out of the reach of children on upper shelves or in locked upper cabinets. Never leave any of these product packages on the washing machine; drips could damage machine surfaces.

■Nonsudsing household ammonia, chlorine bleach, and color-safe bleach, color remover such as Rit brand, and commercial stain removers such as Easy Wash and Whizz.

■Mild hand dishwashing detergent for handwashing; dry cleaning fluid or petroleum-based pretreatment solvent such as Spray "n" Wash or K2r Spot Lifter; paint remover; petroleum jelly; rust removers such as Yellow Out, Whink, and RoVer; pre-wash spot remover; towelettes; and white vinegar.

COMMON PROBLEMS

Grayness overall: Causes are insufficient amount of detergent, low water temperature, or incorrect sorting. To solve, increase the amount of detergent, use a detergent booster or bleach, or increase wash temperature. Sort heavily soiled from lightly soiled items and carefully sort by color.

Grayness uneven: Usually caused by insufficient amount of detergent, too low water temperature, or improper sorting. Sort garments by color and rewash with an increased amount of detergent and hottest water safe for fabric. In future, use sufficient detergent and wash in hottest water safe for fabric.

Yellowing: May be caused by buildup of body soil. Increase the amount of detergent; use a product with detergent booster or bleach safe for fabric; or try both methods at once. In the future, use a sufficient amount of detergent.

Blue stains: Detergent or fabric softener may not be dissolving or dispersing. If detergent causes the problem, soak the garment in a plastic container using a solution of 1 cup white vinegar to 1 quart water; soak for one hour; rinse and launder. If you have been using fabric softener, rub stains with bar soap. Rinse and launder. To prevent stains, add the detergent and turn on the washer before adding laundry. If using fabric softener, dilute the fabric softener in water before adding to wash or rinse cycle or to dispenser.

Powder residue: Usually caused by undissolved detergent. Always add detergent before filling tub and adding laundry.

Stiffness or fading: May be caused by hard water. Use liquid laundry detergent or add a water softener to granular detergent.

Lint: Caused by mixing items that give off lint, such as bath

---

FAMILY FRIENDLY

Deal with Dirt

•

Allow the mud on clothes to dry. Brush off as much as possible. If lightly stained by the dirt or mud, pretreat with a paste of granular laundry detergent and water or liquid detergent. Launder. Presoak heavy stains in a laundry detergent.

Treat Tablecloth Stains

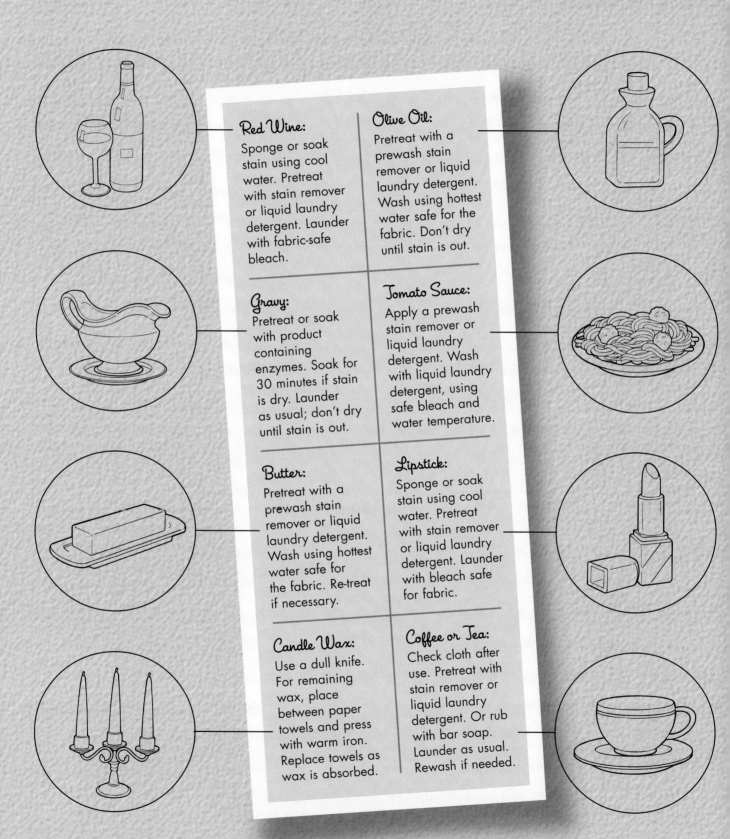

Red Wine:

Sponge or soak stain using cool water. Pretreat with stain remover or liquid laundry detergent. Launder with fabric-safe bleach.

Olive Oil:

Pretreat with a prewash stain remover or liquid laundry detergent. Wash using hottest water safe for the fabric. Don't dry until stain is out.

Gravy:

Pretreat or soak with product containing enzymes. Soak for 30 minutes if stain is dry. Launder as usual; don't dry until stain is out.

Tomato Sauce:

Apply a prewash stain remover or liquid laundry detergent. Wash with liquid laundry detergent, using safe bleach and water temperature.

Butter:

Pretreat with a prewash stain remover or liquid laundry detergent. Wash using hottest water safe for the fabric. Re-treat if necessary.

Lipstick:

Sponge or soak stain using cool water. Pretreat with stain remover or liquid laundry detergent. Launder with bleach safe for fabric.

Candle Wax:

Use a dull knife. For remaining wax, place between paper towels and press with warm iron. Replace towels as wax is absorbed.

Coffee or Tea:

Check cloth after use. Pretreat with stain remover or liquid laundry detergent. Or rub with bar soap. Launder as usual. Rewash if needed.

towels and napped velour or corduroy fabrics. Wash such items separately or with like fabrics. A clogged washer lint filter or full dryer lint screen may be the culprit. Tissues left in pockets also cause this problem. Check pockets before washing and check washer filter frequently. Clean dryer lint screen after every load.

Pilling: This is a wear problem and a characteristic of some synthetic and permanent-press fabrics. If necessary, use a lint brush or roller with masking tape to remove pills. Adding a fabric softener in the washer or dryer may also help. When ironing, use spray starch or fabric finish on collars and cuffs. Use a medium setting to avoid scorching delicate synthetic fabrics.

Shrinking: Avoid the problem by following care instructions on labels. Shrinkage is irreversible. Reduce drying time and remove garments when they are are slightly damp, which is especially important for cotton knits.

ANTIQUE LINENS

Hold up fabrics to the light to check for worn spots, tears, broken threads, and holes. Very old lace or fabrics may tear if washed. Linens that you find at antiques fairs usually are already cleaned and pressed, but if you find fabrics at a garage sale or hidden away at an antiques shop, you'll want to clean them.

Test a piece of embroidery for color-fastness by gently dabbing the thread on the back of the piece with a damp white cloth. If no color comes off on the cloth, you can wash the piece safely. (If color does come off, you'll need to have the piece dry-cleaned.) It's usually safe to machine-wash embroidered dresser scarves, pillowcases, hand towels, and table runners from the 1930s and 1940s if the fabric is not worn or fragile. Press pieces while they're still damp for the smoothest look.

To clean fine linen or pieces with handmade lace, fringe, or crocheted edging, presoak them for about 15 minutes in clear water to loosen dirt. Then gently swish the linens in warm water with mild, nonabrasive, phosphate-free soap. Avoid using bleach because it can damage the fibers. Rinse textiles at least twice in clear water to remove all soap residue.

Old stains may be impossible to remove, but you can try soaking them in a textile enzyme cleaner such as Biz or Axion, diluted with water, before laundering. Or add a nonchlorine bleach to the wash water. The old-fashioned method for bleaching white fabrics is to rub lemon juice and salt over the stain. Hang on a clothesline or spread the fabric out to dry in the sun.

Wash chenille in the washing machine and dry it in the dryer. If you need to iron it, lay the fabric tufted side down on a well-padded ironing board and press using the cotton setting. Have draperies, bedding, or other bark cloth professionally dry-cleaned.

SAFETY ALERT

Sleepwear Care

•

Children's sleepwear must be flame-resistant unless pajamas fit snugly. Never use bleach on flame-resistant fabrics. It reduces the effectiveness of the treatment chemicals and might ruin treated fabrics. Follow care label instructions.

9

Homeowner Tools

- BASICS TO OWN, 233, 251
- PLUMBING AND ELECTRICAL TOOLS, 234
- SAFETY DEVICES, 236

Heating & Cooling

- CARE AND MAINTENANCE, 236
- COMMON PROBLEMS, 237
- WHEN TO CALL A PRO, 237

Fire Safety

- PRODUCTS TO OWN, 239
- SMOKE ALARMS, 240
- CARBON MONOXIDE ALARMS, 240

Plumbing Concerns

- PREVENTING FROZEN LINES, 240
- FROZEN DRAINS, 240
- ANTI-SCALD VALVE, 240

Electrical Questions

- CIRCUIT BREAKER PANEL, 241
- FUSE BOX, 241
- SURGE PROTECTORS, 241

Water Systems

- WATER HEATERS AND WATER SOFTENERS, 242

Lawn Equipment & Tools

- TYPES OF LAWN MOWERS, 245
- LAWN MOWER MAINTENANCE, 246
- DEALING WITH SNOW AND ICE, 248
- SNOWBLOWERS, 250
- LEAF BLOWERS AND VACUUMS, 252
- GARDEN TOOLS AND TILLERS, 252

Outdoor Furniture

- BASIC TYPES; CARE, 253, 254

Garage Door Openers

- WHEN THE POWER IS OUT, 256
- SAFETY AND SECURITY, 256

Fireplaces & Stoves

- STARTING A FIRE, 257
- STOVES AND INSERTS, 258
- GAS FIREPLACES, 260

Security & Safety

- DOORS AND LOCKS; ALARM SYSTEMS, 261

Knowing the Systems

Because they're usually hidden in basements, attics, utility closets, or even outdoors, major household systems such as furnaces, ventilating fans, water heaters, and air-conditioning compressors often fall into the "out-of-sight, out-of-mind" category. Proper maintenance, however, is critical to efficiency. Becoming familiar with your household systems is an important first step toward keeping these systems running well for comfort and safety.

PUT SAFETY FIRST

Safety must be uppermost in your system planning. Basics include installing smoke alarms and carbon monoxide sensors—especially near bedrooms—as well as owning and knowing how to use fire safety equipment, including extinguishers and fire escape ladders. In households with children or elderly family members, practice escape routes so that everyone understands safety procedures and is capable of reacting to emergency situations. Assign capable people to assist ill, elderly, and very young family members in safely exiting the home.

Homeowner Tools

A well-stocked toolbox makes the simplest tasks easier, quicker, and safer because you'll have the right tool for the job.

BASICS TO OWN

Begin with basic tools and add equipment to your toolbox as you become adept at doing it yourself.

Adjustable locking wrench: Firmly holds nuts, bolt heads, and hose connections by adjusting and clamping wrench jaws.

Awl: Start nails or screws in soft wood or use as a hole-punch for leather goods.

Clamps: Hold glued pieces together until dry.

Claw hammer: A 16-ounce curved claw hammer is a basic tool for driving and removing nails.

Duct tape: A multipurpose fabric-tape adhesive. Despite its name, it's NOT for use on furnace ducts. Use mastic on ductwork.

Flashlight: Use a flashlight to see your work under a sink, at the electric service entry, or in crawl spaces.

Pliers: Twist electrical wire, remove a tub drain, or handle similar chores.

Needlenose pliers: Use these pliers to bend and shape wire.

Pen and pencil: Mark areas to be drilled, cut, or sawed.

Putty knife: Stock the 3-inch size for patching small holes.

Home Remedies

FURNACE WOES

Won't Light

For a forced-air gas furnace, look for the flame sensor (a smooth rod next to the pilot). Using a plumber's emery cloth (found at hardware stores), gently abrade rod to clean it. If pilot won't stay on, air intake valves may need adjusting, or a new thermocouple may be needed. Have annual professional furnace inspection, cleaning, and repairs for safe and efficient use.

Warning

Never stick anything into a pilot because you could accidentally enlarge the orifice. Never touch the fragile igniter next to the pilot. **If you smell gas** or think there has been gas buildup, leave the building immediately and call for professional help.

Screwdrivers: Include three basic sizes for home repair—No. 2 phillips, small flat, and medium flat screwdrivers.

Tape measure: A 25-foot metal tape measure is an all-purpose length for most do-it-yourself projects.

Torpedo level: Include a 12-inch model for leveling picture frames as well as desks and tables set on uneven floors.

Utility knife: Stock one to cut drywall and to loosen painted-shut windows, as well as additional practical uses.

EXTRAS

Bucket organizer: Organize with a lightweight 5-gallon bucket equipped with pockets or slots to hold individual tools.

Dripless caulk gun: Dispense caulk, adhesive, and sealant with a squeeze of the trigger.

Electric drill and bits: Buy an electric drill and bits to bore holes. Cordless drills are the most versatile.

Extension cord: Stock a 25-foot 16-gauge ground-fault circuit interrupter (GFCI) cord for safe access to work areas that don't have electrical power.

Framing square and speed square: Use these to check for square when building furniture, hanging shelves, or laying tile.

Hand broom and dust pan: Whisk debris from work space.

Light-gauge or baling wire: Repair or temporarily hold two or more items together.

Nails: Keep 4-penny (4d) and 8-penny (8d) finish nails on hand.

Nail set: Place blunt or cupped pointed end on nail head and hammer flat top to sink finish nails below wood surface.

Painter's tape: Neatly delineate areas to be painted.

Painter's tool: Add a 5-in-1 painter's tool to use as a scraper, a gouge to clean gaps, and to remove paint from a roller.

Plastic sheeting: Protect work areas from spills and scrapes with 2 mil sheeting. Use newspaper or plastic stand under ladders.

Pot magnet: Corral screws and other small metal parts.

Pry bars: Use to remove nails in tight areas. Bars with wide, thin blades allow for low-impact demolition, such as removing door and window frame casings.

Small pull saw: Keep one to cut cleanly on the pull stroke.

Stud locator: Locate support to hang frames and shelves.

Wood chisel: Sharp bevel-edge tool for chipping and slicing wood fiber.

Wood glue: Use for joining wood. Best for indoor projects because of limited water-resistance. Can be sanded and painted.

Wood screws: Stock 1½-inch and 3-inch screws.

PLUMBING

Emery cloth: Use this cloth to clean metal surfaces.

Hacksaw: For cutting metal and nonwood materials.

Forced-Air Gas Furnace

Return Air Duct:
Brings in cool air that passes through the filter before the blower pushes it into the heating chamber.

Plenum:
This large hot-air supply duct leads from the furnace before branching into the duct system.

Flue Connection:
Attaches furnace to flue, a channel that carries combustion gases and vents them to the outside.

Heat Exchanger:
The blower pushes warm air into the plenum. Check exchanger through an inspection port.

Gas Supply Pipe:
Brings in natural gas from fuel source and directs it through the control valve.

Combination Control Valve:
Safety valve shuts off gas if the pilot light goes out.

Burner:
Takes in gas and air from manifold tubes, which are ignited by the pilot light.

Filter:
Basic filters are oil-treated fiberglass in a cardboard frame. Change regularly to maintain good airflow.

Blower:
Belt drives need to be checked for tension and fraying belts. Oil regularly via lubrication ports.

Pipe-joint tape: Better than joint compound around pipe threads to prevent leaks.

Pipe wrenches: Keep two of the 10- or 12-inch size on hand. Use one to hold the pipe still and the other to turn the fitting.

Slip-joint pliers: Versatile pliers adjust from small- to medium-gripping width and have serrated teeth that allow a tight hold.

ELECTRICAL

Combination tool: Measure, strip, and cut wire and cable.

Current detector: Check current in switches and boxes.

Electrical tape: Use to mark wires; attaches cable to fish tape.

Insulated linemen's pliers: Used to cut wires; safety benefit of insulated handles.

Outlet tester: Check whether wires are correctly positioned and whether the ground wire is connected.

Wire connectors: Use the correct size rated for the wire.

SAFETY

Disposable respirator

Gloves

Goggles

Hearing protection

Heating and Cooling

Your comfort depends on your home's heating and cooling capabilities to maintain temperatures and humidity. Well-maintained heating, cooling, and humidity control systems contribute to energy conservation, extend the life of home furnishings, and enhance your well-being. Heating and cooling systems vary greatly; learn what type you have and how to maintain it.

HEATING SYSTEMS

Ducted air systems circulate air from a furnace or air-conditioner via a network of ducts. Blower-driven forced-air systems both heat and cool homes. Water or steam systems distribute heat through radiators, returning cooled water to the boiler for recirculation. Radiant heat systems warm the floor, ceiling, or baseboards via water or electricity. Avoid nailing, boring, or cutting into surfaces of homes with radiant heat until you know where cables are located.

Changing the filter: Forced-air systems rely on a filter to clean the air that moves through the furnace, into the ducts, and back through the furnace. Determine which filter works with your furnace and air-conditioner system and inspect it for contaminants every 30 days. Change or clean the filter every 30 to 60 days for optimum heating and cooling efficiency.

Oil-furnace filter: In addition to an air filter, oil furnaces have an in-line fuel filter that requires changing or cleaning once a year. Some models also have a pump strainer that requires annual

---

BUDGET STRETCHER

Bleeding a Radiator

•

For hot-water units: Let unit cool; open small valve at the top with a screwdriver. Once water flows, close valve. For steam units: Let unit cool; clear by using a thin wire to ream the small hole at top of the conical air vent.

cleaning. Hire a professional to conduct an annual cleaning.

Squeals and squeaks: Noises emanating from the furnace require immediate attention. Causes may be a loose belt between the blower and blower motor, loose ductwork, or a loose furnace door. Correct a loose belt by tightening, aligning, or replacing the belt according to furnace manufacturer instructions. Consult furnace professionals to correct other problems.

Ducting seals: Check exposed ductwork to determine whether duct joints require sealing. If the furnace area is warm during heating season or cool during cooling season, seal both the return air duct and the supply duct with mastic, found in ductwork departments of home centers.

Built-in humidifiers: Humidity levels of 40 to 50 percent are ideal for your health and your home's interior surfaces. Humidifiers attach to the air ducts of the furnace, and humidistat sensors control the humidity level. For humidifier efficiency, check and clean humidifier waterways each time you check the filter.

Gas fireplaces: Gas-fired appliances with ceramic logs are convenient because they can be instantly turned on and shut off. Fuel is provided through a gas line, and the spent fuel from direct vent fireplaces is exhausted outdoors. Unvented units are for short-term use only because by-products that are not combusted enter room air. For safety, insist on an oxygen-depletion sensor that shuts off the appliance when oxygen in the room falls below a safe level. Local codes apply to gas-fired appliances used in bedrooms, bathrooms, and commercial buildings.

COOLING SYSTEMS

Because air-conditioning systems reduce humidity, the cooling process consumes more energy than heating. In addition, cool air falls and warm air rises, making it difficult to push cool air through ductwork for circulation around the home. Central air-conditioning systems use an outdoor condensing unit and an indoor evaporator coil near the blower. Routine maintenance and repair of central air-conditioners is often better left to professionals. In dry climates, homes may have swamp coolers that provide needed humidity.

Clogged condensate drain: Each year before operating the air-conditioner for the first time, unhook the drain line from the furnace and blow through it to clear it. Pour water through the pump reservoir to determine whether the drain empties into the pump. Drain lines may clog during use or freeze when not in use.

Condensing unit: At least once a year, and more frequently if you have a heat pump, use a spray of water to wash away efficiency-inhibiting dust from the condenser coils.

Filter change: Change or clean the air filter every 30 to 90 days to protect the blower motor and clean the air.

Damper adjustment: Note whether your heating system includes dampers near the furnace labeled "summer" and "winter." In two-story structures, the purpose of the dampers is to send warm air to the lower floor during heating season and cool air to the upper floor during cooling season.

Window units: Change filters monthly during the cooling season. If possible, remove from the window opening to store during noncooling months. If your unit or units are more than 10 years old, consider replacing them with energy-efficient units.

Attic fans: In the absence of air-conditioning, attic fans act as an exhaust to cool the home. Install soffit vents so the fan can pull outside air into the house. Attic fans are most effective in climates with temperate summer nights.

Fire Safety

Fire moves quickly and can wreak havoc in a matter of minutes. Homeowners who invest in sprinkler systems and safety alarms are taking precautions to save lives and prevent damage.

WHAT YOU CAN DO NOW

■ Identify, practice, and post escape routes so that everyone in your home knows how to leave in an emergency. Assign a meeting place outside the home.

■ Close bedroom doors at night. Closed doors slow dangerous smoke and gases from entering the sleeping quarters while helping to provide time to respond to fire-detector alarms.

■ Install fire escape ladders in second floor bedrooms and check existing ladders for safety. Practice using the ladders, dropping to the ground, and going to the assigned meeting place.

■ Mount Class ABC multipurpose fire extinguishers in the kitchen and garage, selecting the larger, more efficient extinguisher. Teach family members how to use extinguishers. In the absence of an extinguisher, generously douse a grease fire with baking soda.

■ Replace outlets and light switches that feel warm to the touch.

■ Store flammable chemicals, including machines with gas tanks, in out-buildings or fireproof cabinets.

■ Dispose of oil- or solvent-soaked rags safely to avoid spontaneous combustion. Hang them or spread them to dry thoroughly, allowing combustible elements to dissipate. After they are dry, dispose of them. Never wad them while they are wet; never dispose of them near material that can ignite. Consult local waste-management authorities for requirements for disposal of toxic materials.

HEALTHY HOME

Suspect Your House

•

If a family member is chronically ill from an unknown cause, consider as possible culprits: low levels of carbon monoxide, radon gas, lead poisoning from paint, drinking water even if you have a filtering system, or mold.

Home Fire Safety Tools

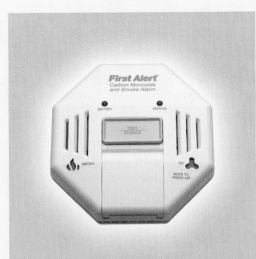

Alarms and Sensors:

A battery-operated combination unit uses separate sensors that monitor the air for smoke and carbon monoxide levels, sounding an alarm if there's danger.

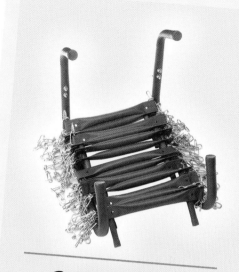

Fire Escape Ladder:

An expandable steel fire escape ladder provides an exit route from a second-story window if halls are blocked. They store under beds and are ready to use in seconds.

Fire Extinguisher:

Many house fires start in the kitchen. Mount a multipurpose Class ABC extinguisher nearby. Teach family members how to use it. Replace or recharge after use.

Baking Soda:

To effectively smother stove or grease fires, cover them with baking soda. Never throw water on a grease fire. It could splatter, spreading flames.

■ If you use live Christmas trees, assign one person to check it and water it daily. Dry trees pose a fire threat each holiday season.

■ Do not leave stovetop burners unattended. Turn off burners when you leave the house even for a short time. Avoid using hot settings for oil and foods that contain oil.

■ Use safety screens in front of fireplaces.

■ Schedule annual professional inspections, cleaning, and repair of fireplace and furnace chimneys, flues, and vents.

SMOKE ALARMS

■ Install at least one alarm on each level of your home, using battery-operated or battery-backup alarms that detect both smoke and heat even in case of power-failure. Ideally, place one in each bedroom and in hallways.

■ Mount alarms on ceiling, away from corners and ductwork.

■ Conduct battery tests every 30 days for every alarm. Most have a push-button for testing. Every six months test the alarm by holding burning incense or a blown-out smoking candle near the alarm.

■ Do not mount smoke alarms or fire detectors in the kitchen, bathroom, utility room, workshop, or garage, where routine heat, smoke, and moisture could trigger the system unnecessarily.

■ Replace the entire smoke alarm every 10 years.

CARBON MONOXIDE ALARMS

■ Carbon monoxide alarms are activated by dangerous levels of the colorless, odorless toxic gas. If family members suffer from chronic headaches or nausea, inspect all gas appliances for leaks.

■ Install at least one alarm, powered with household current with a battery backup, on each level of your home. Avoid installing them close to the kitchen, bathroom, or garage areas that would trigger the alarm unnecessarily.

■ Assign a specific day each month to test the alarm.

Plumbing Concerns

Homeowners are often intimidated by complex plumbing procedures that require specialized tools and technical skills. Learn to do regular maintenance to deter problems and expense.

PREVENTING FROZEN WATER LINES

Wrap water lines in exterior walls or attics with heating tape or insulation. For outdoor water supply lines, install freeze-proof sill cocks or shutoff valves in the pipe to turn off the water supply. Disconnect water hoses from outdoor faucets before cold seasons.

FROZEN DRAINS

In very cold weather, water sitting in drains along exterior walls may freeze. More of an inconvenience than a hazard, the problem can be alleviated by leaving cabinet doors open to the heat in the room.

ANTISCALD VALVES

BUDGET STRETCHER

Saving Water

•

Reduce the use of bathroom water significantly by combining these water-saving methods: Install faucet aerators, use water-saving showerheads, and use water-saving toilet floats.

These devices prevent sudden water temperature changes, particularly in the shower or bath—allowing the water heater to remain at a high setting but limiting the bathroom to a safe 120 degrees F. Many local building codes now require these. If your home does not have an antiscald or pressure-balance valve, home centers stock add-on devices that can be installed on your plumbing.

Electrical Questions

Safety is of utmost concern when working with electricity. Homeowners should hire licensed electricians to accomplish major installations and repairs; however, it is wise for homeowners to learn how to look for problems and perform simple maintenance on their home electrical systems.

CIRCUIT BREAKER PANEL AND FUSE BOX

What's a breaker? Breakers are toggle switches that are located in a breaker box. They automatically shut off electricity to circuits that are overloaded or when a short-circuit occurs. Breakers also are used to turn off circuits for safety when repairing or replacing electrical fixtures.

What trips a breaker? Overloaded circuits commonly trip breakers, a safety measure for your home's wiring. Avoid overloading circuits by becoming familiar with the number of outlets assigned to each circuit, the current consumption of appliances plugged into the circuit, and the total amperage. Circuit breakers normally trip when the load exceeds 15 to 20 amps. Designate specific circuits for major appliances and avoid connecting too many high-amperage appliances, such as hair dryers and microwave ovens, to the same circuit.

A less common but potentially dangerous cause of tripped breakers is a short circuit, which is a result of hot and neutral wires contacting each other in home or appliance wiring.

Breakers are designed to protect the home electrical system, not appliances. For safety measures, see "Smart Ideas" box, above.

What's a fuse? Fuses are sometimes used in older homes that have not had electrical systems updated with breakers. When a fuse blows, a metal strip melts and darkens the glass on the fuse. Replace a blown fuse with one of the same amperage capacity to restart the flow of electricity to the circuit.

If possible, update and upgrade electrical systems by having the fuse box replaced with breaker panels.

Water Systems

Water supply is essential to drinking, cooking, bathing, and cleaning. Maintaining the basic water-supply appliances in your home ensures that water demands are met.

WATER HEATER

Setting the temperature: If your home is not equipped with antiscald devices, set the water heater thermostat at 125 degrees or as low as 105 degrees if you have small children.

Flushing the tank: Water quality and maintenance affect the durability of water heaters. Flush sediment from the water heater at least once a year to extend its life and ensure optimum hot water supply. Follow these steps.

■ Shut off the water supply at the water heater and let the water cool for several hours.

■ Shut off the cold-water supply entering the water heater.

■ Connect a hose to the drain faucet at the bottom of the water heater and run it to a floor drain.

■ Open the water heater drain faucet, allowing most of the water to drain; then turn on the cold-water supply to stir and flush additional sediment from the tank.

■ Close the drain faucet and open a nearby hot-water faucet to prevent air buildup in the water lines.

■ Note: Drain faucets on water heaters might refuse to close completely after being opened. You may have to have a plumber replace the faucet to prevent it from dripping.

■ Follow the appliance manufacturer's instructions for relighting the pilot light. Use a long wooden match to light the pilot light before turning on the gas; do not allow gas to build up before igniting.

Back-draft test: Confirm that carbon monoxide isn't leaking into the home due to improper draft at the water heater. A tightly closed house might have air flowing out of it via a fireplace or vent fan opening that creates a reverse air flow in the water heater flue. Turn down the water heater thermostat and allow the water heater and flue to cool for an hour. Light the fireplace and turn on a kitchen fan. Inspect the water heater flue for corrosion and soft areas. Turn up the thermostat. If the furnace flue connects to the water heater flue, turn off the furnace. Light an incense stick and hold it next to the flue opening at the top of the tank. Smoke should be drawn into the flue; if not, there is a back-draft problem. Call a plumber to correct it.

WATER SOFTENERS

Hard water contains excess calcium and magnesium that causes residue to build up in plumbing, resulting in clogged valves and hard-water deposits. Hard water reduces the efficiency of soap and

---

BUDGET STRETCHER

Maintain Water Tank

•

Water heaters have inexpensive dip-tubes that divert cold water to the tank bottom, allowing the hot water to remain at the top. If the water from the tank is lukewarm, the dip-tube may have broken and require replacement.

Gas Water Heater

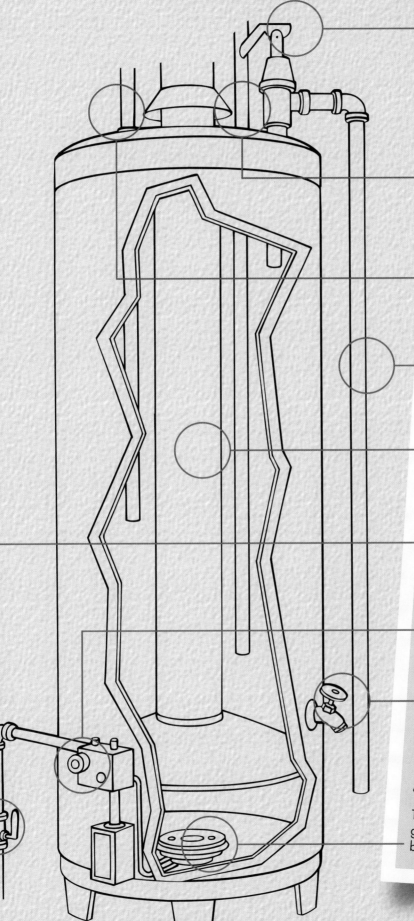

Pressure-Relief Valve:
Safety device prevents steam buildup. Flip valve open. Water should drain from overflow pipe.

Cold-Water Inlet:
Brings in cold water from the main supply line. Should be free of buildup.

Hot-Water Outlet:
Releases hot water into the household plumbing system. Check if water isn't hot.

Overflow Pipe:
Releases water in case of pressure or heat buildup; check during maintenance.

Flue:
Releases combustion gases to the outdoors. Inspect twice a year.

Gas-Inlet Valve:
Brings in natural gas from the fuel supply line to feed the burner; should have its own shut-off valve.

Temperature-Control Knob:
Allows adjustment to prevent scalding.

Drain Valve:
Open every few months to drain a few gallons to remove sediment from the bottom of the tank.

Burner:
Takes in mixture of natural gas and air. This is ignited by the pilot light for heat.

detergent. Treating hard water with sodium, by way of a water softener, eliminates white deposits on shower heads and faucets.

Combating iron: Built-up iron deposits decrease a water softener's effectiveness. Use liquid iron remover made for water softeners that is available from home centers to remove deposits. To prevent iron buildup, use pure salt with an iron remover. Avoid rock salt, which has contaminants that build up in the salt storage tank.

Adding salt: Replenish salt when the salt-tank is nearly empty, filling it only two-thirds full to prevent salt from compacting. Use a broom handle to break up compacted salt.

Seasonal Checklists

Prevent major repairs and expenses by setting aside time each month and especially as the seasons change to review your home maintenance. Prepare and adhere to a checklist of indoor and outdoor chores. Locate and tend to problems in the early stages to prevent costly emergency repairs.

FALL MAINTENANCE CHECKLIST

▶Clean gutter and downspouts.

▶Rake leaves weekly if possible, following city or county guidelines for disposal; or shred leaves with a mulching mower to use as a mulch for soil around plants and shrubs.

▶Build a composter to collect leaves along with garden waste (taking care to discard anything that is insect-infested) and kitchen waste. As the material decomposes, it turns into a rich soil conditioner full of nutrients for your garden in the spring.

▶Clean up planting areas. Remove and discard annuals. Cut back spent perennial stems to the ground. Rake up debris, twigs, broken stems, and discard.

▶Wrap plants that are not winter-hardy. After cold winter weather sets in, shape and trim trees and shrubbery as needed.

▶Plant winter-hardy bulbs, such as tulips, daffodils, and crocuses. Tamp down soil with leaves, or protect bulbs from digging squirrels with bird netting or row cover, available at garden centers.

▶Mow grass as long as it continues growing. Fertilize as appropriate for your climate. Check with local extension services for advice.

▶Drain sprinkler system and hoses. Remove hoses from spigots and store them coiled and flat (hanging causes weak spots). Leaving hoses connected will result in frozen pipes in cold climates.

▶Caulk gaps or cracks in your home's exterior.

▶Close or install storm windows.

▶Have the furnace professionally inspected. Change the air filter. On oil-burning furnaces, clean or change the in-line fuel filter.

▶Test smoke and carbon monoxide detectors and replace batteries.

▶Winterize the lawn mower by draining the gas, sharpening the blade, and changing the oil.

- Test-operate the snowblower.
- Stock up on plant-friendly ice melt, particularly for sloping driveways. Use a handheld fertilizer spreader to distribute.

SPRING MAINTENANCE CHECKLIST

- Inspect step ladders to ensure that the rungs fit tightly as the first step in your chores.
- Test sump pump; pour in water and operate the motor.
- Conduct a water-heater back-draft test. (See page 242.)
- Clear the condensate drain near the furnace. Test condensate pump with water to ensure its operation.
- Test smoke alarms and carbon monoxide detectors. Replace batteries.
- Check fire extinguishers to make sure they are charged.
- Clean gutters, inspecting and repairing loose brackets, bends, or breaks.
- Remove the insulating blanket covering hardy spring bulbs. Spread row cover, available at garden centers, to prevent rodents from chewing on the fresh greens.
- Prepare planting beds for annuals.
- Spread the first lawn-fertilizer application when grass begins to green.

Lawn Equipment and Tools

LAWN MOWERS

Quality lawn mowers make grass cutting easier, efficient, and ecological. Depending on the size of your yard and local environmental regulations, choose from gas or electric self-propelled mower, a riding mower, or a traditional, human-powered push mower. Basic well-maintained mowers provide years of service.

Definitions: Understand lawn-mowing terminology and common terms.

- Deck: The casing that covers the mower's blade assembly and keeps obstacles clear of the blades.
- Two- or four-cycle: Describes the number of piston strokes an engine uses to achieve one combustion cycle of intake, compression, power, and exhaust.

PUSH MOWERS

Mower types: Gas mowers use a combination of gasoline and oil. For two-cycle models, use a gas and oil mixture available at hardware stores and garden centers. For four-cycle engines, the gas and oil are added separately, as in your car. Electric mowers are quieter and easy to start. Corded electric mowers need to be

---

Home Remedies

KEEPING IT LIGHT

Changing Broken Bulbs

Cut a potato in half and stick it onto broken glass to use as a safety handle to unscrew the broken bulb from the socket.

Annoying Buzzing

Lights on dimmer switches sometimes make noise because of vibrating filaments. Replace buzzing bulbs with heavy-duty bulbs, such as those made for ceiling fans. Upgrade old dimmer switches with high-quality switches, available at home centers.

Handling Halogen

Touching bulbs with bare hands reduces its life; wear latex gloves when handling. Use low-voltage, cool bulbs in torcherés, and keep the fire-safety grate that comes with lamps in place.

Gas Tools

plugged into an electrical outlet, so they are limited in the area they can reach. Cordless electric mowers work best on lawns up to a third of an acre. Mowing time on a single charge ranges from 30 to 90 minutes.

Starters: Recoil starters have a retractable cord that is pulled to start the engine. Switch or key starters turn on at the touch of a button or the turn of a key.

Drive systems: Mowers are either push or riding models. Push mowers are self-propelled using engine power, or people-propelled using muscle power.

Discharge style: Standard side or rear discharge refers to the direction clippings are thrown. Some mowers convert to bagging mode with optional accessories.

Cutting width: The size of the swath the blade will cut usually ranges from 12 inches to 33 inches.

Blade types: Rotary blades cut grass at a high speed. They adjust to turf heights and can be sharpened at home. Reel-type blades cut grass with a shearing action, and cutting height is adjustable. Blades move only as fast as the mower can be pushed, and they don't throw debris. Mulching blades reduce clippings to fine organic material that provides nourishment to the lawn when left to decompose.

Options include lawn bags that catch the cut grass, to be disposed of either in the composter or yard waste pickup.

Maintenance: Routine inspections and repair increase mower efficiency and useful life.

▸ Use proper fuel and oil. Check owner's manual.
▸ Clean clippings from the underside of the deck after each use.
▸ Sharpen blades. A sharp blade is crucial to a healthy lawn: Dull blades shred grass tips, which will brown. Check sharpness often.
▸ Replace the spark plug at the beginning of the season.
▸ Clean or change the air filter after every 25 hours of operation.
▸ Lubricate wheels and moving joints every 25 hours of operation.
▸ Change the oil in four-cycle engines after every 10 hours of operation.
▸ Check the condition and tightness of belts and chain drives.

Winter storage:
▸ Drain the fuel tank or add a fuel protectant.
▸ Disconnect spark-plug wire, remove plug, lubricate the cylinder.
▸ Clean dirt and debris from deck with detergent and water.
▸ Follow storage procedures in owner's manual.

Troubleshooting:
■ If your mower has a four-cycle engine, observe the oil level when mowing hilly areas. Gravity may drain oil away from moving parts when the oil pan isn't full. Some engines are designed to

Must-Have Garden Tools

Pruners:

Bypass pruners make trimming small branches simple and cause less trauma injury to the tree or shrub than do standard pruners. Keep sharp for the best job.

Garden Spade:

A spade is not a shovel. It's designed for breaking sod, cutting bed edges, and working amendments into garden soil. Shovels are best for digging.

Watering Can:

Its classic shape, with deep bucket, curved handle, and long spout, makes it easy to carry and use. The rose sprinkler head releases water in a gentle, rainlike flow.

Garden Trowel:

Ideal for digging, the sharp point makes holes for planting. Use a 2-inch trowel for bulbs or seedlings or a 4-inch trowel for transplanting from the garden or pots.

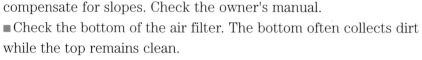

compensate for slopes. Check the owner's manual.

■ Check the bottom of the air filter. The bottom often collects dirt while the top remains clean.

RIDING MOWERS

Two basic types of riding mowers are available. Tractors or riding lawn mowers have conventional drive systems with wheels that work in tandem. Zero-turning-radius machines have wheels that work independently to pivot in tight spaces. Although some are versatile in small areas, push-mowing or string trimming may be necessary near trees and flower beds for trimming up close.

Engine horsepower: As horsepower increases, so does mowing power. The usual range runs from 8- to 25-horsepower.

Deck size: The bigger the deck, the larger the area that can be cut at one time, but this can limit the spaces in which the mower will fit. Decks typically range from 25 to 60 inches.

Fuel tank capacity: Tanks usually hold ¾ to 6½ gallons. Larger tanks require filling less often and run longer at one time.

Turning radius: This is the minimum number of inches a lawn mower needs to make a 180-degree turn. Tighter turning radius fits small spaces and can reduce the need to hand-trim edge grass. Some make such tight turns they're rated as zero turning radius. Large tractors may require up to 35 inches to turn.

Mulching option: Special blades cut clippings into fine pieces and deposit them at the lawn base, adding nutrients to the soil.

Maintenance: Set up and adhere to a regular schedule.
▶ Check tires for proper inflation at each use.
▶ Check the fuel and oil levels before each use.
▶ Clean clippings from the under the deck after each use.

SNOW AND ICE TOOLS

Snow removal is exhausting and necessary work; using the right equipment makes the job manageable. Many city ordinances require snow removal within a specified time as a public-safety measure.

Shovels: Snow shovels are strong and durable. Shovels made of lightweight materials, such aluminum, plastic, or polyethylene make for easier lifting, rust-resistance, and longer wear. Special coatings also prevent snow from sticking to scoop surfaces. Aluminum tube handles are lighter and stronger than traditional wood handles. Some models are ergonomically designed with large D-grips that fit gloved hands for safe use; bent-handle designs that reduce back and shoulder stress; and blade shapes that allow pushing rather than lifting of heavy, wet snow.

Handles, grips, and blades:
▶ Short handles work well in light snow.
▶ Long handles provide leverage in heavy snow.
▶ Bent handles reduce stress on back and shoulders.

Blade width determines the size of the pathway in one push. A 1- to 2-foot blade quickly clears most walkways. Wider blades become heavy and awkward when loaded with wet snow.

A nonstick finish helps snow slide off.

A curved scoop allows pushing of heavy snow.

Travel safety gear:

Shovels with telescoping handles fit in vehicle trunks and extend to 28 to 36 inches for use.

Folding rescue shovels fit in the car and fit backpacks for skiers or snowmobilers.

Shoveling tips and techniques:

Do warm-up stretches before starting.

Use a shovel with a length and weight appropriate to your height and strength.

Shovel the snow while it's fresh and light, if possible.

Avoid picking up too much; fill the shovel only halfway.

Push rather than lift heavy snow.

Lift with your knees, not your back. Slightly bend your knees as you lift the shovel.

Pace yourself; don't overexert. If you feel chest tightness or arm tingling, stop work immediately and get help.

CHEMICAL DEICERS

Some ice-control methods provide traction, and others help keep ice from forming; none melts ice. Chemical deicers work by lowering the melting point of ice and breaking the bond between ice, snow, and pavement to make it easy to shovel or plow. Some communities regulate the use of these chemicals because of concerns about clogging sewer systems, polluting water sources, polluting air with particulates, eroding pavement and vehicle finishes, and burning vegetation. When used and cleaned up correctly, chemical deicers are an option to help reduce ice buildup. They should be used only after shoveling.

Deicer use: Dumping too much on one spot is a common mistake. Spread lightly over pavement according to the manufacturer's guidelines. Some chemicals will erode concrete that's less than two years old. Follow label directions.

■ Rock salt performs best at 15 degrees to 20 degrees F, and is corrosive to concrete and metals.

■ Potassium chloride and urea fertilizers perform best as deicers at 20 degrees to 25 degrees F but high concentrations needed on ice burn grass and pit concrete.

■ Calcium chloride deicers absorb moisture and are efficient down to

TIPTAG №25
Energy Savers

HEATING TIPS:
- Keep thermostat at 68 degrees during the day and 64 degrees at night, or install programmable unit.
- Reduce water heater temperature when on vacation trips.
- Wrap water heater in an insulating blanket available at home centers.

SEASONAL TIPS:
- Seal windows with insulating film.
- Close fireplace dampers and doors when not in use.
- Use ventilation fans sparingly in cold weather.

AROUND THE HOUSE:
- Install low-energy light bulbs.
- Place gaskets behind receptacle covers to reduce drafts.

HEALTHY HOME

Prepare For Winter

•

Stock up on ice melt early in the season, especially if you have sloping walks or driveways. Handheld fertilizer spreaders or empty cheese-shakers make good spreaders, but only if well-labeled as toxic.

-25 degrees F, but they cost more than rock salt.

Gaining traction: Ashes, cat litter, cinders, and sand are common household remedies to keep tires—and people—from slipping. Of these, sand is the most effective. None melts ice or snow.

Underpavement heating systems: Radiant-heat systems use hot-water pipes to warm pavement and melt snow and ice. Although expensive to install under existing pavement, they're environmentally friendly, efficient, and cost-effective over time when installed as part of new construction.

SNOWBLOWERS

Always wear protective eye covering when using a snowblower. Although there is no lifting involved, using a blower in wet snow is heavy work. If the chute clogs, turn off the machine and remove the spark plug wire; then use a stick to clear packed snow. Never put hands or feet in the chute.

Clearing width: This is the path a snowblower clears. "Electric shovel" models clear a 12-inch path and are lightweight enough to use on steps. Standard models usually clear a 36-inch path.

Drive systems: Disc drives use wheels or tracks to propel the snowblower. Auger drives use a screw or auger that comes in contact with the ground surface to propel the snowblower.

Engine types: Two-cycle engines use a mixture of gasoline and oil (available from hardware stores and garden or home centers) in the fuel tank. Four-cycle engines use only gas in the fuel tank. Oil is added separately. Use low-octane regular unleaded gasoline.

Stages: Single-stage snowblowers use fast-moving, rotating blades or augers to pick up snow and throw it directly out of an adjustable discharge chute. Because these models must be pushed, they are better for light snow. Dual-stage snowblowers are self-propelled walk-behind models that use a slow-moving blade to deliver snow to a propeller. The snow is hurled out of a discharge chute that can be adjusted to direct the placement of the snow. Dual-stage models are better for deep snow.

Starters: Recoil starters have a retractable cord to pull-start the engine. Electric starters have a push-button or key.

Seasonal maintenance: Have engine tuned up annually. During plowing season do basic maintenance:
▸Check oil at each use. Change oil and filter after 30 hours of use.
▸Change spark plugs as recommended in the owner's manual.
▸Lubricate moving parts and exposed metal to prevent rust.
▸Run briefly after use to clear snow from blades and deck.

Before storing, complete the following chores:
▸Empty the gas tank by running the snowblower until it stops.
▸Disconnect spark plug wire.
▸Drain used oil and refill with new oil.

Stocking Your Toolbox

Duct Tape:
Despite its name, the plastic-coated fabric adhesive tape serves multiple functions as it holds tight and resists moisture.

Locking Wrench:
Claws adjust and clamp to hold fast to nuts, bolt heads, and hose connections. Must-have for minor plumbing repairs.

Torpedo Level:
Bubbles in liquid-filled tubes indicate level and plumb. Good for adjusting picture frames or other small household projects.

Utility Knife:
The retractable blade is used to score drywall, open packages, cut ceiling tiles, or for general crafts use.

Painter's Tool:
Sturdy metal blade scrapes peeling paint, opens paint cans, and works as a simple flat pry bar for loosening nails.

Pliers:
Groove joint: Grip and turn easily. Slip-joint: Adjust from small- to medium-size grip. Needlenose: Pull nails, cut wire.

Claw Hammer:
A 16-ounce, curved claw hammer is the first tool to own. It drives and pulls nails, making it good for most household jobs.

Steel Tape Measure:
A 25-foot tape locks in place and has easy-to-read markings for taking accurate measurements.

Awl:
To start screws or drill bits in soft woods without slipping, use the awl's sharp point to punch pilot (guide) holes in the wood.

Screwdrivers:
Phillips has X-shape points for use with phillips-head screws. Slotted screwdrivers also pry. Each kind comes in many sizes.

▶ Lubricate as recommended in owner's manual.

▶ Check for damage and repair as necessary.

▶ Clean with mild detergent and water.

▶ Spray exposed metal with lubricant such as WD-40 to prevent rust.

▶ Cover and store in a dry place.

LEAF BLOWERS AND VACUUMS

Leaf blowers and vacuums are easy to use. These yard and garage maintenance machines are noisy, however, and gas-powered engines emit fumes. Be aware of and observe local ordinances concerning the allowed hours of operation.

■ Blowers: Use air velocity to move leaves and debris out of awkward areas and into piles for quick pickup.

■ Vacuums: Leaf blowers with vacuum capability make raking and bagging of leaves and debris easier and faster.

■ Air volume is the amount of air put out by the leaf blower. Volume ranges from 170 to 3,400 cubic feet per minute. The higher the volume, the larger the amount of material it will move.

■ Air velocity is the speed at which air leaves the nozzle. Higher velocities reach farther, extending the efficient working area. Air velocity usually measures from 110 to 260 miles per hour.

Configuration: Lightweight hand-held models work well for small to medium jobs. Backpack models are heavier; because they are carried on the back, they make operation easier as your hands are free to move. Walk-behind blower models offer the most power

Fuel type: Gas models are powerful but require more maintenance, are louder, and cost more. Electric motors are quiet but less powerful and have cords that limit where they can go. Cordless models are available but are better for light work.

STRING TRIMMERS

Whack those weeds with trimmers that use thin line, like fishing line, to cut vegetation. Easy-to-replace cartridges make quick refills.

■ Corded electric trimmers don't have to be recharged or refueled; they do require an electrical outlet near the work area. Dragging a cord becomes a problem over large areas or around trees or plants.

■ Cordless electric trimmers have the advantages of electric trimmers without the disadvantage of a cord.

■ Gas powered trimmers are the most powerful of the three. Because they operate without a cord, they have greater range. They are noisy, however, and they emit fumes.

GARDEN TILLERS

Preparing garden soil becomes a less muscle-wrenching chore with a correctly sized tiller. Be cautious: Too-frequent tilling disturbs soil structure. Use garden tillers to break up soil and to work amendments into the soil; do not use as weeders and cultivators.

■ Mini models till to a depth of 8 to 10 inches with a tilling path

SAFETY ALERT

Leaf
Blowers

•

Don't allow bystanders in the work area. Never point the air nozzle at people or pets. Wear a dust mask, hearing protection, and safety goggles. Check local ordinances for additional operating information and guidelines.

width of 6 to 12 inches. The small size allows them to fit snugly against fences, walls, and plants. Lightweight, at about 20 pounds, they can be picked up and carried as needed and they can rotate at the end of rows.

■ Front-tine or mid-tine models have the engine over the tines, which work like wheels, propelling as they dig. They till up to 12 inches deep and 10 to 36 inches wide. Some have a reverse gear for backing out of tight spots. Optional attachments may include aerators, finger tines for cultivation, or furrowers.

■ Rear-tine models have the engine above the front wheels with tines mounted behind it. These powerful, self-propelled machines work to break up sod or turn under spent crops. They till approximately 8 inches deep with a path 14 to 34 inches wide. Heavy, wide, and sometimes cumbersome, they don't fit closely to structures in the yard and garden.

Outdoor Furniture

Outdoor furniture, in abundant styles and fabrications, is selected for use depending on placement location and style preferences.

BUYING

Porch and patio furniture create outdoor rooms. Because furniture often is sheltered under roofs or awnings, it can be made from a variety of materials. Furniture incorporated into landscape design typically remains outdoors year-round and is selected for durability and design. Although weathering may provide yard furniture with a sought-after patina, maintenance is required for durability.

BASIC TYPES

Aluminum doesn't rust, but it might discolor or become pitted with exposure to pollutants and precipitation. For mild discoloring, wash as usual with detergent and water, adding lemon juice, vinegar, or cream of tartar. For pitting, polish with a soapy steel wool pad, rinse, and dry. Take care to remove steel wool fibers, which rust and stain aluminum. Do not use commercial cleaners on anodized aluminum. Protect aluminum with car wax or silicon spray.

Bamboo, wicker, and rattan deteriorate with extended exposure to sun and rain. They are best used on protected porches. Marine varnish adds some protection when these materials are exposed to weather.

Canvas: Tightly woven cotton sheds water but rots with exposure to weather. Scrub the frame with a stiff brush, using

smart ideas
Building a Fire

BURN GOOD WOOD

Dry, well-aged hardwood burns most efficiently. Use oak, birch, ash, or hickory that has aged at least one year. Avoid soft woods such as pine or spruce, that increase creosote buildup in flues. Never burn chemically treated wood: The fumes are toxic.

AIR VENTS & ASH PITS

A door at the bottom of the hearth covers either an air vent or an ash pit. Look outside on the chimney below the hearth line. If there is a vent, you have an air vent that should be opened for burning. If there is a door, you have an ash pit that is closed for burning and opened for removing ashes.

BUDGET
STRETCHER

Outdoor Cushion Care

•

Protect by tossing a towel over seat and back cushions when using oils or lotions. After summer rains, dry cushions by removing them from the furniture frame and leaning them on their sides to air out all around.

detergent and water. Rinse and dry. Store indoors in winter.

Nylon or vinyl webbing: Replace worn strapping with kits found at home and garden centers and hardware stores. Protect from tanning lotion stains by covering with a towel. Never use abrasives or strong detergents. Clean regularly because buildup of soil, oil, or lotions results in fungus growth. Some furniture features mildew inhibitors incorporated into webbing material.

Painted metal: Baked-on enamel surfaces are the most durable. Paint or enamel applied directly to the metal surface is least durable. Apply automobile liquid wax or paste wax and polish. Store indoors for the winter.

Plastics tolerate weather extremes well. Some have lacquered resin finishes that protect against ultraviolet rays, rain, and salt spray. A resin for plastic tabletops gives a ceramic-like finish. For untreated plastic furniture, applying waxes or protective finishes formulated for plastics provides extra protection. Plastics are easily scratched; never use strong alkalis or abrasive cleaners.

Polyvinyl chloride isn't affected by weather but is scratched with abrasive cleaners. Apply car wax to protect finish.

Polyester mesh fabric coated with polyvinyl chloride: This fabric allows air flow, making seats cool and comfortable.

Redwood resists rot but benefits from the application of a sealer to keep out moisture and retard cracks. Tinted sealers restore redness to grayed wood. Sand rough spots before sealing.

Teak is a dense hardwood with a distinctive leathery aroma of fresh-cut lumber. Teak resists fungal decay, termites, wood-boring insects, water, acids, and metal stains. Finely sanded teak is yellow-brown; wood exposed to the sun gradually bleaches to silvery gray. Periodic oiling slows graying, darkening the wood with a soft sheen.

White woods, such as fir, poplar, or spruce, are used for director's chairs. Use a penetrating sealer or exterior varnish on outdoor furniture, including the end grain at bottom of legs. If cracks occur, refinish to prevent mildew. Avoid leaving unsealed furniture out in the rain. Unfinished wood is used for rustic-style furniture. Treat with an exterior penetrating stain containing a wood preservative and mildew inhibitor. Soak bottom 4 inches of legs in wood preservative, or shield with thin aluminum covering.

Cushion covers are usually made of treated synthetic fabrics that can be left outside all season. Polyacrylics feel like cotton but are water repellent and mildew resistant. Open-weave polyesters are coated with polyvinyl chloride or vinyl. Polyester fillings resist mildew and don't hold water. Seams should be stitched with polyester thread, and covers have buttons that allow water to drain. Cushion covers made of untreated fabrics, or filled with urethane foam, are not weatherproof. Store them indoors.

Plan for Fireplace Safety

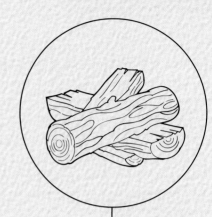

Fire Extinguisher:

Incorrect extinguisher use spreads flames. Set it on hard surface to remove lock pin. Hold upright. Aim nozzle at base of flame. Squeeze levers.

Safety Screen:

Sparks can jump from the firebox onto floors or upholstery. Always use a fireplace screen made of fine steel mesh that fully covers the firebox.

Burn Hardwoods:

Never burn scrap lumber, which could be painted or chemically treated and give off toxic fumes. Soft, oily woods (such as pine) build up creosote in flues.

Fire Logs:

Fire logs made of sawdust mixed with wax light quickly and burn for hours. Never burn more than one: Dangerously large flames could result.

Smoke Alarm:

Smoke rises, so attach detectors to ceilings or high on walls. Never put in corners, which have poor circulation. Install on each level of the house.

Fire Starters:

Never use flammable liquids in fireplaces. They could ignite as they flow, pulling flames back to the container. Toxic fumes are also a risk.

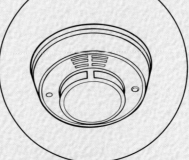

BASIC CARE

Most outdoor furniture can be cleaned with a mild liquid hand-dishwashing detergent and water, followed by rinsing and drying. Products made for cleaning, polishing, and protecting vehicle surfaces are developed to withstand weathering and work well for similar materials in outdoor furniture.

Garage-Door Openers

Convenience and security make good reasons to install an automatic garage door opener or to upgrade to a newer model.

REPLACING A DOOR OPENER

The average life of a garage-door opener is about 12 years. Plan to replace units every 10 to 12 years to avoid problems and to take advantage of advances in technology.

OPENER TYPES

■ Chain-drive systems are the most common and least expensive. An electric motor drives a steel chain that raises and lowers the door. These openers are strong and reliable but can be noisy, which is a lesser concern with a detached garage.

■ Screw-drive systems use a threaded steel rod to lift. These powerful, smooth-running units operate more slowly than chain-drive openers, making them a better choice for one-piece, tilt-up doors.

■ Belt-drive units use a fiber-reinforced rubber belt to lift the door. Top-quality units operate quietly and smoothly.

WHEN THE POWER IS OUT

Garage-door openers have a manual release handle that allows the door to be operated by hand. Once power is restored, a push of a button reconnects the door to the opener.

SECURITY FEATURES

■ Electronic codes: Most newer garage-door openers have a rolling-code technology system that automatically changes to a new electronic code each time the door is used. This deters use of "code grabber" devices by would-be burglars.

■ Lighting: Garage-door openers have a light that comes on when the door is activated; and a built-in timer turns off the light after a few minutes. The light also operates separately from a wall switch.

OPENER MAINTENANCE

Automatic garage-door openers need occasional attention. If the auto-reverse function becomes too sensitive, the "travel" controls need adjustment. These are found on the opener housing mounted on the ceiling. Once a year, lubricate the chain or screw and the rollers with a spray-on lithium product available at home centers.

SAFETY

Automatic garage-door openers are required to have two auto-reversing safety devices.

TIME SAVER

Automatic Openers

•

Most come with two wireless remote transmitters and a hardwired control panel. Wireless keypads that use programmable numeric security codes are available. A keypad mounts outside the garage for convenient opening.

- Contact safety reverse opens the door if the door strikes anything.
- Noncontact safety reverse uses two electric-eye sensors to shoot an infrared beam across the doorway. If anything breaks the beam, the door reverses to open.
- Test auto-reverse mechanisms by placing a roll of paper towels at the base of the doorway. The closing door should reopen immediately as it comes close to or touches the roll. If towels are crushed, adjust the tension.
- Mount control switches out of children's reach.

Wood Heat

The sight, sounds, scent, and warmth of a wood fire spell comfort to many people who relish a roaring fire. Whether building a new home, installing a factory-built unit, or retrofitting an existing firebox, observe building code and environmental protection regulations.

Location of a built-on-site masonry wood-burning fireplace is determined by structural support and venting access.

FIREPLACE ANATOMY:

- Firebox: The opening that contains the fire.
- Hearth: Fireplace floor. Back hearth: Firebox floor. Front hearth: Extends a short way into living space to protect floors from embers.
- Throat: Area directly above firebox and below flue.
- Damper: Movable metal flap covering throat.
- Smoke chamber: Space above throat that stops downdrafts.
- Flue: Inside chimney, with fire-resistant lining.
- Cap: Installed at top of chimney to keep out rain and protect against downdrafts on windy days.
- Ash pit: Ash-collecting chamber under firebox.
- Clean-out door: Ash pit access often found in basement or outside on chimney.

STARTING A FIRE:

- Fully open the exhaust damper.
- Stack a small pile of dry kindling on a grate.
- Stack several 2- to 3-inch-diameter logs on top of kindling, allowing air space between logs.
- Stuff paper under grate or place fire starter sticks in kindling.
- Place crumpled paper on top of logs. Ignite paper.
- When paper burns, ignite kindling or starter sticks.
- Before the fire gets hot, adjust the exhaust damper to halfway, which allows efficient burning by sending heat into the room rather than up the flue.

Home Remedies

SECURING DOORS

Out-of-Line Latches

Normal expansion, contraction, and settling of buildings can push door frames out of alignment. Use a metal file to enlarge latch hole in metal strike plate on the jamb. If this doesn't help, remove strike plate and fill old screw holes. Replace strike plate slightly higher or lower, realigning it to fit latch.

Stubborn Locks

Lubricate keyholes with powdered graphite, available in squeeze tubes at hardware stores.

Self-Closing Doors

For interior doors that swing open or shut on their own, remove one hinge pin and bend it slightly with a hammer. Return pin to secure, and test the door.

SAFETY ISSUES:

▸ Use a screen. Burning fires will spark and send hot cinders flying.

▸ Creosote is combustible. Burning cinders dropping down through the damper indicate a chimney fire.

▸ In case of a flue fire, get everyone out of the house and call the fire department. Only if it seems safe to do so without risk of getting burned, use a fireplace tool to close the damper and glass firedoors. Some flue fires smolder for a long time before flaring up.

▸ Don't burn waste materials, especially treated wood or colored papers, which release harmful fumes.

▸ Install smoke detectors.

▸ Install carbon monoxide sensors.

▸ Keep mantel decorations away from firebox opening.

▸ Fire-resistant hearth rugs protect floors when the hearth doesn't extend outside firebox; never use ordinary rugs near a firebox.

▸ An untended fire is a hazard.

▸ Never use water to put out a flame. Let it burn out. If it must be extinguished, use baking soda, sand, or cat litter to smother it.

MAINTENANCE:

▸ Have a professional chimney sweep inspect and clean flue annually.

▸ Check regularly for loose firebricks or damage to the crown that surrounds flue liners. Seal or repair before using the fireplace.

▸ Regularly check masonry mortar joints, and tuckpoint as needed.

▸ Clean glass firedoors with commercial soot removers or use #0000 (very fine) steel wool that won't scratch tempered glass.

STOVES AND INSERTS

When a fireplace isn't a suitable option, or an old firebox requires updating, consider installing a stove or a fireplace insert.

Stoves: Freestanding wood and pellet stoves provide efficient heating in styles that suit any decor. Stoves certified by the federal Environmental Protection Agency are clean-burning. High temperatures encourage complete combustion of particulates and gases. Select a unit with a Btu rating compatible to the size of the room. Professional installation ensures compliance with building code and safety regulations. Maintain stoves by removing ashes regularly, never overstoking fires (which contributes to creosote buildup), and scheduling annual inspections and cleaning by certified chimney sweeps.

Fireplace inserts: These upgrade existing masonry fireboxes into safe wood- or gas-burning units. Installation is specific to the individual fireplace, so have the work done by a professional. Inserts must meet strict EPA standards for combustion efficiency and pollution control. Usually made of cast iron or heavy-gauge steel, inserts weigh up to 1,000 pounds and come with glass firedoors that insulate the firebox while keeping flames fully visible. Designs that

SAFETY ALERT

In Case Of Fire

•

Teach every family member escape routes and practice. Assign helpers for the elderly or the young. Agree on an outdoor meeting place. Close bedroom doors at night to retard spread of fire or toxic gases.

Know Your Door Locks

Cylinder Lock:
Cylinders hold the locking mechanism. Look for a key-in-knob lock with a separate tongue latch that can't be sprung with a credit card between latch and door frame.

Dead Bolt Lock:
These have bolts that extend at least 1 inch into the door frame. Vertical dead-bolts cannot be removed with a pry bar between the door and frame.

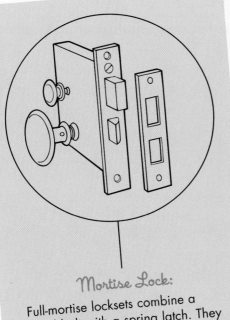

Mortise Lock:
Full-mortise locksets combine a dead bolt with a spring latch. They fit into a deep slot in the door's edge so that they are secure against attempts to break off knob.

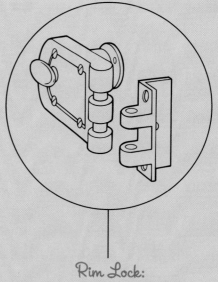

Rim Lock:
A spring-latch rim lock is surface-mounted, heavy duty hardware. As secure as a mortise lock, it doesn't require cutting into the door for proper installation.

protrude slightly out of the firebox allow for better heat radiation into the room, although some styles fit flush and release heat through grills. Optional electric blowers help circulate warmth. Inserts do not include chimneys. They require venting systems, or a connection to an existing chimney through a sealed collar. Flues may require relining for resizing and ensuring safety in old lines. Hire a professional to safely handle this complex job.

Gas Fireplaces

Natural gas fireplaces are increasingly popular in new home construction and home remodeling because they provide the ambience of a crackling fire with greater energy efficiency and less work. Environmentally friendly, vented units emit 99 percent less soot and dust particles. They also emit 95 percent less carbon monoxide than wood-burning fireplaces. Easy to use, some even work with a remote control, and the flames are instantaneous and maintenance-free. Vent-free or direct-venting units have 75 percent heat-efficiency ratings and work in awkward spaces where outside venting would be difficult. Both natural gas or propane are efficient room heaters. Propane gas fireplace systems cost between 30 and 60 percent less per hour of operation than wood-burning fireplaces and emit 40 times fewer emissions than wood burners. Propane gas fireplaces turn off with a switch, eliminating concerns about hot embers.

Outdoor Cooking

Outdoor cooking evokes the taste of flavorful meats and vegetables fresh off the flame. Methods can be as rustic as a metal rack over a campfire, as simple as a tabletop charcoal hibachi or freestanding charcoal kettle grill, or as elaborate as an outdoor kitchen with gas or electric cooktops. Many backyard barbecues fall somewhere in the middle, using charcoal, gas, or electric-start grills.

CHARCOAL GRILLS

These often are less expensive than gas or electric grills, and the ability to add aromatic flavoring fuels, such as mesquite or apple wood chips, to the coals makes for savory meats and vegetables that appeal to many outdoor cooks. Charcoal grills come in several varieties: open grills, covered kettles, and smokers.

What to look for: Pick a grill with a cooking area adequate to the kind of food you'll be grilling and the number of people you'll be feeding. Cooking area typically ranges from 70 to 1,140 square inches. Grills with lids cook faster while conserving fuel and can use aromatic wood chips to season foods. Smokers slow-cook foods while saturating them with flavor from aromatic wood chips.

Maintenance and safety: Ash pans beneath the coals collect ash and embers during cooking. Look for easily removable pans for cleaning. Never discard hot ashes or embers. Once cool, they can be put in the trash. (Wood ash is good for some plants, but do not apply coal ashes to garden soils.) Wheels make units easier to move for seasonal storage or access to eating areas. Do not use charcoal grills on wooden decks because falling embers could start a fire.

GAS GRILLS

Quick-starting and convenient, with propane, natural gas, or electric starters that flip on with a switch, these grills provide adjustable cooking flames and make no ashes to clean up. Gas fuel models can be connected to natural gas lines, but many take bottled propane fuel so they can be used anywhere. Electric grills require a receptacle, limiting their placement.

What to look for: Some units come with rotisseries, warming racks, and side burners that make cooking for crowds, or cooking a variety of foods, easier. Accessory options include smoker units that allow use of aromatic wood chips for flavoring. A cart makes the unit mobile for storage. Removable drip pans collect grease for easy cleanup and avoidance of flare-ups.

Maintenance and safety: Never store propane bottles inside a house or attached garage. Grill units have gauges that alert users to low fuel. Have bottles professionally refilled. Check burner pipes often and clear any blockages.

Security and Safety

Basic steps make your home less appealing to burglars: Lock your doors: Most burglars walk right in, but they won't spend more than a minute trying to open a secure door.

THE TWO P'S

■ Perimeter: Take a look around the yard and assess nighttime lighting. Tools or ladders left out become keys for illegal entry. Inadequate outdoor lighting makes a house inviting to thieves.
■ Points of entry: Exterior doors and windows are obvious, but also consider access through attached garages or crawlspaces.

DOORS AND LOCKS

▶ Avoid using hollow-core doors on exteriors because they are easy to break through. Solid doors are safer and more energy-efficient.
▶ Reinforce door frames by replacing short screws with 3-inch screws. This will ensure a tight fit so the door can't be wedged open with a pry bar.
▶ Choose shatterproof security glass for sidelight windows.
▶ Install—and use—a peephole.

TIPTAG NO 26
Security Alert

TAKE INVENTORY:
• Do it now.
• Note everything, including contents of closets and drawers.
• File receipts for big-ticket items as proof of ownership and value.
• Photograph special collections.
• Keep inventory in a safe-deposit box or other off-site location.

SPECIAL STORAGE:
• Create a security closet: Line the interior of an existing closet with ½-inch plywood. Install a solid-core metal-clad door with three hinges, using extra-long screws. Add a dead-bolt lock.
• Never leave valuables in sight.
• Always use bicycle locks.

▶Install a quality dead-bolt lock with a rectangular bolt that extends at least 1 inch into the door frame. Locksmiths can help you decide on the best locks for your doors and install them.

▶Install a strike plate (the protective metal plate surrounding the bolt hole) with 3½-inch screws, which are difficult to pry out.

WINDOWS

▶Install locking window latches, or install lag screws in sashes, to keep windows from opening wide enough for human entry.

▶Secure sliding windows with key locks and threshold bars that keep windows from sliding along the track.

▶Install grills, grates, or locking shutters over basement windows.

LIGHTING

▶Light doorways, including the garage, and safety-egress windows.

▶Install floodlights or decorative lighting along sidewalk approaches and under shrubbery to eliminate hiding places.

▶Install motion-detector lights over windows to discourage entry.

▶Use timers on indoor lights when you're away from home.

YARD MAINTENANCE

▶Trim overgrown foundation shrubbery to eliminate hiding places.

▶Fencing and gates that lock or have safety latches make access difficult, as do thorny hedges.

▶Signs of pets, especially large dogs, discourage trespassers.

ALARM SYSTEMS

Some alarm systems are simple noisemakers, while others are wired into security-service offices. The right one for you depends on your budget and your lifestyle. Insurance companies usually lower premiums for homes with alarms. Wired systems use low-voltage wires to connect sensors to a master control panel. Wireless systems use radio transmitters to connect sensors to the control panel; these units are mobile and can change homes with you. Both types can take options such as motion detectors or remote access that allow checking on the system by telephone. Systems that connect to security offices can be linked to smoke detectors.

Elements of an alarm system:

▶A master control panel uses a central processing unit to receive information from sensors.

▶The keypad is the command center that allows you to program and monitor how the system functions.

▶Door and window sensors use magnetic contacts. Once contact is broken, sensors alert the master control panel to sound the alarm.

▶Alarm screens, which replace regular window screens, contain sensors that alert the master control if the screen is removed or cut.

▶Acoustic sensors activate the alarm at the sound of breaking glass.

▶Sirens and strobe lights wake the neighbors, but they also show law-enforcement officers or firefighters which house needs help.

SAFETY ALERT

Scare Off Burglars

Battery-operated portable alarm units incorporate motion detectors and alarms. Made to sit on tabletops or hang from doorknobs, they are good for use in apartments.

10

....

Household Pets

- CHOOSING A DOG, 265
- CHOOSING A CAT, 266
- OWNER RESPONSIBILITIES, 265, 268
- PET EXERCISE AND SAFETY, 266
- PET HEALTH; WEIGHT PROBLEMS, 268-269
- DOG AND CAT FIRST AID, 268
- POCKET PETS, FISH, BIRDS, REPTILES, 270

Household Pests

- FLEAS AND TICKS, 274
- IDENTIFYING COMMON INSECTS, 275
- COCKROACHES AND HOUSEFLIES, 276
- ANTS AND TERMITES, 276
- SPIDERS; SCORPIONS, 277
- NATURAL PREVENTION, 277, 279
- HOUSEPLANT PESTS, 278
- STORAGE PESTS, 278
- RODENTS, 280
- PROFESSIONAL PEST CONTROL, 280

Indoor Air Comfort

- HUMIDIFIERS, 281
- DEHUMIDIFIERS, 282
- MAINTENANCE TIPS, 281-282

Indoor Air Quality

- INDOOR POLLUTANTS, 282
- SAFE MATERIAL DISPOSAL, 283
- AIR PURIFIERS, 284
- RADON ALERT, 285
- HOUSEPLANTS, 285

Water Quality

- ACTIVATED CARBON SYSTEMS, 286
- BOTTLED OR BULK WATER, 286

Concerns for Children

- SMOKE-FREE HOME, 286
- POTENTIAL POISONS, 288
- LEAD POISONING, 288
- PLANTS, 288
- PLAY EQUIPMENT, 288

Pets in the Household

DOGS

It's a cliché—and it's true: Dogs are true and loyal friends. Carefully select a canine companion, consulting a veterinarian or breeder for information on breed traits and lifestyle needs.

Should you acquire a dog? Keep these factors in mind:

■ Do you work late or travel often? Puppies eat four or more times a day and urinate or defecate at least that often. Adult dogs left alone may get bored or develop separation anxiety, resulting in excessive barking or destructive behavior.

■ Can you provide a comfortable environment? Descendants of den dwellers, some dogs take comfort in confined quarters. Others, bred to herd or hunt, prefer open spaces. All need shelter from hot sun, excessive heat, cold, wind, and precipitation.

■ Where do you live? Know and observe contract agreements regarding pets. Apartments, condominium units, and cities have restrictions concerning the size and number of dogs allowed.

■ Do you have time to train your pets? Obedience training benefits stay-at-home dogs as well as field-event dogs. Well-trained animals stay healthier and are fun to be with.

■ Do you have time to groom a dog or to arrange professional grooming? Heavy coats require more care than thin coats. Some dogs are difficult and time consuming to groom.

■ Do you have the financial ability to provide necessary feed, medications, and regular veterinary care? The larger the dog, the more it eats. Routine vet visits for checkups and immunizations are essential to good health.

Reasons for wanting a dog: Consider why you want a pet:

▸ Companionship: Children learn responsibility and receive unconditional love. Adults gain exercise partners. Elderly people gain friendship.

▸ Assistance: Guide or service dogs are trained to work with people with physical disabilities; potential owners must apply for dogs and attend training.

▸ Security: Guard dogs with proper training are alert, protective, and sociable family members.

▸ Sporting: Field-event dogs run obstacle courses and retrieve objects with ease, whether for competition or fun.

Breeding: The origins of a pure breed influence personality

smart ideas

The Pet for You

CLIMATE CONCERNS

Short-hair dogs may need sweaters and boots in winter. Heavy-coated dogs can benefit from a cooling summer trim. Fur acts like a mop to track muddy water into your home. How willing are you to go for a walk in a sleet storm or during a heat wave?

CITY OR COUNTRY

In cities, consider traffic, close neighbors, and proximity to green spaces. Small-to-medium size, low-to medium-energy breeds are best. Obey leash and cleanup laws in cities and suburbs. Be prepared for encounters with wildlife, such as skunks, in rural areas. Most breeds adapt to suburban or rural life.

traits. Learn about the dog's origins; mixed breeds often carry the best of their lineage and make delightful pets. "Puppy mill" animals, overbred in response to market trends, often are sickly or unstable.

Showing: Dogs inbred to achieve show traits may be emotionally unstable or have genetic health problems. Research carefully, know your breed, and purchase from reliable, responsible breeders.

Size: Consider a dog's adult weight, build, and height. A small, hefty breed won't necessarily be a good lap dog.

Transportation: Will your dog fit in a pet crate for safety?

Disposition and personality: Breeds have common characteristics that determine which are more aggressive, passive, active, or restrained, yet each dog has its own personality. Determine which traits best suit your lifestyle needs; if possible, spend time with the dog before making a decision.

Genetic or congenital predisposition: Responsible breeders screen for genetic factors before mating animals. Large breeds, such as golden retrievers, may develop hip dysplasia. Dachshunds tend to have spinal problems; giant dogs tend to have short life spans; toy breeds may suffer from slipping patellas (kneecaps); dalmatians often are genetically deaf and prone to kidney disease; pug-face animals tend to have respiratory problems. Check with a veterinarian for specific concerns.

Energy and exercise: Size and breed traits both determine how much exercise dogs need.

■ High-energy breeds include Jack Russell terriers, dalmatians, Border collies, and retrievers that need walking several times each day, plus plenty of outdoor playtime.

■ Medium-energy breeds include large spaniels, boxers, Great Danes, Akitas, and German shepherds. They need daily moderate-distance walks and a weekly chance to romp outdoors.

■ Low-energy breeds include small spaniels, basset hounds, beagles, dachshunds, and bulldogs. Short daily walks, playtime and toys, and careful diet keep them fit and happy.

CATS

Cats are enigmatic creatures. Despite their reputation for aloof independence, cats require daily attention. Indoor cats live longer and are healthier than outdoor cats. Apartment or condominium dwellers often choose cats because they are litter-box trainable. Check leases and contracts for specifics about pets.

Choosing a cat: Have you chosen a cat, or have you been chosen to be its human? Either way, consider breed traits. Cats can have long hair, short hair, or no hair.

Grooming: It's not cat hair, but the proteins in saliva, dander, and urine that cause human allergic reactions. Fastidious groomers, cats clean themselves several times a day. Regular combing removes

---

FAMILY FRIENDLY

Kids and Dogs

Introducing a new family member to an established pet requires patience. Avoid jealous behavior by providing usual attention. Supervise young children and dogs while they become gradually acquainted.

Grooming Dogs and Cats

Medium-Hair Dogs:

Dogs such as this Welsh corgi need daily brushing. Extra-long-hair or double-coated dogs may require special equipment and benefit from regular professional grooming.

Long-Hair Cats:

Long-hair cats, such as the Javanese, benefit from daily combing. Extra-long-hair cats, such as Persian or Angora, need twice-a-day combing to avoid tangles.

Short-Hair Dogs:

Although shorter hair, as on this larger dog, seems to need less-frequent grooming, daily brushing keeps the coat cleaner and reduces shedding around the house.

Short-Hair Cats:

Short hair does not mean there will be no shedding. Brush at least weekly. Breeds with very short hair or no hair will sunburn or may take a chill in cool temperatures.

excess saliva-covered fur and dander to reduce allergens. Because cats swallow fur, grooming results in fewer hair balls.

Disposition: Veterinarians and breeders are good sources of information on cat traits. Cat personalities range from demonstratively affectionate to very reserved. Most are nocturnal, sleeping during the day and prowling after dark.

Exercise: Cats like heights, so offer something other than furniture to climb. Cat jungle gyms are available at pet supply stores.

Litter-box basics: One litter box per cat is the minimum; some experts suggest additional boxes in large homes or for finicky cats. Odors are the primary reason that cats avoid a litter box. Self-cleaning litter boxes, powered by batteries or electricity, automatically rake litter into a disposable container. Cleaning is activated by an electronic motion detector about 10 minutes after the cat leaves the box. Although these boxes are initially more convenient, multiple nooks and crannies are time-consuming to disinfect. Stackable grate-type litter boxes have similar disadvantages. Disposable boxes, filled with litter for one-time use, are expensive yet convenient.

■ Location: Place boxes in low-traffic areas; cats have private elimination habits.

■ Litter: Varieties include recycled pelleted paper products, scented and unscented scoopable clays, gravel-type clay, silica gel crystals, and biodegradable processed corncobs. Lightweight silica gel beads absorb urine and odor but are among the most expensive. Gravel litter is the least expensive. Clumpable litter is easy to scoop, but the fine grit adheres to fur and easily tracks out of the box. Experiment with several litter varieties to find which works best to maintain health and cleanliness for your home and your pet.

■ Liners: Plastic litter box liners ease cleanup. Scoop solids from litter using regular liners or try sifting liners, which come in packages of 10 and are installed all at once. Lift out the top perforated liner, sift reusable litter back into the box, and toss liner with solid wastes into the trash.

■ Cleanliness: Remove solid waste daily; experts recommend twice-daily scooping. Discard litter weekly; wash the box in hot soapy water with bleach or a household antibacterial cleaner. Rinse and dry the box. Place 4 inches of clean litter in the box. Keep the area around litter boxes sanitary. Sweep up tracked or spilled litter. Wash floors under and around boxes with hot soapy water or a household antibacterial cleaner.

DOG AND CAT FIRST AID

First aid does not substitute for veterinary treatment; it does provide quick lifesaving attention for a sick or injured pet.

Pet first aid kit: Keep the following supplies handy in a lunch

---

HEALTHY HOME

Clean Up Tools

•

Indoors, prompt cleanup eliminates odors from paper-trained dogs and prevents coprophagia, a common illness. Outdoors, carry plastic bags, a small plastic shovel, or a two-handle scoop (from pet stores) for stool cleanup.

box or cleaning-tool tote
- Veterinarian's office and emergency phone numbers, and the 24-hour hotline of the ASPCA's National Animal Poison Control Center: 888/426-4435
- Gauze
- Adhesive tape
- Scissors or pocketknife to cut gauze and tape
- Nonstick bandages (Telfa pads)
- Towels and cloth
- Hydrogen peroxide (3 percent)
- Milk of magnesia or activated charcoal (to absorb poison)
- Eyedropper (for oral medications)
- Muzzle
- Rectal thermometer and lubricant (petroleum jelly)
- Styptic powder to stanch bleeding
- Diphenhydramine (such as Benadryl) for antihistamine relief of insect bites or stings

General tips: Pain or illness makes pet behavior unpredictable. Never muzzle a vomiting animal; it could suffocate the animal. Wrap cats in thick towels, making sure they can breathe.

■ Animal bites: See cuts.

■ Automobile accident: Find or create a firm surface (stretcher, board, mat, or blanket). Slide it under animal and lift gently. Keep animal warm while you take it to a veterinarian or animal emergency clinic.

■ Bleeding: Apply direct pressure with a clean cloth.

■ Bloat: A dog's distended abdomen may be a symptom of a life-threatening illness. Get to a veterinarian immediately.

■ Broken bones: Do not disturb or move the bone. Splint fractures with a magazine or newspapers loosely rolled around limb. Tape just above the splint, continue down the leg; do not cover toes. Do not attempt to splint a struggling animal.

■ Burns: Apply cool compresses. Don't immerse animals that have burns over large areas; they may go into shock. Dress small burns with sterile nonstick bandages. Do not apply ointments, butter, or petroleum jelly; they retain heat and attract infection.

■ Choking, coughing, or gagging: Choking may signal a tracheal obstruction or defect. Coughing is common after strenuous exercise and should subside when pet rests. Frequent coughing may signal illness. Gagging in cats often indicates a difficult hair ball ejection. Purchase special pet foods, treats, and gels for reducing hair balls from pet suppliers. Or rub white petroleum jelly on paws. Cats will

swallow this during grooming, easing hair ball ejection.
■Cuts: Wash with mild soap, rinse well, and pat dry with clean towel. Gently dab with hydrogen peroxide. Apply an antibiotic salve.
■Punctures or large wounds: Get immediate veterinary attention.
■Eye injury: Check for obvious foreign bodies; flush with mild saline drops. Scratches or irritations may require medicated eyedrops or salves. Cover eye with damp gauze to prevent pet from rubbing.
■Frostbite: Discoloration indicates freezing injury. Get pet into warm place. Warm injured skin slowly with tepid water.
■Heatstroke: Soak overheated pet in tepid water; provide fresh drinking water. Never leave pets in cars. Provide well-ventilated outdoor shelter in hot weather.
■Insect stings: A swollen muzzle or face indicates a possible sting. Apply a paste of baking soda and water, or a topical antihistamine. Respiratory difficulty signals allergic shock: Get to a vet.
■Poisoning: Three common poisons are antifreeze, rodenticide, and moldy garbage. In all cases—even if only a suspicion—get immediate veterinary care. Symptoms take as long as 24 to 72 hours to manifest, which may be too late for lifesaving treatment.

POCKET PETS

Pets suitable for small spaces come in many varieties. Look for alert animals that have a healthy coat and bright eyes. Purchase from a clean, reputable pet store.

Hamsters and gerbils: Choose golden (Syrian) or dwarf varieties. Golden hamsters prefer to live solo and will fight other goldens. Dwarf hamsters are happy in same-sex pairs. Gerbils are a cousin to hamsters and are curious and solitary.

Guinea pigs: These personable small pets have a life span of three to five years, and they require daily Vitamin C supplements.

Ferrets: Personable carnivores that have a mild, musky skin odor and may have genetic biting traits. Ferrets are easily litter trained, but may become lost in small spaces, such as heating vents.

Rats and mice: When bred as pets, rats are tame, alert, active, and personable. Some experts say pet rats are friendlier than pet mice, which tend toward skittishness and may bite.

Life span: Tiny pocket pets have short life spans. Some gerbils live only 18 months, but other small pets live up to 5 years. Vets say this limited lifetime often unhappily surprises devoted owners.

Habitat: Aquariums with wire mesh covers protect against drafts and escapes, confine bedding materials, and provide a clear view. Solid-bottom wire cages provide good ventilation and climbing surfaces, although some rodents gnaw wires. Select the appropriate size cage to provide exercise space for your pet. Also provide pets with enrichment toys to occupy and mentally stimulate them: chew and rolling toys, branches, and cardboard tubes, for example.

HEALTHY HOME

Parasitic Illness

Only cats that are permitted outdoors are exposed to toxoplasmosis (a parasitic flu like illness); they become contagious about one day after exposure. The best defense: Keep cats indoors, clean litter boxes daily, and wash your hands when handling cats and litter.

Protect Home from Pets

Electrostatic Duster:

Disposable cloths fit snugly on pads that rotate on long handles to reach under furniture and into awkward spaces. Cloths attract dust and pet hair like a magnet for easy cleanup.

Pet Beds:

Providing pets with their own beds keeps dirty paws and pet hair off of the family furniture. Launder pet bedding once a week to keep pet odors and insect pests at bay.

Lint Roller:

An essential for "pet people," it has a sticky surface that removes pet hairs from clothing and furniture. Some use tape that strips off after use. Electrostatic models rinse off.

Shedding Blade:

Familiar to horse groomers, these serrated tools work well on dogs and cats for gently removing loose hairs embedded in their coats. Use with care to avoid cuts or scrapes.

Avoid Vet Emergencies

Learn the pet Heimlich Maneuver: Bend over animal, wrap hands around its chest, and perform a quick jerking movement. Items toxic to pets include antifreeze, cigarettes, and chocolate (poison to dogs, cats, and birds). Keep these items out of reach.

FISH

Soothing to watch as they dart and swim, fish make a relaxing and rewarding hobby.

Species: Saltwater fish, highly sensitive to changes in temperature, salinity, and chemical content, require larger tanks and careful monitoring. Freshwater fish better tolerate change and often are recommended for first-time owners.

Setup: Aquarium sizes range from desktop to wall-size units. Basic equipment includes filter, light, heater, thermometer, air pump, gravel, and a small net. Advance planning before bringing fish home is crucial because water must stand long enough to remove chlorine and adjust saline or pH levels. Fresh plants help oxygenate water and provide hiding places. Old-fashioned round fishbowls have openings too small to absorb oxygen and need covers to keep out other pets.

Location: Keep tanks convenient to a water source and electrical outlets. Keep them away from windows as well as heating and cooling vents. Use a nearby storage area to keep fish food and tank supplies handy.

Cleanliness: Water quality is vital. Monitor chemical levels daily. Ammonia buildup becomes toxic, and dirty water results in fungal diseases on fish. Frequent partial water changes put less stress on fish, but occasionally draining the tank allows for complete cleaning. Between water changes, small vacuums remove detritus from gravel. Magnetic scrapers remove algae from inside tank glass.

Temperature: A fluctuation of more than 2 degrees a day causes stress. Most fish like temperatures between 75 and 80 degrees F.

Nutrition: There are five types of fish food. Processed flakes or freeze-dried foods are most common. Frozen, fresh, or live foods also are available from aquarium suppliers.

BIRDS

Beautiful jewel-tone feathers evoke exotic images of equatorial rain forests. Songbird canaries warble lovely music. But think seriously before buying a bird. If ornamental decor is the goal, a bird replica is a better choice. Real birds require daily care.

Life span: Parrots live up to 80 years, although usually less in captivity. Other large species live up to 10 years. Small songbirds have 3- to 6-year life spans.

Socialization: More than an adage, "birds of a feather flock together" describes domestic birds' need for social interaction. Cockatoos especially crave attention from owners: They love being stroked and hate being alone. Neglected birds develop behavior problems, including screaming, squawking, and feather pulling that leads to bald spots.

Housing: Birds feel secure in elevated cages in which they can fully extend their wings. Stainless steel wire cages that have horizontal and vertical bars on alternating sides are well-ventilated and easy to clean.

Environment: Birds, tropical in origin, require moderate warmth and sunlight. Keep cages away from heating and cooling vents, windows, and lamps. Use cage covers or place cages in rooms that can be darkened for birds to rest. Keep birds away from kitchens: Fumes from nonstick coatings are fatal to birds. Birds require behavioral enrichment and love to chew shiny metallic objects, which may result in toxicolis from ingestion of zinc. Provide branches with bark and cardboard to chew. Select toys carefully to avoid zippers, pulls, cage locks, and jewelry.

Feeding: Nutritional requirements vary among species. Complement commercial pellets with seeds, fruits, and vegetables, and consistently provide fresh water. Supplement with Vitamin A to prevent deficiency, which is a serious problem for some birds. Chocolate, avocado, and rhubarb are toxic to birds.

Cleanliness: Birds challenge owners who hope for low maintenance pets. Birds have messy habits, molt seasonally, and drop feathers when they play.

Grooming: Birds love water. Bathe or mist them daily, or provide an in-cage birdbath.

Health: Parasites and avian tuberculosis are common. Psittacosis is also common and is a potential human infection. Visit with a veterinarian regarding tests. Practice good sanitation and grooming, and provide regular veterinary checkups.

REPTILE PETS

Reptiles, or herps, are far from cold-hearted. They often develop emotional attachments to humans. Estimates show that herpetological pets are in about 3 percent of U.S. households.

Cautions: Reptiles can be sources of salmonella. Use precaution: It is impossible to determine which are infected. Wash hands immediately after handling them, and don't keep herps as pets in households with children under age 5. Pregnant women and seriously ill people should avoid herps.

Life span: Varies widely, depending on species and care. Some reptile pets require lifelong commitments. Experts warn that 90 percent of household herp pets die within one year because owners are unable to meet care requirements. Average ages of reptiles are as follows: gecko, 7 years; iguana, 15 years; king snake, 20-plus

TIP TAG № 27

Pocket Pet Pals

AVOID GREAT ESCAPE:
- Tiny, nimble, and fast, gerbils, hamsters, cavies (guinea pigs), and mice will scamper into danger—furnace vents, under cabinet spaces and so on—if left to roam.
- Keep pocket pets in solid-bottom cages or an aquarium with a screen across the top. Wire bottom cages cause feet problems and infections.

PROVIDE EXERCISE:
- In-cage wheels keep pocket pets fit.
- Hamster balls allow them to run around the house; take care they don't tumble down stairs or get trapped beneath furniture.
- Cardboard tubes make tunnels that tiny pets love to explore.

years; boa constrictor, 25 years; turtle, 40 years; alligator, 50 years.

Size: Pet reptiles average 1 to 2 feet long. A healthy full-grown iguana can be 7 feet long; snakes grow to several yards long.

Care: Reptiles need warmth, special lighting, water, and food. Some can get liquid only from chewing on moist leaves; others drink from bowls. Herbivore turtles and lizards need calcium but can only metabolize it under specific ultraviolet light spectrums. Special lightbulbs are available from pet supply stores. Carnivores require 12 hours of light each day. Cold-blooded creatures all require temperatures between 80 to 85 degrees F.

Habitat: Humidity from misting and natural plants duplicates native tropical homes. A terrarium, solarium room, or greenhouse is ideal for housing reptile pets. Slow-moving snakes curl contentedly in aquariums, but lithe, agile geckos need space to exercise.

Feeding: For carnivores, whole frozen animals can be bought from pet suppliers. Herbivores require specific plant diets. Some reptile pets require nutritional or vitamin supplements.

Household Pests

Indoor pests either invite themselves in through windows or doors or hitch rides on pets or items people bring into their homes.

GEOGRAPHY

Entomologists track common pests. With billions of insects known worldwide, this list isn't intended to be all inclusive. Human mobility spreads pests into new areas daily. The following lists are guidelines.

Nationwide: Carpenter ants, houseflies, stable flies, fleas, dog ticks, silverfish, grain and storage pests, cockroaches, mites, aphids, scales, black widows.

Northeast: Deer ticks

Midwest: Brown recluse spiders, eastern subterranean termites, millipedes, crickets, carpet beetles, fruit flies, yellow jackets

South: Formosan termites, fire ants, black-legged ticks

Southwest: Sun spiders, fire ants, scorpions, desert centipedes

West: Africanized bees, dampwood termites

Hawaii: Formosan termites

FLEAS AND TICKS

Both carry diseases, including Rocky Mountain spotted fever and Lyme disease, infecting humans and animals. Ticks have a teardrop shape and eight legs. Fleas are up to $1/8$ inch long, wingless, and flat, with piercing-sucking mouthparts.

Cat and dog fleas also feed on rodents and humans. Scratching can move them to pet bedding, so launder often. Eggs in the carpet, which hatch into fleas, can be a problem.

American dog ticks will infest animals and humans, but do not survive well indoors.

BUDGET STRETCHER

Houseplant Rescue

•

Lightly wash infested plants with insecticidal soap from garden suppliers. Discard heavily webbed or scaly plants. Spray a strong jet of water on the affected area to wash off insects. Dabbing insects with rubbing alcohol is also effective.

Identifying Common Pests

Cockroach:
From ⅝ inch to 2⅛ inches at maturity, brown or tan, with wings covering their abdomens.

Spider:
Arachnids have two body parts and eight legs. Some are blood feeders; others suck plant sap.

Black Ant:
Usually ¼ inch long, workers vary in size. There are more than 20 species of house ants in the U.S.

Cricket:
Field crickets are up to ¾ inch long and shiny black. They "chirp" by rubbing their wings together.

Clothing Moth:
Only larvae eat natural fabrics; the presence of adults with pale wings suggests larvae at work.

Termite:
These have wings of equal size, no waists, and straight antennae. There are 47 species in the U.S.

Centipede:
Up to 1½ inches with multiple legs, they're poisonous but rarely bite. They prefer to infest damp areas.

Mosquito:
These annoying bloodsuckers breed in standing water and wet areas. Some carry disease.

Housefly:
The most common pest, these ¼ inch insects carry disease from their filthy habitats and feeding habits.

Flea:
Wingless, biting insects, up to 1⁄16 inch long, they have flat bodies and long back legs for jumping.

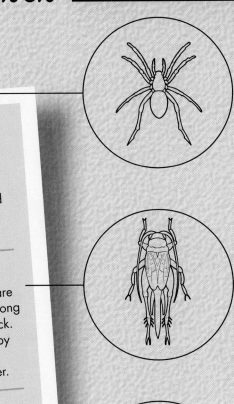
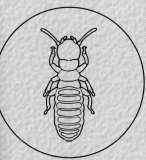
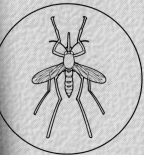

HEALTHY HOME

Pest Control

•

Keep trash tightly covered. Keep windows and doors tightly closed and screens in good repair. Trim branches that touch buildings to remove insect trails. Bait mouse traps with chewy candy or gumdrops.

Brown dog ticks are primarily southern pests, but sometimes live in northern houses and kennels. They seldom bite humans. After feeding, they drop off their hosts and often are seen on walls and furniture.

Black-legged ticks include the deer and bear tick found east of the Mississippi River and the western or Pacific tick along the West Coast and into Arizona.

WOOD CHEWING INVADERS

Carpenter ants are up to ½ inch long, and are black, red, or brown. Areas where water leaks occur, including roofs, soffits, bathrooms, and kitchens, require regular inspection. Rustling in walls or the presence of wood shavings indicates a carpenter ant colony. They don't eat the wood they chew while creating nests, but they still do serious damage if left unchecked.

Termites in the United States number three in major species: subterranean, Formosan, and dampwood. They have broad abdomens, unlike narrow-waisted ants. Termites eat the cellulose in wood, causing significant damage to buildings, books, and furniture.

ANTS

Fire ants: Small, red, and aggressive, with painful stings, they were a southern pest but are spreading into other warm areas.

Little black ants nest under stones, in lawns, and in areas lacking vegetation. Tiny craters mark the nest entrance. They also nest in rotting wood, behind woodwork or masonry in buildings, under carpeting, in old termite galleries, and in wall voids. They eat houseplant aphids but also feed on meat, grease, and sweets.

Odorous house ants and crazy ants are often seen marching across floors or carpets. Odorous ants get their name from their rancid smell when crushed; crazy ants run erratically when searching for food. They nest in wall or floor voids, around hot water pipes and heaters, and in crevices around sinks and cabinets. They prefer sweets but eat almost any household food or trash.

COCKROACHES

German cockroaches (up to ⅝ inch long when mature, light brown to tan, with wings) are the most common household insect in the United States. They will live anywhere there is food, water, and privacy. They feed on nearly anything, including human and pet food, toothpaste, soap, and glue.

American cockroaches up to 2⅛ inches long, red-brown, with wings are abundant in sewers; they prefer warm, damp places. Although uncommon in homes, heavily populated areas, including apartment buildings, are likely locations.

Brown-banded cockroaches prefer warm, dry places off the floor, hiding behind crown molding, picture frames, and wall hangings, and in closets, furniture, and seldom-used appliances.

Oriental cockroaches like damp, secluded places. They produce a pungent odor (as do German and American cockroaches). They eat starches and decaying organic matter.

SPIDERS

Spiders are arachnids, not insects. Most prefer secluded spots, such as undisturbed basement corners, crawlspaces, and rafters. Vacuum webs and egg sacs. Immediately wrap filter bag in a plastic garbage sack and discard to prevent reinfestation.

Black widow: Females are about ½ inch long and glossy black with globelike abdomens. They have two triangular red spots on the underside that look like an hourglass. Males are smaller. These spiders are venomous, sometimes causing anaphylactic (shock) reactions when they bite humans.

Brown recluse: Known as "fiddle back" or "violin" spiders for their markings, they're up to ¼ inch long, with long legs and six eyes in a semicircle. Painful bites develop into slow-healing ulcers.

SCORPIONS

Close relatives of spiders, they are common in the desert Southwest, although they've been seen as far north as Baltimore, St. Louis, and San Francisco. Scorpions that enter buildings seeking water and shelter are most often found in bathrooms, crawl-spaces, attics, dry stone walls, foundations—and clothes and shoes left on the floor. Stings are comparable to a wasp's sting.

NATURAL PREVENTION

Try these ideas before calling in a professional:

Cockroaches, crickets, and silverfish will consume a bait called Niban, which is made from boric acid.

Household ants can be controlled with products such as Advance Dual Choice Ant Bait (5 percent orthoboric acid), a low toxicity, boric-acid based, weather-resistant bait. Carpenter ants can be controlled with products such as Advance Carpenter Ant Bait. Ants can also be killed with a mixture of 1 part dish soap to 10 parts water. Baits are available at home centers and hardware stores. They can also be purchased online.

Spiders are easily captured by inverting a glass over them and sliding a piece of stiff paper under the glass. After entrapping the spider, carry it outside in the glass.

Crickets are attracted to duct tape. Place a piece of duct tape, sticky side up, on the floor near where you hear crickets.

Flies can be kept out of the house by filling resealable sandwich

smart ideas
Indoor Comfort

WATCH MOISTURE LEVELS

Humidity levels above 50 percent allow moisture to build up indoors and condense on surfaces, where bacteria and fungi can settle and grow. Levels below 30 percent are too dry, causing physical discomfort and damaging furnishings. Measure humidity with an hygrometer, available at hardware stores.

BREATHE EASY

When used in steam humidifers, medicinal inhalants, such as eucalyptus help clear stuffy noses. Take care—scalding is a risk. Clean units often with a bleach solution to prevent mold or bacteria growth.

bags with water, zipping them shut, and taping them to the outside of the door. The water bags will repel flies. Inside, use old-fashioned fly swatters instead of spray insecticides.

Earwigs can be trapped by rolling up newspaper, dampening the paper, and placing it outside near exterior doors.

HOUSEPLANT PESTS

Plants grown in poor conditions—with too-little humidity, insufficient lighting, or improper watering—are most susceptible to pests.

Aphids: Yellow, stunted, or curling leaves signal infestation. Tiny sucking insects come in almost any color, winged and wingless. Wash off and spray with an insecticidal soap.

Spider Mites: These tiny insects are the most common houseplant problem. Look for fine webs on the underside of plants. Spider mites like warm, dry conditions. To eradicate, remove all old soil, wash the leaves, repot, and spray with a horticultural oil.

Mealybugs: These soft-bodied insects secrete a cottony white covering, distorting new plant growth. To control, remove the white masses with a cotton swab dipped in rubbing alcohol or horticultural oil.

Scale: These soft-bodied insects suck sap, then secrete a hard shell over themselves. Eggs form under the shell, which hatch into crawlers. Use insecticidal soaps and oil to control at the crawler stage. Use oils to control adult scale.

Whiteflies: Whiteflies are closely related to aphids, mealybugs, and scale insects. Found on the undersides of leaves, infestations spread quickly. Remove damaged leaves. Sticky traps from garden suppliers attract and hold adults for removal. Small vacuums, such as for computer keyboards, gently suck up infestations at egg stage.

STORED FOOD INSECTS

These enter even scrupulously clean households by way of groceries or on fabric or dried flowers. Among the most common household pests, they include flour beetles, granary and rice weevils, drugstore beetles, saw-toothed grain beetles, and flour and meal moths. Flour, sugar, starch, nuts, cereal grains, pastas, dried fruits, and dry pet foods are pest favorites. Buy packaged goods in quickly usable quantities, or store them in the freezer. Toss outdated packaged foods. Wash shelves with warm water, detergent, and white vinegar. Rinse and air-dry before replacing foodstuff. Store fresh foods in containers with tight-fitting lids.

GENERAL STORAGE PESTS

Moths prefer dark closets, attics, basements, or other storage areas where they can lay eggs. Adult moths don't eat, but new larvae have voracious appetites for wool, fur, silk, feathers, and leather.

Carpet beetle larvae have tastes similar to moths. Vacuuming

HEALTHY HOME

Ticks and Disease

•

Tick-borne illnesses include Lyme disease. Wear long sleeves, pants, and boots when hiking and picnicking, and use tick repellent. Check people and pets for ticks daily. Remove ticks with tweezers close to tick head to prevent leaving mouthparts.

Natural Pest Remedies

Bay Leaves:

Household folklore says bay leaves are effective against cockroaches and ants. Scatter in kitchen cabinets and under sinks. Keep leaves away from children and pets.

Boric Acid:

Mix boric acid with oat flour (not meal) and leave for ants or cockroaches to eat. It kills these insects by disrupting their digestion. Harmful to children and pets.

Cucumbers:

Both the rinds and the pulp have been cited as popular home remedies for cockroaches and ants. Leave mashed cukes on dishes in areas of infestation.

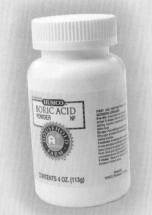

Hot Pepper:

To repel ants, use a mixture of water, liquid soap, and cayenne pepper, sprayed on hard surfaces, or sprinkle chili powder or cayenne along the outside of doorways.

Basil:

Place pots of fresh basil or pennyroyal to grow on windowsills or kitchen counters. Hang sprigs from doorways and porches to repel flies and mosquitoes.

Garlic:

Ants and cockroaches are supposed to dislike garlic. Leave whole cloves on cabinet shelves and under sinks, or place along known ant trails. Replace when dried out.

removes larvae that create infestations. Include closets and seldom-used areas in cleaning routine.

CALLING PROFESSIONAL PEST CONTROL

Termite, flea, tick, or cockroach infestations are difficult to control and may require professional help.

■ Obtain bids. Get an in-home estimate; do not accept prices given over the phone or by e-mail. Discuss both costs and chemical usage.

■ Ask if a monthly contract is required. Experts report that few households need monthly service.

■ Ask to see license and insurance certificates.

■ Ask for copies of labels and Material Safety Data Sheets (MSDS) so you'll know which pesticide a company plans to use.

■ Get references. Find out whether the pest-control operator has experience with the problem you have.

RODENTS

Although usually content to ignore humans, wildlife rodents can cause problems if they get indoors. Squirrels enter attics through loose roofing. Use a humane trap (local pest-control experts often lend or rent them) and release them outdoors. Look for entry points and seal or screen; squirrels are territorial and will attempt to return. Skunks, raccoon, or porcupines try to shelter under porches or decks; cover open areas with lattice.

The house mouse lives throughout the United States. It nests in dark, quiet areas. Favorite foods include seeds and cereals. Salmonella and leptospirosis (a bacterial illness treatable with antibiotics) are major human health risks carried by these mice. House mice squeeze through gaps as small as $\frac{1}{4}$ inch. Routine maintenance to fill holes is important to block entry.

Deer mice are seldom a problem in urban residential areas, but suburban and rural areas may have infestations. Deer mice nest in hollow logs, tree stumps, abandoned bird nests, and shallow burrows. In cold weather, they enter houses, cabins, garages, outbuildings, and seldom-used vehicles such as campers. They are potential carriers of hantavirus.

Rats continue to be a major environmental health danger in large urban areas. Fleas that feed on rats carry disease, including leptospirosis. Rats destroy property by gnawing or fouling it. Vigilant sanitation is the best defense. Try trapping when necessary. Tightly cover trash bins, and keep alleys clean of garbage.

Bats eat mosquitoes and other flying insects. Bats avoid human contact, but fecal droppings in attic, garage, or shed roosts increase human risk of contracting histoplasmosis, a fungal infection with respiratory and intestinal symptoms. Cover potential entry points with screens, sheet metal, or metal wool. Experts suggest sealing all but one or two openings at first, allowing bats a way out. Seal

HEALTHY HOME

Not Too Humid

•

If dampness occurs around a humidifier, turn down the output volume or use only intermittently, not continuously. Don't allow nearby absorbent materials to become damp, which could cause mold or mildew. Stop using; contact physician if respiratory problems develop.

remaining entries after bats emerge in the evening. One-way flaps allow exit only.

Indoor Air Comfort

Household comfort depends on countless variables. Heating and cooling units, geographic temperature ranges, and seasonal changes all play a role. Maintaining proper moisture levels is a balancing act: Too little humidity results in physical discomforts of dry nose, throat, lips, and skin; too much encourages dust mites, molds, and fungus. Maintaining sufficient moisture in winter alleviates problems such as static electricity and cracks in paint and furniture.

HUMIDIFIERS

Central units are built into heating and air-conditioning systems. Consoles have the capacity to humidify several rooms. Portable units are available at drugstores and other retailers such as discount stores.

■ Cool-mist units come in two types. One uses evaporation to produce moisture through a belt, wick, or filter. The other, an impeller, uses a tube to draw water as centrifugal force from a high-speed rotating disk creates large water droplets.

■ Steam vaporizers heat water with electrical elements or electrodes. Vaporizers also include teapotlike steamers for use on wood stoves. Warm-mist units add warmth to rooms without scalding risk—steam is slightly cooled before dispersal, producing vapor.

■ Ultrasonic humidifiers disperse cool mist by sound vibrations.

Performance is rated in output per 24 hours. The more the humidifier puts out, the larger the area it will humidify.

Capacity refers to the amount of water unit holds.

Cleaning and maintenance means following manufacturer's directions. When scrubbing the tank, take care not to damage the motor or scratch the inner surface, which could create niches for mold. Clean or replace filters or belts. Use demineralization cartridges or filters if recommended for your unit. Drain and clean tanks before seasonal storage, checking first that parts are dry. Discard used cartridges, cassettes, or filters. Store in a dry location. Clean again before use and often during heating season. If using disinfectant, rinse well to avoid harmful fumes.

DEHUMIDIFIERS

Excess humidity makes people feel sticky and miserable and invites growth of allergens.

Home Remedies

MOLD & MILDEW

Keep Things Dry

Quick leak repairs prevent the spread of mold spores. For humidity problems, use desiccants available at home improvement centers. Discard soaked ceiling tiles or paper goods. Flood-damaged clothing, upholstery, and carpets need professional attention.

Clean It Up

Mildew stains and odor are often permanent. Try this on durable fabrics, tent canvas, or shower curtains: Wash in solution of ½ cup liquid disinfectant to 1 gallon of hot water. Rinse with a mixture of 1 cup lemon juice and 1 cup salt to a gallon of hot water. Then wash with detergent and bleach (color-safe bleach on color fabrics). Rinse in clear water. Dry before storage.

Temperature: Dehumidifiers work best in warm, moist conditions. At temperatures below 65 degrees, coils frost up. Units with automatic deicers shut off, restarting once frost thaws.

Air flow: Keep units 6 to 10 inches away from walls or furniture. A central location is best for efficient multiple-room drying.

Maintenance: Some units also purify the air. Clean or replace filters monthly. Clean cooling coils annually with detergent and water. Wash water pans weekly with a weak bleach solution or household antibacterial cleaner.

FLOOR DRAINS

Inspect for standing water, which attracts pests or develops algae, bacteria, or molds. Pour a solution of hot water and detergent down the drain to keep it clean. Call a plumber to clear stoppages.

Indoor Air Pollution

Poor air quality poses a special concern for an estimated 40 million Americans with allergies and for an estimated 17 million people with asthma. However, while asthma is mainly a concern from biological contaminants, such as dust mites, pets, and molds, some pollutants can be health risks to anyone if exposure is at unsafe levels.

Asbestos: A mineral fiber once common as insulation and as a fire retardant. It requires professional removal.

Benzene: A chemical now mainly found in tobacco smoke.

Carbon monoxide: Carbon monoxide is a deadly colorless, odorless gas. Install detectors, similar to smoke detectors. Schedule annual checks for heating systems and gas appliances. Don't warm up cars inside garages.

Formaldehyde: Comes from cigarette smoke. In addition, outgassing from some building materials, cleaning products, unvented fuel-burning appliances, adhesives, paint preservatives, and coating products releases formaldehyde into the air.

Fungal outgassing: Molds and fungi grow in moist, warm places and release acetone, benzene, and hexane. A musty odor could signal bacterial or fungal breeding ground. Vacuum with HEPA filter bags. Clean visible molds with a detergent solution.

Lead: A major household threat to children's health. Homes built before 1970 often contain lead paint; remodeling can release it. Lead comes in unexpected forms as well: Candles with metal wicks, now banned by the federal government, give off soot with high lead concentrations. Unglazed ceramics also have high lead concentrations, so use as decorations, not food servers.

Mercury: Silvery, slippery highly toxic heavy metal found in thermometers, fluorescent and HID lights, and thermostats. If a household spill occurs, collect beads with an eyedropper and place them in a widemouthed jar. Never vacuum mercury spills; motor

HEALTHY HOME

Humidifier Cleaning

•

Distilled water reduces film and scale buildup. Change water daily in room humidifiers and clean unit every third day with bleach or peroxide. Never add fresh water to sitting water—empty tank and refill. Clean before storing.

Careful Disposal Required

Paint Thinner:
Buy in very small quantities. Store out of reach of children and away from heat or flames.Check about toxic disposal pickups.

Flea Collars:
Place in paper or plastic bags and seal before tossing. Keep away from children. Check with your vet about medications for flea control.

House Paint:
Buy only as much as you need. Leftovers should be stored in garage or shed. If you must dispose, call your city or county about current regulations.

Gasoline:
Buy in small quantities. Store away from heat or flames. Never pour out or down storm drain. Check with your city or county for options.

Medications:
Keep all prescription and over-the-counter medicines out of reach of children. Dispose of out-of-date ones. Check with pharmacist for safety tips.

Pesticides:
Buy in smallest possible quantities. If you must dispose of it, call your city or county about pickup days for difficult-to-dispose-of items.

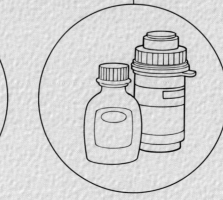

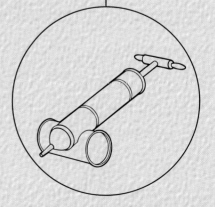

heat vaporizes mercury causing toxic fumes. Contact local solid waste authority for information on toxic waste disposal.

Methylene chloride: Found in paint strippers, adhesive removers, and aerosol spray paints, it has been found to cause cancer in animals. Use methylene chloride products outdoors when possible; use indoors only in well-ventilated areas.

Nitrogen dioxide: A colorless, odorless gas that irritates the mucous membranes in the eyes, nose, and throat and causes shortness of breath after exposure to high concentrations.

Ozone: Relatively low amounts can cause chest pain, coughing, shortness of breath, and throat irritation. Ozone exposure may worsen chronic respiratory diseases such as asthma.

Perchloroethylene: Widely used in dry cleaning; people breathe low levels while wearing and storing dry-cleaned clothing. Dry cleaners remove some of this chemical during pressing and finishing. Look for a dry-cleaning service that uses processes requiring little or no perchloroethylene, if possible.

Pesticides: Use strictly according to manufacturer's directions. Mix or dilute outdoors. Apply only in recommended quantities. Increase ventilation when using indoors. Take plants and pets outdoors before applying pesticides inside. Use natural, nonchemical methods whenever possible. Store pesticide containers locked up outside the home. Dispose of empty containers; safely follow toxic waste laws in your city or county.

Radon: Odorless radioactive gas occurring naturally in the Earth's crust. Found in many buildings, including apartments below the third floor.

Tobacco smoke: A complex mixture of more than 4,000 compounds—more than 40 of which are known to cause cancer.

Volatile Organic Compounds: VOCs come from many indoor sources. Low-VOC paints are available, but may emit formaldehyde fumes. When having carpet installed, ask about Carpet and Rug Institute emission-reduction guidelines. Run fans for 48 to 72 hours after painting or carpet installation.

Indoor Air Quality
AIR PURIFIERS

Systems range from tabletop models to whole-house systems. Air cleaners usually don't effectively remove gases such as radon. Effective air-purification depends on both filter efficiency at trapping particles and the amount of air that passes through it. Air-conditioners, humidifiers, and dehumidifiers filter some pollutants.

Whole-house systems: Furnace filters remove a small percentage of breathable particles, so they qualify as air purifiers.

■ Basic furnace filters usually are made of fiberglass or synthetic fibrous material in cardboard frames. Filter fabrics are sometimes coated with oily substances, which act as adhesives for particulates. These filters are inexpensive. They are less than 20 percent efficient at trapping particulates, according to standards set by the American Society of Heating, Refrigeration, and Air Conditioning Engineers (ASHRAE). Replace monthly.

■ Medium- to high-efficiency filters contain cellulose or activated charcoal. They trap smaller particles and remove odors. Others are made of pleated cotton or polyester in die-cut frames. They range from 20 to 25 percent effective by ASHRAE standards. These last about three months before needing replacement.

■ High-efficiency filters include permanent metal-mesh and pleated or extended-surface fabrics with an electrically charged media. Some include antimicrobial treatment to retard mold and bacteria growth on the filters. Many are permanent but should be washed monthly. Electronic air cleaners are 10 to 20 times more efficient than standard filters but are more expensive. Charged particles attach to grounded plates for holding until washed away.

Portable air cleaners: Tabletop or console units use filters ranging from fibrous to electronic. Some portable units will clean air in only one room; large units may clean air in two or more rooms. Both work by using fans that pull air through the charging area and return the cleaned air to the room. Check that inlet and outlet vents are clear of obstructions, including walls and furniture. Clean or replace filters weekly or monthly, depending on unit capacity.

Whole-house fans: Ventilation units pull cool air through the house and move stale air out via roof vents. These fans are an integral part of radon removal systems.

Heat exchangers: These increase ventilation by discharging seasonally heated or cooled indoor air to the outdoors and bringing in fresh air.

Houseplants: Although there's a wide range of scientific opinion on their effectiveness, plants are worth including in an air-purification plan, if healthy and well maintained to avoid molds. Foliage and root systems work together in removing impurities. Research on "sick-building syndrome" suggests the possibility of a living air cleaner, plants potted in soil that has been mixed with activated carbon, which degrades the chemicals it absorbs. Avoid flowers if you're allergic to pollen. Two plants are sufficient for 100 square feet of space. The following plants are especially helpful:

■ Philodendron, spider plants, and golden pothos remove

TIPTAG №28
Radon Alert

EARLY DETECTION:
• Levels vary daily and seasonally.
• Test kits are available from hardware stores and home centers.
• Contact the American Lung Association at 212/315-8700 for more details.

MITIGATION MEASURES:
• Sub-slab and soil depressurization methods use pipes and fans for removing radon gas from beneath concrete floors and foundations. The gas is vented above the roof for safe dispersal. Never turn off fans.
• Radon-reduction repairs should be made by an EPA- or state-certified contractor. Check your local Yellow Pages for contractors.

formaldehyde and carbon monoxide under test conditions.

■ Gerbera daisies and chrysanthemums have been shown to be effective in removing benzene.

■ Chinese evergreen, ficus, aloe vera, dieffenbachia, and English ivy also are good general indoor air cleaners.

Water Quality

Pure liquid is vital to good health. No in-home system removes every contaminant. Household filtration depends on preference in taste; treatment may be only a temporary measure for water quality concerns. Boiling water for at least two minutes kills organisms, so is a good method for purifying small quantities in emergencies.

Activated carbon (AC) systems filter water as it is dispensed. These commonly come as water pitchers or units that attach to faucets or under sink pipes. Filters are easily replaceable. This is the most common method in use for home water purification. Products are readily available at hardware and discount stores. Activated carbon collects contaminants in its porous surface area. Filter effectiveness depends on how long water remains in contact with the activated carbon. AC filters work best at removing organic compounds, such as pesticides, benzene, some metals, and radon. Some newer-designed AC filters remove water supply contaminants, including lead, and bacteria such as giardia.

Point-of-use systems mean the AC filters clean water as it is dispensed. Use is simple: Filter cartridges insert into units, allowing water to pass through. Point-of-use systems may include bypass filtering, increasing useful filter life and reducing time between replacements. Carefully read labels when purchasing low-cost filters. Look for activated carbon, not plain.

Point-of-entry systems are whole-house units that filter water as it enters household plumbing and may be installed during home construction. These require professional installation.

Water coolers, bottled water, or bulk water can be the pure-water source in a household. A refrigeration-cooling dispenser usually is in in the kitchen. Small dispensers sit on countertops; standing coolers require floor space in a convenient spot. Many come with a large (5-gallon) plastic water bottle on top; others are bottleless, concealing the water source inside the unit. Many include reverse osmosis or other filtering systems. Check for a UL or NSF label, which indicates the watercooler has undergone testing and meets approval standards. Care of refrigerated water chillers and coolers often comes with the rental service contracts. Choose a model with removable reservoirs so you can clean at each water change. Dishwasher-safe models are especially nice. Check local Yellow Pages for distributors.

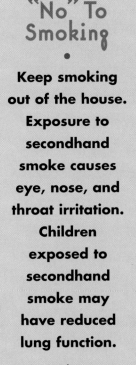

FAMILY FRIENDLY

"No" To Smoking

•

Keep smoking out of the house. Exposure to secondhand smoke causes eye, nose, and throat irritation. Children exposed to secondhand smoke may have reduced lung function.

In-Home Water Filtration

Faucet Attachment:

Most often used when the water taste or smell is a concern. Filters have a limited life; package estimates may not be accurate for your water use.

Pitcher:

A simple system with no installation. Used for improving taste and removing odor; may also remove some organic compounds. Follow instructions for effective use.

Sink-Mount:

Easy to attach with minimal tools, these units are added at the sink. Check filters. Different brands remove organic compounds (radon) or water supply contaminants.

Under-Sink:

This style has the advantage of being hidden under the sink. Choose the filter that addresses your water purity, taste, or smell concern and change frequently.

Filter:

The activated charcoal filter is the basis of point-of-use systems. Make sure the filter is activated charcoal, which removes more contaminants than plain charcoal.

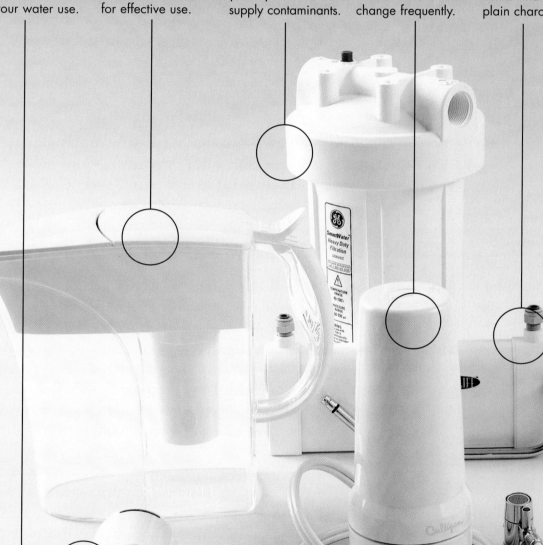

Special Needs for Children

Children are inquisitive and love to touch and taste whatever they find, so take care to keep them safe from household hazards.

■ Cleaning agents: Lock up. Never use unmarked containers.

■ Diaper pails: Bacteria grow rapidly in dark, moist places like diaper pails. Launder diapers daily in hot water with detergent and bleach to kill bacteria on the cloth. Wash pails with a detergent-and-bleach solution or antibacterial cleaner; rinse and dry.

■ Furnishings: Inexpensive children's furniture sometimes is particleboard joined with formaldehyde-based adhesives. Choose solid wood, or seal surfaces with water-based paints or sealers.

■ Hand washing: This is the most effective way to avoid disease. Teach children to wash their hands often and thoroughly. Make hand-washing fun by teaching them to sing a verse of a song while sudsing, and another verse while rinsing their hands. After wiping their hands on a towel, show them how to rehang the towel.

■ Holidays and special occasions: Alcoholic beverages are poison for young children. Clean up quickly during and after parties. Keep strings of lights and ornaments high enough to avoid electric shocks or cuts from breaking glass. Don't leave burning candles on tablecloths or decorative fabric; a pull on the cloth topples candles, causing burns or starting fires. Gift wraps with loose ribbons or trinkets can cause choking, so put them out of reach.

■ Lead: A child who gets adequate calcium and iron in the diet absorbs less lead if exposed. A simple blood test by a pediatrician determines health risk and treatment. Be especially alert if you live in an older (pre-1970s) house or apartment.

■ Pesticides: Store locked up outside the house.

■ Pets: Keep pet areas clean. Keep vaccinations current and have dogs and cats wormed with a broad-spectrum wormer. While uncommon, children can contract parasites from dogs and cats.

■ Water temperature: Lower the temperature of the water heater to 105 degrees F to prevent burns. Also consider thermostatic faucets, which can be set to reduce scalding risks.

Play equipment: Annual inspection and maintenance of swing sets and climbing equipment keep play areas safe:

■ Cover chains with rubber sleeves to prevent pinching.

■ Check that all nuts and bolts are tight and fix any protruding threads that could snag clothing or scratch.

■ Gliders can be battering rams that hit young children. Remove them when children under age 4 will be present.

■ Cover the ground under and around swing sets or climbing equipment with shredded bark or other mulching material, play sand, ground rubber, or pea gravel to cushion falls.

SAFETY ALERT

Dangerous Plants

•

Plants best kept away from children include caladium, clivia, croton, crown of thorns, dumbcane, English ivy, ficus, fishtail palm, flamingo flower, peace lily, philodendron, and Swiss-cheese plant. Keep high on shelves or in hanging baskets out of reach.

Table Settings
- FINE AND CASUAL CHINA,291
- SILVER AND SILVER-PLATED FLATWARE,294
- STAINLESS-STEEL FLATWARE,294
- CRYSTAL AND GLASSWARE,295
- TABLE LINENS,296
- CENTERPIECES,296
- SETTING THE TABLE,305

Entertaining
- KNOW YOUR STYLE,298
- FOOD CONCERNS,299
- SETTING UP A BUFFET TABLE,300
- BUFFETS AND COCKTAIL PARTIES,300,302
- GUEST RESPONSIBILITIES,300,304
- BUDGET STRETCHERS,300,306
- ALCOHOL-FREE PARTIES,302
- POTLUCKS AND PROGRESSIVE DINNERS,303
- PARTY CHECKLIST,303
- SUPPER CLUBS,304

Parties for Weddings
- ANNOUNCING THE ENGAGEMENT,304
- SHOWERS, LUNCHEONS, AND DINNERS,304,306

Children's Parties
- OUTDOOR FUN,307
- BIRTHDAYS,307,308
- HOLIDAY PARTIES,308

Family Celebrations
- ANNIVERSARIES,306
- SPECIAL BIRTHDAYS,307
- REUNIONS,307

Special Holidays
- CHRISTMAS,310
- KWANZA,310
- HANUKKAH,311
- PASSOVER,311
- EASTER,312
- SHARING WITH FRIENDS,311

Seasonal Holidays
- HALLOWEEN,312
- FOURTH OF JULY AND LABOR DAY,312
- THANKSGIVING,314
- NEW YEAR'S EVE AND DAY,314
- TWELFTH NIGHT,314
- MARDI GRAS,314
- PARTY SAFETY,314

Table Settings

Setting the table is a skill: When you learn the basics, you are more comfortable inviting people to your home. The basics are easy, as you'll see in the following sections. If you are occasionally confused about a placement, refer to this section for a quick refresher. The trend is toward more informal settings that mix dinnerware and flatware. Although it is wonderful to have complete sets of inherited or acquired fine china and silver, colorful, well-designed place settings from discount or import stores are equally inviting.

FINE CHINA

Selecting: What is typically called fine china is either bone china or porcelain. These differ in material composition, but both are delicate and strong. See page 293 for comparison information. Traditionally, brides and grooms select and register their fine china patterns when they become engaged. Pieces are purchased by place setting or individually, such as by plate. Buying open-stock pieces makes it easy to add place settings and serving pieces, replace damaged ones, and expand your service through the years. When you select a pattern, take your time: You will own it for a long time. Think of the color scheme you have or plan for the future, remembering that tastes and lifestyles change. Classic white patterns with minimal ornamentation or simple gold or silver banding are timeless.

In general, matching china patterns are used for each course. For example, use all the same pattern for the main course, but use a different pattern for dessert and coffee. Some sets have different but coordinating salad or dessert plates. If you use different sets—your own and an inherited pattern, for example—they should have the same general degree of formality and quality.

People choose china patterns they can add to over the years. Department stores and jewelry stores may have plans tailored to installment purchases of fine china as well as silver and crystal.

For entertaining, place settings for eight are a starting point. Place settings for 12 are nice to have if you have a large extended family or like to entertain. The all-matching place setting is a traditional choice. However, if you want to add interest to a table setting, consider selecting a salad or dessert plate in a design that complements your main pattern. China discovered at an estate sale or antiques shop can create beautiful table settings. Choose carefully: Pieces made before the 1920s and antique items from the

TIPTAG NO. 29
Serving Pieces

FLATWARE:
- Useful pieces include salad servers, two to three large serving spoons, slotted serving spoon, serving fork, carving set.
- Helpful are butter knife, pie server, sugar spoon, gravy ladle, cake fork.

CHINA:
- Items to add through the years are one or two open vegetable dishes, trio of serving platters, gravy boat, sugar bowl, creamer.

SILVER OR SILVER PLATE:
- Pieces to acquire include salt and pepper shakers, Revere-style bowls in various sizes, water pitcher, butter dish, coffee service, tea service, round tray, large oval tray.

Personal Patterns

If you enjoy bargain shopping at flea markets or estate sales, collect deliberately mismatched antique or vintage china and silverware or silver plate. Complete with vintage crystal, tablecloths, napkins, and serving pieces.

18th and 19th centuries may be too delicate for practical use.

Storing: Store fine china so it cannot get chipped, nicked, or damaged. The round, zippered containers with padded lining available from home furnishing specialty stores are excellent for protecting fine china when it is not in use. These cover-ups are available in every place size; a design is also made to hold cups. Another protective strategy is to sandwich rounds of felt between each plate to keep plates with elaborate decorations or touches of gold from being scratched or marred. Felt rounds can be purchased at home furnishing shops. You can cut circles of felt using a paper template slightly smaller than the dimensions of the actual plate.

Care: Most fine china currently manufactured is dishwasher-safe. If you are in doubt, check with the store where it was purchased or the manufacturer. Securely arrange pieces in the machine's dish rack so that the plate and cup rims do not knock against one another. Gold and silver are soft metals, and edging detail will be damaged by automatic dishwashing detergents, which are abrasive.

If you own estate china or treasured inherited pieces, or if you are hesitant to put fine china in the dishwasher, wash it by hand. To avoid damage, use a plastic dishpan in the sink. Fill the pan with hot water and a mild dishwashing detergent. Let plates soak to remove sticky food; wash off with a soft sponge—avoid any abrasive product that could permanently scratch the fine china—and rinse with hot water. Set pieces to drain in a sturdy draining rack, carefully arranging them so that the edges aren't vulnerable. Wipe dry with a clean dish towel. The gilding on gold-decorated china may discolor if acidic food, such as vinegar or pickles, is allowed to remain for any period of time or if the plate is not washed thoroughly.

Formal service for 8 or 12: Formal services usually include dinner plates, salad plates, cups and saucers, bread and butter plates, creamer and sugar bowl, salt and pepper shakers, and rimmed soup plates.

Five-piece place settings include dinner plates, salad plates, bread and butter plates, and teacups and saucers. Soup plates are often used for pasta dishes.

Serving pieces in formal china service are serving bowls, platters, and the gravy boat as well as tea- and coffeepots.

CASUAL CHINA

Selecting: Stoneware, earthenware, and pottery are the typical materials for everyday or casual china. With renewed interest in mid-20th-century design, some mass-market retailers are selling plastic dinnerware reminiscent of the 1950s and 1960s. Depending on the style and material, casual dinnerware is purchased in sets or place settings.

Informal service for 8 or 12: Services include dinner

Choose Your Service

Porcelain:
Imported from Europe, this ceramic is associated with formal beautifully detailed and translucent glazed dinnerware.

Fine Bone China:
Traditional for formal tables, translucent bone is made with bone ash for strength. Gold or silver detailing is often used.

Stoneware:
Durable and heavier than bone china, stoneware is a good choice for everyday use. New stoneware is dishwasher-safe.

Ironstone:
This white ceramic is typically decorated with reliefs, rather than color. Weight is between china and earthenware; for general use.

Fine China:
Depending on ornamentation and thickness, it is appropriate for everyday use and for special occasions; often dishwasher-safe.

Earthenware:
This glazed ceramic is among the heaviest in use. Some imported pieces require hand washing; care is needed to avoid chips.

plates, dessert or salad plates, bowls, cups and saucers (or mugs), and sugar bowl and creamer.

STERLING SILVER AND SILVER PLATE

Registering or investing in sterling silver or less-expensive silver plate is a personal decision. If you have inherited sterling silver or silver plate, treasure it as a valuable family heirloom.

Selecting: New silver is usually purchased open stock. Newly engaged couples select and register a pattern with a department store or jewelry store. Sterling-silver services are typically purchased through open stock. Silver plate is purchased in services or in open stock. If you purchase a service, check that open-stock pieces are available so that you can add to your service or replace lost or damaged pieces. As with fine china, it's wise to think long-term use when you choose a pattern. Consider the style of your china and whether you plan to use your silver every day or only for special occasions. A handsome option is to have the handles engraved with the initial of your last name.

Storing: If your service has a silver chest with a tarnish-resistant interior, use it.

Care: Hand wash sterling and silver-plated flatware and serving pieces. The heat from a dishwasher can cause knife handles to loosen, and automatic dishwashing detergents can dull and gray the finish. Immediately rinse silver that has come in contact with eggs, vinegar, salad dressing, or pickled foods because these cause tarnish. To hand wash sterling or silver plate, add flatware to a plastic dishpan of hot, soapy water. Soak for a few minutes to remove stuck-on foods. Rinse with hot water. To shine, dry while warm with a soft, clean dish towel.

When you polish, especially old silver, be gentle; don't scrub. (See "Polish Pointers," page 295.) Use polish without grit and a soft, smooth cloth, such as an old cotton T-shirt. Don't use paper towels because they can scratch. Try a very soft toothbrush to remove the tarnish from ornate pieces; don't leave polish in the crevices.

Service for 8 or 12: The basic set for each place setting should include dinner and salad forks, teaspoon, soupspoon, and dinner knife. Other possible pieces included with a service or available open stock are shrimp or oyster forks, butter knives, iced tea spoons, steak knives, and dessert spoon and fork combinations.

STAINLESS STEEL

Selecting: Quality pieces hold up to everyday use (including the dishwasher) and are handsome for entertaining as well as for family meals. Inexpensive stainless steel bends easily. If you like a pattern, check to see if it is available open stock so you can add to your service or replace lost or damaged pieces. Patterns of some quality pieces are based on traditional 18th- and 19th-century designs.

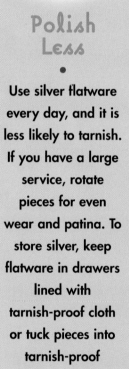

TIME SAVER

Polish Less

•

Use silver flatware every day, and it is less likely to tarnish. If you have a large service, rotate pieces for even wear and patina. To store silver, keep flatware in drawers lined with tarnish-proof cloth or tuck pieces into tarnish-proof flannel rolls.

Brides and grooms may register for stainless steel in addition to or in place of sterling silver or silver plate. Quality stainless-steel pieces are imprinted with the numbers 18/8 or 18/10. The 18 indicates the amount of chromium, and the second number is the amount of nickel. The 18/10 stainless steel costs more because it contains a higher proportion of nickel. Some particularly handsome stainless-steel flatware is imported from Europe.

Storing: Stainless steel is usually stored in drawer dividers. Some families like to use a holder on the kitchen counter for everyday pieces.

Care: It's easy: Wash and dry in the dishwasher.

Service for 8 or 12: With the number of handsome patterns, many pieces available in silver or silver plate are also available in stainless steel. Some of the less-used 19th- and early-20th-century pieces, such as shrimp forks or fish knives, may be more difficult to find in stainless. However, if you want to add more obscure pieces, it's acceptable to mix materials or to introduce gold-plated or bone- or ivory-handle pieces.

CRYSTAL

Selecting: Full-lead crystal, also known as lead crystal, is a long-term investment comparable to fine china and sterling silver. Lead crystal is made of 25 percent lead oxide and may be handblown, etched, or engraved. The term "crystal" correctly refers to glass made with a small amount of red lead oxide. Use lead-crystal liquor decanters for entertaining, but do not store alcohol in them; over time, lead from the crystal leaches into the liquor. Choose a pattern that is compatible with the style and formality of your china and silver. Classic, understated patterns are the most versatile. For a formal table setting, the traditional arrangement of crystal stemware includes a large goblet for water, a red wine glass (its larger bowl is designed to allow the wine to breathe), and a slightly smaller and narrower white wine glass. Some hosts may vary this, using the red wine glass as an all-purpose wine glass, or substituting a champagne flute for the white wine glass if they intend to serve Champagne with the dessert course.

Storing: Store lead crystal upright, with enough space between each glass so that the delicate edges aren't chipped.

Care: If you prefer to wash crystal in the dishwasher, securely cradle the stems and bases. Avoid overloading the dishwasher—the edges of the crystal may knock against each other or the sides of the dishwasher while it is operating. If you own fine or heirloom crystal,

Home Remedies

POLISH POINTERS

Recognize Patina

Tarnish isn't dirt, and a certain amount provides added shading. Antique metals acquire a patina that can't be duplicated and that makes the object more valuable. Whether—or when—you polish depends on the patina you want.

When You Polish

Wear cotton gloves to avoid transferring acid from your hands. Use mild liquid polish. Look for a formula containing jeweler's rouge. (See sources on page 366.) Use paste if the item is extremely tarnished. Never use a dip. Wash in mild soapy water, dry immediately, and polish with a clean, soft cloth. Don't overpolish silver or silver plate; some detailing can be lost.

wash it by hand. Use a plastic dishpan, filling it with enough hot, soapy water to cover the glasses. Soak each glass a few minutes; rinse with warm water and place on a soft surface—a counter protected by a dish towel is ideal. Wipe glasses dry with a soft, clean towel to prevent streaks.

Service for 8 or 12: Include water goblets or water glasses (sometimes called iced-tea glasses), and general purpose wine glasses or white and red wine glasses. Other choices include champagne flutes, brandy snifters, and port or cordial glasses.

GLASSWARE

Selecting: Basic pieces of fine crystal—wineglasses, goblets, and water glasses—are available in a range of crystal and glassware. The weight and smoothness are indicators of quality. Pressed glass and handcrafted glass work well for table settings. If you prefer a more delicate rather than a chunkier wineglass, look for handblown glass stemware with light-catching panels. Tempered-glass tumblers can be a sturdy, attractive choice for everyday glasses.

Storing: Everyday glassware is stored in the kitchen. Store goblets and wineglasses in the dining area, such as in a china cabinet or corner cupboard, if space allows.

Care: Most new glassware is dishwasher-safe. However, it's safest to wash fragile or thin glassware by hand. See the preceding section on crystal for more information.

Service for 8 or 12: Pilsner glasses for beer, glass mugs, and smaller juice glasses are often included in sets or open stock.

LINENS

If you have a handsome wood or glass-top table, the trend is to use a tablecloth for only the most formal occasions. However, if you prefer not to show off your table or if you like linens, use the tablecloth that fits your look. Traditionally, white damask (a particular weave) or plain white linen, with or without lace inserts or embroidery, is used for formal dinners. The damask weave, rather than the Jacquard weave, is considered the most formal. Use a table pad with a formal cloth and setting.

If your table is set up as a buffet table, the cloth should drop to the floor. Otherwise, the cloth drop below the top of the table should be 8 to 18 inches. For a formal dinner, napkins should match the tablecloth. For informal settings, the fun is in the mix and match.

Sizes: Napkin sizes vary, but traditionally cocktail napkins are 6 inches square; luncheon napkins are 20 inches square; and dinner napkins are 24 inches square. Some linen stores sell larger linen dinner napkins, which are known as European size.

Care: See page 229 for a chart on tablecloth stain removal.

CENTERPIECES

Formal: Centerpieces go in the center of the table—unless the

---

BUDGET STRETCHER

Stylish Flatware

•

For every day, look for forged stainless-steel flatware with colorful Bakelite handles. For dressier stainless-steel flatware, shop for faux-wood (resin) or pewter handles. Or consider reproduction hotel silver (silver plate).

Stemware Shapes and Sizes

Pilsner:
Tall and slender with a weighted base, pilsner glasses are traditional for beer, ale, stout, and similar beverages. Often part of barware sets.

General-Purpose Wine:
Used when wine is served as a cocktail or in informal place settings; appropriate for red, white, and rosé.

Champagne Flute:
The tall slender shape conserves the bubbles of champagne and sparkling wines; style has replaced wider glasses for general use.

Red Wine:
The bowl shape allows red wine to breathe; used for cocktails and for meals. Larger ones sometimes used as festive water goblets.

Martini Glass:
Traditionally used for martinis but works for specialty drinks such as margaritas or frozen drinks. Can fill in for champagne glasses.

White:
Smaller and narrower than red wine glasses because white wine doesn't require breathing; included with general barware.

Highball/Water:
Used for drinks made with mixers (also called highballs); the shape and size also work well for nonalcoholic drinks and for water.

Old-Fashioned:
Part of barware sets or sold individually; used for drinks "on the rocks" or for mixed drinks traditionally served in smaller glasses.

table is quite long. Then two centerpieces may be used. Centerpieces are most often fresh flowers, but fruit and vegetables may be used instead or mixed with flowers. Art objects are another possibility. Choose a centerpiece that doesn't obstruct the view of guests sitting across from each other. A tureen or low bowl is ideal.

Informal: For casual dinners, there are no real rules—except that guests should be able to see over the centerpiece. Flowers are always appropriate—especially freshly picked ones from your garden or a casual arrangement you do yourself. Topiaries, fruit, vegetables, and dried materials are other ideas. For luncheons or brunches, a small arrangement is often done for each place setting.

PLACE CARDS

They are used for formal occasions—such as wedding or rehearsal dinners—or if you are entertaining a crowd and would like to arrange seating. If you host a formal event, consult with a stationery store for the proper card for your event. If your event is informal, purchase cards and handwrite the names.

Entertaining

Inviting people into your home is a warm, friendly gesture. Think of entertaining as sharing your home and hospitality with your family and friends—or as a pleasant way to turn acquaintances into friends. Entertaining is a gracious way to thank people for special help or to recognize noteworthy occasions. If entertaining seems daunting, tell yourself you are having friends over. That's easy.

MAKE IT FUN

Know your entertaining style: Choose what works for you, your lifestyle, your budget, and your home. Do what is comfortable, affordable, and fun for you. You don't have to entertain as others do. Guests enjoy gatherings more that are different. Creativity, not what you spend, is the key. The most casual occasions—such as chili or a Cajun gumbo supper—can be the most fun.

Know your limits: Don't spend more time and money than you can afford. Decide if you can do everything yourself. If not, consider hiring someone to assist with preparation, errands, and cleanup. Or plan a potluck or progressive dinner, which moves from house to house, where the work is shared.

Be inclusive: Casual get-togethers or parties are an easy way to introduce a new friend, neighbor, or coworker to others in your area. If a family is new to your area, plan an event where children are welcome.

Reciprocate your way: According to etiquette experts, if you accept two or three dinner invitations or attend several parties at a person's home, you should reciprocate—if you would like to continue the social relationship. This doesn't mean you have to

---

FAMILY FRIENDLY

Extra Guests

•

Always ask before bringing an uninvited person— even your child—to a social gathering. Don't be offended if your hosts can't accommodate an extra guest or child. When you can accommodate an extra guest, it's a nice gesture.

entertain in the same style. A formal dinner can be returned graciously with a casual Sunday supper. A fancy cocktail party can be returned with a picnic in the park. If you are unable to entertain, treat your friend to a restaurant meal or a movie with treats. The gesture and the hospitality are what count.

Collect party menus and ideas: Look for simple do-ahead meals, dinner salads, or grilled meats or seafood that use fresh, seasonal ingredients. You may be inclined to entertain more frequently if you can pull out your own pretested menus and recipes and make them with confidence. If you entertain different groups of friends, perfect one menu and use it several times. Keep a party notebook to record when and to whom you served the menu.

Think of ways to make a party memorable: Serve a special drink, pick a theme, or celebrate a day, such as the first day of spring or the longest or shortest day of the year. Other ideas include a fondue night, make-your-own-pizza night, and wine or beer or cheese tasting. Instead of a cocktail party, throw a chocolate and champagne party or a jazz brunch.

Special cases: Parties, dinners, and other social occasions are sometimes held in homes, restaurants, or clubs to raise money for charities, social causes, and political candidates or groups—or to introduce someone involved in a social or political cause. Hosting such an event is an honorable and respectable way to be involved in the community. Don't treat this as a purely social event, however. Send written invitations clearly stating the purpose of the event, the group involved, and the cost of attending. Send invitations only to people who you think may be interested in the group. Inviting someone to such an event doesn't count as reciprocating for a private social event where that person hosted you. It is socially correct to purchase extra tickets and to give them to friends or family who would like to attend such an event.

Special concerns: If you haven't dined with someone before or aren't well-acquainted, be as clear as possible about the invitation. For example, mention barbecuing steaks or grilling fish as a clue to what you are serving. Guests may be vegetarians, or have food allergies, or have religious restrictions on what they eat or drink. Always offer nonalcoholic drinks in every social setting and never press a guest who declines an alcoholic beverage.

Etiquette opinion differs on what to do if you are a guest with food concerns. If you are invited to a large buffet-style gathering or potluck, the best course of action normally is to say nothing. You will usually find something you can eat or drink. If you have a medical condition that is affected by diet (such as diabetes), it may be wise to eat something before attending a party.

A small sit-down dinner or backyard barbecue in someone's home is another matter. If you have legitimate food limitations and you suspect there will be little or nothing you can safely eat or drink, tactfully mention it to the host beforehand. Most hosts prefer to be prepared. If you are trying to cut back on fats or sugars or follow a diet, occasionally eating a small quantity of forbidden food may not be a problem. Taking a few bites of the host's famous three-cheese and sausage lasagna and filling your plate with salad is a better solution than making an issue of the lasagna's fat content.

BUFFETS

Buffets are used to serve a complete meal, drinks and hors d'oeuvres only (the cocktail party), dessert and coffee, an open house reception, and other variations. Buffets work well because guests serve themselves and because a guest list larger than your dining table can be accommodated. When you host a buffet, plan traffic flow and arrange your table or server (sideboard) accordingly. Stack plates, flatware, and napkins neatly at a logical beginning point. Arrange condiments next to the dish they accompany. Don't add awkward objects—slender candlesticks or overly large centerpieces. An edible centerpiece—a nicely arranged fresh fruit plate—makes sense when space is tight.

If you are giving a large party, rent what you need, such as chafing dishes to keep food hot and extra wine glasses.

If guests will sit at tables, place water glasses and empty wine glasses on each table before the party. Have an open bottle of wine (or a bottle of red and a bottle of white) and a pitcher or carafe of water at each table. If guests will not be sitting at set tables—but will be sitting in the living room, for example—arrange a separate table with drinks and glasses and a coffee service. Some hosts place desserts on this secondary table.

For an informal buffet, make the table appealing by using colorful napkins, interesting serving pieces, arrangements of fruit or flowers—anything that makes the table colorful and inviting.

If there is no table seating for the meal, make sure guests can serve themselves, cut the food with a fork, and eat easily while sitting with a plate in their laps.

As a guest: If you are unsure what to wear, ask the host about the appropriate attire. Only ask to bring another, uninvited guest if you have an unusual situation, such as a relative or friend visiting from out of town. A small gift, such as a plant, box of candy, or unchilled bottle of wine is always appropriate. Be careful about

BUDGET STRETCHER

Switch and Save

•

Serve a festive wine or champagne punch instead of wine or mixed drinks. Substitute white table wine for tequila in frozen margaritas. Your guests will enjoy something different with less alcohol, and you'll save money.

Using Flatware Correctly

Table Knife:
Also case knife; lay to right of and normally closest to plate. Place across top of plate when not using.

Butter Knife:
Used to butter bread. Traditionally laid across the top of the butter plate, with blade facing left.

Dinner Fork:
Laid to the left of the plate, closest to plate. Laid diagonally with handle on rim when meal is over.

Cocktail Fork:
Also called an oyster fork; normally laid to the far left of the plate because it is typically used for a first course.

Teaspoon:
To stir coffee or tea; laid to right of knife. Laid to left of place spoon or above plate horizontally.

Place Spoon:
Used for soup; may be used for some desserts, depending on service; laid to the far right of the knife.

Iced-Tea Spoon:
If for tea, lay to far right; if for parfaits or other desserts, place horizontally above the plate, facing left.

Salad Fork:
Also used for desserts; laid to left of the plate in order of use; in some settings place above plate.

overfilling your plate. Accidents happen—especially if you are eating with a plate in your lap.

COCKTAIL PARTIES

Although the name cocktail party goes in and out of fashion, this type of open house has always been an easy way to entertain a group of people at one time. It's an ideal way to return social obligations to people who have invited you to their homes—and a way to entertain a visiting friend or relative or introduce someone new to your area. If you are giving a small party and have time, invite friends by telephone. If it is a large party, use printed or fill-in invitations. Include "please respond" or "RSVP." If you specify a time (such as 5 to 7 p.m.), light hors d'oeuvres will be expected. If only the beginning time is given, guests will expect a buffet.

Serve finger food, such as cheese, hors d'oeuvres, and small sandwiches. Include raw fruits and vegetables and dry-roasted nuts for guests who may have food concerns. Stock small plates, glasses, and cloth or paper cocktail napkins. Set out more glasses, plates, and napkins than the number of anticipated guests to allow guests to use more than one glass and plate and several napkins.

Serve beer and wine only or a full bar. Always have a variety of bottled waters, juices, and nonalcoholic drinks on hand. If you like, feature a special drink, such as a Kir Royale, Bellini, or martini. If the gathering is informal, pitchers of margaritas or sangria are festive choices.

Plan how you will handle a crowd. If your budget allows, call a local caterer to get recommendations for hiring a bartender. Ask a young adult in your neighborhood or a family member to help out. If you are giving the party without help, station yourself at the bar or the door to greet guests. Have your spouse or a friend at the other key location.

For a large party or when traffic flow is restricted, set up more than one bar, with nonalcoholic drinks at each one. When weather permits, set up one or more bars outside or on a porch.

How much to buy: Although many hosts only serve beer, wine, and nonalcoholic beverages, it's useful to have a reference for a full bar. The following is a standard general reference for 25 to 30 guests; it can be used for wedding receptions, 50th anniversary parties, and similar occasions. Adjust for your guests, region, and the time of the year.

■Beverages to stock: 4 to 5 bottles (750 milliliter each) of liquor (choice depends on region and personal preference; most hosts include at least vodka, gin, and a whiskey; bourbon, scotch, light or dark rum, and tequila are other common choices); 1 bottle dry vermouth; ½ case dry white wine (Chardonnay is a safe choice; Pinot Grigio is nice for summer.); 1 to 2 standard bottles of rosé; ½

BUDGET STRETCHER

Alternative To Alcohol

•

If you prefer not to serve alcohol, consider festive ideas such as a weekend brunch with coffee and juice, an afternoon open house with a coffee or tea bar, or an evening dessert and coffee party after the dinner hour.

case dry red wine (Merlot or Pinot Noir is a safe choice.) Wines from your state or region can also be interesting for your guests to sample. If you decide to include bottled beer, purchase a case-and-a-half total of an imported beer and nonalcoholic beer and reduce the hard liquor. Ask the liquor store if you are allowed to return any bottles—such as red wine, which isn't chilled—if they aren't opened.

■ Drinks per bottle: A 750 milliliter of liquor equals about 17 drinks; a regular bottle of wine, about six (4-ounce) drinks.

■ Wine and liquor equivalents: A magnum of wine is 51.2 ounces; a liter of wine is 33.8 ounces; a milliliter of wine is 24 to 26 ounces; a milliliter of liquor is 25.6 ounces; a half gallon of liquor is 64 ounces; a gallon of liquor is 128 ounces.

■ Mixers: 8 to 9 liter bottles or large cans of mixers, such as cola, lemon-lime drink, diet soft drinks, tonic water, ginger ale, club soda, bottled water, orange juice, tomato juice.

■ Bottled or sparkling water: 3 to 4 liters.

■ Garnishes: 4 lemons in twists and wedges; 4 limes in twists and wedges (stock more in summer when you may be serving more vodka-and-tonic and gin-and-tonic drinks). A twist is a small narrow slice of rind. Also stock Maraschino cherries, cocktail olives, cocktail onions.

■ Bar supplies: 25 pounds of crushed ice; 80 to 100 cocktail napkins; toothpicks; 18 to 24 wineglasses (some guests use more than one); 2 to 3 dozen (10-ounce) glasses.

Special cases: See buffet section (page 300) for general obligations. The time on the invitation means dropping by between those hours. An hour is long enough unless the party isn't crowded or you are a close friend. If the host is entertaining a special guest, they may be going to dinner after the cocktail party, so don't linger.

POTLUCKS/PROGRESSIVE DINNER PARTIES

Meals where everyone pitches in and shares the work are popular. They work well for casual or organized groups of friends who like to get together. To organize a potluck, decide on an easy plan. It often works well for the host to provide the main dish, such as a ham or roast, and the beverages; the guests bring salads, side dishes, or desserts. During the summer grilling season, the host may provide grilled meat and beverages and ask guests to bring the traditional cookout side dishes.

It's fun to organize your potluck using a theme, such as a Southwestern fiesta. If your guests have moved to your area, consider a sampling party where they bring their favorite dish from

TIPTAG№30
Party Checklist
PLAN; DON'T PANIC:
• Choose a guest list and type of party.
• Select and test menu.
• Shop for food and beverages; make what you can ahead of time.
• Clean the house before party day so you aren't exhausted.
• Decide what you'll wear.
PARTY DAY:
• Do last-minute shopping (fresh bread and flowers).
• Set the table; arrange the flowers; chill the wine and other beverages.
• Prepare last-minute dishes and garnishes; set up bar; grind coffee.
• Relax and enjoy your party.

their home state or country. If you are having a potluck as a welcome or good-bye party, tell your special guest that the honor or his or her company is the contribution to the party.

Progressive dinners work well in neighborhoods where guests walk or drive only short distances between homes. One course, such as the salad, is served at every house. If you have more homes than courses, two couples or friends may pool their resources for the entrée course. These dinners are especially fun during the holidays when homes are decorated for the season.

SUPPER CLUBS

If you and your friends like to entertain, consider setting up a supper club, which meets on a regular, organized basis, such as the second Saturday every month. Create a structure that works well for you and your situation. A typical club includes six couples or six singles so that the club meets twice a year in each home. In some clubs, the hosts do everything for the meal. Other clubs are structured so that the hosts provide the entrée and the guests bring side dishes and desserts. If you and your friends like to cook together, preparing the meal as a group can be integral to the gatherings. Once a year, club members plan who takes what month.

PARTIES FOR WEDDINGS

When parties start and how many are given depends in part on the size and formality of the wedding and local and regional customs. If you are in doubt, ask your future spouse or future in-laws for guidance.

Engagement announcement: Traditionally, this party is given by the parents of the bride or close relatives of the bride. Normally, the invitation does not allude to the engagement. Instead, at the party, the father of the bride makes the formal announcement. The traditional purpose is to introduce the groom to family friends and relatives. Relatives and close friends of the groom are invited. Engagement announcement parties may also be given—usually more informally—by a close friend of either the bride or groom. In that case, friends gather to wish the couple well, but the engagement is generally known before the party.

Showers: Traditional bridal showers are given by the bride's close friends, often the maid or matron of honor or the bridesmaids, two to three weeks before the wedding. Family members of the bride or the groom do not give showers. A traditional bridal shower is held in the middle of the day, at a home or party room of a restaurant. It is a gracious gesture to invite the mothers of the bride and groom as well as grandmothers, great-grandmothers, sisters, and other close female relatives to the main bridal shower. Customs on this vary. When you are unsure, check with the bride or her mother. Anyone invited to a shower must be invited to the wedding

---

FAMILY FRIENDLY

Be a Good Guest

•

Respond promptly to all invitations, even if you can't attend. Once you accept, you are obligated to attend unless an emergency arises. If that happens, call the host as soon as possible and express your regrets.

Standard Table Settings

Formal Dinner:
Arrange knives and dessert spoon to the right in order of use; place forks to the left in order of use, fish fork first. Arrange water goblet, red wineglass, and white wineglasses in descending order. Place bread plate above forks.

Informal Dinner or Luncheon:
Arrange knife and soup spoon to the right; place dinner fork to the left. Place dessert spoon and dessert fork above, facing left and right respectively; water glass and wine glass are above knife.

Casual Family Meals:
For everyday family meals, the knife and teaspoon to the right of the plate, the fork and napkin to the left. The glass is above the knife. A soup spoon and a salad fork may be added; cup and saucer placed to left if used for breakfast.

and to the reception. If multiple showers are planned, they usually have themes, such as kitchen or lingerie. In the case of multiple showers, hosts should consult with each other so the same people aren't asked to give several gifts. If the wedding is canceled, shower and wedding gifts are returned. The bride should write a thank-you note for each gift. For couples with established households, friends may have evening couples showers, such as a stock-the-bar shower.

Bachelor or bachelorette parties: These are given by close friends of the bride and groom several days before the wedding. They are typically given in a private room of a restaurant.

Bridesmaid luncheon: The bride and her mother entertain the bridesmaids, and sometimes other close female friends and relatives, at a small luncheon a few days before or on the wedding day. This is normally held in a restaurant or club or in the home of the bride's mother or other close relative.

Rehearsal dinner: Customs vary, but traditionally the groom's family hosts a dinner in a private room of a restaurant or a club after the rehearsal, the night before the wedding. The dinner may also be held in the home of the groom's parents or the home of a relative or friend. Although the purpose is to entertain the wedding party, which includes both sets of parents, guests who have come from out of town to attend the wedding may also be included. For small weddings or when a couple is giving their own wedding, a small dinner in a private home for the wedding party and out-of-town guests is appropriate. It is always a nice gesture to invite parents, grandparents, great-grandparents, siblings, and their spouses.

BABY SHOWERS

Close friends give the baby shower in a private home or in a convenient location such as the club room of an apartment building. Baby showers are only given for the first child and are traditionally given four to six weeks before the baby is due. This varies around the country. Hostesses may coordinate gift giving or pool their resources and buy a larger gift, such as a baby stroller. Many stores now have registries for the parents-to-be.

A couples baby shower, sometimes held in the evening as an informal supper or potluck, is a fun and increasingly common way to celebrate with the parents-to-be. If the pregnancy ends unsuccessfully, the parents are not expected to return gifts.

Friends will also want to celebrate the adoption of an infant or older child. In such special cases, a close friend should check with the new parent or parents about their preferences.

SPECIAL ANNIVERSARIES

Before the 25th anniversary, celebrations are family affairs with only the couple or the couple and their children. Anniversary parties start at the 25th (silver) and are traditionally given by the children.

If a couple is childless, close relatives, such as nieces and nephews, can give an anniversary party. Close friends or other relatives may want to honor a couple for a major anniversary.

Anniversary parties range from small family parties in a home to a large affair with family friends, relatives, and business associates in a restaurant, hotel ballroom, or club. Plan a party with the degree of formality and size that suits the couple. Gala parties are usually not given before the 40th or 45th anniversary. Unless there are conflicting circumstances such as health concerns, the 50th anniversary is the appropriate time for the special anniversary party. After the 50th anniversary, children or family members might give smaller family parties every year or every five years. The 55th and 60th anniversaries are often times for larger parties.

Traditionally, music preferred by the couple is part of a large anniversary party. The couple should greet guests by the door, if possible. Many families take this opportunity to hire a photographer for formal family portraits or group pictures.

Gifts may or may not be part of the festivities. Ask the couple about their preference and honor it. If gifts are not preferred, write "no gifts please" on the invitation. Guests should honor the request. Children of the couple or other close family members may want to pool their resources to buy a special gift or pay for a special trip for the couple. They should not ask others to contribute to the gift.

SPECIAL BIRTHDAYS

For adults, close friends or family typically give parties for the decade birthdays: 30, 40, 50, 60, 70. Age 75 is often rightly celebrated as a landmark birthday. If invitations are sent or if guests ask, a "no gifts" policy is usually best. However, close family members often pool their resources and buy a special gift, particularly for the 75th, 80th, and 90th birthdays.

Surprise birthday parties are sometimes a feature for 30th, 40th, or 50th birthdays. Arrange such a party only if you are certain your friend or relative will be pleased. In some cases, a quiet family celebration or dinner with friends in a restaurant is a better choice.

FAMILY REUNIONS

If you haven't held a family reunion before, ask a friend or relative who has for tips and suggestions. To get started, consider your immediate family—perhaps your parents and your siblings and their spouses and children. If your family is small, expand the invitation list to include your mother's or father's siblings and their children

smartideas

Kids' Parties

OUTDOOR FUN

Visit a farm and have an old-fashioned hayride and picnic in the country. Plan an afternoon of games at a city or state park. Many parks have pavilions that can be rented for nominal fees—often with grills for cooking hot dogs or hamburgers. In the city, arrange for a visit by an ice cream truck or food pushcart, if available.

FIELD TRIP FUN

The zoo or a natural history or children's hands-on museum is always fun. But what about learning how doughnuts are made—and sampling them warm with milk? How about a ride on a local excursion boat or commuter train?

and spouses. Either way, use this first reunion as a core committee to determine whether you would like to organize a larger and more ambitious reunion.

When you hold your reunion is a matter of personal preference, but many families find it easier to hold reunions in the summer when children are out of school and pavilions at city or state parks are available. Other families—particularly those who have to travel long distances—reserve a block of hotel or motel rooms for a reunion. It's always a good idea to have an activity or two planned, especially if the family has a large number of children. And don't forget the group photograph—have copies made for everyone.

CHILDREN'S PARTIES

It's easy to let parties get out of hand. Creativity, not cost, is the key to party fun. Don't think you have to emulate parties your child may have attended. Often the most fun parties are the least expensive— especially when children are young and enjoy simple activities.

Birthdays: Before age 4 or 5, the simpler, the better. Parents enjoy celebrating the first, second, and third birthdays, but keep in mind that the cake or ice cream will be the most fun for your child. Keep these celebrations simple: Invite the family, grandparents, and perhaps a neighbor child for a 3-year-old's party. Some parents limit the number of guests to the child's age.

For school-age children, plan the party together with your child— with the understanding you will make final decisions. Choose a theme that reflects your child's wishes, but don't overdo. Start planning a few weeks in advance. If you have time, make invitations and decorations together—or visit a party store together. If you are going to hire someone for entertainment, such as a local clown or magician, do it early. Hire someone you've seen or heard about from friends. Or enlist an older child or a relative to help entertain.

Even if you book entertainment, plan a simple game or two or a crafts project to occupy guests until all the children arrive. Have several activities or projects geared to the season, age of the guests, and theme of the party. Plan food that children like—pizza, hot dogs, sandwiches, cake, cupcakes, and ice cream—and that is easy to eat. Cake and ice cream and juice are fine for a small afternoon party for young children. After refreshments, open gifts and hand out a party favor or small gift for each child.

Holiday parties: The start of the winter holidays, spring break, and the end of the school year are fun times for your child to have friends over. Consider something easy in the winter, such as helping kids make gingerbread houses from components you've baked in advance. Even easier: Have a cookie decorating and hot chocolate party.

SPECIAL HOLIDAYS

If you love the holidays, especially the busy winter ones, enjoy them

---

FAMILY FRIENDLY

Teach Kindness

•

Use your child's birthday party to reinforce sensitivity to others. For school-age children, invite the entire class or no more than half the class (if the latter, send invitations to their homes). Encourage your child to include a new classmate.

Candles and Holders

White House Tapers:

The rolled finish adds detailing to a style that complements the contemporary candlesticks shown here, or more ornate, traditional candlesticks.

Pillars in Hurricanes:

Larger-diameter—such as 3-inch—candles are called pillars. Hurricane lanterns, traditionally used to protect the flames from wind, are safe candleholders.

Beeswax:

Pure beeswax candles, used for centuries, are good choices because they burn slowly, are smokeless, and drip very little; often used with traditional candlesticks.

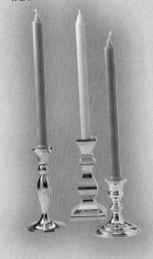

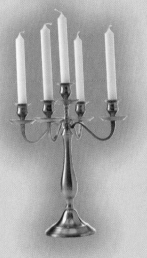

Beeswax Pillars:

Known as honeycomb pillars; heights of 4 and 6 inches are versatile and can be displayed on wide glass candleholders sized for these 3-inch-diameter candles.

Candelabra:

Displayed on dining room sideboards or pianos; affordable reproduction candelabras are also used on dining tables and mantels and for decorative accents.

Votives in Holders:

Often part of dining table settings or displayed on holiday mantels, votives are arranged on plates or trays or protected by their own clear or colored glass holders.

by giving a party or two. If you are frazzled by all the fuss, wait and give a midwinter party when nothing is happening or a spring or summer party when you can entertain outdoors.

Christmas: Celebrating the birth of Jesus, Christmas is commemorated in many different ways around the world. In the midst of lavish events, Christmas is a nice time of year to give a party for your neighbors. After all, Christmas is a family time, and good neighbors look out for each other as family members do. Neighborhood parties are easy for the guests because they can walk over, and you can keep it casual. Such parties are often given on a Sunday afternoon before Christmas, but consider having yours the day after Christmas—especially if Christmas is on a Thursday, Friday, or Saturday. By then, families, including those with out-of-town visitors, are often at the "What do we do now" stage. Ask your neighbors to bring their children and their houseguests too.

If you give a party after Christmas, be organized and stash party food in the freezer well before the holiday. Keep the menu simple: hot wassail, some spirits, coffee, light nibbles, and desserts.

■ Holiday brunch. This works well if you have a group of friends you'd like to entertain during the holidays. Give them each a small tin of cookies—homebaked or fancy ones from a bakery—to take home.

■ Cookie swap. Near the holidays, who has time to bake all the varieties of cookies they'd like to try? Invite close friends to bring two dozen cookies—one to share and one to swap.

■ Food pantry or shelter party. Ask your guests to bring one canned item or toilet articles to donate to pantries or shelters. If animal shelters are in need in your area, add pet food or other items to your lists.

■ Christmas caroling. This isn't new, but it's still fun. It works well for a neighborhood party, for children, or with a small group of friends. Serve hot chocolate or wassail and cookies after caroling.

Kwanza: African-Americans observe Kwanza (from December 26 to January 1), celebrating their heritage and focusing on the principles that nurture a sense of identity, community, and self-esteem.

Kwanza is a Swahili word that means "the first," referring to the first fruits of the harvest. To emphasize the harvest theme, some people like to use whatever is available at the market for the centerpiece; others prefer to highlight tropical foods, such as mangoes, papayas, and plantains. Other symbolic elements for the centerpiece include the following:

■ Mkeka, a straw mat representing tradition as the foundation on which everything rests.

■ Kinara, a seven-branched candleholder symbolizing ancestors; shaped like the Star of David. The kinara holds black, red, and

SAFETY ALERT

Consider Children

•

Holidays can be fraught with dangers for small children. Never leave a child alone with the Christmas tree or lighted candles. Don't let children wander around parties where they could sip from alcoholic beverages.

green candles that symbolize the African-American people, their bloodshed, their continuing struggle for freedom, and the land and life.

■ Mshumaa, the seven candles representing the principles that are the focus of the celebration—unity, self-determination, collective work and responsibility, cooperative economics, purpose, creativity, and faith.

■ Muhindi, ears of corn representing children (or the potential for children) and hence posterity.

■ Kikombe cha umoja, the Unity Cup, used for pouring a libation to honor the ancestors.

■ Zawadi, small gifts that reward personal achievement.

Arrange these elements as simply as you like, or for a large neighborhood or family gathering, build a more lavish display on a table or a table and chest. Collect baskets and wooden or crockery bowls to hold the vegetables and fruits. To use fewer materials and still achieve a look of abundance, fill the baskets and bowls with crumpled newspapers and then arrange the fruits and vegetables on top of them.

Hanukkah: Hanukkah brings light to the darkest time of the year and joy to the Jews of the world. The celebration of Hanukkah, the Festival of Lights, commemorates a victory won by the Jews over the Syrian occupiers more than 2,000 years ago. During the eight nights and days of Hanukkah, Jewish people around the world celebrate with special foods. In America, the most commonly eaten food is potato latkes, crisp-fried and served with applesauce. Some people also eat preserve-filled, sugarcoated little doughnuts, called sufganiyot.

Other celebratory foods in the Jewish tradition include challah, a soft, rich bread, and rugelach, a flaky rolled cookie filled with raisins and other dried fruits and nuts. (According to Jewish law, recipes that include dairy products cannot be eaten alongside or following a meat dish.)

To set a festive table for Hanukkah, cover the table with silver lamé fabric; then lay a runner of blue fabric down the center of the table. Arrange a variety of clear glass vases on the runner and fill each with one of the following: hazelnuts in the shell, almonds in the shell, silver-wrapped candies, and blue-foil-wrapped candies. Insert glitter-sprayed dried flowers from a crafts store or florist's supply shop into the nuts and candies. Stretch a Star-of-David garland (from a party-supply store) along the runner.

Passover: The Passover holiday lasts for eight days, the dates

Summer Parties

•

If you like the idea of an annual party, throw yours in the summer. Guests can be outside, and the menu, such as grilled burgers, can be easy and inexpensive. Crank ice cream or serve chilled watermelon for dessert.

varying according to the Jewish calendar. Passover commemorates the Israelites fleeing Egypt to freedom. Generally, it falls around Easter; the Last Supper was a Passover Seder. The Seder, a series of celebratory meals and gatherings of family and friends, is the focus of Passover. Special foods are served, and the Haggadah from the Book of Exodus is read, with family members taking different parts. Music and dancing can be part of the festivities as well. In observant Jewish homes, foods must be kosher for Passover. Yeast cannot be used; this law honors the Israelites who had to flee so quickly that they had no time to let their bread rise.

Easter: The most holy holiday of the Christian year is still celebrated primarily as a religious and family holiday. The traditional Easter dinner or brunch is usually a meal with family and close friends. As with other holidays, it is a considerate gesture to invite someone who celebrates the holiday. On the secular side, Easter egg hunts with pretty, egg-filled baskets are a traditional rite of spring. If you live in a neighborhood with young children or have young children, Easter egg hunts are fun and easy to organize.

SEASONAL HOLIDAYS

Halloween: Halloween is becoming increasingly popular, especially with adults. It's the time of year you can indulge your fantasies and take on a new persona. Consider a grown-up Halloween party with prizes for the best costumes. Pick a theme if you like—politics, celebrities, a certain decade. Serve spiked hot cider, cool drinks if you live in a warm climate, a nonalcoholic libation, something made with pumpkins, and assorted snacks. Set the mood with jack-o'-lanterns and votives for lighting. Specialty stores sell tapes of scary sounds, and video rental stores stock old scary movies that set the scene.

For children, parties have become more important because of safety issues with trick-or-treating. Liven up parties with pumpkin-carving contests or have the guests make their own trick-or-treat bags. Have the party in the late afternoon, early evening, or the dinner hour, depending on the age of the children and if it is a school night. Serve snacks or a light sandwich meal.

If trick-or-treating is done in your neighborhood, invite all the children and their parents over for hot dogs, chips, and soft drinks before they start their rounds or have the goblins and their escorts stop by for cookies and hot chocolate when they're finished.

Fourth of July and Labor Day: Red, white, and blue; grilled hamburgers and hot dogs; and watermelon are traditions in the United States. Vary the themes and menus as much as you like, but keep it simple so you and your guests can enjoy a summer afternoon outdoors. If you live in an area with Fourth of July fireworks, invite friends over for a backyard picnic or cookout before the fireworks.

Folding Dinner Napkins

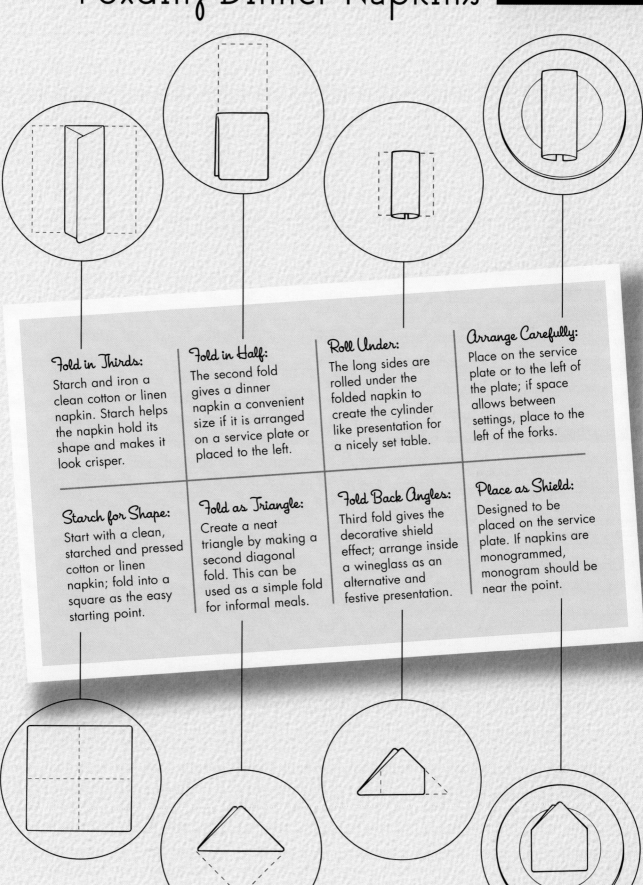

Fold in Thirds:
Starch and iron a clean cotton or linen napkin. Starch helps the napkin hold its shape and makes it look crisper.

Fold in Half:
The second fold gives a dinner napkin a convenient size if it is arranged on a service plate or placed to the left.

Roll Under:
The long sides are rolled under the folded napkin to create the cylinder like presentation for a nicely set table.

Arrange Carefully:
Place on the service plate or to the left of the plate; if space allows between settings, place to the left of the forks.

Starch for Shape:
Start with a clean, starched and pressed cotton or linen napkin; fold into a square as the easy starting point.

Fold as Triangle:
Create a neat triangle by making a second diagonal fold. This can be used as a simple fold for informal meals.

Fold Back Angles:
Third fold gives the decorative shield effect; arrange inside a wineglass as an alternative and festive presentation.

Place as Shield:
Designed to be placed on the service plate. If napkins are monogrammed, monogram should be near the point.

Or organize a picnic you all carry to the fireworks viewing area.

Thanksgiving: This family holiday is a good time to think of others—and teach sharing by example to your children. Invite a friend or coworker who can't travel home for the holiday or share the American holiday with a foreign exchange student.

For a big extended-family celebration, develop the tradition of having different family members cook their specialty dishes for the day. For example, the host does the turkey, and family and family friends bring the side dishes.

New Year's Eve and New Year's Day: If you like to have a New Year's Eve party, consider an open house with coffee and cake as well as Champagne; then friends can drop by on their way to other parties or events. Some people like to be safely home early, so consider starting as early as 7:30 or 8 p.m. But keep the traditional Champagne toast (with a nonalcoholic alternative) at midnight.

If you have preschool or elementary school children, take a cue from the increasingly popular "first night" celebrations and make your party a family affair with games and activities planned for the children. Invite other families to celebrate with yours.

If you entertain on New Year's Day, consider a late-morning brunch, casual lunch, or early supper as a low-key event that winds down the festivities. Keep such a party simple and serve some of the foods, such as black-eyed peas, traditionally eaten for good luck. (Good-luck foods vary by region of the country; if you are new to a city and in doubt, ask your neighbors or call the food editor at the local newspaper.)

Twelfth Night: If the holiday season seems overcrowded, consider the alternative of giving a Twelfth Night party in January. Traditionally, Twelfth Night commemorates the Magi's visit to the baby Jesus. In cities in Europe, Latin America, and the United States that celebrate Mardi Gras (or carnival), Twelfth Night is the start of the carnival season—the pre-Lenten season. Depending on regional customs, decorations and food are in the Christmas spirit or in the colors (purple, green, and gold), spangles, beads, and music of Mardi Gras. If the Twelfth Night party has a Mardi Gras theme, the traditional "King Cake" is often served.

Mardi Gras day: In New Orleans and other cities that celebrate Mardi Gras, the day before Ash Wednesday is called Fat Tuesday—a day of revelry, food, and fun before the austerity and penitence of Lent, the 40 days leading up to Easter. The religious roots of Mardi Gras are no longer a major factor in this raucous celebration, and people of all backgrounds and faiths participate in Mardi Gras. Parties typically feature Louisiana cuisine—gumbo, red beans and rice, jambalaya—and jazz, blues, and zydeco are the music of choice.

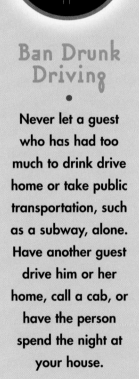

SAFETY ALERT

Ban Drunk Driving

Never let a guest who has had too much to drink drive home or take public transportation, such as a subway, alone. Have another guest drive him or her home, call a cab, or have the person spend the night at your house.

Good Manners
- WHY MANNERS ARE IMPORTANT,317
- EXAMPLES TO FOLLOW,317
- TEACHING CHILDREN,317,318
- CLASSES FOR CHILDREN,318

Table Manners
- THE FAMILY TABLE,318
- SPECIAL COURTESIES,318,320
- TEACHING CHILDREN,318,321
- IN PUBLIC AND AT PARTIES,318,319
- SIGNALS FROM THE HOST,320
- RESTAURANT BEHAVIOR,321
- DINING DILEMMAS,321

Introductions
- HOW TO INTRODUCE PEOPLE,322
- CONFIDENCE-BUILDING TIPS,322

Social Correspondence
- PERSONALIZED STATIONERY,323
- SAMPLE CORRESPONDENCE,324
- THANK-YOU NOTES,325,328
- SYMPATHY AND CONCERN NOTES,328
- ISSUING INVITATIONS,329
- RESPONDING TO INVITATIONS,329

Modern Communications
- PERSONAL E-MAIL,330
- CELLULAR PHONES AND PAGERS,330

Polite Conversations
- BE A GOOD GUEST AND GOOD LISTENER,330
- CONVERSATION STARTERS,332
- SAFE TOPICS; TOPICS TO AVOID,332,333
- GENTLE REMINDERS,333

Other Situations
- WELCOME TOUCHES FOR YOUR GUESTS,331
- HOUSEGUESTS,333
- WHEN YOU ARE A HOUSEGUEST,333
- GUESTS WITH DISABILITIES,334
- DIVORCED OR SEPARATED COUPLES,334
- GUESTS WHO WON'T LEAVE,334
- IMPOLITE GUESTS,334

Etiquette

The Golden Rule of treating other people as you would like to be treated is the basis of etiquette, manners, and getting along at home and in the business and social worlds. Societies set up rules of behavior so people know how to act and conduct themselves. This is what etiquette and manners are all about. These rules can be useful because they make it easier to converse and interact with people and to live pleasantly day to day. If you know how to dine with others and how to meet and introduce people, you are naturally more at ease in personal, business, and social settings. The elaborate social rituals and arcane rules of the 18th, 19th, and early 20th century have been relegated— and rightly so—to the dustbin of history, but being kind, thoughtful, and considerate of other people will never go out of style.

Good Manners

Manners smooth the rough edges of life. Please, thank you, no thank you, excuse me, pardon me, I'm sorry, and all the polite phrases that children learn are important for adults. So too is the sense of fair play and taking turns that children learn at school and on the playground. Treating people of all walks of life and ages with respect and courtesy is the right thing to do. It's also good business to practice thoughtful manners. Some corporations send executives to school to brush up on manners, and many job interviews include social or dining settings that test how well a person comports him or herself.

TEACHING CHILDREN

Teach with kindness and firmness. From infancy, your child notices what goes on around him or her—and how you react to others. Emphasize please and thank you in your child's vocabulary. Teach your children to respect you and others. An important early lesson for children is to not interrupt when others are speaking. Allow your child plenty of time to talk without rushing, and don't interrupt him or her, or others in your child's presence. If you give your child blocks of your undivided attention every day, he or she will have less need to interrupt.

You and others will enjoy your child more if he or she knows how to behave from an early age. Some parents take a traditional approach to teaching manners: They instruct their children to call all adults by their last names, as in "Mrs. Jones." If this is your preference and background, teach your children this way and don't

smart ideas
Learn by Example

PAY ATTENTION

When you are unsure of what to do in a social or business situation, watch people around you for clues. In business or educational settings, observe supervisors or the most senior person present. In a private home or restaurant, watch the hosts to see how they hold a utensil or eat a certain food.

RECOGNIZE DIFFERENCES

If you are traveling overseas or across the country, pay attention to how people conduct themselves. Err on the side of manners and respect in public behavior, clothing, eating, and smoking. Overseas, learn the cultural phrases to express please, thank you, and greetings.

let others derail your efforts. Teach your children to always first use Mr., Mrs., Ms., or Miss when speaking with an adult. If the adult prefers to be addressed by his or her first name, he or she will say so. A good family rule is to instruct children to wait until an adult has asked several times before beginning to address him or her by the first name.

However, if you have close family friends whom the children see often, consider allowing them to call your friend "Uncle Bob" or even "Bob" instead of "Mr. Roberts." In some parts of the United States, children are taught to say "yes, sir" and "yes, ma'am" to their elders, particularly to their parents, grandparents, and teachers, as a sign of respect.

Set reasonable behavior expectations for your child. Even the brightest 3- or 4-year-old isn't a miniature adult. Adult events, such as art gallery openings, films, or dinners at sit-down restaurants, can be too long and too confining for young, energetic children. Instead, choose family-friendly events, such as zoo picnics and family-oriented restaurants, where both you and your child can have fun. As children grow up, expose them to nice "dressier" restaurants so they'll know how to behave in such settings.

CLASSES CAN HELP

In some cities, there are schools or individuals who teach manners and etiquette to children in lighthearted, fun settings. Some department stores also offer similar classes. If your child enjoys group activities based on positive reinforcement, these work well.

Table Manners

For everyday family dining, family members should be expected to come to the table when they are called and sit in place until everyone is present. Unless family members serve themselves from a sideboard or casually from the kitchen, the table should be set. Family-style service means food dishes are placed on the table and passed around, or plates are passed to one parent to serve. Plates may also be passed to one parent to serve the meat or main course, and then other serving platters and bowls passed. Many families say a blessing before meals or before the nighttime meal.

In public or with guests: When you are dining with guests, in a home or a restaurant, pay attention to what the host or hosts do and take your cues from them. (If you are the host, mind your manners.) Traditionally, men remain standing until women are seated. This is an especially nice gesture when guests are of different generations, such as grandsons showing courtesy and respect to their grandmothers. Men assist women with their chairs unless the waiter or host does. Men rise when a woman leaves the table and rise again when she returns. However, this can be a tricky

---

FAMILY FRIENDLY

Never Too Young

•

Start teaching table manners at home as soon as your child sits at the table. Buy colorful plastic dinnerware and child-size utensils. Teach with positive reinforcement and patience. Reward good behavior; don't dwell on mishaps.

Dinner Table Manners

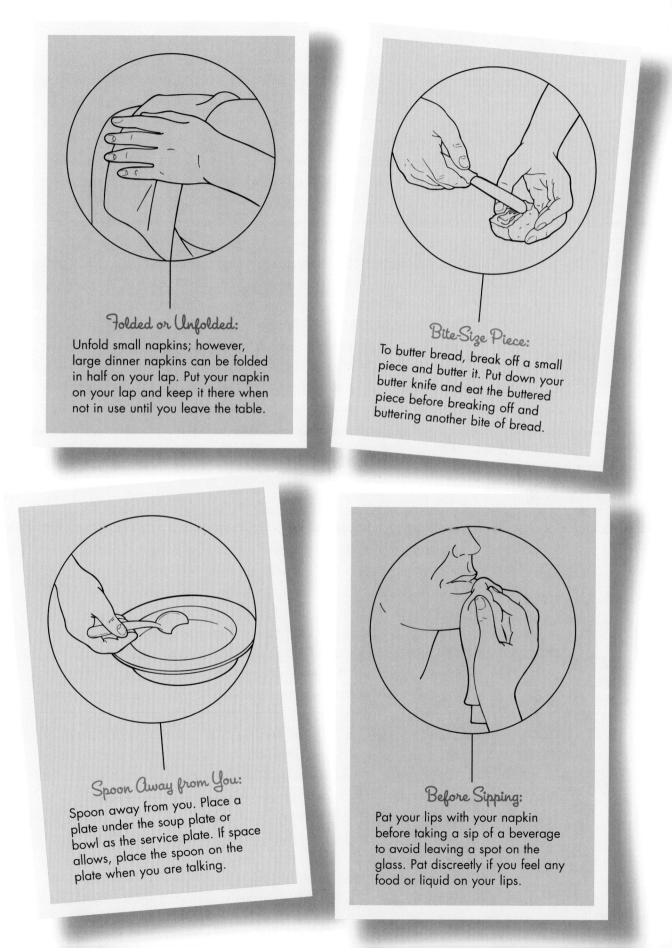

Folded or Unfolded:
Unfold small napkins; however, large dinner napkins can be folded in half on your lap. Put your napkin on your lap and keep it there when not in use until you leave the table.

Bite-Size Piece:
To butter bread, break off a small piece and butter it. Put down your butter knife and eat the buttered piece before breaking off and buttering another bite of bread.

Spoon Away from You:
Spoon away from you. Place a plate under the soup plate or bowl as the service plate. If space allows, place the spoon on the plate when you are talking.

Before Sipping:
Pat your lips with your napkin before taking a sip of a beverage to avoid leaving a spot on the glass. Pat discreetly if you feel any food or liquid on your lips.

situation, particularly with booth or banquette seating. Use your own judgment. It is accepted practice for only the man seated next to a woman to rise as she leaves the table and returns. Other men should not feel compelled to do so. However, if a woman approaches a man's table in a restaurant—or even a company cafeteria—it is appropriate for the man to stand until she is seated or while she is talking at his table. (If the woman wants to linger, she should accept an offer of a chair and sit to talk.)

At the table—at home or in public: As soon as you sit down, place the napkin on your lap. Always wipe your mouth before sipping a beverage or if you feel food or liquid on your lips.

At the table, sit up straight; no elbows on the table. Don't lean back in your chair. You may lean lightly with your arms or wrists on the table. As the meal begins, take silverware from the outside of the place setting for the first course and work your way in toward the plate. (If in doubt, watch your host and other diners.) Never put used flatware back on the table.

Although there are variations of where and how to lay the knife and fork during the meal, the American style is accepted and easy to remember: Lay the knife across the back of the plate, slightly to the right, handle on the right side. During the meal, lay the fork at an angle to you, the handle on the rim.

■ Passing dishes. If dishes are passed family style, pass to the right, person to person, to whoever asks for the dish. Don't pass over someone—unless the diner is a small child who is unable to hold a large bowl or platter. Always pass the salt and pepper shakers together, even though only one may be requested.

■ More formal setting. Pass dishes and place them in front of the person next to you, rather than handing them directly to the person.

■ Finger food. If in doubt, watch the host or other guests or other diners in a restaurant. If still in doubt, use utensils.

■ Talking. Chew and swallow before you talk. Keep your mouth closed while you are chewing. Don't talk with food in your mouth.

■ Spills. Accidents do happen to everybody. If you spill something, apologize and mop it up. In a restaurant, if necessary, ask the waiter for help.

■ Smoking. Don't smoke at the table. It is no longer acceptable.

■ End of meal. Lay the knife and fork across your plate with the handles at four o'clock (think of a clock face) to signal that you have finished eating. Make conversation at the table until everyone has finished eating. If the meal involved a soup course, the spoon should be on the service plate, not in the soup plate or bowl. However, if this is awkward, leave the spoon in the bowl or notice how other diners are handling the situation.

When you are hosting at home: If you are serving guests,

FAMILY FRIENDLY

Wait for Everyone

Wait until everyone is served before starting to eat in a private home or restaurant. For family meals, the mother starts first. Guests should wait for the hosts. No one should leave the table until everyone is finished.

serve from the diner's left and clear from the right. However, as glasses are on the right, wine and water are poured from this side.

Wait until all your guests are finished with a course before clearing the table. Some guests eat more slowly than others. Don't rush guests or family.

TEACHING CHILDREN

The best way to teach table manners to your children is to eat meals with them every day—and to make dinner a special, pleasant family time. Banish arguments and disagreements. If your spouse works late or if you enjoy an occasional later adult meal, sit with your children and have a light snack while they eat. Don't force food on children or set up battles of will. If you do, mealtime in general and manners in particular will get off to a rocky start. Offer simple, nutritious food and allow your child to eat what he or she wants. If you don't make an issue of food, your child won't either. Teach your children that when they are guests, they should take only what they can eat and at least try a little of everything being served.

Practice good table manners, and your children will learn by example. As your children grow up, it is appropriate to gently remind them—when no guests are present—if they are forgetting their manners. Teach your children how to set the table, and as soon as they are old enough, turn this chore over to them. Dinnertime is a good opportunity to set the example of listening to others and not interrupting. Help your children get into this admirable habit.

RESTAURANT BEHAVIOR

Look the server in the eye and smile; it's impolite not to acknowledge service from others. In a conventional, full-service restaurant, tip 20 percent of the bill for good service. This is easy to calculate—figure 10 percent of the bill and double it. Keep in mind that your dining companions may notice if you leave an inadequate tip—and think less of you as a result. Serving is a difficult and demanding job, and servers depend on tips. If you dine at a buffet or similar restaurant, where only your drink is served, 10 percent is adequate. In cafeterias, leave a dollar or two for the person who clears the tables.

Some restaurants no longer calculate separate checks for dining parties. If you are dining with several people or a larger party at a restaurant, find out in advance whether they provide separate checks and which credit cards they accept. An easy way to avoid the annoyance of splitting a bill is for everyone in your party to have

TIPTAG № 31
Dining Dilemma

PLATES AND BOWLS:
• A large plate on a set table is a charger or service plate. It stays on the table throughout the meal unless removed with the soup course.
• Finger bowls are small bowls filled with water, sometimes with lemon slices added. They are occasionally used at formal dinners and when meals include food such as lobster. Dip your fingers briefly into the bowl and wipe on your napkin.

BONES AND PITS:
• If you have something in your mouth that you can't swallow, turn your head slightly down, cover your mouth with your napkin to spit it out. Return your napkin to your lap.

adequate cash in small bills.

Splitting the bill evenly only works if everyone ordered entrées of roughly the same price and agreed on ordering wine. Dine in moderate-price restaurants with friends a few times to gauge their dining habits before venturing into more tony establishments. Another workable solution is to appoint one friend the accountant and have him or her tell everyone else what they owe. If you like to dine with groups of friends, don't worry about dividing the bill to the last penny. It's far better to pay an extra dollar or two than to quibble with your friends in a restaurant.

To share food in a restaurant, carefully place a small portion on your bread and butter plate and pass it to your companion. In informal situations with a spouse or close friend, a forkful of food, carefully passed and not dripping is fine. Don't feel compelled to share food, and don't press others into tasting all the dishes.

Introductions

The higher-status person (your boss, your father, the minister, the mayor), an older person, or a woman is spoken to first. The other person is introduced to them. This means you introduce a man to a woman, a child to an adult, and a younger person to an older person. When introducing both a man and a woman to someone else, say the woman's name first. The people being introduced should then shake hands.

For example, "Rita, I'd like for you to meet Bob Brown. Bob, this is Rita Young, a new partner in our firm."

To introduce an older person to a child: "Mrs. Clausen, I'd like for you to meet Cindy Wilson. Cindy, this is my friend, Mrs. Clausen."

Try to be friendly and relaxed when making introductions. Say the names distinctly. In a group or at a party, in particular, it is helpful to say something brief about the person to get the conversation going. For example: "Rita, Bob lives in Addison Heights; he and his wife, Sue, are restoring the old Andrews house." Or "Bob, Rita is a fellow music lover. She studied the cello last fall in New York."

If introduced to someone, pay attention to the full name and try to remember it; ask the person to repeat it if necessary so you are sure of the pronunciation.

If you meet someone you've met before or whom you haven't seen for a long time, help the person by giving your name again: "Hello, I'm Susan Banks; we met last year at the fund-raiser for Ferry Park." If someone approaches you in this way, take a cue that the person may not remember your name and reintroduce yourself as well. When you must introduce yourself to someone whose name you have forgotten and hinting doesn't work, confess politely with a smile: "Please help me with your name. I have such an awful

BUDGET STRETCHER

Ethnic Food

•

If you enjoy dining with friends in restaurants, look for unfamiliar cuisines to sample. Take turns and vary the cuisine you choose. Neighborhood ethnic restaurants often feature reasonably priced entrées and interesting decor.

Personalized Stationery

Folded Informals:
First and last name; first names and shared last name of a married couple; or the full names of a married couple with different last names.

Traditional Titles:
Mrs. with the husband's full name, or Mr. and Mrs. with the husband's full name. Mrs. with a woman's first and last name when divorced.

Informal Cards:
First and last name; husband's and wife's first names and shared last name or different last names; for notes and informal invitations.

Stationery:
Printed at the top as Mrs. with husband's name or with first and last names; used for personal letters with matching envelopes.

Calling Cards:
Mr. and Mrs. with husband's full name or first and last name; used by couples and singles for enclosures; substitute for business cards.

Children's Cards:
May be printed with full name when a baby is born; attached with pink or blue bow to birth announcement. Enclosed with gifts from the child.

Monograms:
For women and couples, last name initial in the middle; first or middle name initials to left and right; men use their initials in order of name.

memory sometimes." Or "I'm so sorry. I enjoyed talking with you at the conference last year, but I've forgotten your name."

When someone introduces him or herself for the first time, introduce yourself back. For example, at a child's birthday party another mother may say: "Hi, I'm Joan Smith, Suzy's mother." That is your cue to say, "It's so nice to meet you. I'm Jane Sanders, Billy's mom. Our children are in Mrs. Lambert's class."

Social Correspondence

Social correspondence is expressing a sentiment—such as congratulations, good wishes, or condolence—to a friend or acquaintance, or issuing or responding to an invitation. Social correspondence began long before the days of telephones, when written or verbal messages were how people communicated. Don't worry about following prescribed forms or wording: If you sincerely express your sentiment in a handwritten note or if you respond promptly to an invitation, you will be doing the right thing. If you need to respond to a formal invitation, a reply card is often included. If it isn't, follow the tone of the wording in the invitation.

To accept a formal invitation:

Mr. and Mrs. Gerald LeBlanc
accept with pleasure
the kind invitation of
Mr. and Mrs. Michael O'Brien
to dinner
on Saturday, the 29th of October
at eight o'clock

To decline:

Mr. and Mrs. Henry Chavez
regret that they are unable to accept
the kind invitation of
Mr. and Mrs. Benjamin Stern
to dinner
on Friday, the 18th of September

PRINTING STATIONERY

Stationery and department stores sell fine-quality, tasteful stationery for personal correspondence. Art museums and museum catalogs also sell beautiful note cards for informal correspondence. If you would like to have your own printed note cards or stationery, consult with a stationery shop. White or ecru printed or engraved with black or dark navy blue ink is standard. However, strict rules are no longer the norm. See "Personalized Stationery," page 323, for more on personal stationery and cards.

TYPICAL CORRESPONDENCE

Use plain correspondence notes or cards or those imprinted with

---

FAMILY FRIENDLY

Polite Children

•

Teach your children to stand up and shake hands with adults when they are introduced. Teach children to say "excuse me" or "pardon me" when they don't hear a question or request. Refrain from using profanity around your children.

your name, initial, or monogram for regular correspondence. If you prefer, decorative stationery or folded note cards are fine for casual correspondence with family and friends.

Thank-you notes: By far the most important thing is to write them. A quick "thank you" dashed on a postcard is acceptable if that is all the time you have. The recipient will be pleased with the effort.

Gifts: Send a written thank-you if someone has taken the time and effort to select and mail you a gift—whatever the occasion. If you don't, the giver doesn't know if you have received the gift. If you absolutely don't have time to write within a week or two, call or e-mail that you have received the gift and express your appreciation. Then, when you can, write a personal note to acknowledge the gift. It's also a nice gesture to write a note for gifts, such as holiday or shower gifts, received in person. For example:

■Dear Aunt Alice,

Thank you so much for the place setting in our china pattern. Warren and I were so pleased and surprised with your generous gift. We set the table last night for the first time—we've been unpacking for days—and the china looked beautiful on our table. The next time you are in town, please come see us. Thank you again for thinking of us.

Love,

Ann

Hospitality: If you have been an overnight guest in someone's home or if someone has done something extra special, such as giving a party for you, a written note is a must. If you present your host with a gift during your visit, also write a note when you get home, expressing your appreciation. A telephone call or e-mail isn't enough. A thank-you note after a dinner or party in someone's home is always appropriate, especially if you are new friends or acquaintances. For example:

■Dear Mary and Mark,

Bob and I really enjoyed ourselves at your open house Saturday afternoon. The food was wonderful, especially your fabulous dessert, and we met many interesting people. Thank you so much for including us. We hope to see you soon.

Sincerely,

Martha

Help or special kindness: When someone has done something especially nice for you or your family, such as bringing food or baby-sitting during an illness, write a note. After a death in the family, acknowledge sympathy cards, food, and flowers that were sent in condolence. It is nice, if you can, to write a personal line or two on the card, especially if the sender was close to your relative. If this is daunting because of the large number of cards to acknowledge, several family members can share the task. For example:

■ Dear Mrs. Witosky,

Thank you for your note and for the generous memorial contribution after Grandmother's death. She spoke fondly of you through the years, and I know how much your friendship meant to her. Thank you again for thinking of our family.

Sincerely,

Anita Aquino

Or helping in other ways, such as a job reference:

■ Dear Mr. Wong,

Thank you for your reference to Multi Media. I learned so much working for your company last year and from the many experiences I had with Lake Publishing. I appreciate the time you took to write the personal note to Ms. Halkias. Thank you again for your consideration and encouragement.

Sincerely,

William Jackson

School or business world: Handwritten thank-you notes have their place here too. After a school or job interview, a brief, handwritten note thanking the interviewer for his or her time is always appropriate. It is also polite to thank anyone else who was helpful during your interview process.

■ Dear Mrs. Cortez,

Thank you for spending extra time with me today. I didn't expect the tour of Standard Computers, and it was fascinating to see how your plant operates. I believe I have the educational background and work experience to make a contribution to your marketing efforts. Please let me know if I can provide any additional information or references. Thank you again for your consideration today.

Sincerely,

Melissa Romano

Congratulations: When a friend, relative, coworker, or acquaintance has a new baby, noteworthy achievement, happy event, or success, write a note on your personal stationery. If you send a card, write at least a line or two. If a married couple sends a joint note, only the writer signs but the other should be mentioned. Cards are usually signed with both names. For example (for a note):

■ Dear Sally and Al,

John and I are so happy to hear that Maria Louise is here. Cathy told us what a doll she is—with pretty curls and long eyelashes. We

BUDGET STRETCHER

Personal Cards

•

When you need a housewarming gift, have note cards printed with your friend's new address. If your friends are married, be sure you know how they like to be addressed; some couples prefer first names to Mr. and Mrs.

Gifts Mark Anniversaries

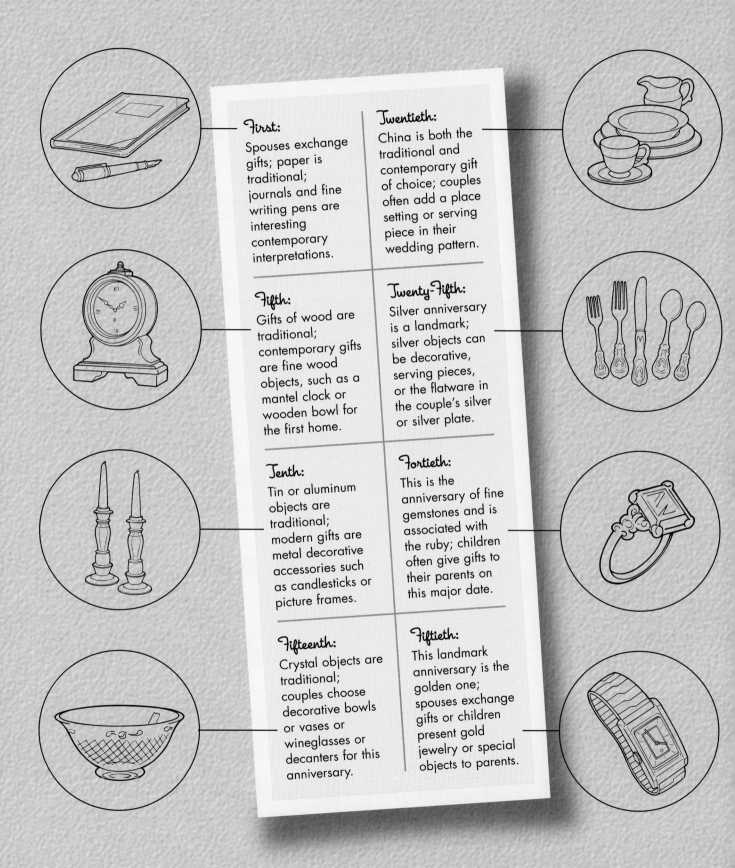

First:
Spouses exchange gifts; paper is traditional; journals and fine writing pens are interesting contemporary interpretations.

Fifth:
Gifts of wood are traditional; contemporary gifts are fine wood objects, such as a mantel clock or wooden bowl for the first home.

Tenth:
Tin or aluminum objects are traditional; modern gifts are metal decorative accessories such as candlesticks or picture frames.

Fifteenth:
Crystal objects are traditional; couples choose decorative bowls or vases or wineglasses or decanters for this anniversary.

Twentieth:
China is both the traditional and contemporary gift of choice; couples often add a place setting or serving piece in their wedding pattern.

Twenty-Fifth:
Silver anniversary is a landmark; silver objects can be decorative, serving pieces, or the flatware in the couple's silver or silver plate.

Fortieth:
This is the anniversary of fine gemstones and is associated with the ruby; children often give gifts to their parents on this major date.

Fiftieth:
This landmark anniversary is the golden one; spouses exchange gifts or children present gold jewelry or special objects to parents.

can't wait to meet her. I'll call next week after things have settled down to see when it's a good time for us to drop by for a few minutes. Congratulations again. We are so happy for you all.
With all good wishes,
Carol

Sympathy: Writing a note on your own stationery is always in good taste. If you use a printed card, choose carefully, especially if you aren't sure of the family's faith background. This kind of note isn't easy to write, but it will mean a great deal to the family. If you can, include a warm, personal memory of the deceased. If you know the family well, and if it is appropriate, you may mention keeping them in your prayers. Write something on a printed card, even if it is just a sentence or two.

Here are examples of appropriate phrases: "I was distressed to learn of your mother's recent death. Please know you are in our thoughts and prayers at this difficult time." Or "We heard of your wife's death with great sadness. Our memories of her will be precious to us. We hope you find comfort at this difficult time knowing that we and others are thinking of you."

If you knew the deceased well, add something personal or say how much you will miss him or her. An example (when you know the family well):

Dear Elizabeth,

I was so sorry to hear of your mother's death. When we were in college, I looked forward to Sunday supper at your parents' house. Mrs. Benson always made your friends feel welcome and at home. She told me many times how proud she was of you and your career and what a good daughter you were. You and your family are in my thoughts and prayers.
With sincere sympathy,
Lee Ann

Serious illness: When someone is seriously injured or ill, use the tone of a sympathy note—the person and family are on your mind or in your prayers, and you are offering comfort. It's tempting in a sympathy or concern note to make empty offers of help. If you do want to help, be more specific. The traditional way to help in these difficult situations is to take food to the house or to call a family member or close friend of the family to see what is needed. If you learn of other specific needs, such as child care, shopping, or yard work, make a firm offer.

Personal notes/difficult situations (not illness or death): Divorce cards are on the market. Don't send them. Cards with humor or sarcasm aren't appropriate. If someone is your close friend, write a brief note to say that you are thinking of the person, but don't offer sympathy.

TIME SAVER

Thanking a Crowd

•

If coworkers have done something special for you, write individual notes if the group is no more than 8 to 12 people. For a large group, write a thank-you note and ask that it be posted or circulated in the office.

Other difficult situations —loss of job, child in trouble, business failure—should be handled equally diplomatically. Only write notes to intimate friends and close family. Only express your concern and support. Don't offer unsolicited advice or suggestions; don't be specific about what you know of the situation.

ISSUING INVITATIONS

For formal occasions, such as engagement announcement parties, weddings, or 50th anniversary dinners, consult with a good stationery shop on the standard formats and formal paper. A respected and widely used source for this information is *Crane's Blue Book of Stationery: The Styles and Etiquette of Letters, Notes, and Invitations.* Stationery shops may use this or similar books as a reference; books of this type are generally available in public libraries.

Use your own personal informal stationery and informal cards for invitations to informal parties. If you are inviting more than 20 or so guests, have invitations printed. As an alternative, purchase preprinted invitations from a stationery store or stationery section of a department store. Preprinted invitations are good choices for children's parties or theme parties, such as baby showers.

For small gatherings, call or invite your guests in person. Be clear about the event—a barbecue or picnic, for example—so your guest will know what to wear and what kind of activity to expect.

RESPONDING TO INVITATIONS

This is nonnegotiable. When you are invited to dine in someone's home, you have to respond. There are no excuses—other than serious crises—for violating this rule. If you are hesitant or want to keep the evening open, decline politely. It's impolite to not give people a definite answer in a reasonable time period. If you are married or are part of a couple, it's fine to say you have to check the other person's plans before you accept an invitation.

Casual parties, cocktail parties, and open houses where meals aren't served don't require a commitment of your entire evening— unless you are the guest of honor. On weekends, especially during the holidays, you may be invited to several events. If you plan to drop by early or late or stay only a few minutes because you have another engagement, simply mention that to your host when you accept the invitation. People who entertain expect this.

RSVP: This is an acronym for a French phrase that means "please respond." "Please respond" may be used as a less formal alternative.

smart ideas

Inviting Guests

BE CLEAR WITH DETAILS
Whether you are calling a few friends or mailing printed invitations, clearly specify the event, time, date, and place. If it is an informal event, where everyone pitches in, mention clearly what you would like guests to bring. This saves guests the embarrassment of arriving empty-handed.

MAKE IT EASY
If you mail invitations or leave voice messages, include your telephone number so guests can call you back. If it is helpful, include a line such as "casual dress." If guests have trouble getting baby-sitters, such as during the holidays, hiring a neighborhood teen is a nice gesture.

If either of these appears on an invitation, you must respond whether or not you plan to attend. Most invitations now include a telephone number, and most people have answering machines, so it is easy to respond. Return cards with stamped envelopes addressed to the hosts are often used for wedding dinners or other events when the hosts must know how many people are attending.

Regrets only: Hosts use this phrase rarely because it has proven to be ineffective. It means only respond if you are not planning to attend.

PERSONAL E-MAIL

Giving out your e-mail address means you need to check it daily, as you would a telephone answering machine. If you use your home computer only occasionally, don't give your e-mail address because messages from friends may languish unanswered.

Don't type in all caps because this is comparable to raising your voice in conversation. Generally use punctuation and capitals; if you dash off frequent e-mails, all lowercase is acceptable. Remember that e-mail is not as private as a sealed letter; don't gossip or give out privileged information. If you like to send out jokes, ask the recipient if he or she would like to be included on your list; some people consider this to be junk mail. Don't get involved with chain letters. Enjoy the speed of e-mail with friends who also do. But don't let it replace the written note.

CELLULAR PHONES AND PAGERS

Unless you are on call for professional reasons, turn off cellular telephones and pagers and don't visibly carry them in restaurants and private homes. If you must make a telephone call during a social event in a home or in public, leave the table or gathering and do so in private. It isn't polite to make business calls at a dining table (including a restaurant table), children's party, or sporting event.

BE A GOOD GUEST

Entertaining is stressful—hosts want everything to go well and for their guests to have a good time. When you are a guest, think about how you would feel in the host's place.

Know when to arrive: Never arrive early. Your hosts may be dressing or doing last-minute preparations, and it is disconcerting to have to stop and greet guests. If you are a very close friend, it's acceptable to ask whether the hosts would like for you to come early to help or to greet early-arriving guests.

If you are invited for dinner at 7:30, it is acceptable to arrive 10 to 15 minutes after the appointed time. (If you are the guest of honor at a dinner, shower, or other party, arrive on time or a few minutes early so you can greet the first guests.) Don't arrive later than 20 minutes after the appointed time because you may interfere with the serving time. In some parts of the country, people arrive at the

Pamper Your Houseguests

Carafe:

Place a water carafe with its own glass on the bedside table. Styles are traditional and contemporary. Consider adding bottled water as a special touch for guests.

Alarm Clock:

Remember the alarm clock, especially if guests have morning appointments or an airplane to catch. Midcentury styles with large numbers are easy to read.

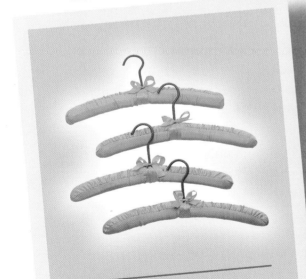

Padded Hangers:

Stock your guest closet with padded hangers so guests' clothes will hang well while they visit. Wooden or well-made plastic hangers are other options.

Luggage Rack:

Make unpacking easy with a sturdy hotel-style rack, sold by home furnishing stores and catalogs. Between visitors, keep it folded up in your guest closet.

appointed hour—or later than 30 minutes after the stated hour. If you have any doubts, ask your hosts or other friends or coworkers.

If an unforeseen mishap occurs and you have to be later than 30 minutes to a dinner party, call your hosts. If you are going to be extremely late, insist they start dinner without you.

Know when to leave: People work hard, and an hour or two after dinner is over, your hosts may be getting tired. If they plead with you to stay after you make the first move to leave, stay. But if they say how much they enjoyed the evening, go. It's always better to leave a little early than to exhaust your hosts. Another sign: All the other guests have departed.

Although it is important not to overstay your welcome, it isn't polite to bolt from the table unless you have an emergency. Traditionally, a guest should stay at least an hour after dinner. However, if you have small children or need to be home at a certain hour because of a family concern, mention your time frame when you accept an invitation.

Be discreetly helpful: When you are attending a large party, introduce yourself and talk with guests who aren't mingling. They may know few if any other guests at the party. At multigenerational parties, help your hosts make everyone feel welcome. Sometimes children or teens feel left out or awkward. Introduce yourself to family members of the host. At a small dinner party, offer to help serve, clear the table, or clean up.

Polite Conversations

Social conversation: Meeting new people and renewing friendships are part of the fun of going to parties. If you haven't met someone and haven't been introduced, introduce yourself. If you meet a guest you think your spouse or another friend at the party would enjoy meeting, introduce them. Train yourself to catch and remember the person's name. Appropriate opening lines include a simple statement about how you know the host, a pleasant, positive comment about the party or event, or a remark about the weather or season. Refrain from immediately asking what the person does. Do not solicit professional advice or business tips from other guests.

Listen to others: Find out something interesting about the person as soon as you can—such as a hobby or recent trip—so you can ask questions. Encourage other people to talk, and listen attentively to what they say. Be positive and more interested in other people than you are in yourself.

Respect other people's right to have different views on politics, religion, social issues, culture, and sports. As a guest, you have an obligation to be polite and congenial. Never raise your voice. Don't talk over people or interrupt them. If you have strong opinions on

FAMILY FRIENDLY

Leave Gracefully

When you attend a large private party or business social function, find and thank the hosts before you leave. Teach your children to thank the parents and hosting child when they attend a birthday or other children's party.

certain topics, steer clear of them until you know people well.

Appropriate topics: Read a newspaper or two and a news magazine the day of a party if you think you may need conversation topics. Express genuine interest in a topic. Read book, film, and restaurant reviews and travel stories for congenial starter topics. People generally enjoy talking about their own children, grandchildren, pets, and hobbies.

Gossip and humor: Refrain from gossiping about people or repeating stories. If you like to use humor, find things about yourself to laugh at; don't make your spouse or another guest the butt of your jokes. Avoid stories that embarrass another person, including family members.

Watch your language and jokes: In a reaction to vulgar popular entertainment and culture, people are beginning to decry rough and crass language. Stifle the impulse to use four-letter words or to tell off-color stories, especially if children or people of an older generation are present. Jokes or negative comments relating to faith and religion or ethnic, racial, regional, or gender themes are never appropriate. Commenting on or attempting to imitate someone's accent is also not appropriate.

Other Situations

HOUSEGUESTS

If you live a distance from family and old friends, encourage them to visit you and your family. Welcome them with an activity or two planned for their interest and your free time together. When grandparents or other relatives are visiting, include quality time, such as an afternoon outing, with your children. If possible, purchase any needed tickets, such as to sporting events, in advance to avoid standing in long lines.

When you have to work during part of the visit or if your guests like to do shopping or sight-seeing on their own, provide them with a set of house keys, maps, brochures, and directions to area attractions. Consider having them meet you for lunch.

Create a comfortable environment by including extras such as a clock radio, small television, books, and current magazines in your guest room. Fresh flowers, bottled water and glasses, and a basket of treats, such as wrapped cookies and fresh fruit, are nice touches.

If your den or other living space doubles as a guest room, give your guest privacy and provide a place to hang clothes and store luggage. Special touches, such as an alarm clock, an extra blanket or pillows, and water carafe, are welcome.

TIP TAG No. 32

The Houseguest

CONSIDER YOUR HOSTS:
- Be clear about when you are arriving and when you are leaving.
- Arrange your own transportation from the station or airport if it is difficult for your hosts to meet you.

TREAT YOUR HOSTS:
- Bring your hosts a gift, traditionally called a bread-and-butter gift.
- If you are unsure of what they might need, wait until you visit and then buy the gift before you leave.
- Offer to baby-sit for an afternoon or evening if a couple has small children. Or offer to take the children out for the afternoon.
- Take your hosts out for dinner.

FAMILY
FRIENDLY

Family
History
•

Teach your children
to broaden their
conversation skills:
Have them ask
relatives or family
friends to share
stories about life
when they were
your children's
ages—or about
their memories of
historic events such
as World War II.

WHEN YOU ARE A HOUSEGUEST

Visit at a convenient time. Remember that people who live in resort areas and major cities can get inundated with guests. If you plan to be in the area, call in advance and ask if you can get together. If your friends want you to stay with them, they'll insist that you do.

Unless someone is an intimate friend or close relative, limit your visit to two or three nights maximum. While visiting, be as helpful as possible. For example, offer to shop, cook, and prepare a meal or two, or to walk the dog or stroll with the baby. Be respectful of your friends' home and possessions. If you want to see other friends in the area, visit them in their homes or meet in a public place. Use a prepaid telephone card or credit card to make long distance calls. When you are leaving, ask if you should make or strip the bed.

GUEST WITH DISABILITIES

Be as inclusive as possible but be honest about steep steps or narrow doorways. If possible, make arrangements so you can include everyone in a group. If it is your turn to host an organization or group and your residence is inaccessible, meet at another spot, such as a restaurant, where everyone can attend.

DIVORCED OR SEPARATED COUPLE

When you invite them both to a function, let them both know ahead of time unless you are absolutely sure they are on friendly terms. If you are friends with both members of the divorced or separated couple, invite one or the other on different social occasions, if necessary, to avoid taking sides.

GUESTS WHO WON'T LEAVE

The French have a great custom: When hosts are ready for the party to end, they serve orange juice. Guests know when they see the orange juice that it is time to ask for their coats.

When lacking such a clear signal, more tact is required. If guests make no move to leave and you are tired, don't offer any additional drinks or coffee. If you are truly desperate and exhausted, politely stifle a yawn. A cocktail party often extends beyond the prescribed hour, but when you are ready for it to be over, close up the bar.

IMPOLITE GUESTS

If you entertain long enough, you'll eventually have a guest who is rude to you or another guest—or who makes an offensive or off-color remark. Handle the situation tactfully, but firmly. If other guests are present, change the subject to a less controversial topic—and don't invite the person back. If the behavior was truly offensive, call your other guests the next day and apologize. It's a good idea to have people over several times before including them as guests at crucial times. When you entertain your boss, a key client, or a future in-law, you want guests who are interesting and congenial but who will not make inappropriate comments.

13

Home Records Storage
- SETTING UP A SYSTEM, 337
- RECORDS TO KEEP, 338
- HOME LOCKBOX, 339
- RENTED SECURITY BOX, 338
- RECORDS ON COMPUTER, 340
- TAX PROGRAMS, 340

Family Photographs
- PRINTS, 341
- NEGATIVES AND SLIDES, 341
- PROFESSIONAL RESTORATION, 341

Scrapbooking and Artifacts
- SCRAPBOOKING SUPPLIES, 342
- CONTENTS, 342
- PRESERVING WEDDING DRESS, 344
- PRESERVING CHRISTENING GOWN, 344

Family History
- EXTENDED FAMILY, 344
- HOME COMPUTER, 345
- INTERNET SEARCH, 345
- PRESERVATION, 345

Video Library
- DIGITAL VERSATILE DISCS, 346
- VIDEO CASSETTES, 351
- STORAGE AND CARE TIPS, 351

Music Library
- COMPACT DISCS, 348
- RECORD ALBUMS, 348
- AUDIO CASSETTES, 351
- STORAGE AND CARE TIPS, 351

Electronic Equipment
- OPTIMUM ENVIRONMENT, 349
- WORKING AT A KEYBOARD, 349
- COMPUTER SAFETY AND PRECAUTIONS, 349, 350
- CLEANING SUPPLIES AND TIPS, 349
- PAPER FOR PRINTER, 350

Home Library
- REFERENCE BOOKS, 347, 352
- NEWSPAPERS, 352
- READING LISTS, 353
- CHILDREN'S BOOKS, 353, 354

Home Record Storage

Maintaining complete, neatly organized, and accessible records—short term and long term—is an important part of making your home run smoothly. Start with the bills. Open them immediately and check the due date. Keep bills in one place where you'll notice them. Set up a routine: Designate a time each month or each week to write checks. Mail payments five to eight days before they are due. If you have a loan coupon book, keep it and addressed, stamped envelopes together. Check your bank statements if you've arranged for automatic deductions and record the payments.

SETTING UP A FILING SYSTEM

Set up a filing system to organize your paper trail. File any coupons you clip by category and expiration date. Organize recipes in a divided box, pocket notebook, or plastic-covered page binder; record the source on the recipe. Create a similar system for newspaper or magazine clippings.

When you order entertainment or travel tickets in advance, file them in envelopes in a logical place; replacements can be difficult and costly at the last minute. Save appliance manuals and warranty information in one place. Computer manuals are most useful near the computer. Record serial and model numbers on each manual; attach the original bill for reference. Store master software disks (including compact discs) and registration numbers near your computer. You need the original disks to reinstall software in case of computer system failure, and you need the registration number for technical support. It's always better to be safe with what you save and store.

WHAT TO KEEP OR SHRED

Label and date folders or boxes for easy identification. After you open mail, file materials promptly. Save bank statements, credit card statements, receipts for purchases (in case of return), investment statements, utility statements, canceled checks or copies, pay stubs (including direct-deposit forms), and family medical records such as immunizations.

Don't let anyone steal your Social Security, bank account, or credit card numbers. Such numbers will be on payment statements, copies of credit card slips, and numerous other financial, purchasing, and personal records. To be safe, invest in a wastebasket shredder; prices are around $30 at office supply stores. Separate the shreds when you throw them away.

Home Remedies

ADDRESS BOOK

Your Big Book

Your personal address/telephone book should be a work in progress. Update when you learn of a change. Use a computer database program, an index card file box, or a letter-tabbed book to keep track of relatives and friends. (Write in pencil if your friends move frequently.) List birthdays, anniversaries, and personal information.

For Purse or Briefcase

Use a small address book, day planner, or computer organizer to keep information that you may need with you. Examples include telephone numbers that you call frequently and family Social Security numbers.

TIME SAVER

Ready for Tax Time

•

Start a file on January 1 for that year. Keep documentation of donations, dues, mortgage interest, and property taxes. Add to the file throughout the year. Keep copies of previous tax returns for at least seven years.

SECURE PROTECTION

Providing secure protection for some of your records is important—crucial for items that aren't a matter of record elsewhere. On-site or off-site location is a matter of personal preference and convenience. At home, you can use a waterproof, heat-resistant metal lockbox or a safe. Waterproof containers are double-walled and insulated. Fire protection for up to one hour at 1,700 degrees F is best; paper chars at 350 degrees F. The smallest metal security boxes are about 12×8×4 inches and hold flat paper and small containers. Don't keep the key in the lock. Keep it in a safe, easy-to-find location. Safes have interior dimensions as small as 8×10×1 inches; or they can be as large as sheds. Safes can be freestanding, in a wall, or buried. Combination locks, electronic locks, and key locks are available.

Off-site, consider the safe-deposit-box service at your bank. Standard size for families without voluminous records is 24 inches deep by 3 inches high by 5 inches wide; annual rental starts at $20 or more. Bank lobby hours determine the availability of access to your box. The renter has a key; and the bank or other financial institution retains a key. Both keys are necessary for entry. Check with an attorney in your state about whether you should keep your will in the safe-deposit box. Some states freeze assets, including bank boxes, in the event of death.

RECORDS TO KEEP

Keep these documents and objects in a safe, secure location, either at home in a lockbox or at a financial institution:

- School records
- Account numbers
- Bonds, securities, stock certificates
- Social Security cards
- Passports
- Birth certificates
- Blueprints/house plans
- Loan papers, contracts
- Mortgage papers/lease
- Abstracts and deeds to property
- Vehicle, boat titles
- Adoption, marriage, divorce, military discharge papers
- Safe-deposit box key and inventory of contents (keep at home)
- Will: one copy at home; one copy in bank box (original retained by your attorney)
- Insurance policies
- Inventory (list, videotapes, or photographs) of household possessions for insurance
- Jewelry, stamps, coins, valuable silver, or other treasures
- Valuable negatives

Home Lockbox Contents

Passport:
Keep passports belonging to you, your spouse, and children. It is easier to renew (every 10 years) if you have current one.

Heirloom Jewelry:
Protect from fire or storm damage; only store in a hidden or large and heavy home safe if you are worried about theft.

Disks of Records:
Store backup computer records, such as manuscripts, family research, and financial records; also keep in safe-deposit box.

Insurance Inventory:
Protect from fire or storm; easy to update if kept at home; also keep copy in safe-deposit box for additional security.

Home Deed:
Store deed and any other crucial personal financial records if not in bank box; also keep a copy of your will for convenience.

Family Letters:
Protect originals here, stored in acid-free envelopes. Or keep photocopies here and originals in your safe-deposit box.

Safe-Deposit Key:
Keep the key to your box here in case of fire or severe damage. Make sure you can easily access the key to your home lockbox.

Birth Certificate:
Store for all members of your family. If possible, obtain multiple copies from your state; photo copies not usually accepted.

▶ Computer disks with backups of sensitive files

Review your personal property insurance coverage annually. Actual cash value subtracts depreciation from the cost of replacing a damaged item. Full-replacement-value insurance costs more but allows replacement without a depreciation deduction. If you own expensive or one-of-a-kind items, consider adding riders for them. Musical instruments, jewelry, electronic equipment, artwork, furs, guns, antiques, and items of exceptional value may not be covered by your homeowners policy. You'll need an appraisal or documentation of worth to determine the insurable value. Your peace of mind is worth the extra premium.

RECORDS ON COMPUTER

Home computers allow you to handle a number of functions simply. Use an electronic calendar to record special days, appointments, and your to-do list. Start a folder for recipes or travel ideas on your hard drive. Use the data management capabilities of your word processor, spreadsheet software such as Excel (Microsoft), or database software such as FileMaker Pro (FileMaker, Inc.). You will be able to manage the data more effectively in Excel or FileMaker when it is a large list. Make a "virtual" address/phone book. You can even add columns—"fields" in database language—in your holiday card list for cards sent and cards received. Let the software's mail merge capability pull names and addresses from a list for a form letter. Turn your address book file into envelope labels. (Or use a label-making program such as Avery Label Maker.) Use the address book in your e-mail program for easy routing of your electronic messages.

PHOTOS ON CD

This option with film processing allows you to store your photographs on CD-ROM. Programs such as Photoshop (Adobe), Print Shop Photo Pro (The Learning Company), or Picture It! (Microsoft) allow you to view, print, or, in some cases, alter your photos. These digital photo files also can be combined with text in applications with layout capabilities such as Word (Microsoft), PageMaker (Adobe), and XPress (Quark).

TAX PROGRAMS

Use programs such as Intuit's Turbo Tax (sometimes included on Quicken) and Tax Case (The Learning Company) to record personal tax information throughout the year. These programs store information on the correct tax form and do the calculations. The programs print hard copies of your returns if you want to file by mail or keep a paper record; or you can file electronically. Check that your program is current or can be updated to reflect changes in tax laws. You may need special programs for individual state-tax returns.

A federal law that took effect in October 2000 made digitally

BUDGET STRETCHER

Money Managing

Use a program such as Quicken (Intuit) or Microsoft Money to monitor accounts, reconcile your checkbook, track investments, and write and print checks. Some versions create budgets and financial plans.

signed documents legally binding. Your hard drive may eventually store as many legal documents as your filing cabinet or safe-deposit box does now. To be safe, transfer important files electronically to a secure website for off-site backup. These virtual safe-deposit boxes on the Web are open all day every day. Enter your code, and your box opens. Send modified files or retrieve stored files when you need them. Understand, however, that Internet systems can fail, erasing your data, and even the best sites may not be totally secure. If you don't want hackers accessing your legal records, do not store them on the Internet.

Family Photographs

Humidity, fingerprints, light, and dust damage photographs; handle prints by edges only. Keep loose photos in containers in cool, dry places. The packet enclosing developed prints works for storage, especially if you keep it in the outer envelope. On the envelope, mark the dates, if they aren't printed on the print, and the subject of the contents. Store in acid-free paper or inert plastic boxes, separated by date or subject. Put a package of silica gel inside the box to absorb moisture. Never write on the surface of a print; write on the back only with special photographic marking pens. Write captions under pictures in albums.

NEGATIVES AND SLIDES

Reprinting from negatives results in better quality than copying photos themselves, so keep negatives safe. Never touch the surface of negatives and never cut them apart. Use uncoated polyester or polypropylene sleeves enclosed in paper envelopes for storage; and indicate which set of pictures came from the negatives. Keep in a dust-resistant case or import the disk of negatives to your hard drive for digital storage.

If you use slides instead of prints, remember that slides are originals. No negatives of these transparencies exist. Protect slides by storing them in acid-free or metal, baked enamel-finish boxes or in polypropylene slide pages. Leaving slides in projector carousels subjects them to moisture, which causes warping, and dust contamination. Keep slides—and all photographic images—out of attics and basements.

SAFE DISPLAY

Mat favorite photos for framing with lignin (wood pulp)-free, 6- to 8-ply mounting board and attach with archival-quality adhesives. The frame should be deep enough so that the image does not touch the glazing that filters ultraviolet light; otherwise, processing chemicals can cause the photo to adhere to the glazing. Use a moisture barrier behind the mat if the frame will hang on an outside wall. Avoid environmental extremes such as exposure to intense light (direct sun) or ultraviolet light (mercury-vapor lamps) or exposure to high humidity (bathrooms and kitchens).

Scrapbooking/Artifacts

Archiving your memories and personal artifacts to save and protect them for the future is an enjoyable pastime. It's also a method of organizing, displaying, and showcasing personal and family milestones. Make scrapbooks for specific events, years, or individuals. Let your scrapbooking be a work in progress: You can add pages or start a new volume.

GETTING STARTED

From the start of a meaningful period in your life—marriage, first house, new baby, child starting school—keep the artifacts that come your way. For children, save report cards, representative artwork, projects, ribbons, awards, and certificates.

SUPPLIES

Visit a scrapbook or crafts store to get an idea of what you need. An expandable binder, purchased or made at home from wood or cardboard, makes adding pages easy. Or choose a blank bound book if it offers enough pages to record memories of a specific event, such as a retirement party or anniversary celebration. Save a section for other guests to write messages to the guest of honor.

Buy only archival-quality supplies, items that are chemically stable, for long-term preservation of your memories. Look for the term "acid-free" on paper labels or buy an acid-testing pen to test paper you already have. Don't use newsprint: It contains lignin, wood fibers that cause discoloration and brittleness. Avoid adhesives such as rubber cement, pressure-sensitive tapes such as cellophane, spray adhesive, and adhesives with odors; all of these contain gases that can damage photos. Instead, use photo splits (double-sided adhesive tabs that are secure but can be moved); glue sticks that dry clear; liquid glue pens and glue cartridges; photo corners; and special photo tape.

Check catalogs or stores for recommended brands. See sources on page 366.

CONTENTS

Anything can go into your scrapbooks. Photos are usually included. (Use a special "red eye" pen to correct photographs with this common problem.)

Preserve invitations, announcements, report cards, greeting cards and notes, and certificates directly on the pages. Buy or make

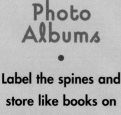

TIME SAVER

Photo Albums

•

Label the spines and store like books on shelves to avoid weight on prints. Use only acid-free paper pages and nondamaging materials for attaching—photo splits, photo corners, or photo-safe glue sticks. Use archival plastic cover sheets.

Safe Storage of Photographs

Archival Boxes:

Work well if you keep loose photographs, negatives, or slides. Add labels. Organize with acid-free glassine sleeves to preserve your memories.

Leather Albums:

Choose classic albums if you display with your books. Select archival albums; if pages are magnetic, check for PVC-free plastic. Use pH-neutral adhesive.

Flip Display Boxes:

Enjoy current snapshots—new baby, trip, big event—that you like to flip through or show to friends. Designed for quick updates with new photographs.

Fabric Albums:

Ask for acid-free paper and archival glue and photo corners. Check that page protectors are archival-quality to avoid having them stick to or discolor photos.

sleeves or pockets so you can include small objects and mementos. Use photos of larger objects. Make photocopies of newspaper clippings to avoid deterioration. Or spray the original clipping with deacidification spray, mount on buffered paper with water-based glue, and place in a polyvinyl chloride (PVC)-free protector. Plastic sheets containing polyethylene or polypropylene are usually safe.

ITEMS FOR SPECIAL ATTENTION

Wood objects: Keep out of direct sunlight and heat. Use a soft dust cloth. Wash with oil soap; don't use silicon-based polish.

Silver: Keep small pieces in tarnish-proof bags or wrap in acid-free tissue paper, not in plastic bags.

Quilts: For hanging, use a fabric tube across the top edge to distribute the weight over the entire width of the quilt. Don't poke sharp objects through the fabric. Wrap unused quilts in acid-free tissue paper or a large pillowcase and store in individual acid-free boxes. Wash once a year and refold in a different pattern to reduce fiber stress. Check with a quilt store about products designed to gently wash quilts.

Wedding dress or christening gown: Use a reputable professional dry cleaner's preservation service or wrap the cleaned garment in acid-free tissue paper and place in an acid-free, airtight box. Store in a cool location (not a cedar chest). A vinegar smell or yellowing indicates that acid is attacking the fibers.

Family History

Begin family research with living relatives. Design or purchase a data organizer for questionnaires and interviewing. Gather facts about given names, birth, education, interests and hobbies, occupations, and general health (useful for tracking genetic predisposition to disease). Use their memories to glean details about their immediate ancestors (especially birth information) to help you dig deeper. Seek their aid in identifying people in old photographs. Make notes and transcribe soon after an interview. Or store the information in a database on your computer for access. The database format allows for sorting by topics. Use audio- or videotape to save the stories your relatives tell about their lives.

Visit the hometowns of your ancestors. Walk through the cemetery; headstones reveal names and dates—sometimes more. Look through records in churches and issues of local newspapers. Access birth, marriage, death, property ownership, and other official records at county courthouses. The local library has books about family history, which contain other sources and tips from genealogy buffs. States and some regions maintain genealogy libraries open for public research; the librarian can help you or refer you to someone else.

NETWORK WITH EXTENDED FAMILY

FAMILY FRIENDLY

Scrapbook Extras

•

Personalize your scrapbooks with tools such as decorative-edged scissors, printed papers, rubber stamps, special inks, and diecuts. Some supply stores offer classes to teach techniques, or join a scrapbook club to share skills.

Track down second and third cousins, in-laws, and as much extended family as you can if you are planning serious genealogical searching. The more tiers of relatives you locate, the more information you'll uncover, especially name changes and differences in spellings. In the 19th and early 20th centuries, immigration officials often Americanized surnames, modified spelling, or completely translated a name into English. (For example, the German name Holzbauer might have become Carpenter.) Try a round-robin letter or e-mail chain with your relatives. E-mail makes it easy to quickly contact distant relatives and other sources; you may receive answers from any point on the globe.

USE YOUR HOME COMPUTER

Take advantage of your personal computer for genealogy research. With software such as Family Tree Maker (Broderbund) and Generations Family Tree (Sierra Home), you can use stored data or transfer it to the program's templates to make graphic family trees. Some programs allow you to import photographs and illustrations. Sophisticated versions of these programs include CD-ROMs with searchable databases of immigration records, military records, Social Security death indexes, ship passenger lists, and other records.

Choose software that allows you to convert your stored data to GEDCOM (Genealogy Data Communication) format. Then you can share files with other researchers via e-mail (or disk), even if their genealogy information is on another software program. (It's similar to translating from Beta to VHS video format.) Sharing information is the basis of genealogical research; this file format makes sharing much easier.

PRESERVE FAMILY HISTORY

Ask about items that have always been in the family. Store handed-down family papers—letters, diaries, journals, and others—with special care. Preserve the integrity of the original. Do not write on it, glue it to anything, or keep it in the open. Don't laminate papers: Lamination causes damage and is not reversible. Keep paper flat in airtight plastic boxes. (Avoid cedar chests; the acidic oil and exuded gas can eat through and discolor paper.) Make archival-quality photocopies of deteriorating paper, especially newsprint. Treat originals with deacidification spray and place them inside polyester film sleeves or folders; store in a cool, dark place.

Video Library

Renting allows you to revisit a favorite film or avoid high ticket

TIPTAG No.33

Internet Search

GETTING STARTED:
- Take advantage of telephone books; search internationally at www.infospace.com.
- Use the RootsWeb site, www.rootsweb.com for free searches of 650 million names.
- Some sites are not free. Don't sign up for a service you don't want.
- National Adoption Clearinghouse, www.calib.com/naic, contains databases of birth records.

GOVERNMENT RECORDS:
- Check the National Archive and Records: www.nara.gov/genealogy.
- Search the Library of Congress texts: lcweb.loc.gov/rr/genealogy.

prices, but if you want to watch a film or tape many times, buying the video makes sense. The purchase price usually equals three or four rentals. Remember that home videos are for home viewing only. Copying a video—rented or purchased—is illegal; every commercial tape begins with that copyright warning. Some tapes include scramblers so that you can't copy.

If you plan to keep your own taped programs—such as all the episodes of a television mini series—label the tape and the container. Include the airdate. To make the tape permanent, break the tab on the edge. If you record the same program frequently, use the same tape. Standard speed makes better quality and longer-lasting tapes than extended and slow speeds. Rewind and eject tapes when you have finished viewing.

CARE

Heat, humidity, and direct sunlight cause tape deterioration that appears as dropouts—flashes, white spots, or streaks on the screen.

Fast-forward and rewind your tapes every year or so if you haven't watched them (at that point decide if you want to keep them). An inexpensive rewind machine applies constant pressure.

Avoid dirt and oil contamination by not opening the cassette or touching the tape.

Avoid demagnetization by not keeping your tapes on top of the television, videocassette recorder (VCR), or speakers. Don't store on the bottom shelf of a video cabinet as the vibration from the vacuum cleaner will erase the tape.

Keep a dust cover on your VCR. Clean the VCR monthly with a commercial cleaning tape and solvent to remove dust that could scratch your tapes.

DIGITAL VERSATILE DISC (DVD)

The digital versatile disc, also called the digital video disc, is the same size as a compact disc but holds seven times more data than a CD due to file compression. The DVD is also multimedia, allowing audio and visual recording and playback, plus tracks for overlaid subtitles, graphics, or spoken commentary. You can watch a DVD movie on a compatible computer as well as on television. Not every DVD will be compatible with your player because DVD movies carry region codes, indicating the country of sale. The region codes on the disc and player or computer drive must match. This code protection is an effort by the movie studios to prevent unauthorized duplication of copyrighted material. Check the region code on the DVD box for compatibility before you buy.

FILMING YOUR HISTORY

Taping family events with a video camera is an enjoyable way to preserve family history. Make the process worth your time by buying the best-quality tape you can afford. If you'll be in one spot for a

TIME SAVER

Family History

•

The Church of Jesus Christ of Latter-Day Saints maintains and shares genealogical records in their free Family History Centers. The only charge is for microfilm or microfiche records. Check out www.familysearch. org for details.

Reference Books at Home

Atlases:
Use the oversize road atlas to plan trips and routes; turn to the world atlas to look up facts and for help with homework projects.

First Aid:
Mark poison charts for quick reference. Write emergency numbers in the book, such as poison control or doctor's office.

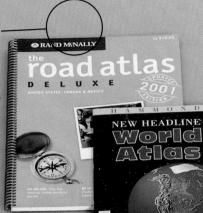

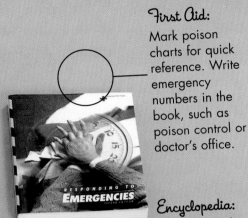

Medical Guide:
Choose from a respected source, such as a leading medical school. Use the index or table of contents to quickly find information.

Encyclopedia:
This is a quick reference for facts and for current and historical information. Paperback editions are available.

Dictionary:
Buy a hardback to stand up to years of use. Every home needs a quality dictionary to look up words and correct spellings.

Almanac:
The index is in the front to make it easier to use; updated annually. Cover date is for year after the book is published.

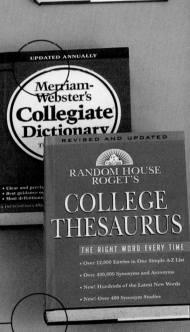

Thesaurus:
Use it to widen your word choices for professional or personal writing; helpful when you have a student in your home.

Desk Reference:
Handy and concise for general reference and cultural and historical facts. Helpful for homework and school projects.

while, use a tripod to avoid shaking the camera. Video is a visual medium, so consider the background composition of shots, including lighting and other action as well as the object of your focus.

Avoid taping just a talking head by varying the camera angle and range (close-up, wide-angle) throughout the session. Use camera features such as fading and on-screen titles to blend between shots and sessions. Remove the tape and carry it in a zippered plastic bag. Also consider making a videotape of all valuables, showing serial numbers where applicable.

Music Library

Expand your music library with a format that fits your playing equipment. When you want to expand your musical experience, switch radio stations. Try some chamber music, jazz, easy listening, big band—whatever you can find. If you like what you hear, call the station for a playlist. Continue your sampling at the library; borrow compact discs that interest you. If you have children, introduce them to a variety of music and musical experiences at an early age.

LISTENING STATIONS

Many stores provide listening stations so you can hear before you buy. They also give collection advice. Both in print and online, Borders offers "Music Essentials" suggestions for blues, children's music, classical, country, folk, international, jazz, New Age, rap, rhythm and blues, show tunes, big band, British Invasion, and soundtracks. So does *All Music Guide*, in print and at allmusic.com. Watch film credits for titles of featured music. Search *Phonolog*, the weekly loose-leaf publication at record stores, to locate popular songs by album, song title, or performers. The annual guides *Schwann Spectrum* (pop and rock) and *Schwann Opus* (classical) provide album and artist reviews. Libraries carry back issues.

CARE

LPs and 45s: Sheathe the records and their covers in polyethylene-lined sleeves; this frosted plastic protects records from dust, leaves no residue, and reduces static buildup. Place records vertically on strong shelves—they weigh as much as 45 pounds per shelf foot—away from direct sunlight and high heat. Avoid touching the grooves. Use isopropyl alcohol from the drugstore to clean the surface, wiping in a circle from the center out with a soft, lint-free cloth. Wipe with a very lightly damp cloth and pat dry. Cover the turntable and clean the stylus after each session with a stylus-cleaning brush such as Disc-Washer.

Compact discs: Dusty or scratched compact discs do not play. Clean CDs by wiping in a straight line from the center out—not in a circle, because this can leave scratches. Use a damp, lint-free cloth. It may be possible to repair a shallow scratch by rubbing automobile

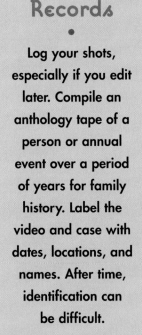

FAMILY FRIENDLY

Video Records

•

Log your shots, especially if you edit later. Compile an anthology tape of a person or annual event over a period of years for family history. Label the video and case with dates, locations, and names. After time, identification can be difficult.

paste wax into it, then smoothing with a lint-free cloth. Clean the optical mechanism inside the player with CD lens cleaner at least once a month to remove dust. If you own a CD burner, copy your CDs and keep the originals for copies to replace in case of loss or scratching.

Electronic Equipment

Protect the investment you made in your computer. The biggest enemies of hardware are dust, high (or low) heat, humidity, and smoke. Anything that leads to contamination or loss of data can be fatal to software. Don't use a magnet to attach notes to the computer. Self-adhesive notes work well. Guard against static electricity near hardware by putting plastic mats under your chair and under any machines near the floor; or misting antistatic clothes spray on the carpet once a week.

Give your computer hardware a clean, comfortable environment for a long, healthy life: Place the computer away from sources of heat. Shield from direct sunlight; this protects all the equipment and reduces screen glare. Don't smoke in your computer room. Unless the computer is designed to be portable, don't move it except when you must do so. Choose a workstation with room for all your hardware. Don't pack the computer into a small space. The CPU or central processing unit (the component with the vents and fan), needs room to breathe—at least 2 inches all around—to prevent overheating.

Opinions vary about when to turn off the computer. As a commonsense approach, turn off the monitor if you are going to be away from the computer for more than two hours. However, newer units rarely experience screen burn, so this is primarily an energy-use issue. If you don't restart occasionally, you'll miss screen prompts for backups and updates. Don't test the limits of your surge protector or UPS. Always turn off and unplug during electrical storms.

WORKING AT THE KEYBOARD

Hours at the keyboard can lead to repetitive strain injury, muscle damage caused by overuse of shoulders, arms, or hands. Be ergonomically savvy. Position your chair directly in front of the keyboard and an arm's length away from the monitor, with your feet on the floor or on a footrest. The backs of your knees shouldn't touch the chair. The lower the keyboard the better; a lap-level keyboard tray with room for the mouse is best. Invest in an

smart ideas

Computer Safe

PROBLEM POWER SPIKES

Plug into one surge protector power strip. If you are on-line, buy one that includes a grounded phone cord if you're not connected via a cable modem. Prevent circuit overload by not plugging anything other than your equipment into that outlet. Plug the power strip into an uninterruptible power supply (UPS) with a rechargeable battery that keeps the computer running during a power outage until you can exit.

WATCH THOSE CORDS

Computer stores and office outfitters carry a variety of UPS setups. This adds up to lots of cords; make sure they are well out of the walking path.

ergonomically designed keyboard, available at computer stores.

CLEANING PRODUCTS

Cotton swabs, isopropyl alcohol, tweezers: Take your mouse apart. Swab or lift out dust particles regularly. Wipe the ball and rollers with alcohol.

Mini vac: Use this handled tool to pull dust away from vents and surfaces. Also vacuum the mouse pad.

Nonabrasive wipes or lint-free cloths: Wipe the cases frequently with a clean, soft cloth slightly dampened in water. Never use an ammonia cleaning product. Never spray the computer casing or screen; however, wipe the screen with a cloth slightly dampened with window cleaner. Note that accidental liquid contamination can do serious harm to a computer.

Dustcovers: Cover regularly when not in use. ALWAYS cover if you are painting or sanding nearby.

PRECAUTIONS

Keeping your software and data pure involves a few routine precautions:

Save frequently while you work. Delete files you no longer need. Back up current programs and data.

Print hard copies only after you've saved the file, in case a glitch occurs during printing.

Make disk copies of individual files to keep off-site—away from the computer in a dust-free disk case. Keep sensitive files in your safe-deposit box.

Use a Zip or Jazz drive (both Iomega) or CD-burner to back up the entire hard drive or specific programs. Or export your files to a secure server via the Internet.

Record software registration numbers and store master discs or CDs once the programs are loaded. Keep hardware and software manuals and technical support telephone numbers nearby.

PAPER

Paper choice depends on what you are printing. Lightweight, 20-pound copier grade serves the purpose for most jobs, especially draft copies. Ink-jet paper rated 24 to 28 pounds with 92 or higher brightness works better with graphics. Look for decorated and high-rag-content paper for projects such as holiday letters. Store paper flat in moisture-proof wrapping to protect from humidity and wrinkles, both of which lead to printer jams.

Home Library

Every home needs a collection of basic references, sources to consult for specific information; they aren't meant to be read from cover to cover. Keep your reference material in one specific location—the den, the home office, a special shelf—wherever you

---

TIME SAVER

Data Protection

•

Install an antivirus program such as Norton Anti-Virus or McAfee VirusScan. Buy updates, or download updates regularly from the Internet. Online support agreements send screen prompts to remind you when you need to update.

Caring for Recordings

Compact Discs:
Keep out of the sun and away from direct heat; store upright, not stacked, in plastic cases inside a larger case if possible. Handle only by edge or within the center hole.

Video Cassettes:
Store in inert plastic boxes sold by video stores with the tape in the cassette at bottom of reel. Handle with care; dropping can break the housing and loosen tape.

Audio Cassettes:
Protect in their plastic cases at home or in your automobile. Don't leave in a tape player; eject and store. Keep out of the sun and away from heat and direct sunlight.

Digital Versatile Discs:
Store in their holders to reduce dust and scratching. Avoid touching the surface. Clean with a soft cloth sprayed with window cleaner; wipe in straight line from the center.

think you'll need it most.

Choose references that are current, comprehensive, and user-friendly. Check the copyright date of books already in your collection as well as new purchases. Always buy the latest edition.

REFERENCES

In addition to basic reference books (see page 347), include a version of the Bible, the Talmud, the Koran, or other faith source. Other helpful books include the following:

Usage guide: Everyone occasionally has a grammar, punctuation, or word-usage question. Unless you have a college composition handbook or other reference, you can only guess and wonder. Helpful books include *The Gregg Reference Manual,* which provides examples and an easy-to-use index. *The Chicago Manual of Style* is the standard source for publishing. Specialized manuals include *Words into Type, The New York Times Manual of Style, The Associated Press Stylebook and Libel Manual,* and the *MLA Handbook for Writers of Research Papers.*

Foreign language dictionaries: Include paperback foreign language dictionaries if you travel, are bilingual, or have a language student in your household.

Special-interest guides or dictionaries: Consider a literary source book such as *The Oxford Companion* series or *Benet's Reader's Encyclopedia* if you are an avid reader. A crossword dictionary, rhyming dictionary, bad-speller's dictionary, and a quotation sourcebook, such as the well known *Bartlett's Familiar Quotations,* are handy to have in a home library.

Encyclopedia: Think about what you need. Some home computers are sold already loaded with basic encyclopedias; you can also buy CD-ROM encyclopedias. Neither kind can be updated unless you buy a new program. You also can visit encyclopedia sites on the Web. If you own a set of bound encyclopedias, keep them—especially if you have a student in the household. The historical information is helpful and often interesting.

Etiquette: If you occasionally have etiquette or social questions or are planning a wedding or other major occasion, add a revised and updated version of a standard guide. Well-known ones include *The Amy Vanderbilt Complete Book of Etiquette* and *Emily Post's Etiquette.*

THE NEWS

Don't forget the daily news. The local newspaper features information about your area—local events, meetings, entertainment, school news—that you can't find anywhere else in one place. Consider the regional edition of a national newspaper, such as *The New York Times* or *The Wall Street Journal,* or weekly news magazines (*Time, Newsweek, U.S. News and World Report*) for

---

TIME SAVER

Public Library

Your library card gives you access to references sources. Large public libraries offer online patrons access to the collection for the availability of specific titles and sets. Library Web sites may provide links to on-line reference sources.

perspectives on national and international topics and culture.

LITERATURE AND CULTURE

Books bring the world, the past, and even speculation about the future into your home. Create a home library that will enrich you and your family. Your interests and needs will determine the contents of your library. But whatever your passions, indulge them with books. Children who grow up with books and see their parents reading learn the value of reading at an early age.

What to read: To find titles you'd like to read, keep track of best-sellers or join a subscription book club or book discussion group. Visit bookbrowser.com on the Web for reading lists and book reviews. Many "best lists" are available too. Examples include The Radcliffe Publishing Course "100 Best Novels" of the 20th century and the Modern Library lists of "100 Best Novels" chosen by readers and the board of directors. These lists and others are on the Random House website; similar lists are available at your public library. Bookstores often create displays of staff favorites.

Award winners: Keep up on annual award winners and books nominated for major awards. Pulitzer Prizes are given for American poetry, drama, fiction, nonfiction, and other literary genres. The Nobel Prize for literature goes to an international author for the body of his or her work. The National Book Award, in various categories, honors new American titles; the Booker Prize is the British equivalent. Among the other well-known annual awards by type are the James Beard (culinary), Spur (western), RITA (romance), Hugo and Nebula (science fiction, fantasy), and Agatha and Edgar (mystery). Bookstore staff can help you find current or past award-winning books.

Proper shelving: Enhance the ambience of your home and protect your books with proper shelving, whether you arrange the volumes for accessibility or aesthetics. Shelves can be freestanding or built-ins. Wood is a good choice for either because it can be stained or painted and is rigid if it has proper support. (For more on shelving dimensions and supports, see page 17.) Keep often-used books where they are most useful—cookbooks in the kitchen, how-to manuals with equipment, for example. Store treasured books where they cannot be damaged by children or pets.

How to shelve books: The Library of Congress recommends shelving books, especially old ones, by height to prevent warping. However, you may prefer to arrange a large collection by subject or author—being able to find your books is important. Never jam on

TIP TAG № 34
Nurture Reading

START YOUNG:
- Introduce books with interactive volumes, such as alphabet, counting, and picture-identification books (animals, shapes, colors). Read every day, particularly at bedtime.
- Choose classic editions or try modern retold versions; both should have quality illustrations. Familiarity with the characters and plots enriches cultural literacy.

MAKE READING FUN:
- Stock age-appropriate audio-books for long automobile trips.
- Include pop-up books and books featuring hands-on tasks such as lacing, snapping, and zipping.

SPACE SAVER

Readers Share

•

Read and weed. Keep your collection manageable by recycling books, especially paperbacks. Donate extra books to charity sales or shops. Check the public library's wish list: You may have an out-of-print title they need.

shelves. Leave enough room so that you can remove a book by its whole spine, not the loop at the top, to avoid damaging the binding.

Care: Avoid temperature extremes, excessive light, and uneven humidity levels. Placement above a hot radiator dries out bindings and makes the paper brittle. Keep out of direct sunlight—facing a window—as colors fade. Allow books to breathe. If your bookcase has glass doors, open them occasionally for air circulation.

Dust your bookshelves and books. For shelves and book covers, wipe covers with a clean dust cloth lightly scented with lemon oil, oil of cloves, or oil of lavender to add a pleasant scent and to repel insects and molds. Protect dust jackets with polyester clear covers (such as Reddi covers or Just-A-Fold III), available from library and school supply stores. If you see green or orange mold, it is growing and should be removed by a professional conservator. Brush or vacuum off dried mold. Work outside or on a porch and wear a mask to protect yourself from inhaling mold. Don't eat while reading because grease marks are difficult to remove. Cornstarch sprinkled on a fresh stain, patted dry, and brushed off may work.

Repairing damage: If you would like to attempt to straighten a warped book cover: Weigh down the book in a humid area, such as in a bathroom with the shower on. After the book has straightened, let dry it out completely in a non-humid area before reshelving.

Accidents: Take care of your books as you build your library. Here are suggestions for dealing with mishaps:

■ Sandwich a damp page between paper blotters or heavy-weight paper towels. Press with a medium-hot iron until dry.

■ Lay wet books on clean window screening supported by bricks or building blocks. Separate wet pages with waxed paper and air-dry.

■ Use non-abrasive erasers to remove stray pencil marks from pages.

■ Don't write margin notes in ink because ink can bleed through.

■ Use self-adhesive Filmoplast or special book tape to fix tears. Cellophane or other pressure-sensitive tape can become brittle. As an alternative, place waxed paper under the tear, dab white glue on the torn edges, and rub a strip of white tissue paper into the glue along the entire length of the tear. Apply some weight until the glue dries. Then remove the excess tissue paper by pulling toward the tear from both sides.

Children's books: Encourage reading at a very early age. Take your children to the library and to bookstores for story hours. Notice what appeals to them. Make books valued gifts by including a bookplate or an inscription. Teach children respect for printed material by providing bookmarks. Don't let children damage books. Choose fabric or hardback books for young children. Introduce your children to your own childhood favorites, either those saved by your family or new editions you purchase.

Extension Services
- CONSUMER PUBLICATIONS, 357
- WEBSITES, 357
- E-MAIL ADDRESSES, 357

Federal Agencies
- CONSUMER PUBLICATIONS, 358
- WEBSITES, 358
- E-MAIL ADDRESSES, 358

Museums & Libraries
- WEBSITES, 359
- E-MAIL ADDRESSES, 359

Sources by Chapter
- CONSUMER ASSOCIATIONS, 357
- NATIONAL SHOPPING SOURCES, 358
- SAFETY ASSOCIATIONS, 358
- PROFESSIONAL ASSOCIATIONS, 358
- TRADE ASSOCIATIONS, 358
- NONPROFIT FOUNDATIONS, 358
- SPECIALIZED SHOPPING, 359

Special Needs
- ACCESSIBILITY INFORMATION, 358
- ENVIRONMENTAL RESOURCES, 362, 363, 365
- HEALTHY LIVING RESOURCES, 363
- PET CARE AND PET HEALTH, 365
- NEIGHBORHOOD RESOURCES, 365
- FAMILY HISTORY, 366

Special Thanks
- PROFESSIONAL CONTRIBUTIONS, 367
- CONTRIBUTORS, 368

Extension Services

EAST

Rutgers Cooperative Extension Department of Family and Consumer Sciences, www.rce.rutgers.edu Consumer Publications: www.rce.rutgers.edu/pubs/index.html

MIDWEST

Iowa State University Extension, Ames, IA, 50011 515/294-4111, www.extension.iastate.edu, E-mail: answer@iastate.edu; Consumer Publications: www.extension.iastate.edu/Pages/pubs/; Extension Distribution Center, 119 Printing and Publications Building, Iowa State University, Ames, IA 50011-3171, 515/294-5247, Fax: 515/294-2945

Michigan State University Extension, 108 Agriculture Hall, East Lansing, MI 48824-1039, 517/355-2308, Fax: 517/355-6473, www.msue.msu.edu, E-mail: msue@msue.msu.edu; Consumer Publications: http://ceenet.msue.msu.edu/bulletin/ctlgmast.html

University of Minnesota Extension, consumer information: http://www.extension.umn.edu/housing

SOUTHEAST

University of Florida Cooperative Extension Service, Institute of Food and Agricultural Sciences Gainesville, FL 32611, 352/392-1971, E-mail: info@ifas.ufl.edu; Consumer Publications: http://edis.ifas.ufl.edu/

SOUTHWEST

Texas Agricultural Extension Service Family and Consumer Sciences, Texas A&M University, 311 History Building, 2251 TAMU, College Station, TX 77843-2251, 979/845-3850, Fax: 979/845-6496, E-mail: fdrm@tamu.edu, http://fcs.tamu.edu/

WEST

Oregon State University Extension Service Extension Family & Community Development, 161 Milam Hall, Corvallis, OR 97331, 541/737-0997, http://osu.orst.edu/extension/, Consumer Publications: Publication Orders; Extension and Station Communications, Administrative Services A422, Corvallis, OR 97331-2119, Oregon State University, 541/737-2513, Fax: 541/737-0817

General Information

WEBSITES

www.learn2.com Use search to find information on nearly any topic;

TIPTAG №35

Consumer Help

Check out these sites or call for more information from these well-known consumer groups.

CONSUMER FEDERATION OF AMERICA:
- 1424 16th Street NW Washington, DC 20036
Phone: 202/387-6121
Fax: 202/265-7989
Internet: www.consumerfed.org

CONSUMERS UNION:
- 1666 Connecticut Avenue NW Suite 310 Washington, DC 20009-1039
Phone: 202/462-6262
Fax: 202/265-9548
Internet: www.consumersunion.org

www.organizedhome.com Practical articles, how-to tips, and links on housekeeping matters; **www.built-e.com** Information for environmentally conscious consumers and building professionals.

U.S. Federal Agencies

Advisory Council on Historic Preservation (citizen's guide to federal regulations protecting historic buildings), 1100 Pennsylvania Ave., NW, Suite 809, Old Post Office Building, Washington, DC 20004, 202/606-8503, E-mail: achp@achp.gov, www.achp.gov

Federal Trade Commission, Consumer Line (information including heating and cooling efficiency, home equity loans, mortgage services, and tips on assessing lawn services), www.ftc.gov

United States Department of Agriculture (website has consumer information on food safety and other topics), 14th & Independence Ave., SW, Washington, DC 20250, 202/720-2791, Fax: 202/720-2166, www.usda.gov

U.S. Department of Energy, Energy Efficiency and Renewable Energy Clearinghouse, 800/363-3732, www.eren.doe.gov

United States Department of Housing and Urban Development (safe and healthy home information), 800/483-7342, www.hud.gov

U.S. Environmental Protection Agency is a valuable source of consumer information, including such topics as residential air-cleaning devices, indoor air quality, and asthma facts available on its website and as brochures and booklets. Public Information Service, 401 M Street, Washington, DC 20460, 800/438-4318, www.epa.gov

Sources by Chapter
CHAPTER 1: ORGANIZATION

Albright Lighting & Interiors, 3029 Ingersoll Ave., Des Moines IA 50312, 515/255-2906

American Occupational Therapy Association, 4720 Montgomery Lane, P.O. Box 31220, Bethesda MD 20824-1220, 301/652-2682, TDD: 800/377-8555, Fax: 301/652-7711, E-mail: praota@aota.org, www.aota.org

Barrier Free Environments, P.O. Box 30634, Raleigh NC 27633, 919/782-7823

Bed, Bath & Beyond, 800/462-3966, www.bedbathandbeyond.com

Burlington Coat Factory, 800/444-2628, www.bcfdirect.com

The Container Store, 2000 Valwood Parkway, Dallas, TX 75234, 888/266-8246, E-mail: contain@containerstore.com, www.containerstore.com

Crate & Barrel, 800/323-5461, www.crateandbarrel.com

SAFETY
ALERT

**Where
To Start**

•

U.S. Consumer
Product Safety
Commission,
Washington, DC
20207-0001;
Consumer Hotline:
800/638-2772;
phone: 301/504-
0990; TTY:
800/638-8270; fax:
301/504-0121;
Internet:
www.cpsc.gov

Eddie Bauer Home, 800/625-7935, www.eddiebauer.com/ebh/

Get Organized, 800/803/9400, www.shopgetorganized.com

Gracious Home, (Eastside store), 1217 & 1220 Third Avenue, New York, NY 10021, 212/517-6300, Fax: 212/249-1534, E-mail: eastside@gracioushome.com, www.gracioushome.com

Gracious Home, (Westside store), 1992 Broadway, New York, NY 10023, 212/231-7800, Fax: 212/875-9976, E-mail: westside@gracioushome.com, www.gracioushome.com

Hold Everything, 800/421-2264, Catalog sales: 800/840-3596, www.holdeverything.com

Horchow Home, 800/456-7000

IKEA, 800/434-4532, www.ikea.com

Kmart, 800/355-6388, www.bluelight.com

Linens 'N Things, 800/568-8765, www.lnthings.com

Lowe's, 800/445-6937, www.lowes.com

Pier 1 Imports, 800/447-4371, www.pier1.com

Pottery Barn, 800/922-9934, 800/922-5507, www.potterybarn.com

Target, 888/304-4000, www.target.com

CHAPTER 2: CLEANING ROUTINES

A Place for Mom (senior housing and Alzheimer's care referral service), 877/666-3239, www.aplaceformom.com

Alzheimer's Association, 800/272-3900, www.alz.org

Eldercare Locator Service of the U.S. Administration on Aging, 800/677-1116, www.aoa.gov

Immigration and Naturalization Service, 800/870-3676, www.ins.gov

Internal Revenue Service, www.irs.gov

International Nanny Association (information on hiring child-care professionals), 856/858-0808, www.nanny.org

Social Security Administration, 800/772-1213, www.ssa.gov

United Way, (general information and to find local chapter), www.unitedway.com and www.unitedway.org

CHAPTER 3: SURFACE CARE

Armstrong Flooring, www.armstrongfloors.com

Gracious Home, see above

Hardwood Information Center, 400 Penn Center Boulevard, Suite 530, Pittsburgh, PA 15235, 800/373-9663, Fax: 412/829-0844, www.hardwood.org., Publications: www.hardwood.org/write_us.htm

smartideas

When You Need To Know

LIBRARIES & MUSEUMS

Library of Congress
1101 Independence Ave. SE
Washington, DC 20540;
Phone: 202/707-5000
E-mail: vso@loc.gov
Internet: www.loc.gov

KENNEDY LIBRARY & MUSEUM

Columbia Point
Boston, MA 02125
Phone: 877/616-4599
TTY: 617/929-1221
Fax: 617/929-4538
E-mail: library@kennedy.nara.gov
Internet: www.jfklibrary.org

VIRTUAL MUSEUM OF ART

http://virtualmuseumofart.com

T I M E
S A V E R

Appliance
Questions

•

Association of
Home Appliance
Manufacturers
1111 19th Street
NW Suite 402,
Washington, DC
20036,
202/872-5955,
Fax: 202/872-
9354,
www.aham.org

Kmart, see page 359

Lowe's, see page 359

Marble Institute of America, 30 Eden Alley, Ste. 301, Columbus, OH 43215, 614/228-6194, Fax: 614/461-1497, E-mail: stoneassociations@hotmail.com, www.marble-institute.com

National Paint & Coatings Association (including information on dealing with lead paint and leftover paint), www.paint.org.

National Paint and Decorating Retailers Association, www.pdra.org

National Wood Flooring Association, 16388 Westwoods Business Park, Ellisville, MO, 63021, 800/422-4556, Fax: 636/391-5161, E-mail: info@nwfa.org, www.woodfloors.org

Porcelain Enamel Institute, 5696 Peachtree Parkway, P. O. Box 920220, Norcross, GA 30092, 770/242-2632, Fax: 770/446-1452, E-mail: penamel@aol.com, www.porcelainenamel.com

Restoration Hardware, 800/762-1005, www.restorationhardware.com

Seabrook Wallcoverings, 800/238-9152, www.seabrookwallcoverings.com

Target, see page 359

The Home Depot, 800/553-3199, www.homedepot.com

Tile Council of America (for professionals only), 100 Clemson Research Blvd., Anderson, SC 29625, 864/646-8453, www.tileusa.com

Wallcoverings Association, 401 N. Michigan Ave., Chicago, IL 60611, 312/644-6610. www.wallcoverings.org

Williams Sonoma, 800/541-2233, www. williams-sonoma.com

CHAPTER 4: FURNISHINGS CARE

Eddie Bauer Home, see page 359

Gracious Home, see page 359

Sotheby's, www.sothebys.com; 800/444-3709. To purchase Sotheby's Restoration professional furniture wax: www.sothebys.com, or call 800/444-3709 for information.

Williams Sonoma, see above

CHAPTER 5: KITCHEN KEEPING

American Homeowners Foundation, 6776 Little Falls Rd., Arlington, VA 22213, 800/489-7776, www.americanhomeowners.org

American Institute of Architects, 1735 New York Ave. NW, Washington, DC 20006, 800/242-3837, www.aia.org

American Society of Interior Designers, 608 Massachusetts Ave NE, Washington, DC 20002, 800/775-2743, www.asid.org

Association of Home Appliance Manufacturers, 1111 19th St. NW, Suite 402, Washington, DC 20036, 202/872-5955

Better Homes and Gardens Magazine, www.bhg.com

Chefs (professional restaurant equipment for home chefs), 800/338-3232, www.chefscatalog.com

Cookware Manufacturers Association, Box 531335, Mountain Brook, AL 35253, 205/802-7600, Fax: 205/802-7610, E-mail: hrushing@cookware.org, www.cookware.org

Hold Everything, see page 359

International Solid Surface Fabricators Association, (information online about solid-surface material used for countertops), www.issfa.com

Kitchen Collage, 2745 100th St., Urbandale, IA 50322, 515/270-8202

National Association of Homebuilders, 1201 15th St. NW, Washington, DC 20005, 800/368-5242, www.nahb.com

National Association of the Remodeling Industry, 780 Lee St., Des Plaines, IL 60016, 847/298-9200, Fax: 847-298-9225, www.nari.org

National Kitchen and Bath Association, 687 Willow Grove St., Hackettstown, NY 07840, 908/852-0033, www.nkba.com

Restoration Hardware, see page 360

Rubbermaid, Inc., www.rubbermaid.com

Sears PartsDirect, consumer help to find parts and accessories from 400 manufacturers for household items such as appliances, power tools, lawn and garden equipment, and home electronics. Site also contains owner's manuals for most major appliance brands. Parts: 800/366-7278, General information: 800/469-4663, www.sears.com/partsdirect

Target Stores, see page 359

The Home Depot, see page 360

Williams-Sonoma, see page 360

CHAPTER 6: LIVING & DINING ROOMS

ABC Carpet & Home Outlet, 777 S. Congress, Delray Beach, FL 33445, 561/279-7777

Albright Lighting and Interiors, see page 358

American Lighting Association, P.O. Box 420288, Dallas, TX 75342-0288, 800/274-4484, www.americanlightingassoc.com

Calico Corners, 800/213-6366, www.calicocorners.com

Carpet and Rug Institute, see Expert Care Tips box above

The Curtain Exchange, 3947 Magazine St., New Orleans, LA 70115, 504/897-2444; Fax 504/269-8488; thecurtainexchange.com

Home Remedies

EXPERT CARE TIPS

These trade associations provide help and product information to consumers.

Soap and Detergent Association
1500 K St. NW, Suite 300
Washington, DC 20005
Phone 202/347-2900
Fax: 202/347-4110
E-mail: info@sdahq.org
Internet: www.sdahq.org

Carpet and Rug Institute
310 Holiday Ave.
Dalton, GA 30720
Consumer Information: 800/882-8846
Fax: 706/278-8835
Internet: www.carpet-rug.com;
Consumer publications: Order online.

The Curtain Exchange, 1183 Howell Mill Road, Atlanta, GA

Design Store at the Door Store, 1201 3rd Ave. at 70th Street, New York, NY 10021; 123 W. 17th Street, New York, NY 10011; and 67 Old Country Rd. Carl Place, Long Island, NY

Door Store, 1 Park Ave., New York, NY 10016, 877/366-7786, E-mail: info@doorstorefurniture.com, www.doorstorefurniture.com

Forythe Fabrics and Furniture, 1190 Foster Place NW, Atlanta, GA 30354, 404/351-6050

GE North America Lighting Institute, 800/327-0533, www.gelighting.com/na/home/; Consumer Publications: Available online

International Association of Lighting Designers, Suite 9-104, The Merchandise Mart, 200 World Trade Center, Chicago, IL 60654, 312/527-3677, www.iald.org

Lexington Furniture Industries, (dropleaf table on page 163), 800/539-4636; www.lexington.com

Osram Sylvania, www.sylvania.com

Philips Lighting (information on compact fluorescent technology), 800/555-0050, www.lighting.philips.com/nam

Projects Contemporary Furniture, (nesting tables on page 229) 501 E. Locust St., Des Moines, IA 50309, 515/557-1833

Room & Board, 800/486-6554, E-mail: shop@roomandboard.com, www.roomandboard.com

Swedish Blonde Corporation, (demilune table on page 229), 800/274-9096, www.swedish-blonde.com

Waverly Fabrics, www.waverly.com

Whittier Wood Products (unfinished furniture), 3787 W. 1st Ave., Eugene, OR 97402. Locate dealers: 800/653-3336

CHAPTER 7: BEDROOMS & BATHS

Albright Lighting, see page 358

Bath Enclosure Manufacturers Association, 2945 SW Wanamaker Drive, Suite A, Topeka, KS 66614-5321, E-mail: bema@glasswebsite.com; www.glasswebsite.com/bema

Bed, Bath & Beyond, see page 358

Better Sleep Council, www.bettersleep.org

Burlington Coat Factory, see page 358

Calico Corners, see page 361

Chambers, (bed and bath linens), 3025 Market St., Camp Hill, PA 800/334-1254

The Company Store, 800/285-3696, www.thecompanystore.com

Cotton Incorporated World Headquarters, 6399 Weston Parkway, Cary, NC 27513, 919/678-2220, Fax: 919/678-2230, www.cottoninc.com

Eddie Bauer Home, see page 359

Garnet Hill (bed and bath linens), 231 Main St., Franconia, NH

SAFETY ALERT

Help with Radon

For a general clearinghouse on radon concerns: AirChek Radon Information Center, 570 Butler Bridge Road, Fletcher, NC 28732-9365; 828/684-0893; Fax: 828/684-8498; www.radon.com

03580-4803, 800/622-6216, www.garnethill.com

Gracious Home, see page 359

Hold Everything, see page 359

Hunter-Douglas, 800/937-7895, www.hunterdouglas.com

Hunter Fans, 800/448-6837

IKEA, see page 359

JC Penney Home Store, 800/322-1189, www.jcpenney.com

Kmart, see page 359

Lands' End, 800/963-4816, www.landsend.com

Linens 'n Things, see page 359

National Kitchen and Bath Association, see page 361

Pottery Barn Bed + Bath, 888/779-0557

Target, see page 359

Williams Sonoma, see page 360

Younkers, Des Moines IA 515/244-1112

CHAPTER 8: LINENS & LAUNDRY

Amana Appliances, Attn: Consumer Affairs, 2800 220th Trail, Amana, IA 52204, 800/843-0304, www.amana.com
Consumer Publications: Online or by fax 800/843-0304 (option "2")

Bed, Bath and Beyond, see page 358

Burlington Coat Factory, see page 358

Cotton Incorporated, see page 362

Gracious Home, see page 359

JC Penney Home Store, see page 362

Kmart, see page 359

Linens 'n Things, see page 359

Maytag, Maytag Customer Service, 240 Edwards Street, Cleveland, TN 37311, 800/688-9900, www.maytag.com

Pottery Barn Bed + Bath, see page 362

Soap and Detergent Association, see Expert Care Tips box on page 361

Target, see page 359

Whirlpool, 2000 N. M-63, Benton Harbor, MI 49022-2692, 800-253-1301, E-mail: Whirlpool_CIC@email.Whirlpool.com www.whirlpool.com, Publications: Order online

Williams Sonoma, see page 360

Younkers, see above

CHAPTER 9: HOUSE SYSTEMS

Chimney Safety Institute of America, 8752 Robbins Rd Indianapolis, IN 46268, 800/536-0118 (recording/takes voicemail only), Fax: 317/871-0841, E-mail: csia@csia.org, www.csia.org

TIPTAG N⁰ **36**

Health & Safety

Check out the websites for consumer information and safety tips.

NSC ENVIRONMENTAL HEALTH CENTER DIVISION:
• 1025 Connecticut Ave., NW
Suite 1200
Washington, DC 20036
Phone: 202/293-2270
Fax: 202/293-0032
Internet: www.nsc.org/ehc.htm.

NATIONAL SAFETY COUNCIL:
• 1121 Spring Lake Drive
Itasca, IL 60143-3201
Phone: 630/285-1121
Fax: 630/285-1315
Internet: www.nsc.org

Fluidmaster Inc. (information on common plumbing problems), 30800 Rancho Viejo Rd., San Juan Capistrano, CA, 92675, Technical services: 800/631-2011, Fax: 949/728-2485, E-mail: professorflush@fluidmaster.com, www.fluidmaster.com

Gas Appliance Manufacturers Association, 2107 Wilson Blvd., Ste. 600, Arlington, VA 22201, 703/525-7060, Fax: 703/525-6790, E-mail: information@gamanet.org, www.gamanet.org, Publications: Order online

GE Answer Center, 800/626-2000, www.geappliances.com/geac/index.htm

GE North America Lighting Institute, see page 362

Hard-to-Find Tools, 877/468-3580, www.brookstone.com

Hearth Education Foundation, 1601 N. Kent St., Ste. 1001, Arlington, VA 22209, 703/524-8030, Fax: 703/522-0548, E-mail: info@hearthed.com, www.hearthed.com

Hearth Products Association, (HPA), 1601 North Kent Street, Suite 1001, Arlington VA 22209, 703/522-0086, Fax: 703/522-0548, E-mail: hpamail@hearthassociation.org, www.hearthassoc.org

The Home Depot, see page 360

Home Ventilating Institute, a division of AMCA International, 30 W. University Drive, Arlington Heights, IL 60004, 847/394-0150, Fax: 847/253-0088, E-mail: general@hvi.org, www.hvi.org, Consumer Publications: www.hvi.org/directory

Kinsman Company Inc. (gardener's catalog), P.O. Box 428, Pipersville, PA 18947, 800/733-4146, www.kinsmangarden.com

Langenbach, (garden tools), 800/362-1991, www.langenbach.com

Lowe's, see page 359

MidAmerican Energy, 888/427-5632, www.midamericanenergy.com

National Chimney Sweep Guild, 8752 Robbins Rd., Indianapolis, IN 46268, 317/871-0030, Fax: 317/871-0841, E-mail: office@ncsg.org, www.ncsg.org

National Fire Protection Association, 1 Batterymarch Park, P.O. Box 9101, Quincy, MA 02269-9101, 800/344-3555 or 617/770-3000, Fax: 617/770-0700, www.nfpa.org

Rumford Fireplaces (for a printed catalog, call Superior Clay Corp., 888/254-1905), Buckley Rumford Fireplace, 1035 Monroe Street, Port Townsend, WA 98368, 360/385-9974, Fax: 360/385-1624 www.rumford.com

Smith & Hawken (garden tools), 800/940-1170, E-mail: smithandhawkencustomerservice@jcplsh.com, www.smith-hawken.com

The Stanley Works (tools), 1000 Stanley Dr., New Britain, CT 06053, 860/225-5111, Fax: 860/827-3895, www.stanleyworks.com

ToolSource (online source for power and hand tools with more

BUDGET STRETCHER

Lower Utilities

•

The Alliance to Save, a nonprofit organization, offers information on-line on reducing energy waste in the home. The Home Energy Checkup section calculates efficiency improvements using climate types and energy prices, www.ase.org.

than 11,000 products from 100 brands), 888/220-8350,
www.toolsource.com

Vent-Free Gas Products Alliance, 2111 Wilson Blvd., Ste 600,
Arlington, VA 22201-3001, 703/875-8615, Fax: 703/276-8089,
E-mail: mscsmitty@cs.com, www.gamanet.org/consumer/ventfree
Consumer Publications: Order online

CHAPTER 10: HOME ENVIRONMENT

American Animal Hospital Association, 12575 W.
Bayaud Avenue, Lakewood, CO, 80228, 800/883-6301,
www.healthypet.com, Consumer Publications: Healthypet
Bookstore, AAHA, Dept. 945, Denver, CO 80291-0945,
303/986-1700

American Association of Poison Control Centers,
www.aapcc.org

American Lung Association, (in-home air quality,
asthma, and radon information), 1740 Broadway, New
York, NY 10019, 800/586-4872, E-mail: info@lungusa.org,
www.lungusa.org, Consumer Publications:
www.lungusa.org/pub

American Veterinary Medical Association,
1931 N. Meacham Rd., Ste. 100, Schaumburg, IL
60173, 847/925-8070, Fax: 847/925-1329, E-mail:
avmainfo@avma.org, Veterinarian locator (by state):
www.avma.org/care4pets/othrstlo.htm

**ASPCA National Animal Poison Control
Center,** Emergency Hotline: 888/426-4435, 1717 S.
Philo Road, Suite #36, Urbana, IL 61802, 217/337-
5030, Fax: 217/337-0599, napcc.aspca.org

**Asthma and Allergy Foundation of
America,** 1233 20th St. NW, Ste. 402,
Washington, DC 20036, 800/727-8462, E-mail:
info@aafa.org, www.aafa.org

**Energy Efficiency and Renewable Energy
Clearinghouse,** P.O. Box 3048 Merrifield, VA 22116; 800/363-
3732, www.eren.doe.gov

Indoor Air Quality Information Clearinghouse, P.O. Box
37133, Washington, DC 20013-7133, 800/438-4318, Fax: 703/356-
5386, E-mail: iaqinfo@aol.com, www.epa.gov/iaq/

International Society of Arboriculture (information on tree
care and preventing tree loss). To find a certified aborist in your area,
call 217/355-9411, E-mail: isa@isa-arbor.com, www.isa-arbor.com

National Asthma Education and Prevention Program of
the National Heart, Lung, and Blood Institute, (guidelines for the
diagnosis and management of asthma), 301/592-8573,
www.nhlbi.nih.gov/about/naepp/

smart ideas

Community Info

REAL ESTATE WEB SITES

Considering moving to a new
community or want to know
more about neighborhoods in your
area? The following information is
easy to access from the Internet:
crime statistics, area school statistics,
local maps, assessed property
values, agent, lender, and builder
locators, credit reports, mortgage
rates, insurance rates, loan
calculators, home listings.

HELPFUL SITES WITH LINKS

National Association of Realtors
(NAR), www.realtor.com;
National Association of Exclusive
Buyer Agents (NAEBA); Cendant
Mobility's www.cendantmobility.
com/moving/int_mov.html

Petco (articles, coupons, and more information for pet owners), www.petco.com

Water Quality Association, 4151 Naperville Road, Lisle, IL 60532, 630/505-0160, E-mail: info@mail.wqa.org, www.wqa.org

CHAPTER 11: ENTERTAINING

Ballard Designs, 800/367-2775, www.ballarddesigns.com/home

Beverly Bremer Silver Shop (matching silver flatware), 3164 Peachtree Road, Atlanta, GA 30305, 800/270-4009, www.beverlybremer.com

Croghan's Jewel Box, 308 King St., Charleston, SC 29401; 843/723-3594

Gracious Home, see page 359

Joseph's Jewelers, 320 Sixth Ave., Des Moines, IA 50309; 515/283-1961

Pier One Imports, see page 359

The Silver Queen (replacement and matching sterling silver and silver plate), 730 N. Indian Rocks Rd., Belleaire Bluffs, FL 33770, 800/262-3134 ext. 5000, E-mail: sales@silverqueen.com, www.silverqueen.com

Sotheby's, see page 360

S. Wyler Inc. (silver polish source) Silversmiths since 1890, 941 Lexington Ave., New York, NY 10021, 212/879-9848

Younker's, see page 363

CHAPTER 12: ETIQUETTE

The RSVP Shoppe, Ltd, 328 King St., Charleston, SC 29401, 843-577-9740; Fax: 843/577-0064

CHAPTER 13: RECORDS & REFERENCES

American Homeowners Foundation, see page 360.

Exposures (catalog source for archival photograph albums, scrapbooks, framing materials, and other supplies. Outlet stores in Norwalk, CT and Oshkosh, WI), 800/222-4947, Fax: 888/345-3702, E-mail: csr@exposuresonline.com, www.exposureonline.com

Kolo (colorful photo albums and journals), www.kolousa.com

Light Impressions (archival albums, storage and presentation, frames, and framing accessories), 800/828-6216, Fax: 800/828-5539, www.lightimpressionsdirect.com

Mayflower Transit and United Van Lines (websites offer helpful checklists and information to prepare for a move), www.mayflower.com, www.unitedvanlines.com

The Statue of Liberty-Ellis Island Foundation, American Family Immigration History Center, Department W, 52 Vanderbilt Ave., New York, NY 10017-3898, 212/883-1986, Fax: 212/883-1069, www.ellisisland.org

Additional Sources

These websites provide consumer information, product descriptions, helpful hints, and online order forms for hard-to-find products.

ABC Carpet & Home, 881 and 888 Broadway, New York, NY 10003; 212/473-3000, www.abchome.com

Arm & Hammer, Church & Dwight Co. Inc., (Brands include Arm & Hammer Baking Soda products, Brillo, Cameo Cleaners, Parsons' Ammonia, Snobowl), 469 North Harrison St., Princeton, NJ 08543, 609/683-5900 Fax: 609/683-5902, Cleaning tips website: www.armhammer.com; Corporate information website: www.churchdwight.com

Clorox, 510/271-7000, E-mail: info@clorox.com, www.clorox.com/products

Colgate-Palmolive Company, (Brands include Ajax, Dynamo Laundry Detergent, Fab Laundry Detergent, Hill's Pet Foods, Murphy Oil Soap, Palmolive Dishwashing Liquids), 300 Park Ave., New York, NY 10022, 212/310-2000, www.colgate.com

The Dial Corporation, (Brands include Purex detergents and bleaches, Renuzit, Zout), 15501 North Dial Boulevard, Scottsdale, AZ 85260-1619, 800-528-0849 or 480/754-3425, E-mail: Dial@2RCS.com, www.dialcorp.com

Hill's Pet Foods, 800/445-5777, www.hillspet.com

HomePortfolio, (a website that helps shoppers use the Internet to find retail showrooms that carry the home design products they want. The site lists showrooms nationwide. Each listing has the dealer's address, telephone number, hours, and short description of the showroom and its focus), www.homeportfolio.com

ImproveNet, (a website geared to home improvement, with contractors, architects, and designers, includes information on professional references and legal and credit histories), www.ImproveNet.com

Murphy's1 Oil Soap, 800/486-7627, www.murphyoilsoap.com

OxiClean, Orange Glo International, 8765 East Orchard Road, Suite 703, Englewood, CO 80111, 877/836-5934, E-mail: orangeglo@protocolusa.com, www.oxiclean.com

Restoration Hardware, see page 360

SC Johnson Co. (Brands include Drano, Fantastik, Glade, Off, Pledge, Raid, Saran Wrap, Scrubbing Bubbles, Vanish, Windex, Ziplock), 800/494-4855, www.scjbrands.com

Western Red Cedar Lumber Association, www.wrcla.org

TIP TAG №37

Pest Control

FOR QUESTIONS:

- "Ask the Bug Man," Richard Fagerlund, Integrated Pest Management, University of New Mexico, Albuquerque, NM 87131; phone 505/277-9904; E-mail: fagerlun@unm.edu; Internet: www.askthebugman.com

OR CHECK THESE SITES:

- Iowa State University, Department of Entomology; Insectary Building, Iowa State Ames, IA 50011 3140; Internet: www.ent.iastate.edu.
- National Institute of Environmental Health Sciences, P.O. Box 12233, Research Triangle Park, NC 27709 phone: 919/541-3345; Internet: www.niehs.nih.gov

Special Thanks

Texas Agricultural Extension Service, Family and Consumer Sciences, Texas A & M University, College Station, TX

University of Minnesota, Department of Design, Housing and Apparel, St. Paul, MN

Iowa State University Extension, Ames, IA

American Furniture Manufacturers Association, High Point, NC

The Container Store, Dallas, TX

Sotheby's, New York, NY

Crate and Barrel, New York, NY

Mike Gavin, Gateway Computers, West Des Moines, IA

Albright's Lighting and Interiors, Des Moines, IA

Kitchen Collage of Des Moines, Des Moines, IA

Richard Fagerlund, University of New Mexico, Albuquerque, NM

Gracious Home, New York, NY

Josephs Jewelers, Des Moines, IA

Jim Haas, Audio Labs, Des Moines, IA

Maytag Corp., Newton, IA

MidAmerican Energy, Des Moines, IA

Dr. Dennis Riordan, DVM, Riordan Pet Hospital, Des Moines, IA

Drs. Allison and Tom Sullivan, DVM, Sullivan Family Pet Hospital, Johnston, IA

Resilient Floor Covering Institute, Rockville, MD

Seabrook Wallcoverings, Memphis, TN

Tile Council of America, Anderson, SC

Carpet and Rug Institute, Dalton, GA

Soap and Detergent Association, Washington, DC

U.S. Environmental Protection Agency, Washington, DC

United States Department of Agriculture, Washington, DC

Contributors

Tim Abramowitz, Janet Anderson, Susan Andrews, Lynn Blanchard, Jennifer Darling, John DeMers, Brenda Dunbar, Larry Erickson, Kristi Fuller, Brice Gaillard, Sandra Gerdes, Gretchen Kauffman, Lynn McBride, Carol McGarvey, Mell Meredith, Burns Mossman, Jerry and Joetta Moulden, Cynthia Pearson, Marilyn Rogers, Michael Satterwhite, Wade Scherrer, Colleen Sculley, Donald Severson, Margaret Smith, Pete Stephano, Carroll Stoner, Donna Talley Wendt, Charles Worthington

HEALTHY HOME

Indoor Air Quality

•

Research Products Corp. offers free information on indoor air quality, including tips on choosing a humidifier, call 800/545-2219. The Air Conditioning and Refrigeration Institute (ARI) provides consumer information on climate control. 4301 N. Fairfax Drive, Suite 425, Arlington, VA 22203 E-mail: ari@ari.org www.ari.org/consumer

INDEX

A

Accessible design, 28, 30, 151–152, 202
Acetate upholstery fabric, 166
Acrylic
    carpets, 181
    clothing, 225
    upholstery fabric, 166
Address books, 337
Afghans, cleaning, 124
Air cleaners and purifiers, 284–285
Air-conditioners. *See Cooling systems*
Air quality, indoor, 282, 284–285
Alarm systems, 262
Alcohol
    alternatives to, 302
    children and, 288, 310
    entertaining and, 299–300, 302, 314
    stains, removing, 80
    stocking, 299
    storing, 20, 22, 26, 27
Allergies
    bedding and, 197
    indoor pollutants and, 282
    to pets, 266
    vacuum filters and, 81
Aluminum cookware, 132, 134
Aluminum outdoor furniture, 253
American Lung Association, 285
Ammonia, 101, 102
Anniversary parties and gifts, 306–307, 327
Anodized aluminum cookware, 134, 141
Antibiotic ointments, 41
Antiques
    china, 292
    furniture, caring for, 112–113
    linens, cleaning, 230
    rugs, cleaning, 120
Anti-scald devices, 241, 288
Antiseptic solutions, 41
Ants, 275, 276, 277
Apartments, storage in, 46–48, 207–208
Appliances, large, 140–148, 150, 152–154
Appliances, small
    basic, 127, 128, 145
    care and maintenance of, 136, 138–140
    safety measures, 128
Armoires, 144, 172–173, 208
Art, cleaning, 122
Artifacts, preserving, 342, 344, 345
Asbestos, 282
Aspirin, 41
Attics, 44, 45, 46, 238
Au pairs, 66
Automobiles, travel gear for, 249

B

Baby showers, 306
Baby-sitters, 66
Backsplashes, wallpapered, 92
Bacteria control, 100, 158

Baker's racks, 27
Bakeware, 127, 128, 129, 136
Baking soda, 101, 238, 239
Bamboo furniture, 111, 253
Bar storage, 20, 22, 26, 27, 299
Basements, 44–46, 48
Baskets, for storage, 11, 13, 23, 29, 30, 31, 43
Bathrooms
    accessible design of, 202
    children's, 204
    cleaning, 56, 58, 92, 199, 203
    fixtures, 199, 200–202
    guest supplies in, 40, 42
    lighting in, 204
    medicine cabinets, 40, 41
    in one-room apartments, 47–48
    skirted vanities, 40
    storage in, 39–42
    ventilation in, 201
Bats, 280
Bed linens, 55, 187, 193–197, 208, 210–211. *See also Sheets*
Bedrooms
    children's, 34–35, 197–198, 200
    cleaning, 58, 60
    furniture, 32, 185–186, 188–189
    guest, 211
    lighting in, 176, 189–190, 191
    storage in, 31–35, 189, 190
    window coverings in, 192–193
Beds
    bunk, 200
    buying, 186, 188–189
    children's, 34, 35, 197–198, 200
    daybeds, 189
    fold-down, 32
    futons, 185
    making, 187, 193–197
    sofa, 188
    split box springs, 185
    storage under, 31, 34
    water, 188
Bedspreads, 196
Benzene, 282
Bills, organizing, 13, 23, 337
Birch furniture, 169, 174
Birds, as pets, 272–273
Birthday parties, 307, 308
Blankets, 196, 197
Bleach, chlorine, 59, 101, 102
Bleached wood, 173
Blenders, 136
Blinds
    in bedrooms, 192, 198
    cleaning, 115, 117, 119
    safety measures, 192
Blood stains, removing
    from carpets, 79
    from clothing, 224
    from hard surfaces, 82
Bookcases, 18, 23, 34, 244
Books
    care of, 353–354

Budget Stretcher Index

A – B

Alcoholic beverages
    alternatives to, 302
    serving, 300
Appliances, painting, 150
Beds, buying, 188
Bookcases, 18

C

Cabinets, restoring metal, 100
Carpets
    colorfastness test for, 78
    pads for, 182
China, vintage, 292
Clothing, ironing, 220
Coffeemakers, cleaning, 138
Cookware, nonstick, 142
Cork floors, care and cleaning of, 88
Cleaning, hiring baby-sitter during, 58
Computerized money management, 340
Curtain care, 118
Cushions, furniture, 254

D – F

Disposals, garbage, 154
Ethnic restaurants, 322
Fabric weaves, 166
Fireplaces, gas, 260
Flatware, everyday, 296
Floors, cork, 88
Furniture
    "aged" metal, 116
    mahogany alternatives, 174
    upholstered, shopping for, 162, 166

G – K

Garbage disposals, stalled, 154
Gas logs, 260
Houseplants, insects on, 274
Housewarming gifts, 326
Ironing clothing, 220
Irons, caring for, 224
Kitchens, storage in, 30
Continued on page 372

for children, 353, 354
recommended reading, 352–353
recycling, 354
reference, 347, 350, 352
storing, 45
Bookshelves
built-in, 19, 24, 26, 32, 42, 47
constructing, 17, 23, 35
for display, 22
floor-to-ceiling, 23, 26, 32
using, 353
Boxes, storage, 32, 37
Box springs, 185, 186, 188
Brass, cleaning and polishing, 122
Bread machines, 136
Breakers, circuit, 241
Brick, cleaning and sealing, 84, 92–93
Bridal showers, 304, 306
Brocade upholstery, 108
Brooms, 99
Brushes, bathroom, 203
Buffets, 300, 302
Bunk beds, 200
Burned-on food, removing, 134
Burner grates, cleaning, 143
Business thank-you notes, 326
Butcher block, 100, 155
Butler's pantries, 26–27
Buttons, extra, 56

C

Cabinets
bathroom, 40
built-in, 24
in butler's pantries, 26–27
china, 24
cleaning, 96–98
computer, 20
hinges, repairing, 98
in home offices, 42
kitchen, 28, 30, 96–97
medicine, 40, 41
metal, 97, 100
television, 20, 22, 23
Cages, bird, 272–273
Calamine lotion, 41
Candles and holders, 309
Candlesticks, cleaning, 122, 124
Cane furniture, cleaning, 111
Canvas furniture, 108, 253
Carbon monoxide, 58, 237, 239, 240, 242, 282
Carpet beetles, 278, 280
Carpets
all-purpose stain remover for, 80
buying, 180–182
cleaning, 57, 77–81, 82
cleaning services for, 57, 67
colorfastness test for, 78
crayon marks on, 93
fibers in, 180, 181, 182
measuring for, 181
pads for, 182
protectors for, 75
stain removal, 79, 80–81, 82

VOCs in, 284
weaves of, 167
Carports, storage in, 46
Cassette tapes, caring for, 351
Cast iron cookware, 134, 135, 141
Cats, 266–270
CDs, caring for, 351
Cedar closets, 38–39
Cedar furniture, 170
Ceiling fans, 94, 190
Ceilings, cleaning, 93, 94
Cell phones, etiquette and, 330
Centerpieces, 296, 298
Ceramics
accessories, 122
cookware, 135–136
dinnerware, 293
Chairs. *See also Upholstered furniture; Wood furniture*
buying, 162, 164, 173
dining, 173, 175
styles, 175
unusual materials for, 111
Chandeliers
bulbs for, 179
cleaning, 55, 94, 121–122
hanging, 178
Checks, restaurant, 321–322
Chemicals, storing, 46, 48, 50, 238
Cherry furniture, 171
Chests of drawers, 185–186, 208
Chimney sweeps, 67
Child-care options, 64, 65–66, 68–70
Children
bathrooms for, 204
bedroom furniture for, 34, 35, 197–198, 200, 288
etiquette and, 317–318, 321, 324, 325, 332, 334
holiday safety and, 288, 310
household hazards and, 139, 156, 158, 286, 288
parties for, 307, 308
pets and, 266, 288
reading by, 353, 354
recycling by, 156
sleepwear for, 230
storage for, 34–35
tobacco smoke and, 286
as uninvited guests, 298
China, 291–293
China cabinets, 24
Chintz upholstery, 108
Chlorine bleach, 59, 101, 102
Chocolate stains, removing, 226
Christening gowns, preserving, 344
Christmas, 240, 310
Chrome furniture, cleaning, 111
Cigarette burns, on laminate floors, 88
Circuit breakers, 241
Cleaning. *See also specific materials, rooms, and surfaces*
center, 56
fall, 60, 61

Budget Stretcher Index

Continued from page 371

L – O

Lampshades, 124
Laundry, sorting, 214
Liquor cabinet, converted, 20
Mahogany furniture, alternatives to, 174
Metal cabinets, restoring, 100
Metal furniture, cleaning, 116
Money management, computerized, 340
Nonstick cookware, 142

P – R

Pantries, in vintage armoires, 144
Parties
budgets for, 306
in summer, 312
Pillows, replacing, 186
Radiators, bleeding, 236
Renting storage space, 50
Restaurants, ethnic, 322

S – T

Servers, 24
Sheets, mixing and matching, 208
Shirts, laundering, 218
Sideboards, 24
Sinks, re-enameling, 150
Slipcovers, 106
Storage
bookcases, 18
containers, 12, 26
in dining rooms, 24
in kitchens, 30, 144
liquor, 20
rental units, 50
in vintage furniture, 144

U – Z

Upholstered furniture, buying, 162, 166
Water conservation, 240
Water heaters, maintaining, 242
Window frames, cleaning and repairing, 98
Wood cleaners, 110

frequency, 53–54
for holidays, 60, 94
outdoors, 58, 59
products, 56, 59, 101–102, 110, 203
routines, setting up, 53
safety measures, 101–102
service professionals, 57, 61–65, 67
shortcuts, 54, 56
spring, 55, 57–58, 60
supplies, 56, 59, 73, 99
tools, 56, 99
Clocks, caring for, 122
Closets
    cedar, 38–39
    children's, 38
    cleaning, 56
    home offices in, 47
    humidity in, 284
    laundry rooms in, 43
    linen, 207–208
    mildew in, 39
    nooks in, 22
    organizing, 33, 36–39
    for secure storage, 261
    space guide, 39
Clothing
    donating, 14–15
    dry cleaning, 38, 225, 284
    fabric care, 224
    folding, 220
    hanging, 39, 44
    ironing, 219, 220, 223
    laundering, 60–61, 216, 218–219, 221, 228
    seasonal cleaning and, 57–58, 60
    shirts, washing and ironing, 218, 219, 220
    stain removal from, 218, 224, 226–228
    storing, 31, 34, 37, 44, 45. See also Closets
    trading, 15
Clutter, preventing, 53
Cockroaches, 275, 276, 277
Cocktail parties, 302–303
Coffeemakers, 136, 138, 145
Coffee stains, removing
    from carpets, 80
    from clothing, 229
    from tile, 82
Coffee tables, choosing size of, 172
Cold packs, 41
Collectibles, étagères for, 23
Colorfastness, testing for
    carpets, 78
    embroidered linens, 230
    laundry, 218
Comforters, 194–196
Compact disks, caring for, 351
Compactors, trash, 155–156
Composite furniture, 170
Computer cabinets, 20
Computers
    care and cleaning of, 349–350

data protection, 350
digital photos and, 340
document storage, 339
money management programs for, 340
paper for, 350
power surges and outages and, 349
researching family history on, 345, 346
tax programs for, 340
useful functions of, 340
Concrete
    cleaning, 84, 92–93, 100
    painting, 84, 86
Condos, storage in, 46–48
Consignment shops, 15
Convection ovens, 142–143
Conversations, social, 332–333, 334
Cooking
    outdoors, 260–261
    safety measures, 139, 260, 261
Cooktops, 142, 143, 148
Cookware
    basic, 127–129
    caring for, 134–136
    choosing, 132, 134–136, 141
    make-do, 127
    nonstick, 142
    storing, 27–28, 30, 54
Cooling systems, 67, 237–238
Copper cookware, 134, 141
Cork
    floors, care and cleaning of, 88
    wall coverings, cleaning, 92
Correspondence, 324–326, 328–330
Cotton
    clothing, 225
    sheets, 210
    upholstery fabric, 166
Countertops, cleaning and protecting, 94–95, 98, 100–101
Crates, plastic, 35
Crayon marks, removing, 86, 88, 92–93, 226
Cribs, 36, 198, 210
Crickets, 275, 277
Crockery cookers, 138
Crystal, 295–296, 297
Cupboards, 24, 27
Curtains, care and cleaning of, 116–117, 118
Cushions, on outdoor furniture, 254
Cutting boards, 155, 158

D
Damask upholstery, 108
Dampers, 238
Daybeds, 189
Day care, 64, 65–66, 68–70
Deep-fat fryers, 139
Dehumidifiers, 281–282
Deicers, 249–250
Delicates, washing, 218, 221
Dens, storage in, 19, 22
Desiccants, homemade, 284

Family Friendly
Index
A – B
Accessible design
    bathrooms, 202
    kitchens, 152
Ad for nanny, 68
Au pairs, 66
Basements, sports gear in, 46
Bathrooms
    accessible design of, 202
    guest amenities in, 42
Beds, children's, 200
Birthday parties, children's, 308
C
Carpet stains, 82
Child-care options, 66
Children
    beds for, 200
    closets for, 38
    dogs and, 266
    etiquette and, 324, 334
    tobacco smoke and, 286
    as uninvited guests, 298
Closets, for children, 38
Clothing, dirt and mud on, 228
Comforters, down, 194
D – H
Dogs, children and, 266
Etiquette, children and, 324, 332, 334
Fabrics
    for sofas, 164
    laminated, 108
Garages, sports gear in, 46
Guests
    bathroom amenities for, 42
    uninvited, 298
H – Q
Homework, organizing space for, 34
Invitations, responding to, 304
Light, reading, 176
Organization of homework, 34
Paint finishes, 90
R – Z
Rugs, stains on, 120
Safety measures, 244
Scrapbooks, 344
Sofa fabrics, 164
Sports gear, storing, 46
Stains, on rugs, 120
Storage, 46
Table manners, 318, 320
Videotaping family events, 348

Healthy Home Index

B – E
Bacteria, on dishcloths and sponges, 158
Cats, and toxoplasmosis, 270
Desiccants, homemade, 284
Dishcloths, bacteria on, 158
Dogs, cleaning up after, 268

F – K
Floors, pet stains on, 74
Furniture, removing odors from, 112
Grout, removing mildew from, 94
Humidifiers, 280, 282
Humidity, in closets, 284
Ice-Melt Chemicals, 250
Illnesses caused by house systems, 238

L – Q
Lyme disease, 278
Medicine cabinets, 40
Mildew, removing from grout, 94
Odors, removing from refrigerators, 140
Pest control, 276
Pet stains, 74

R – Z
Refrigerator odors, removing, 140
Sponges, bacteria on, 158
Stains, pet, 74
Ticks and Lyme disease, 278
Toxoplasmosis, 270
Vinegar, cleaning with, 102
Wood floors, pet stains on, 74

Desks, 32, 34, 35, 42, 43
Detergent, 102, 229
Diapers and diaper pails, 288
Digital Versatile Disks (DVDs), 346, 351
Dimmers, light, 178, 180, 245
Dining areas
 decluttering, 53
 furniture for, 24, 26, 169, 173, 175
 storage in, 24, 26
Dining tables, buying, 169, 173
Discoloration, in laundry, 228
Diseases carried by animals, 270, 284
Dishes, 24, 26–28, 30. *See also China*
Dishwashers, 146–148, 153
Displays
 in children's rooms, 200
 in dining areas, 24
 in kitchens, 28, 30
 plates, 24, 28
 shelving options for, 22, 23
Disposals, garbage, 154–155
Dogs, 265–266, 267, 268–270
Donating to charity, 14–15
Doors
 locks for, 259, 261–262
 repairing, 257
 security measures for, 261–262
Down comforters, 194, 196
Drains
 air-conditioning, 237
 clogged and slow, 101, 155
 frozen, 240
 garbage-disposal, 155
Draperies, care and cleaning of, 116–117
Drawers
 in bedroom chests, 185–186
 dividers for, 27, 29, 30, 189
 in storage units, 172–173
Dresses, ironing, 223
Dry cleaning, 38, 225, 284
Dryers, 214, 216, 218–219, 223
Duct tape, 251
Dusting tools, 115
Duvets, 194, 196
DVDs (Digital Versatile Disks), 346, 351
Dye stains, removing, 82, 86

E
Earthenware, 293
Earwigs, 278
Easter, 312
Ebony furniture, 169
Elder care, 70
Electric blankets, 197
Electricity
 breakers, 241
 fuses, 241–242
 for laundry rooms, 214
 tools for working with, 236
E-mail, 330
Employees, household, 68–70
Enameled cookware, 135, 141

Enamel-finished wood, 173–174
Energy use
 dishwashers, 147, 152
 dryers, 223
 refrigerators, 146, 152
 tips for reducing, 249
 washers, 215–216
Engagement parties, 304
Entertaining. *See also Guests*
 alcohol and, 299–300, 302, 314
 anniversary parties, 306–307
 baby showers, 306
 birthday parties, 307, 308
 budget for, 306
 buffets, 300, 302
 children's parties, 307, 308
 china for, 291
 cocktail parties, 302–303
 faith holidays, 310–312
 family reunions, 307–308
 food preferences and, 299–300
 fund-raising events, 299
 holiday parties, 308, 310–312, 314
 kitchen equipment for, 128, 130
 party checklist, 303
 place cards for, 298
 planning, 299
 potlucks and progressive dinners, 303–304
 seasonal holidays, 312, 314
 setting table for, 301, 305
 stocking food for, 131–132
 storing cookware for, 27
 summer parties, 312
 supper clubs, 304
 wedding-related parties, 304, 306
Entries, organizing, 15–18
Étagères, 23
Ethnic restaurants, 322
Etiquette
 cell phones and pagers, 330
 children and, 317–318, 321, 324, 325, 332, 334
 conversations, social, 332–333, 334
 correspondence, 324–326, 328–330
 difficult situations, 328, 334
 at dinner parties, 330, 332
 e-mail, 330
 guests. *See Guests*
 introductions, 322, 324
 invitations, 298–299, 304, 324, 328–330, 334
 in restaurants, 321–322
 table manners, 318–322
 thank-you notes, 324–325, 328
 in unfamiliar situations, 317

F
Fabrics
 caring for, 225
 flame-resistant, 230
 laminated, 108
 removing pet hair from, 105
 smoothing naps on, 105

types of, 166
upholstery, 107–109, 164–166, 168
wall coverings, cleaning, 90, 91
weaves, 166, 168
for window treatments, 116
Fading, of laundry, 228
Fall cleaning chores, 60, 61
Fall maintenance checklist, 244–245
Family history
    researching, 344–345, 346
    taping, 346, 348
Family reunions, 307, 308
Fans
    attic, 238
    bathroom ventilation, 201
    ceiling. *See Ceiling fans*
    whole-house, 285
Faucets, 150, 151, 199, 202, 240
Feces stains, removing
    from clothing, 227
    from floors, 81
    from rugs, 118
Fiberboard furniture, 172
Fiberglass draperies, cleaning,
    116–117
Fibers, 108–109, 165, 180, 181, 182
Filing systems, 337
Filters
    for heating and cooling systems,
      236, 237, 238, 284
    for water, 286, 287
Finishes
    upholstered furniture, 168–169
    wood furniture, 173–174
Fire building, 253, 257
Fire extinguishers, 58, 238, 239, 255
Fireplaces
    anatomy of, 257
    gas, 237, 260
    inserts, 258
    maintaining, 258
    safety measures, 240, 255, 257–258
Fires, grease, 156, 238, 239
Fire safety, 238–240, 255, 257–258
First aid
    for pets, 268–270, 272
    supplies, 41
Fish, as pets, 270, 272
Flame-resistant sleepwear, 230
Flatware
    everyday, 296
    serving pieces, 291
    silver, 294
    stainless steel, 294–295
    storing, 27, 29, 30, 294, 295
    using correctly, 301
Flea collars, disposing of, 283
Fleas, 274, 275
Flies, 275, 277
Floors
    brick, 84
    cleaning, 59, 73–76, 81–86, 88–89
    concrete, 84, 86
    cork, 88

crayon marks on, 93
    laminate, 83, 88, 93
    linoleum, 88–89
    protectors for, 75
    removing wax buildup from, 77
    resilient, 85
    sealing, 76, 77, 82, 84
    stone, 83, 84, 93
    tile, 81–84, 85, 93
    vinyl, 83, 85–88, 89, 93
    waxing, 74, 76
    wood, 73–76
Fluorescent lightbulbs, 151, 176, 179
Food
    emergency supplies of, 131
    ethnic, 322
    frozen, 146, 158
    processors, 138–139
    safety, 146, 155, 158
    stains, 79, 80–81, 229
    stocking, 130–132, 137
Food storage
    containers for, 28, 30
    dry staples, 28, 130–131
    refrigerated, 130
    spices, 28, 29, 30
Formaldehyde, 282
Fourth of July, 312
Freezers, 144, 146, 149
Front entries, organizing, 15–18
Fryers, deep-fat, 139
Fuel
    stains, removing, 226
    storing, 50
Fungi, 282
Fur, storing, 44, 45
Furnaces
    filters in, 237, 384
    forced-air gas, 233, 234, 235
    gas odor from, 233, 237
    inspecting, 61, 233
    lighting, 233, 234
    maintaining, 236–237
    oil, 236–237
    parts of, 235
    professional services for, 237
Furniture. *See also Upholstered*
    furniture; Wood furniture;
    specific pieces and rooms
    antiques, 112–113
    for apartments and condos, 48
    construction techniques, 172
    donating, 14–15
    fine, 112–113
    fitting into rooms, 168, 185
    floor protectors for, 75
    gilded finishes on, 114
    glass, 114
    hardware, 113
    inlaid, 113–114
    laminate, 114, 172
    metal, 114, 116, 254
    odors, removing, 112
    old, 112–113, 114

Home Remedies Index

A – E
Address books, 337
Allergies, bedding and, 197
Bedding, 197, 211
Burner grates, cleaning, 143
Children, thank-you notes from, 325
Cooktops, cleaning, 143
Dimmer switches, noisy, 245
Doors, repairing, 257

F – J
Faucets, cleaning, 151
Floor wax, removing, 77
Food, emergency supplies of, 131
Furnaces, problems with, 233
Furniture, vintage, 165
Gas odors, 233
Halogen lightbulbs, handling, 245
Hard water deposits, removing, 151
Hooks, organizing with, 19

K – Q
Kitchens, storage in, 27
Leather upholstery, dyeing, 109
Lightbulbs, handling, 245
Mineral deposits, removing, 151
Mold and mildew, 281
Organization, pegs and hooks for, 19
Pegs, organizing with, 19
Pillows, refreshing, 211

R – Z
Range tops, cleaning, 143
Sealing floors, 77
Silver, polishing, 295
Storage, 19, 27
Thank-you notes, from children, 325
Walls, scrubbing, 93
Wax, removing from floors, 77

Safety Alert Index

A – E
Alarm systems, portable, 262
Alcohol and entertaining, 314
Blind cords, 192
Children and holidays, 310
Cribs, 198, 210
Day-care centers, 64

F – J
Fires, 156, 258
Flame-resistant sleepwear, 230
Food, thawed, 146
Freezer outages, 146
Furnaces, lighting, 234
Furniture, painted, 114
Garden power tools, 252
Gas grills, 248
Gas-powered yard machines, 246
Grease fires, 156
Guests, drinking and, 314
Gun safety, 48
Houseplants, toxic, 288

K – Q
Knives, kitchen, 132
Lead in paint, 114
Leaf blowers, 252
Lightbulbs, 180
Nannies, and car insurance, 70
Painted furniture, 114
Parties, children's safety during, 310
Pets, first aid for, 272
Propane gas, 248
Power tools, garden, 252

R – Z
Ranges, 156
Security systems, portable, 262
Sleepwear, flame-resistant, 230
Small appliances, 128
Stoves, 156
Tables, corners of, 170

outdoor, 60, 253–254
painted, 113, 114
ready-to-assemble, 173
special finishes on, 113–114
unfinished, 173
veneer, 113, 170, 172
vintage, 112–113, 144, 165
waxing, 110, 112–113
Fuses, 241–242
Futons, 185

G
Garage, storage in, 44, 46, 48
Garage door openers, 256
Garage sales, 14
Garbage disposals, 154–155
Gardens, maintaining, 244–245
Garden tools, 247, 252–253
Gas grills, 48, 50, 248, 261
Gasoline
    disposing of, 283
    stains, removing, 226
    storing, 48, 50
Gas logs, 260
Gas odors, 233
Gas-powered yard machines, 246
Gas water heaters, 243
Genealogy, researching, 344–345, 346
Gerbils, 270, 273
GFCIs (ground fault circuit interrupters), 241
Gifts
    anniversary, 307, 327
    baby shower, 306
    birthday, 307
    bridal shower, 306
    for hosts, 333
    housewarming, 326
    thank-you notes for, 325
Gilded finishes, cleaning, 114
Glass, cleaning, 96, 114
Glass cookware, 135–136
Glassware, 26, 27, 30, 296. *See also Stemware*
Glue, for laminate, 97–98
Granite surfaces, cleaning, 83, 100
Grass stains, 226
Grease fires, 156, 238, 239
Grease stains, removing
    from carpets, 79
    from hard surfaces, 82, 88
Great-rooms, 20
Green cards, and household employees, 69–70
Grills, 48, 50, 139, 248, 260–261
Grooming pets, 266–267
Ground fault circuit interrupters (GFCIs), 241
Grout, cleaning, 82, 94, 100
Guests
    difficult situations with, 334
    etiquette rules for, 330, 332, 333–334
    fold-down beds for, 32
    inviting, 304, 324, 328–329, 334
    linens for, 211
    supplies for, 40, 42, 331, 333
    uninvited, 298
Gum, removing
    from carpets 80
    from tile floors, 82
Gun safety, 48
Gutter-cleaning services, 57, 67

H
Halloween, 312
Halogen lightbulbs, 151, 176, 179, 245
Hampers, 31, 61
Hamsters, 270, 273
Hand washing, 288
Hanukkah, 311
Hard water deposits, 151, 242, 244
Hardwoods, 169–170, 174
Hazardous materials
    disposing of, 283
    storing, 46, 48, 50, 158, 238, 288
Hearths, outdoor, 253
Heat exchangers, 285
Heating systems, 67, 236–237, 249, 250
Herbicides, storing, 46
Holidays
    children's safety during, 288, 310
    cleaning chores, 60
    of faith, 310–312
    parties, 308, 310–312, 314
    seasonal, 312, 314
Home maintenance checklists, 244–245
Home offices, 42–43, 47
Homework, organizing space for, 34
Hooks, organizing with, 12, 19, 21, 28, 36, 40
Household employees, 68–70
Housekeepers, 61–65
Houseplants
    as air cleaners, 285
    caring for, 123
    pests on, 274, 278
    toxic, 123, 288
Humidity and humidifiers, 237, 277, 280, 281–282, 284
Hydrocortisone cream, 41

I
Icemakers, 146, 149
Ice removal, 249–250
Illnesses caused by house systems, 238
Incandescent lightbulbs, 151, 174, 176, 179
Ink stains, removing
    from clothing, 226
    from floors, 82, 86, 88
Insects. *See Pests*
Insurance
    child-care givers and, 70
    housekeepers and, 64
    personal property, 338–339

Introductions, 322, 324
Invitations, 298–299, 304, 324, 329–330, 334
Iodine stains, removing from floors, 84
Ipecac, 41
Ironing
    boards, 44, 217, 220, 222–223
    clothing, 219, 220, 223
    tablecloths, 223–224
    zippers, 222
Iron in water softeners, 244
Irons, 217, 220, 222, 224
Ironstone dinnerware, 293

J – K

Jars, storing food in, 30
Juice stains, removing
    from carpets, 79
    from clothing, 226
    from floors, 82, 86
Kitchens
    accessible design of, 151–152
    bacteria control in, 100, 158
    basic equipment for, 127–129
    cabinets, 28, 30, 96–98
    child-proofing, 139, 156, 158
    cleaning, 54, 56, 57, 58, 95, 99–101
    lighting in, 150–151
    linens, 207
    safety measures in, 139, 146, 156, 158, 238, 240
    storage in, 26–30, 54, 56, 144, 156, 158, 207
    ventilation systems in, 143–144
Knives
    care and cleaning of, 132
    safety measures, 132, 158
    sharpening, 136
    types of, 157
Kwanza, 310–311

L

Lace curtains, washing, 117
Lacquer finishes, 174
Ladders, fire escape, 238, 239
Laminate
    cabinets, cleaning, 97
    countertops, cleaning and protecting, 95, 100
    floors, cleaning, 83, 88, 93
    furniture, 114, 172
    gluing, 97–98
Lamps and lampshades
    for bedrooms, 191
    cleaning, 121
    table, 178
    updating, 124
Laundering
    antique linens, 230
    bed linens, 211
    clothing, 60–61, 216, 218–219, 221, 228
    delicates, 218, 221
    diapers, 288
    draperies and curtains, 116–117
    folding, 220

by hand, 219
    pillows, 124, 211
    problems with, 228, 230
    routines, 60–61, 216, 218–219, 221
    rugs, 118, 120
    shirts, 218
    sorting, 214, 228
    stained items, pretreating, 218, 224, 226–228
    textiles, 124
    towels, 212, 214, 215
    water temperature, 218, 221
Laundry rooms, 43–44, 56, 214–215, 216, 228
Lawn equipment and tools, 245–248
Lawn maintenance, 67, 244–245
Lawn mowers, 50, 245–246, 248
Lazy Susans, 29, 30
Lead, 114, 244, 282, 288
Leaf blowers and vacuums, 252
Leather
    clothing, storing, 44, 45
    dyeing, 109
    upholstery, 108–109
Lemons, cleaning with, 102
Letters, social, 324–326, 328
Libraries
    home, 23, 26, 350–354
    public, 352
Lightbulbs
    broken, 245
    choosing, 179
    fluorescent, 151, 176, 179
    halogen, 151, 176, 179, 245
    incandescent, 151, 174, 176, 179
    replacing, 97, 245
    safety measures, 180
Lighting. *See also specific rooms*
    accent, 178
    ambient, 150–151, 176–177
    dimmers, 178, 180, 245
    fixtures, cleaning, 94, 121–122
    overhead, 176–177
    for reading, 176
    for security, 262
    spot, 178
    task, 151, 178
    wall, 177, 178
Linen closets, setting up, 207–208
Linens. *See also Sheets; Table linens*
    antique, 230
    bed, 55, 187, 193–197, 208, 210–211
    cleaning, 55, 230
    folding, 213, 220
    kitchen, 207
    monograms on, 207
    storing, 27
Linoleum floors, 88–89
Lint, in laundry, 228, 230
Lipstick stains, removing
    from clothing, 229
    from vinyl, 86
Liquor. *See Alcohol*

Smart Ideas Index

A – C

Allergies, and vacuum filters, 81
Appliances, caring for, 147
Bars, stocking, 299
Box springs, 185
Cookware, seasoning, 135
Cat care, 269
Children's parties, 307
Clothing, trading in, 15
Clutter, preventing, 53
Computer power surges, 349
Consignment shops, 15
Cookware, 135

D – F

Dining areas, 53
Dogs, choosing, 265
Dryer efficiency, 223
Etiquette, 317, 329
Fall routines, 61
Fire-building, 253
Furnace care, 61
Furniture
    ready-to-assemble, 173
    unfinished, 173
    upholstered, 161
    wood, 113
Futons, 185

G – M

GFCIs, 241
Hearths, 253
Holiday invitations, 311
Home offices, planning, 43
Household employees, 69
Humidifiers, 277
Invitations, sending, 329
Lightbulbs, replacing, 97
Linens, cleaning, 215
Living areas, decluttering, 53

N – S

Napkins, 227
Pans, self-cleaning, 135
Parties for children, 307
Pet hair, 215
Photographs, 341
Shades, roller, 193
Storage, 35, 43, 53
Surge protectors, 241

T – Z

Television storage units, 177
Towels, 215
Toys, storing, 35, 53
Upholstered furniture, buying, 161
Vacuum filters, 81
Waxing furniture, 113
Wood, for fires, 253
Wood furniture, care, 113

Litter boxes, 268
Living areas
  decluttering, 53
  displaying collectibles in, 23
  storage in, 18–20, 22, 23
Lockboxes, 339
Locks, 259, 261
Luggage, storing, 36, 38
Lyme disease, 274

M

Magazines, organizing, 13, 23
Mahogany furniture, 171, 174
Mail, organizing, 13, 16, 23
Maintenance checklists, 244–245
Manners. *See Etiquette*
Maple furniture, 171
Marble floors, cleaning, 83, 93
Mardi Gras, 314
Marks on surfaces, removing, 74, 86, 88, 89, 92–93
Mattresses, 185, 186, 188
Measuring tools, 133
Meat thermometers, 133
Medicine cabinets, 40, 41, 58
Medicines, safety measures for, 283
Mercurochrome stains, removing from floors, 84
Mercury spills, 282, 284
Metal cabinets, 97, 100
Metal furniture, 114, 116, 254
Methylene chloride, 284
Mice
  as pests, 280
  as pets, 270, 273
Microwave ovens, 143, 145
Mildew
  in basements, 44, 45
  in closets, 39
  on grout, 94
  removing, 39, 94, 281
Mineral buildup, removing, 102, 151
Mirrored walls, cleaning, 92
Mixers, electric, 138, 145
Moisture in basements, 44–46
Molds, preventing and removing, 281, 282
Moldings, cleaning, 93–94
Money management software, 340
Monograms, 207, 323
Mops and mopping, 73, 84–85, 99
Mosquitoes, 275
Moths, 275, 278
Mucous stains, removing, 227
Mudrooms, organizing, 18
Musical instruments, storing, 20
Music libraries, 348
Mustard stains, removing, 227

N

Nail polish, removing
  from clothing, 227
  from floors, 86, 88
Nannies, 66, 68
Napkins
  folding, 313
  paper vs. cloth, 227
  sizes of, 296
National Association of Professional Organizers, 15
Newspapers
  organizing, 13, 23
  reading, 352
  recycling, 23, 25
  saving clippings from, 342, 345
New Year's celebrations, 314
Nightstands, 189
Nitrogen dioxide, 284
Nonstick cookware, 142
Nurseries, 36, 198
Nylon
  carpets, 181
  upholstery fabric, 166
  webbing, 254

O

Oak furniture, 171
Odors, removing
  from old furniture, 112
  from refrigerators, 140
Offices, home, 42–43, 47
Oil
  for floors, 76
  wood finish, 174
Oil stains, removing from carpets, 79
Olefin
  carpets, 181
  upholstery fabric, 166
Organization. *See also Storage*
  in children's rooms, 200
  in closets, 33, 36–39
  in entries, 15–18
  in home offices, 42–43
  homework, 34
  hooks for, 12, 19, 21, 28, 36, 40
  linen closets, 207–208
  mail, 13, 16, 23
  in mudrooms, 18
  newspapers and magazines, 13
  pegs for, 12, 19, 21, 31, 34
  planning for, 11–12
  professionals, 15
Outdoor furniture, 60, 253–254
Ovens, 142–143, 148
Ozone, 284

P – Q

Pagers, etiquette and, 330
Paint
  disposing of, 283
  family-friendly finishes, 90
  storing, 50
  VOC-free, 284
Paint, removing
  from carpets, 80
  from clothing, 227
  from floors, 86–87, 88
  from windows, 96
Painted furniture, 113, 114, 174
Paneling, cleaning, 92
Pans, baking, 129, 134, 135

Space Saver Index

B – E

Backsplashes, wallpapered, 92
Beds, fold-down, 32
Bedside shelves, 190
Books, recycling, 354
Chandeliers, hanging, 178
Coffee tables, choosing size of, 172

F – R

Furniture, fitting into rooms, 168
Guest rooms, 32
Kitchens, storage in, 28
Plate racks, for storage, 22

S – Z

Shelves, bedside, 190
Storage
  fold-down beds, 32
  in kitchens, 28
  over-the-door, 14
  plate racks, 22
Wallpapered backsplashes, protecting, 92

Pantries
    butler's, 26–27
    finding space for, 28
    stocking, 130–132, 137
    storage in, 26–27
    in vintage armoires, 144
Particleboard furniture, 170, 172
Parties, 303. *See also Entertaining*
Passover, 311–312
Paste wax, 74, 76, 110, 112, 113
Pegs, organizing with, 12, 19, 21, 31, 34
Pendant lights, 190
Perchloroethylene, 284
Permanent marker stains, removing, 88
Perspiration stains, removing, 227
Pesticides
    disposing of, 283, 284
    safe handling of, 284
    storing, 46, 50, 288
Pests. *See also specific pests*
    controlling and preventing, 276, 277–280
    on houseplants, 274, 278
    identifying, 275
    insects and arachnids, 274–278
    natural remedies for, 279
    professional services for, 280
    rodents, 280
    in stored food, 278
Pets
    allergies to, 266
    birds, 272
    cats, 266–270
    children and, 266, 288
    diseases carried by, 270, 273
    dogs, 265–266, 267, 268–270
    first aid for, 268–270, 272
    fish, 270, 272
    fleas and ticks on, 274, 276
    gerbils, 270, 273
    grooming, 266–267, 271
    hamsters, 270, 273
    picking up hair from, 105, 118, 215, 271
    poisons and, 270, 272, 273
    rats and mice, 270, 273
    reptiles, 273
    stains from, 74, 79
Photographs
    displaying, 341
    restoring and reprinting, 341
    storing and protecting, 45, 341, 342, 343
Pianos, caring for, 20, 122
Picture frames, cleaning, 122
Pilling, 230
Pillows
    care and cleaning of, 58, 124, 194, 211
    replacing, 186
    types of, 193–194
Pine furniture, 170, 171

Place cards, 298
Plants, indoor. *See Houseplants*
Plants, outdoor, 244, 245
Plastic crates, 35
Plastic outdoor furniture, 254
Plate racks, 22, 28, 30
Plates, storing and displaying, 24, 26–28, 30
Playground equipment, 288
Plumbing
    concerns about, 240–241
    for laundry rooms, 214
    professionals, 237
    tools, 236
Plywood furniture, 170
Poisons, 123, 270, 272, 273
Polishing
    brass, 122
    candlesticks, 122, 124
    floors, 76
    furniture, 110, 113
    pointers for, 295
    silver, 294
Pollutants, indoor, 282, 284–285
Polyester
    carpets, 181
    clothing, 225
    mesh, on outdoor furniture, 254
    upholstery fabric, 166
Polyurethane sealants, 76
Polyvinyl chloride outdoor furniture, 254
Poplar furniture, 169
Porcelain dinnerware, 293
Potlucks, 303–304
Powder rooms, organizing, 40
Power tools, garden, 252
Pressure cookers, 139–140
Progressive dinner parties, 304
Professionals
    cleaning, 57, 61–65, 67
    child-care, 64–70
    heating and cooling, 237
    household, 67
    organizing, 15
    plumbing, 237
Propane gas, 48, 50, 248, 260

Q – R

Quilts, care and cleaning of, 124, 196, 344
Racks, storage, 22, 27–28, 30–31, 43–44
Radiators, bleeding, 236
Radon, 284, 285
Ranges, 140, 142, 143–144, 156
Rats
    as pests, 280
    as pets, 270, 273
Rattan furniture, 111, 253
Rayon upholstery fabric, 166
Recessed lighting, 178, 190
Recordings, caring for, 351
Records, protecting and storing, 337–341

Time Saver Index

B – C

Bed-making, quick, 196
Burned-on food, removing, 134
Candlesticks, 122
Cleaning
    for holidays, 60
    routines, 54, 56
    service professionals, 62
    windows, 96
Closets, organizing, 36
Computer data protection, 350
Concrete floors, painting, 86

D – H

Duvets, 196
Family history, 346
Floors
    concrete, painting, 86
    tile, cleaning, 84
    waxing, 76
Food, stocking refrigerator, 130
Front entry organizers, 16
Garage door openers, 256
Garage storage, 44
Holiday cleaning chores, 60
Housekeepers, hiring, 62

I – R

Invitations, 330
Ironing zippers, 222
Knives, sharpening, 136
Laundry, timing of, 216
Ovens, cleaning, 148
Pans, removing burned-on food from, 134
Photograph albums, 342
Public library, 352
Refrigerator, stocking, 130

S – Z

Shower curtains, 204
Silver flatware, 294
Sizing and starching fabric, 226
Storage, garage, 44
Stoves, cleaning, 148
Tax time, preparing for, 338
Thank-you notes, 328
Tile floors, cleaning, 84
Towels, displaying, 212
Vacuums, unclogging, 80
Waxing floors, 76
Windows, cleaning, 96
Zippers, ironing, 222

Tip Tag Index

B – C

Bedroom storage, 189
Blinds, cleaning, 117
Carbon monoxide detectors, 237
Carpet fibers, 181
Children, reading, 353
Cleaning
  kitchens, 57
  products, natural, 101
Closets, 39, 47
Cookware, make-do, 127
Cutting boards, 155

D – F

Dining etiquette, 321
Dining table size, 169
Drawer dividers, 189
Energy savers, 249
Etiquette for guests, 333
Fabrics, 105
Family history, 345
Fans, ventilation, 201
Floors
  tile, rating systems for, 85
  vinyl, caring for, 89
  wood, cleaning, 73
Food safety, 155
Furnace problems, 237

G – L

Gas leaks, 237
Guests, etiquette, 333
Heating tips, 249
Home offices, 47
Housekeeper calendar, 65
Ironing shirts, 219
Kitchens, 57, 139

M – R

Mail, organizing, 23
Monograms on linens, 207
Newspapers, organizing, 23
Party checklist, 303
Pet hair, 105
Pets, tiny, 273
Radon, 285

S – Z

Security measures, 261
Serving pieces, 291
Shirts, ironing, 219
Storage, 11, 23, 31
Table manners, 321
Tables, choosing size of, 169
Tile floors, 85
Vacuuming wood floors, 73
Ventilation, 201
Vinyl floors, caring for, 89
Window shades, 121
Wood floors, cleaning, 73

Recycling, 13, 25, 30, 156
Redwood outdoor furniture, 254
Reference books, 347, 350, 352
Refrigerators
  cleaning, 149
  features of, 144, 146, 149
  removing odors from, 140
  stocking, 130
  temperature setting of, 158
Renting storage space, 50
Reptile pets, 273–274
Resilient floors, caring for, 85
Restaurant etiquette, 321–322
Rice cookers and steamers, 140
Rodents, 280
Rosewood furniture, 169
RSVPs, 329
Rugs, buying and caring for, 117–118, 120, 181–182
Rush chair seats, cleaning, 111
Rust stains, removing
  from carpets, 79
  from metal, 101
  from vinyl floors, 88

S

Safe-deposit boxes, 338
Safety measures. *See also separate Safety Alert Index*
  basic, 233, 244
  for children, 139, 156, 158, 200, 230, 286, 288, 310
  cleaning routines, 101–102
  cooking, 139, 156, 260, 261
  fire, 238–240, 255, 257–258, 260
  food, 146, 155
  garage door openers, 256
  guns, 48
  knives, 132, 158
  nurseries, 198, 210
  storage, 48, 50, 139, 156, 158
  tools for, 236
Salt, cleaning with, 101–102
Satin sheets, 210
Sconces, 177, 190
Scorched fabrics, 227
Scrapbooking, 342, 344
Scratches
  on countertops, 101
  on wood floors, 74
  on wood furniture, 112, 113
Screens, cleaning, 96
Sealing
  floors, 76, 77, 82, 84
  metal furniture, 114
Security measures, 256, 261–262, 337–338
Servers, 24, 26
Serving pieces, 291
Sewing centers, 56
Shades, window, 121, 192, 193
Sheds, storage, 46
Sheer curtains, washing, 117
Sheets, bed
  folding, 213

materials used in, 208, 210
  organizing, 207
  sizes of, 208
Shelf paper, 98
Shellac, 174
Shelving
  in bathrooms, 39–40
  in bedrooms, 32, 189, 190
  built-in, 19, 24, 26, 32, 42, 47
  in children's rooms, 34–35
  constructing, 14, 17, 22, 23, 35
  floor-to-ceiling, 23, 26, 32
  in home offices, 42
  in kitchens, 28
  roll-out, 12
  in small spaces, 47
  units, 49, 172–173
Shirts, washing and ironing, 218, 219, 220
Shoe polish, removing from floors, 88
Shoveling snow, 248–249
Shower cleaners, 92
Shower curtains, 204
Showerheads, 199, 202, 240
Shrinkage, in laundry, 230
Shutters, cleaning, 119
Sideboards, 24, 26
Silicone polishes, for floors, 76
Silk clothing, caring for, 225
Silver and silver plate
  selecting and caring for, 294
  serving pieces, 291
  storing, 24, 27, 294
Sinks
  cleaning, 199
  features of, 150, 201–202
  materials used in, 148, 150
  removing mineral buildup in, 102
Sizing, fabric, 226
Slacks, ironing and hanging, 220, 223
Slate surfaces, cleaning, 83, 100
Sleepwear, flame-resistant, 230
Slipcovers, 106
Smoke alarms, 58, 239, 240
Smoking, 284, 286
Snow blowers, 250, 252
Snow removal, 248–249
Soap scum, preventing, 92
Sofas. *See also Upholstered furniture*
  buying, 162, 164
  fabrics for, 164
  sleeper, 188
Soft drink stains, removing, 79, 80
Soft woods, 170
Soil retardants, 105-106
Solvents, 50, 283
Spices
  stocking, 130, 131, 132, 137
  storing, 28, 29, 30
Spiders, 275, 277
Sponges, bacteria in, 158
Sports gear, storing, 16, 18, 46, 48
Spot removal. *See also Stain removal*
  upholstery, 106, 108

walls, 89, 90
wood furniture, 109
Spring cleaning, 55, 57–58, 60
Spring maintenance checklist, 245
Stained glass, cleaning, 96
Stained-wood furniture, 174
Stainless steel
    cookware, 135, 141
    flatware, 294–295
Stain removal
    antique linens, 230
    carpets, 79, 80–81, 82
    ceilings, 93
    clothing, 224, 226–228
    countertops, 95, 100–101
    fabric guide to, 224, 226–227
    food, 79, 80–81, 229
    grout, 82
    laminate floors, 88
    laundry, 218, 224, 226–228
    products, 228
    rugs, 118, 120
    stone surfaces, 100–101
    tablecloths, 229
    tile, 82, 84
    vinyl floors, 86, 88
    wood floors, 74
Starch, 226
Stationery, personalized, 323, 324, 329
Stemware, 27, 295–296, 297
Stone surfaces, cleaning and sealing, 84, 92, 93, 100–101
Stoneware, 293
Storage. *See also specific items and rooms*
    accessible, 28, 30
    in apartments and condos, 46–48, 207–208
    in attics, 44–46
    in basements, 44–46, 48
    baskets, 11, 13, 23, 29, 30, 31
    bookcases, 18, 23, 34
    boxes, 32, 37
    built-in, 14, 16, 18, 19, 20
    containers, 12, 13, 26, 30, 31, 32, 37
    cubes, 31
    in drop-off spots, 11
    fold-down beds, 32
    in garages, 44, 46, 48
    of hazardous materials, 46, 48, 50, 158, 238, 288
    over-the-door, 14, 27
    racks, 22, 27, 28, 30, 31, 43, 44
    of records, 337–341
    rental units, 50
    safety measures for, 48, 50, 139, 156, 158
    security measures for, 261
    servers and sideboards, 24, 26
    sheds, 46
    space for, 14
    trunks, 32, 35, 43, 47
    under-bed, 31
    units, 172–173, 177
    in vintage furniture, 144
Stoves, 140, 142–143, 148, 156, 258
Suede upholstery, 109
Supper clubs, 304
Surge protectors, 241
Sympathy notes, 325–326, 328

T

Table linens
    ironing, 223–224
    stains on, 229
    storing, 27
    using, 296
Table manners, 318–322
Tables
    buying, 169, 173
    choosing size of, 169, 172
    safety measures, 170
    styles, 162, 163
Table settings, 291–298, 301, 305
Tarnish, preventing, 24, 27
Tar stains, removing
    from carpets, 80
    from hard surfaces, 82, 88
Taxes
    computer software for, 340
    documentation for, 338
    for household employees, 69
Teak furniture, 169, 254
Tea stains, removing
    from carpets, 80
    from tile, 82
Television cabinets, 20, 22, 23, 177
Termites, 275, 276
Textiles, care and cleaning of, 124
Thanksgiving celebrations, 314
Thank-you notes, 324–325, 328
Thermometers, 41
Throws, cleaning, 124
Ticks, 274–276, 278
Tile
    care and cleaning of, 81–84, 92, 100
    crayon marks on, 93
    rating systems for, 85
Tillers, garden, 252–253
Tipping servers, 321
Toasters, 139, 145
Tobacco smoke, 284, 286
Toilets
    buying, 200–201
    cleaning, 199
    water-saving, 240
Tools
    basics and extras, 233–234, 236, 251
    garden, 247, 252–253
    storing, 44, 46
Toxoplasmosis, 270
Towels, bath, 209, 211–212, 214, 215, 220
Toys, storing, 35, 45, 53
Track lighting, 178, 190
Trash compactors, 155–156
Trimmers, string, 252
Trunks, 32, 35, 43, 47

U.S. Units To Metric Equivalents

To Convert From	Multiply By	To Get
Inches	25.4	Millimeters (mm)
Inches	2.54	Centimeters (cm)
Feet	30.48	Centimeters (cm)
Feet	0.3048	Meters (m)

Metric Units To U.S. Equivalents

To Convert From	Multiply By	To Get
Millimeters	0.0394	Inches
Centimeters	0.3937	Inches
Centimeters	0.0328	Feet
Meters	3.2808	Feet

Tubs, 199, 202
Turpentine, storing, 50
Twelfth Night parties, 314

U

Universal design, 28, 30, 151–152, 202
Upholstered furniture
  buying, 161–162, 164–166, 168–169
  cleaning, 55, 105–109
  crayon marks on, 93
  fabrics, 107–109, 164–166, 168
  finishes, 168–169
  trim, cleaning, 124
  weaves, 166, 168
Urine stains, removing
  from clothing, 227
  from floors, 81
  from rugs, 118
Utensils, storing, 27–28, 30, 54

V

Vacuuming
  carpets, 77–78, 80, 81
  upholstery, 105
  wood floors, 73
Vacuums, 77–78, 80, 81, 87
Vanities
  buying, 201
  lighting, 190
  storage in, 40
Varnish
  removing from vinyl floors, 86–87
  removing from windows, 96
  wood finish, 174
Velvet and velveteen upholstery, 108
Veneer furniture, 113, 170, 172
Ventilation systems
  in bathrooms, 201
  in kitchens, 143–144
  whole-house fans, 285
Videotaping family events, 346, 348
Videotapes, 345–346, 351
Vinegar, cleaning with, 80, 102
Vinyl
  floors, 83, 85–88, 89
  wallpapers, 90, 91
  webbing, on outdoor furniture, 254
Volatile organic compounds (VOCs),
  284
Vomit stains, removing
  from carpets, 81
  from clothing, 227

W–Z

Waffle irons, 140
Wallpapers, care and cleaning of,
  90–91, 92, 93
Walls
  cleaning, 59, 89–90, 92–93
  crayon marks on, 93
  mirrored, 92
  tile, 81
Warranties, 152, 154, 188
Washers, 214–215, 216, 218–219
Water
  conserving, 240
  damage caused by, 93, 94, 95

dispensers, 146, 286
  filters and purifiers for, 286, 287
  frozen lines, 240
  softeners, 242, 244
  temperature of, 156, 204, 241, 242,
    288
Water beds, 188
Water deposits, hard, 151, 242, 244
Water heaters, 241, 242, 243
Water marks, removing from wood
  floors, 74
Wax
  on candlesticks, 122
  for floors, 74, 76, 77
  for furniture, 110, 112–113
  removing, 77, 81, 82, 122, 229
  Sotheby's, 113
  wood finish, 174
Wedding gowns, preserving, 344
Wedding-related parties, 304, 306
White vinegar, cleaning with, 80, 102
White wood outdoor furniture, 254
Wicker furniture, 111, 253
Windows
  cleaning, 55, 59, 94, 96
  cleaning services, 57, 67
  frames, 98
  security measures for, 262
Window treatments
  for bedrooms, 192–193
  care and cleaning of, 115, 116–117,
    118, 119, 121
Wine, storing, 26
Wine stains, removing
  from carpets, 79
  from clothing, 229
  from vinyl, 86
Woks, electric, 140
Wood
  cabinets, 98
  cleaning, 59, 92, 93, 98, 100
  countertops, 100
  for fires, 253, 255
  floors, 73–76
  types of, 169–172
Wood furniture
  buying, 169–174
  caring for, 45, 109–110, 112–113
  finishes, 173–174
  outdoor, 254
  polishing, 110, 113
  ready-to-assemble, 173
  restoring, 112
  scratches on, 112–113
  Sotheby's advice for, 112–113
  unfinished, 173
  waxing, 110, 112, 113
Wool
  carpets, 180, 181
  clothing, 220, 225
  upholstery fabric, 166
Workers' compensation, 70
Yards, maintaining, 244–245, 262
Zippers, ironing, 222

**Equivalents:
U.S. =
Australia/U.K.**

⅕ teaspoon = 1 ml
¼ teaspoon = 1.25 ml
½ teaspoon = 2.5 ml
1 teaspoon = 5 ml
1 tablespoon = 15 ml
1 fluid ounce = 30 ml
¼ cup = 60 ml
⅓ cup = 80 ml
½ cup = 120 ml
⅔ cup = 160 ml
¾ cup = 180 ml
1 cup = 240 ml
2 cups = 475 ml
1 quart = 1 liter
½ inch = 1.25 cm
1 inch = 2.5 cm

Making a
Home